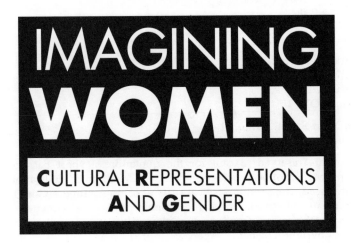

IMAGINING
WOMEN

CULTURAL REPRESENTATIONS
AND GENDER

Edited by Frances Bonner, Lizbeth Goodman,
Richard Allen, Linda Janes and Catherine King

POLITY PRESS   in association with    The Open University

Selection and editorial material copyright © 1992 The Open University

First published in the United Kingdom by Polity Press in association with
Blackwell Publishers and The Open University

Editorial office:
Polity Press
65 Bridge Street
Cambridge CB2 1UR, UK

Marketing and production:
Blackwell Publishers
108 Cowley Road
Oxford OX4 1JF, UK

238 Main Street, Suite 501,
Cambridge, MA 02142, USA

Edited and designed by The Open University

ISBN 0 7456 0973 2
ISBN 0 7456 0974 0 (pbk)

A CIP catalogue record for this book is available from the British Library
and from the Library of Congress.

Typeset in Palatino on 10/12 pt
by Photo·graphics, Honiton, Devon
Printed in Great Britain by T.J. Press (Padstow) Ltd, Padstow, Cornwall

This book is printed on acid-free paper.

CONTENTS

LIST OF PLATES

BLACK AND WHITE PLATES

INTRODUCTION:
ON IMAGINING WOMEN

This book is about women's images and images of women. It addresses writing and reading, creativity and imagination, image making and interpretation, subjectivity and self-representation. The title, *Imagining Women*, was chosen (as were the others in the series) in the recognition that it is unfixed, that it slides as it is read. One moment women are being imagined, and the next are doing the imagining. In this way the very title is characteristic of the field of women's studies.

CULTURAL REPRESENTATIONS

The book's subtitle, 'Cultural Representations and Gender', indicates its concern with one of the first areas where women's studies began critical work – cultural representation. This was roughly concurrent with the spread of another area, known, initially in the UK, as cultural studies. The 'culture' that was being studied was not that known as high culture, but a much wider field which looked at everyday life and was informed by a consideration of the culture industry and all its products, especially the neglected and castigated area of popular culture. The two interdisciplinary areas (women's studies and cultural studies) interacted and were frequently complementary. For instance, the concern with popular culture echoed the concern in the women's movement with the activities and interests of 'ordinary women'.

Most of the articles in this book could be described as examples of feminist cultural studies. They are concerned with the processes of production, dissemination and consumption of texts; they ask questions about how audiences (and particularly female audiences) use texts, how meaning is made from them and how they are incorporated into everyday life. There is also a special concern with how they evolve and grow *from* everyday life.

In referring to cultural *representation*, this book looks at how women are represented, how we represent ourselves, and what we do with the representations we encounter. It is important to note the distinction between representation and reflection. The latter term is not used in this book because it implies that there is a direct correspondence between phenomena (events, people, things) in the 'real' world and their appearance in texts. Representation, however, indicates that some kind of modulation or interpretive

1

process is involved in re-presentation. Some manipulation or transformation is unavoidable. Not even photographs are reflections – they are two dimensional representations which we learn to read and interpret in many different ways.

FEMINIST PERSPECTIVES

Defining 'feminism' is, ironically, one of the most common themes of feminist criticism, complicated not only by the multiplicity of different feminist perspectives, but also by the origins of the term 'feminist' itself. The question of whether 'feminism' is a white, middle-class word is an important one. Feminism as a *word* has most often and most extensively been defined and employed by middle-class white women, predominantly in Europe, the USA, Canada and Australia. But the larger project of feminism – its implications, its perspectives, its strategies, its possibilities – appeals (albeit in varying degrees) to women of all cultures, ages, races, religions and classes.

There is not one feminism, but rather several different branches of feminist thought. The tripartite division into liberal, radical and socialist feminisms no longer accurately describes the great diversity of positions. One basis on which feminist perspectives can be distinguished is the degree to which they are described as 'essentialist'. 'Essentialism' is simplistically characterized by the argument that women are 'born, not made', that 'womanhood' is innate rather than socially constructed. Yet few feminists deny the sociocultural construction of gender. Feminist critic Teresa de Lauretis argues that it is still possible to talk about the 'essence' of woman:

> . . . it is the specific properties (e.g. a female-sexed body), qualities (a disposition to nurturance, a certain relation to the body, etc.), or necessary attributes (e.g. the experience of femaleness, of living in the world as female) that women have developed or have been bound to historically in their differently patriarchal sociocultural contexts which make them women not men.

> *(de Lauretis, 1989, pp. 5–6)*

Feminists vary, de Lauretis argues, in the emphases they place on the various qualities, properties and attributes of sex and gender, as well as in the valuing of them. None the less, she asserts that a modified essentialism is the very basis on which feminist thinking differs from non-feminist thinking, enabling all the different branches of feminist thought to be termed 'feminist'. The extent to which her description of women's 'essence' incorporates constructivist positions is an indication of how the positions are becoming reconciled. Diana Fuss, writing in *Essentially Speaking* from an anti-essentialist position, concludes similarly that social constructivism needs to recognize the essentialism which informs it (Fuss, 1989).

The merging of what previously were opposed positions is central to the discussion of cultural representation in this book. Investigations of women's or feminist 'ways of seeing' or of the female gaze can easily be labelled essentialist and, since the term is often used as one of abuse, dismissed. When we use such terms we are not invoking some eternal immutable female essence, but historically and socioculturally inflected ideas and arguments which can contribute a great deal to developing feminist cultural studies. We must remember, however, that definitions of terms such as essentialism in different cultural contexts do not always coincide precisely.

THE VALUING OF WOMEN'S WORK

Women's work in different media is 'valued' or judged and criticized in a variety of ways, but nearly always within the context of patriarchal culture and its norms. As a consequence, women's work *in the* of all kinds has been undervalued and under-represented through *media* the years. One aim of feminist criticism has been the reclaiming of women's work. But this is easier said than done, since years of marginalization have effectively erased women's contributions to many different areas of cultural representation. As well as reclaiming the past, feminist activists have engaged in diverse contemporary activities from 'reclaim the night' marches to women poets' vigils: all public acts of protest against the marginalization of women's space and creativity.

When women write, or sing, or paint, or take photographs, or stand for election they are called 'women writers', 'women singers', 'women artists', 'women politicians'. This is significant because it shows the male bias of society and language in the clear assumption that women, when they are creative or active, are taking positions normally occupied by men, and must be labelled accordingly. There are no 'male writers', only 'writers' and 'women writers'. It is also significant that women writers are generally seen to be representative of all women while men are seen to be unique individuals, representative only of themselves. Again, the male is privileged and seen as the 'norm', while the female position is seen as 'other' and therefore easily conflated with that of all females.

Other norms operate in conjunction with the patriarchal. Lesbian experience is viewed as 'deviant' from the 'norm' of heterosexuality. Where heterosexuality is the supposed norm for all women in images, regardless of individuals' sexual preferences, lesbians experience special difficulty in making and taking meaning from dominant cultural representations. Similarly, the experience of people of colour and of working-class people has been traditionally viewed as 'other' in relation to the 'main' issues represented by middle-class white values.

The privileging of male experience in patriarchal society has had direct and long-term effects on the ways in which women's experience has been and is viewed. As well as asking whether this male bias has also influenced the way in which women view, see, think and create, some feminist theory also asks whether there is a difference between 'women's experience' and 'feminist experience'; women's creative work and feminist creative work. These distinctions are taken up and examined in some of the articles in this book.

THE LOOK, THE GAZE, SEEING AND BEING SEEN

A major concern in much feminist writing on visual matters has been the gaze, or the look. The idea of 'the gaze' overlaps and intermeshes with the literary concept of 'point-of-view'. There is only space here to sketch out a little of what the term refers to; particular applications will be mentioned later. The article at the centre of much concern with the look and the gaze is Laura Mulvey's 'Visual Pleasure and Narrative Cinema' (Mulvey, 1975). It used Freudian and Lacanian psychoanalytic theory to argue that mainstream Hollywood cinema constructed the spectator as male and legitimized his fetishistic looking at the women displayed on the screen by directing his 'gaze' at them through the intermediary of the camera or of some 'looking' male figure within the film. The suggestion, which Mulvey later modified, that women could only view such films from a 'male' position, has been much debated within film studies and has been used in a number of other contexts, such as television studies, photographic criticism and art history, in each case amalgamating with extant conceptions of looking.

Perhaps as a result of the contestation, migration and merging, little of Mulvey's original formulation remains. Yet it has focused attention on the gendered character of looking and being looked at. Mulvey referred to women connoting 'to-be-looked-at-ness' in a way which men did (and could) not. This was in keeping with early women's movement activity disputing the presentation of women as 'sex objects', in beauty contests for example. (Mulvey had herself participated in and written about the protest at the 1970 Miss World Contest). The idea that women, and images of women, are constructed in order to be looked at by men was consonant with theories in art history, especially those about the female nude.

Feminist activists, artists and critics have all worked at changing this asymmetry and with some success. Considerable attention is now paid to the female spectator, or spectatrix. The increasing presence of men as spectacle, however, probably owes as much to the growth of consumer culture and the usefulness of men's as well as women's bodies in advertising, as to feminism.

The specificity of gendered looking and the possibility of a female gaze remains problematic. The power of women to control the gaze within (and at) certain cultural representations has been increasingly explored, for example, in the collection entitled *The Female Gaze* (Gamman and Marshment, 1988). Yet despite these changes, a certain asymmetry persists. Men still have greater power to look, their gaze is more controlling, not least in the highly practical way that the 'looks' relayed to us – in films, on television, from gallery walls and magazine pages – are still more likely to have been framed and chosen by and for the male eye. For example, in pornography, the power of the male gaze and the powerlessness of the female spectacle is at its most explicit. If there has been any variation in the asymmetry here, it has been difficult to recognize in the proliferation of pornographic material and its increased availability in the last twenty or so years.

Feminist performance, however, offers a very different perspective, largely because the performer is physically present during the performance. Feminist performance may instigate social change through the transformation of the relationship between performance and audience. Like other feminist activity, including feminist criticism, such transformation aims to produce active spectators, able to question their positioning by texts. Throughout the book we will explore various texts and contexts which can be similarly re-framed, or transformed through active questioning of norms and refocusing of the gaze.

READING AGAINST THE GRAIN/THE GAZE

One question which was raised in a great deal of feminist work, from the late 1980s on, was: what is the relationship between feminist theory and a feminist way of seeing and being in the world? The phrase 'ways of seeing' was coined by John Berger as the title of a television series and book (Berger, 1972). The phrase, which is not limited solely to the visual, has become a commonplace for the expression of the multiplicity of different perspectives, different opinions, views, and 'ways of seeing' ourselves in relation to representation and culture. But the question of whether there is a feminist 'way of seeing' (or, perhaps, a set of different ways of seeing which are all feminist, allowing for differences within the feminist movement itself) has been formulated in most relevant disciplines.

In literature, a great deal of attention has been given to the idea of 'reading against the grain', or 'reading between the lines'. The idea is that women's experience is rarely contained in the literary canon, composed of what is considered to be the 'great' works of literature, mainly written by (dead) men. In her famous novel *To the Lighthouse*, Virginia Woolf did not give her character

Mrs Ramsay a first name. Mrs Ramsay is only Mrs Ramsay: a strategy devised by Woolf to make the point that women's lives are not fully represented in traditional narrative forms and structures. But contemporary women's fiction provides female characters with first names, and also with full rich lives and 'ways of seeing' and of speaking all their own. In reading most contemporary fiction, it is no longer necessary to read between the lines in order to determine what a female character's name is, what she is like or what she might be thinking. In fact, much recent feminist fiction has told us nothing *but* what the female characters are thinking.

Similarly, in the visual arts images have been made 'against the grain', asserting the possibility of a distinct 'women's creativity' and pointing out the erasure of women's inventiveness in the past. In her photographic exhibit *Muses*, for example, Maud Sulter depicted nine black women skilled in different arts. Alice Walker is one, portraying the Muse of Comedy. Sulter's images assert the way in which Eurocentric interests have depicted the creative principle as white, and thereby erased the possibility of black (female) creativity. By making Muses into creative women in their own right, Sulter opposes the right of individualized male artists to take inspiration from anonymous female Muses. Sulter's Muses take, and make, inventive images of their own.

The increased emphasis on the spectator, which has been referred to already, has not been regarded as unequivocally desirable by all feminist writers. Jill Dolan has written on the importance of *The Feminist Spectator as Critic*, but has emphasized the potential problems of theories of spectatorship (Dolan, 1988). Elsewhere in her work, Dolan has referred to Roland Barthes' concept of 'the death of the author' in arguing about the increased focus on spectatorship which enhances the role of the audience (readers or spectators) in interpretation of the text or performance. The positions of the playwrights, directors and actors, who had previously had control over creation and production of performances, may be undermined by this displacement or refocusing of attention (Dolan, 1989, p. 59: cf. Barthes, 1977, pp. 142–8).

The balance of creative power between active creators and active receivers or critical audiences is one of the key themes of this book. It affects and informs representations of women and men in all cultural forms, from the visual arts to the media to everyday life, where women's roles are continually played and increasingly complicated by the contingencies of life in the modern world. The same concerns apply outside the theatre. For instance, there are particularly distasteful cases of feminist anti-pornography films being screened for purposes of sexual arousal in 'adult' cinemas.

SITUATED PERSPECTIVES

So far, 'positions' and 'perspectives' have been discussed in a very general way, but there are more precise ways of expressing these ideas. The term 'positionality' refers to the individual's viewpoint, as influenced by such factors as gender, age, race, class, and sexual orientation. Depending upon positioning in these terms, an individual may have a particular perspective, or way of looking at things. But the same individual may have more than one perspective. Cultural critic Donna Haraway has argued, for instance, that the individual may have different perspectives at different points in time, different stages of her life, and under different circumstances. The concept of the situated perspective is invaluable in studying cultural representations of and by women. In Haraway's words:

> Feminism is about the sciences of the multiple subject with (at least) double vision. Feminism is about a critical vision consequent upon a critical positioning in unhomogeneous gendered social space.
>
> (Haraway, 1988, p. 589)

This double vision is present in the shift from created to creator, represented to representer, as we examine the category 'woman' of which we are also part (and analogously as men examine the category 'man', if they perceive its gendered specificity and do not envisage its being coterminous with 'humanity'). The critical position from which feminism operates depends upon acknowledging a gendered position. By its name, feminism privileges gender, but Haraway insists that this is neither all nor sufficient. The 'gendered social space' is unhomogeneous. Women are not all alike. The social space in which we are positioned is marked in many different ways. The women we imagine and the women imagined by other people are distinctive in many ways.

Haraway advocates writing from a situated perspective which involves acknowledging both that a particular person (rather than a general unmarked voice) is writing and, as the quotation indicates, that the particular person is a multiple subject. The space from which such a person writes is characterized not only in gender terms, but also in other ways: power is unequally distributed in ways determined in part by factors such as age, race, class, sexuality, level of education and physical abilities, all of which may intervene in the individual's ways of interacting in society.

One of the characteristics of a situated perspective is that it is acknowledged in the style of writing. Different authors in this book acknowledge their positions in different ways. Few authors write impersonally; most write as feminists; many use the first person (I, me, my); and some address readers as 'you'. This introduction has a particular problem in being situated. It has been written collaboratively by two members of the editorial group with additional input from members of the whole group. Our pronoun then is inevitably plural, but how exactly are 'we' situated and what positions are assumed in this 'we'? We are not here assuming a unity with our readers. We write as feminist academics, one Anglo-Australian and one American, both resident in the UK. We use the impersonal voice a little more than may seem good feminist practice, but do not do so with a claim to universality or objectivity (as 'malestream' academic writing often does).

LANGUAGE AND THE ACADEMIC 'NORM'

One issue which is repeatedly raised in this book is that of *academic* norms, or standards, and the possibilities for feminist subversion of them. The standard (male) academic convention is of speaking and writing in the third person. It is argued that the third person is more 'objective' than the first person, but this assumption is challenged in women's studies. Standards are about power. The most powerful people in the public sphere in most contemporary societies are, and have long been, men. The masculine has therefore come to be associated with 'objectivity' and with power. The masculine has also tended to subsume the feminine: a point which is best illustrated with reference to the English language, wherein gendered power relations are inscribed in remarkable ways.

The most obvious example of gendered language usage influenced by a male-dominated culture is the common English use of masculine pronouns as 'generic'. The 'Pronoun Problem' is described in *The Handbook of Non-Sexist Writing*:

Use of the pronouns *he, his* and *him* to refer to any unspecified or hypothetical person who may be either female or male is usually justified on two grounds. First, the practice is said to be an ancient rule of English grammar long and faithfully followed by educated speakers and writers. Second, it is asserted – somewhat paradoxically, if the usage is thought to distinguish the educated from the uneducated – that everybody knows *he* includes *she* in generalizations. Historical and psychological research in the past few years has produced evidence to refute both claims.

(*Miller and Swift, 1981, pp. 44–5*)

The use of 'generic' pronouns is only one example of the patriarchal marginalization and suppression of women's voices. Feminist criticism and cultural representation have uncovered and begun to shift the balance of power in this and other areas. The process has not been restricted to written language and the conventions of pronoun usage, but has carried over into areas such as word order as well. For instance, in this book (as in much feminist writing), the standard ordering of gendered words is reversed: 'female and male', 'women and men', 'her or his' are the phrases used in this text. The contraction 's/he' is sometimes used as well: this is shorthand for 'she or he', a usage which has caused considerable academic protest. The fact that the adoption of this linguistic contraction has met with such hesitation (and some open hostility) may actually support the idea that the ordering of pronouns in 'standard' usage *is* related to – indeed, is an expression of – gender and power after all.

POSITIONALITIES AND DIFFERENCES

Individual authors as well as editorial groups may encounter problems of positionality. The position of an individual author can – and usually will – change over time, and be influenced by shifting cultural contexts as well as by personal circumstances and political contingencies. For instance, Susan Bassnett, a feminist historian and critic as well as a linguist and dramaturg, closed one of her books (in 1986) with reference to her feeling of being positioned at a particular historical moment in the development of the modern women's movement. She wrote:

> This recognition of one's perception of the world as something at once unique, shared and different is the principal lesson I have learned from being part of the process of changing consciousness of women of my generation. The final result of a process of comparison is never likely to be the clarification of absolutes, but rather perception of the greater complexity of the web of problems that surround each individual and a recognition by the individual of where she stands in the web.
> (Bassnett, 1986, p. 182)

The 'web' Bassnett describes is one which entangles women and men of different generations. The web is culture, and cultural representations are the strands which compose it. They mingle and mix, cross and intersect. The web is composed of complexities and contradictions. Existing as an active subject within this web demands flexibility and determination, the taking and changing of positions, the raising of consciousness and the changing of minds.

It is issues such as language and power, positionality and difference which enrich all the readings in this book and which inspired the title: *Imagining Women*. Because feminist critics, writers and readers have achieved so much in re-viewing the structure of society, language and all other power structures, it is now possible to discuss an idea as seemingly vague as 'Imagining Women' and to have people know, not only what the phrase might mean, but also that its importance lies in its potential to mean so much.

THE ORGANIZATION OF THE BOOK

This book pays particular attention to texts and images created by women in literary forms, the visual arts and performance. In considering film and television, and pornography, the texts are primarily created by men, but are very relevant to women. In looking at film and television, we are concerned with mainstream representations and the ways in which a female audience may use and derive pleasure from them. Because pornographic images are primarily of women, they are an important form of cultural representation related to gender. Our decision to include a discussion of pornography in this book was based on its importance in feminist debates and the particular impact such representations have on the lives of women.

The book is divided into six chapters. The first chapter introduces the key concepts of the book including representation, genre and women's language, developing these concepts to facilitate understanding of the readings in the following chapters. The question discussed here of a 'women's language', as distinct from the language and 'ways of speaking' common to patriarchal society, is one of the most commonly debated issues in feminist cultural studies. The idea that there may be a female way of writing (the French feminist conception of *écriture féminine*) is discussed in the essay by Dinah Birch, and the possible existence of a specifically female 'way of speaking' is explored by Joan Swann. Both of these ideas are contentious: some feminists argue that to assume a common 'women's experience' or 'women's language' (written or verbal) is to marginalize, and possibly ghettoize, women. Others argue, conversely, that women do have gender-specific experiences and different ways of communicating, and that these should be recognized and credited, even celebrated. This issue may be relevant to body language and gesture, movement and dress as ways of communicating, as well as to spoken and written language.

The second chapter focuses on women's roles as writers, readers and interpreters of the written word in literatures of various kinds: feminist theory, fiction, poetry and autobiography. The distinction between women's fiction (fiction written by women) and feminist fiction (fiction written by women with feminist political intent) is discussed in the reading on short stories by Lizbeth Goodman, while the idea that feminist science fiction depicts 'better ways of being' is discussed by Frances Bonner. Wendy Webster's essay examines some working-class women's writing, and attempts to evaluate why such a perspective is rare in a textbook of this kind.

The third chapter discusses the particular uses of the term 'representation' in visual art and in creating things; it asks how women's artistic productivity (what women are able to produce artistically) re-presents notions of gender differences. This chapter considers various kinds of self-portrayal and skilled making, as well as the particular interventions of artists with a self-consciously feminist approach to using the arts. The fourth chapter concentrates on the mass media of popular film and television. The emphasis is on the representation of women and the ways in which female audiences make sense of these representations.

Chapter 5 looks at the debates generated by feminist theorists and activists surrounding the issue of pornography. It contrasts different forms of pornographic imagery, including mass-market fiction, but concentrates on hard-core pornographic magazines, photographs and videos (usually made by and for men). This chapter includes a variety of material, from theoretical writing about the pornography problem and the censorship debate to first-hand testimonies of the ways in which pornography can be seen to intersect with sexism and racism in society, touching the lives of individual women. It asks the extremely contentious question of whether there may be a feminist erotica and explores some of the implications of such an idea.

Chapter 6 also examines images of women by focusing on woman-produced images: 'living' images of women in society and the theatre. This chapter argues that humour and theatre are two very distinct areas in which women have 'made spectacles of themselves' by imagining and representing themselves in subversive and liberating ways in the public sphere. Humour and staged comedy are forms of communication with potential for undermining cultural expectations of 'what women should be'. Yet again, there is a distinction to be made between 'women's humour' (humour by women) and 'feminist humour' (humour by and for women with feminist political intent).

The book concludes with Alice Walker's 'In Search of Our Mothers' Gardens'. This was selected because it expresses the book's major concerns in a personal, yet accessible, way. It has not been 'situated' with editorial remarks, but rather stands on its own. The book ends with the last line of Alice Walker's essay.

Each section of the book focuses on two main ideas: the creation and reception of women's images, and the role which feminist theory and criticism may play in individualized interpretation of these images. Just as all the authors included in this book, and all the editors, have different positions in relation to feminist ideas and their (our) material, you as the reader will inevitably find that some of the readings are either more, or less, relevant to your life and your ways of seeing. Your situated perspective will inform your reading and interpretation of the book, will make you its audience and its critic, as well as its subject.

Frances Bonner and Lizbeth Goodman

1
THEMES AND ISSUES: GENDER, GENRE AND REPRESENTATION

This first chapter of the book includes four articles, each of which is intricately related to each of the others. In each article, the concepts of representation, gender and genre are defined and analysed with reference to specific examples taken from a range of media and academic disciplines.

The first article, by Catherine King, addresses the linked concepts of gender and representation. King's piece is written primarily in a third person academic voice. Her examples are taken from the visual and plastic arts: one of the many disciplines in which representation can be seen to be influenced by gender difference. The article refers to the division sometimes defined between 'high' and 'low' forms of art, and between artistic and 'practical' artefacts. King argues that the division is an artificial one, charged with an assumed scale of values which need not be seen to apply to feminist art making.

The second article, by Richard Allen, examines the issue of representation in relation to the concept of ideology, and is supported by a range of examples taken from cultural studies, academic criticism and literature. Allen's piece is written primarily in the first person: a technique which draws attention to the position of the author. This piece is significantly longer than others in the book, because its function is a very important one: it illuminates three of the key concepts of this book – representation, analysis and ideology. This piece serves as a 'way in' to thinking about the relationship between receiving and interpreting images in everyday life and the media, as well as in literature and art.

The third article takes on two more key themes of the book: gender and genre. Dinah Birch evaluates the interconnections between the two with reference to the development of poetry and fiction (the novel) as forms of literary representation. She also develops some ideas about gender difference in written and spoken language usage, with reference to feminist theory. In some ways this piece informs the earlier articles by King and Allen. It develops some of their points and gives specific examples from literature, thereby setting the scene for the next chapter, which focuses on literary representations.

The fourth and last article in this chapter is Joan Swann's 'Ways of Speaking'. Written by a linguist, this piece interrogates the English language in terms of the oral tradition as well as the written tradition. Swann's piece raises many issues of importance to the book as a whole, including the idea that there may be significant differences in women's and men's use of the same language. Women's representation by and through speech is one of the most pervasive and perhaps the most complex form of interpersonal communication, and one which is affected in different ways by gender and power relations. Therefore, Swann's piece focuses on women's everyday speech as a form of cultural representation. Most of the issues which arise in Swann's piece – to do with women's exclusion, the low value attached to women's speech, and the search for alternative ways of speaking – also arise in relation to women's engagement in various other forms of cultural activity. While Swann refers primarily to spoken language, her comments and insights are relevant to gender differences in written language and body language or non-verbal communication as well.

Swann's piece brings this introductory exploration of themes full circle, from representation in the arts, media and literature to representation and language in everyday speech and daily interaction. These four articles have all been specially written for inclusion in this book. Because the context of writing and representation is 'made issue of' in the book as a whole, it is particularly significant that the first part should be composed, not of decontextualized bits of material from other sources, but of unique and interrelated introductory readings. Each of the four authors in this section knew the place and the intended audience of her or his material.

The articles might have been arranged in other orders: they have each been designed to inform the others, and to help identify some of the key themes and issues raised and discussed in the book as a whole. Each chapter in this book points out that cultural representations take many different forms and may intersect at many different levels with theory and practice, representation and 'real life'.

Lizbeth Goodman

Article 1.1
MAKING THINGS MEAN: CULTURAL REPRESENTATION IN OBJECTS

Catherine King

Cultural representation states notions of gender difference in a variety of ways. Although the most obvious kinds of representation entail words and visual images, I want to begin by drawing attention to other powerful ways in which ideas of the feminine are transmitted. For gender is expressed in the rules about who is allowed to make all the things that surround us daily, about the values assigned to women's making, and the way women are supposed to respond to artefacts. Just as the gendering of everyday speech relates to representations of the feminine in literary terms, so the gendering of everyday objects and arts underpins the representation of femininity in the 'Fine Arts'. To consider the positions women have been pushed into, and how they might be able to refuse them, it is important to define art in very broad terms, and to stress the potential openness of art's boundaries and partitions.

Art-making is the skilled production of more or less lasting objects and visual images. The emphasis is strong on the physically tangible, and on sight (as well as scent and flavour). The skills of painting and sculpture, as well as cookery, ceramics, weaving of all diversities, metal work and wood carving, can be considered arts. We can include the dressing, adornment and the shaping of the human body since we use these things to state ourselves. If we include our bodies, we can surely include the forming of the landscape, or gardening. These kinds of making continue into and are part of what we call technology: which is appropriate since *techné* is Greek for skill or *art*. Definitions shift as skilled makers invent new arts. For instance, women have been interested in using the powers of performance art entailing actors, props and costumes. This is a little like drama, but it stresses the visual and physical more than words, because it has been made by artists. Yet we could imagine it shifting *more* towards drama. The American artist, Jenny Holzer, has made art which consists of sentences engraved on large slabs of stone (one reads, 'Men don't protect you any more'). This could be 'literature', except that the epigraph is physically monumental: and the heavy stone validates the words in a way in which a page or voice could not do. Again, women have used video to good effect, and, rightly, this suggests the links with the media of film and television.

These boundaries are fluid and there are continual contests for hierarchies of value within this group. Women are seeking free movement through such categories, the revaluation of our making of things, and the treatment of all these skills as equal. We can point to such masculine-led shifts in the past as valuable precedents, for how flexible these systems are. I refer to three important regroupings of the arts: first, when specialists in the making of figurative images (painters and sculptors) were, in the sixteenth century, prised away from decorative arts like embroidery or utilitarian arts (such as armourers) to create the category of 'Fine Arts', along with architecture; and second, the slightly later groupings of arts linked with mechanized manufacture, to create technology, as distinct from 'craft' and 'art'; third, most recently, 'Design' has been created to form a category allowing 'Fine Art' skills to 'style' both manufactured and crafts goods to be commodified more successfully (thus joining 'technology', 'craft' and 'Fine Art', for commercial gain).

One of the key ways in which gender is represented culturally is through the segregation of certain kinds of art-making to women, which are seen as both feminine and inferior. Lace-making is done by women and considered to represent the delicacy and decorativeness of the feminine, and this can be contrasted with net-making, which entails the same skills, but which is exclusively masculine, and signifies the adventure of men, killing for food, beyond the home. Often a skill is gendered only in so far as, if it is done in the home, it is a feminine craft, while if it is paid employment outside the home, it is an art for men (this applies to knitting, dress-making and cookery, for example). Or if women work alongside men, in paid employment outside the home, as the Birmingham chainmakers did, an 'important' gender difference must be created here, in that women make slightly smaller and lighter chains (Bailey, 1990, pp. 75–8). In the so-called Fine Arts, women are more likely to paint than sculpt (because of the 'unfeminine' heaviness of the material for sculpture) and if they design buildings they will be steered into house, school or hospital work. Within such categories, women must be placed at the least valued end of the ladder: in craft, not painting; or once in painting, they must paint less prestigious kinds of subjects, like the flower-pieces and portraits, or landscapes, made by women in the nineteenth century, rather than producing the highest allegorical and narrative art. Again, women are likely to dabble in all these arts, as accomplishments, while a man will follow an important career, in his profession as painter, sculptor, film maker, photographer or architect.

Most obviously, male control over the representation of gender difference in producing things, and the notion of female inferiority, is effected through the powers of unions and masters in the workplace, such that, for example, women are employed in certain categories, like the surface decoration of pottery but not the throwing or casting of pots (*so* heavy and messy). In this way, women can be represented to others as decorative, and these meanings can be re-presented to the next generation.

Representation of gender difference is also effected through male control over human reproduction, such that women are represented as the main carers of the family of 'man', and are made dependants of men. Women are associated with making things in the home, and are supposed to gain satisfaction from making things 'freely' and without professional training. Men have the power to make women's effortful and painful birth of children characteristic of a delicate and decorative femininity, and the power to make our making of things in the home, private, amateur and secondary to paid work done outside the home. The so-called 'discourses' of the home, of paid work and of human reproduction (that is, ways of valuing and defining the activities included in the scope of, say, 'home'), are all linked to similar 'discourses' in law, medicine, education, leisure and entertainment, to announce that women's making of things is less important than and different from men's. In this way, masculine control of institutions from the family to the state (which is visible, and somewhat vulnerable to being re-formed) is based on vast ideological foundations that seem much more difficult to move.

Important also is the masculine control of the forms of knowledge and values which link notions of gender difference, and the supposed relative weakness of women, to a cluster of binary concepts used to 'make sense of' the world. Such couples as: public versus private; nature versus culture; body versus mind; reason versus emotion, have formed dualities, in which women always take the characteristics of the subordinate, dependent 'partner', which is made to appear opposite. This characterizing of women as body, emotion, nature and private has been used to place women's art-making in connection with the home, the family and our supposedly caring duties. This dualistic thinking has also extended into binaries used in the evaluation of art (such as decorative or functional; ornamental or structural; original or imitative; form or colour, and so on), which can be added to the basic dichotomies to create evaluations of women making things, regarded as emotional, sensuous, colourful, ornamental, derivative and decorative.

Western masculine investment in this system of ideas is intense, but it can be shown that its rigidity ignores the way the 'dichotomies' can be thought of as equal partners (as in 'body *and* mind', or 'public *and* private') and that other characteristics can be placed usefully with them, like 'reason *and* emotion *and* imagination'

17

(perhaps to describe a visual image), or 'functional *and* decorative *and* structural' (perhaps to describe a building). The 'either/or' system, which underpins the categorization of women and men as opposites, could be demolished to create a structure which would be subtly discriminating about our world and allow diverse distinctions of people. The binary system can be seen to achieve self-definition for the man at the expense of the negative concept 'opposed' to his apparent primary quality (of public importance and capacities, of reason, culture and the powers of the mind). Similar categorizations have been shown to operate to create the fictions of racial differences. In both cases, there is a privileged position, apparently independent of, but actually secured by, the subordinate position of the 'other'. And this provides conditions in which, although there may continually be contests to assign oppositional meanings to production, or for the exclusive making of white men to be open to all, strong barriers have been made.

The analysis of the way this binary system works shows how important it is for securing any groups in power: and the core philosophical system of dichotomies appears to be linked to many other attached systems, in areas such as education, law and medicine, and to categories for discussing art practices, each supporting one another in a systemic 'house-of-concept/cards'. This system, once understood, can be refused: Barbara Kruger's *We Won't Play Nature to Your Culture* (Pl. 1) gives a vivid example of such refusal in visual terms. We can call the system into question by showing the way in which the meaning of kinds of art-making will shift, depending on whether women or men are doing it. Thus Cheryl Buckley states:

> Historians have described at length Sonia Delaunay's *'instinctive' feeling* for *colour* while [her husband and design partner] Robert Delaunay is attributed with having *formulated* a colour *theory*. Robert Delaunay embodies the stereotype of men as logical and intellectual, while Sonia Delaunay embodies the female stereotype as instinctive and emotional.
>
> *(Buckley, 1986, p. 401, my emphasis)*

(The designs of Sonia and Robert Delaunay are difficult to tell apart.) Examples can also be found in the area of manufacturing, where all the dirtiest and heaviest kinds of making will be discovered in wartime to be highly suited to women: though illustrations of them doing this making will disappear. Or there may be objects permanently made by women whose womanufacture must be hidden to 'save the phenomena' of gender differentiation. This seems to be the case, for instance, with the brick industry in the Black Country area of the midlands in the UK where women made all the bricks (though men placed them in the kilns) between about 1850 and 1930. Yet it is inadmissible to recognize the brick buildings of the Black Country as substantially woman-made (Roszinska and Wightman, 1990). Definitions of skilled making as gendered will continually shift, from the media used, to kinds of skill, to the location of the skill, to whether it is paid or not, and to its scale or purpose, but always chasing the goal of representing the feminine as 'other'.

Just as the production of things is diversely gendered, so is their use and the attribution of meanings to them. Can women wield power tools? Can a woman use a fishing rod? And what sort of wrist-watch is correct for a man? The spheres of leisure and of paid work, of communication and the home present highly gendered patterns of consuming. For example, in her study of the way women made meanings in Harlow New Town in the 1950s, Judy Attfield highlighted the way in which conceiving of the house as one's place of labour and skill affects responses (Attfield, 1989). The women she interviewed liked old-fashioned parlours. They did not approve of the open-plan systems designed by men in the new houses. Their preferences rested on 'the need for women to have a room where they could relax and escape from unfinished work' (ibid., p. 221). Women could feel strongly about household appliances: 'I felt sick with the excitement of it. I had a refrigerator coming! And there it was – splendid in its packaging and ice-blue inside. It looked beautiful. I'd really arrived' (ibid., pp. 224).

Our responses to large and complex constructions, like the city, are gendered too. A survey of attitudes to the design of the new city of Milton Keynes showed how alienating and dangerous this urbanscape seems – with its beautiful tree-lined walk-ways keeping pedestrians well away from the fast road networks – if you are *not* one of the car-driving men who designed it, but a young woman with children and without transport (Matrix, 1984). This gendering in cultural representation varies dizzily from time to time and place to place (think of the seventeenth-century English aristocrats, for example, who stated their class and maleness with high-heeled shoes, silk stockings and long curling ringlets). The signifiers are always shifting, but what they signify remains the same.

Knowing something of the way the system works, as well as seeing how fluid and contradictory it is, suggests that it can be shifted, both by theoretical dismantling and prising apart, and by campaigning and activity to place women in all fields of making and in the teaching and valuing of things made. A pessimistic view predicts that, while women will be allowed into new areas of making, this will be accommodated so that the evaluative differentials are maintained. We see the pay differentials of medieval Europe sustained, for instance, in modern Britain (Shahar, 1983, p. 243; Coote and Campbell, 1982, p. 78). More optimistically, when the position of 'subordinate other' can be refused by women (*We Won't Play Nature to Your Culture*), *we* begin to define *our* diversities and *our* creativities. Equal others (anothers) have the ability to keep effectively disputing their positioning. They unfix the feminine of cultural representation. They cease to be where 'he' expects and tells them to be producing and using things.

In the subsequent articles in this chapter, authors discuss the representation of gender in visual and verbal images, in everyday speech and in the literary genres made accessible to women writers and readers. It should be pointed out that there are equivalents to these genres in art forms. For instance, women have been allowed to practise the forms of small-scale metalwork in jewellery or silver smithing, rather than founding bronze sculptures for public commemorative purposes. They have been able to make small, delicate, cheap watercolours for domestic display, rather than huge long-lasting frescoes for religious instruction, or full-length feature films, for a world audience. And this pattern meshes with the system of values pinning women to novels rather than poetry, to conversation rather than political speeches, and to making lace, not nets.

According to a masculine, geometrical, circular model of cultural activity, it is difficult to conceive of marginalized statements making real impact on the powerful centre of the system. But if we take another, feminine, model – of the plait – it is easier to imagine that diverse cultural strands could continually cross over one another, occupying both median and peripheral positions.

Article 1.2
ANALYSING REPRESENTATIONS
Richard Allen

A VARIETY OF IMAGES

I began this essay at the end of 1990 as war threatened in the Persian Gulf. Television and other media images concentrated on high technology and men at work, but interest also focused on women in a war zone as front-line members of the regular army. American women soldiers had served in Grenada and Panama, but the scale of the Gulf War made their position both more evident and more newsworthy.

Through one particular day I saw a sequence of different images of women soldiers. First I saw television pictures of women soldiers boarding a plane. Second, there was a close-up picture of a woman sitting cradling a rifle, occupying most of the front page of a newspaper. Then, again on a news-stand, I saw a picture of a woman soldier standing on guard duty, rifle at her side, gazing out across the desert – also occupying most of a page. Later in the day there was a television interview with a woman soldier; the questions focused on how she felt leaving her family.[1] Then, finally, I caught a kind of follow-up to this television interview where the local television station in the UK had discovered that the woman's child was staying with grandparents in the UK. We saw the child watching the television news apparently by chance; as pictures of the woman appeared on the screen the child ran over exclaiming, 'That's my mummy!'.

All the pictures I saw started from the same point – a desire to picture a woman soldier – but the results were very different. The nature of the picture appeared to be controlled as much by the place in which it appeared as by the subject itself. The second picture, for example, appeared in a newspaper which every day carries large pin-up pictures of women; the picture of the woman in the desert appeared to contrast with such pictures but it also picked up something of those sexualized images. In the fourth image, asking the woman how she felt about leaving her family behind showed the news editor particularly associating women with the family in a very conventional way; interviews with men were more likely to raise questions about training and preparedness for battle. Heterosexuality was also the norm – we did not see gay or lesbian soldiers being asked how they felt about leaving their partners. Both these elements are brought out very sharply in my last example. The local television news followed on from the national news so could hardly provide new mainstream coverage but it could provide local – and human interest – variants of the main stories. 'Human interest' easily pushes together women and children and identifies women by their role in the family – as 'mum' or 'mummy'.

The framing and focusing of images in the way I have described must be partly a conscious process – a journalist who moves from the *Financial Times* to *Spare Rib* adopts a new style – but so many of the meanings involved are so familiar that it must also be an almost unconscious process for anyone at home in the media of our society. As I saw the sequence of images, I had my part to play as well. When I saw pictures of women soldiers in different places on the same day, or when I read an account of the same events in two different papers, I could understand how each of the stories or pictures meant the same and yet also meant something different. When I read a newspaper or watch news and current affairs programmes on television, on the surface some things are 'opinion' while some things are 'fact', but the 'factual' images are as much the result of a person writing as 'opinion' is, and I am hardly for a moment deceived into seeing them as absolutely true. When I see an advertisement, I cheerfully understand the 'truths' it contains while understanding exactly the nature of those truths.

Confronted by images, our impulse is to understand rather than to find things incomprehensible. In a familiar culture it is not the difficulty of finding and making meanings which is most striking but the way in which those meanings depend on assumptions shared between the producer of the image and the viewer and on the context in which the image appears at least as much as on the image itself. Seen in a place where images of younger women are almost invariably sexualized, women soldiers offer sexually exciting meanings; seen in a context where women are most associated with family, a woman soldier is really a 'mummy'.

When we come to images from an unfamiliar culture, the situation is more complex. On the day after I saw the sequence of Gulf War images I saw a picture of Saudi-Arabian women training in civil defence; this showed five women standing in a line all wearing the black Islamic clothing which covered everything except their eyes and hands. The right arms of the women were extended, each holding and aiming a heavy pistol. At one level the image was comparable with the images of the women soldiers and, since it appeared in a western paper, it was easy for me to interpret it within the same western conventions. The image resisted this absorption; the dress of the women asserted their femininity, very distinct from the dress of masculinity, but refused the western conventional associations of women with sexuality and the family. But the urge to create meaning was still there. I drew on conventions which identify the nation and patriotism as female – the English have a Queen and Britannia, the French Marianne, or even the image of a woman soldier standing with men saluting the flag. Through these images, patriotism draws strength from the link with femininity and the desire of the mother to protect her child: the image of the Saudi women was more powerful an expression of patriotism than a squad of soldiers would have been. The picture also came close to engaging with other less pleasant conventions from the European colonialist past, which identified non-white women as exotic and sexually exciting and white men as inherently superior. In this respect, the picture is a way of saying something about the distant strangeness of the Gulf War and in a racist way about the superiority of the West; the women may be ready to defend their homes but it is the West which has the high technology weaponry which will protect them. As with the earlier images, meanings that arise here have more to do with the context in which the pictures appear – and what we bring to them. The reality of the women in the pictures is stolen and used for some wider purpose. The 'we' needs to be qualified here, along with the nature of the wider purpose, for all the conventions to which I have referred assume a masculine point of view. As a man, I am plainly involved in that point of view, but the point of view is so very common that it *can* be part of the familiar way of understanding for women and men. From this point of view, the combination of soldiering and femininity is strange; perhaps overall the images 'mean' that, for the conventional male gaze, femininity is somehow strange, even abnormal?

How does this relate to images which do not appear in public, easily recognizable contexts? In my own photograph album I find a picture of someone, probably in his late teens, sitting, half turning in his chair to look at the camera. I know that this is a picture of me, although whether someone would recognize this is a bit doubtful since my facial features have changed since then. How could anyone else recover the meaning of this picture? The place in which it appears – a family album – sets things going. Immediately the picture can be interpreted as a 'portrait' of someone. It might be, too, that you would understand some of the features of the room in the picture to show that it was taken in a school. I am flinging wide my arms in the picture and the expression on my face shows recognizable signs perhaps that I am excited, but how do you know whether I have just come top in mechanical engineering or been told that I can study domestic science at A-level? Without further information about the context, you cannot decipher the original meaning of the picture or the meaning it has for me now.

How can you break the code and know what the photograph is 'about'? We can probably agree generally on the meaning of a picture from our own culture when it shows someone who is sad or happy, but how do we understand the relation between a person and a place or possessions? If we see a picture of a man standing in front of a house, how do we know whether he owns it or not? If the picture shows a woman in front of a house, do we consider the same set of possibilities? Do we understand a man standing in front of a fast car in the same way as when we see a woman standing beside the same kind of car? I know, or should I say, I understand, that my photograph in fact represents me not wanting to be photographed and therefore adopting a pose which would guarantee that the photograph was not an accurate representation of me. Someone else who knows me may say, 'But in fact that is a good representation of you'.

An understanding of a public image seems to depend on shared assumptions whereas the private image seems much more open to interpretation in different ways. Representations of self are explored in more detail elsewhere in this book.[2] Here I will only suggest that a simple division of this kind is impossible. Neutrality – freedom from familiar understandings – is equally impossible. Hardly anyone reads a newspaper in an entirely passive way, and even I read my own photograph within the same cultural framework as I read a newspaper picture. Even the most private level of understanding is formed by conventions; we expect the fragmentary images of old photographs to help explain our present selves.[3]

NAKED AND NATURAL

The idea that the meaning of a representation is created by where it appears and what we bring to it (by its context and conventions) has been commonplace in the study of art for many years but gender has often been absent from the discussion. In his seminal book *Art and Illusion*, Professor Sir E.H. Gombrich writes that 'no artist can "paint what he sees"' (Gombrich, 1960). The book as a whole explores not only how the images artists make are created by pre-existing ideas and conventions, but also how the viewer is involved in a similar process. The 'tendency of our minds' in an art gallery and in everyday life is 'to classify and register our experience in terms of the known'; '. . . I vividly remember the shock I had while I was studying . . . formulas for chubby children: I never thought they could exist, but all of a sudden I saw such children everywhere' (ibid., p. 144). We can see nothing new; all our new understanding and all our new seeing is formed by what we have seen before.

Amongst the many paintings Gombrich discusses is one by the nineteenth-century French painter Edouard Manet, 'Le Déjeuner sur l'herbe' (1863). It shows four people in a rather private and enclosed woodland setting; two are men who sit in a relaxed fashion, fully and rather formally clothed, apparently together. Two are women; one appears to be drying herself by a pool, the other sits with the men – both are naked. When first shown, the picture shocked those who saw it as representing the immoral life lived by artists. Gombrich scorns this moralizing response. He sees it as a masterpiece of composition – something particularly exciting because of the way it echoes and reworks the known. Research shows that the painting is based 'on a print from Raphael's circle' praised at the time as a model of how to compose an image. The image was new and realistic but we can only understand it because it is also 'a very closely knit configuration of relationships which cannot be varied beyond certain limits without becoming unintelligible to artist and public alike . . .' (ibid., pp. 273–4).

Manet's technical skill is beyond doubt, but to me Gombrich's comments cannot help me understand the most peculiar part of the picture – that the men are clothed and the women not – nor can his suggested compositional source, for in the earlier picture all the characters are shown in classical nudity. His understandings do build on meanings shared with, or originating from, Manet himself; one account of the creation of the picture tells us:

> Some women were bathing. Manet had his eye fixed on the flesh of those coming out of the water. 'It appears', he said, 'that I must do a nude. Very well, I'll do one. When we were at Couture's I copied Giorgione's 'Concert Champetre' . . . I want to do that over again in terms of transparent light and with people like these'.
>
> (Richardson, 1972, p. 22)[4]

A wider sense of the involvement of gender in the meaning of the image seems missing from both accounts and this prompts me to want to develop my own reading of the picture. The woman drying herself is set apart from the other people in the picture; this gives her a special significance for the viewer of the picture. Because of the separation and the classical overtones she may appear simply an expression of beauty – so conventionally familiar as hardly to provoke comment. The second woman seems to me inevitably to provoke a sense of disturbance. She is naked but sits in such a way that her body is not 'displayed' for the viewer as it often is in paintings of the nude. One leg is extended and the foot lies between the legs of one of the clothed men quite close to his genitals, but the sexuality of this is half barred because he sits with one arm outstretched, half pointing at the woman and the second man who sits next to her. Sexuality is again avoided by the way the heads of the woman and the second man are painted very separately and the way both look challengingly out at the viewer and not at each other.

The account above represents Manet wanting to create disturbances in art – 'to do that over again' – but apparently unconscious of his act of voyeurism when he saw the bathers and when he painted the picture. Looking at the image now the disturbance and the taking over of the women interact. A good deal of the fascination of the picture lies, as Margaret Walters has commented in *The Nude Male*, in the way the picture works to 'challenge audiences by putting a naked and very contemporary woman into a traditional setting' (Walters, 1979, p. 237). It provokes an understanding of the fundamental convention on which the painting relies – that 'the female nude of the last couple of centuries exists *only* as an incarnation of male desire' (ibid., p. 13). The disturbing nature of the image lies for me in the way it forces those ways of looking into the light. A male viewer, who may, perhaps with a shock, see here the habitual way he sees the female body naked and available to his gaze, must see the image in a different way from a female viewer who will not need a representation to know this oppression. Perhaps because the image is self-consciously provocative as well as exploitative, feminist artists have reworked it, reversing the image to make the men naked and the women clothed, or used it for new kinds of provocations. One of Jean Fraser's photographs in a series called 'Celestial Bodies' shows a group of three figures modelled on the composition of Manet's painting. In the photograph, reproduced in the collection *Stolen Glances: lesbians take photographs* (Fraser and Boffin, 1991), the two men are replaced by women formally and fully clothed in nun's habits while the third woman sits among them naked as in 'Le Déjeuner'.

Reversing and reworking images in this way involves working 'against the grain'; this graphic phrase also nicely emphasizes the way women can appropriate a process, like woodworking, commonly seen as male. Subversion of assumptions which only appear to be shared is a key element in the process, and with that subversion goes the claim that the disorientation is a greater truth than that contained in the original image. The reversal, as with the spray-painted comments on advertisements, offers a later and greater truth. In this respect, it contrasts strongly with any notion that one should search for the truth in the words of the producer of the image.

SYSTEMS OF REPRESENTATION

Pornographic images of women crudely expose the links between the habitual understandings of representation, male desire and the taking over of women's bodies; in the sophistication of Manet's work we get a different sense of the weight of the past as it bears on women in art and in life. On both counts, ways of challenging understandings as they appear in the past and the present then become important for women. Making new ways of representing may involve radical reformulations – which can at first exist only within a small protected area – or be a matter of inch by inch reformulating the conventions operating within the society as a whole. In *The Nude Male*, Margaret Walters writes of women painters who are trying radically to reverse the traditional gender roles of artist and nude:

> For a woman to paint the male nude, as against being painted nude by a man, is a break with our whole art tradition . . . [radical women] artists [do this when they] play jokes with the sexual metaphors we take for granted. Anita Steckel, for example, has done a number of phallic city skylines, sometimes funny and sometimes surreally menacing. Her *Feminist Peep-show* consisted of forty photographs of dignified Victorian gentlemen, bearded and heavily clothed; below the waist, Steckel drew in bare legs and weird and comic penises.
>
> *(Walters, 1979, pp. 314, 317)*

This quotation shows well how battles between radical and orthodox representations can seem almost inevitably like a struggle between something strange and different and something very familiar. Familiar representations woven into the seamless web of historical accounts perhaps only become obviously problematic when they are taken from their contexts. After producing his monumentally successful history of western culture, *Civilisation*, Kenneth Clark published another book – again designed to glorify European culture – *Feminine Beauty*. It consists of a series of images drawn from western art, initially designed to illustrate a historical thesis:

> The discovery of feminine beauty, like so much that we value in civilized life, was made in Egypt in the second millennium BC. It was a sort of miracle . . .
>
> Raphael's concept of feminine beauty had an influence that cannot be overstated. For over three hundred years it was an ideal to which every woman aspired. *'Belle comme une Madone de Raphael'* was a standard expression of praise, and was reflected in the work of dozens of painters from Ingres downwards . . .
>
> *(Clark, 1980, pp. 8, 17)*

But when he comes to the twentieth century Clark's historical framework begins to slip:

> We have all lost self-confidence, and our beauties are not immune. But, as if to show that all such generalisations are nonsense, the book ends with the glorious photograph of

Marilyn Monroe on the beach, doing a high kick . . .

Going back over the plates one has the feeling that, although almost everything else in the world has changed, feminine beauty has remained constant.

(*Ibid.*, p. 33)[5]

We are told that confidence is restored, but at the expense of shifting from the specifics of history to some vague 'constant'. Then there is the uneasy shift in pronouns and point of view – 'we' and 'our' shift to 'the book ends' and to 'one'. All conceal the masculine point of view and the partiality of the account. If the 'one' has the same timelessness as the 'constant', we are left with some kind of crudely simple image of gender relations. If 'one' like 'everything else' changes, the image is of man changing through history while woman remains a kind of perpetual beautiful child (the choice of Marilyn Monroe as representative is significant here).

Clark's representations of femininity show the normalizing process as it operates at a level of ideals and high art: the contents of this book will indicate how widely the notion of 'representation' can be applied. Going beyond the widest boundaries of what might be called art, it can also be applied to our daily lives – we represent ourselves through what we choose to wear, through make-up, body language and so on, and other people read those representations when they see us. As Alison Lurie writes in *The Language of Clothes*:

Long before I am near enough to talk to you on the street . . . you announce your sex, age and class to me through what you are wearing . . . By the time we meet and converse we have already spoken to each other in an older and more universal tongue . . . clothing is a language . . .

(*Lurie, 1983, p. 3*)

The equation of the process of representation with language is helpful since it emphasizes how much representation is a system of communication; something that only exists when there is someone to receive the meaning as well as someone producing it. The analogy also prompts us to recognize not only the omnipresent nature of representation but also the need to acknowledge that there are different representation systems as there are different languages.[6] The danger of the analogy with language is that it may carry with it undesirable implications, such as that there are sets of abstract rules, or that we are only concerned with words, or that there are correct forms and so on. The term 'discourse' is ultimately more useful because it stresses the dynamic flowing nature of the process and because it stresses meaning rather than, for example, the rules of grammar. In 'Le Déjeuner' one might then say, analysing the representation, that meaning is created, or the painting is constructed, within the discourse of 'nature and the natural', the discourse of

28

'femininity' and the discourse of 'art'. Femininity unavoidably foregrounds gender but frequently in the discourses of art and nature gender has been either absent or concealed – as in Manet's own comment. If this is so, the apparently genderless discourses of art and nature may succeed in neutralizing the gendering. On the other hand, an awareness of the powerful gendering in the discourse of femininity may succeed in gendering nature and art.

Examples of discourses could be multiplied; I will refer only to one other very different example, namely that which contains the simple words 'we' and 'our'. Such words appear to refer to some kind of group and something shared, but at other times they represent something different covering over differences. For example, if I write here 'in this picture we understand . . .', I may be referring to an understanding that we share but I am more likely to be claiming a common meaning, coercing you into accepting that meaning as something we share. In this case I might be said to be using a discourse of commonality in order to give authority to my words and conceal the possibility of a different view. Authors often use a similar strategy by using a discourse of impersonality – 'It was a dark night . . .' or 'Once upon a time there was . . .' – to establish a poem or story as something independent of themselves and therefore having greater authority.

DEGREES OF FREEDOM

As with language, I would want to stress not only that a discourse operates across boundaries but also the need to acknowledge the particularity of meanings and discourses. On the one hand, the meaning of nature in a picture is in some way akin to the meaning of nature in a garden, but on the other hand the representation of nature in a French painting of the 1860s operates in a different world from my 1990s English garden. The meanings which arise in a specific medium are in many respects specific to that medium; we understand pictures in newspapers in terms of other pictures in newspapers, films in terms of other films and so on.

Particular forms are known as 'genres' so we can think of these meanings as 'generic' understandings.[7] We have given particular prominence to the generic forms of literature in this book – in the next article Dinah Birch concentrates on poetry and in Chapter 2 there are discussions of the short story and science fiction. Here I will use as my example the novel, arguably the most important and fruitful generic form for women.

The novel has particular importance for women from a historical point of view because its growth in the eighteenth and nineteenth centuries was involved with the increase in the number of women working as writers producing material for public sale. The novel was originally 'novel'; a new and unconventional form hardly taken more seriously than avant-garde writing today. By the nineteenth century it was seen as dominated by women writers, women's issues and by a style of writing we call 'realism'. In simple terms, this meant that novels echoed non-fictional writing and engaged with the issues of the real world. Increasingly, the special and generic understandings and conventions of fiction and the novel slipped into what appears as the transcribing of the generic understandings of everyday life. In realistic novels, descriptions of men's and women's dress, for example, are bound by the same conventions as in life; decent women may wear trousers but only after 1920 – decent men may not wear skirts, unless they are in the Far East and foreign. In realistic fiction unorthodox behaviour is understood as wayward or wicked.

Realistic novels by women (and occasionally men) have achieved extraordinary insights into the situation of women in society and have been the starting point for many people's thinking about feminism and gender issues, putting on paper and thus into public view aspects of women's lives which had hitherto been almost secrets. But the genre itself has limits. Gillian Beer has put this point in the context of the work of Mary Ann Evans who wrote in the mid-nineteenth century as George Eliot. Evans herself lived a strikingly unorthodox life but only some of this is carried through into her fiction where in the end:

> The individual [woman] is directed into a restricted time, space and activity . . . Although she cannot know all the conditions that have brought her there, they are, according to this arrangement of experience, ineluctably present, intertwined and matted so thick that there is no space, no interruption, no moment, which can escape from sequence. [In the novels we find] determinism [which] emphasises relations, but relations fixed in a succession which more or less acutely delimits and characterises. It is a process which we recognise in *Middlemarch*'s melancholy . . .
>
> (Beer, 1979, p. 81)

Evans' use of deterministic discourse then builds into her novels a strong sense that the world is naturally a place, in Beer's words, of 'inherent and irreversible order' (ibid.). One might suggest that this discourse is gender blind – that it affects men as well as women – but this would hardly be true given that in this context it fixes masculinity as different from but superior to femininity. The determinism in representations of masculinity includes the freedoms men can partake of in society – travelling freely, determining whom to have a relationship with and pursuing that person, work etc.

The realistic discourse and the genre of the novel allowed women to write about the present oppression of women in society. Logically, to represent a more radical future a writer had to break free of realism or at least fracture the realism in some ways. Mary Ann Evans does attempt this (for example, by feminizing a male character) but such is the strength and power of the realism that this radicalism is overwhelmed and for many readers appears only as artistic failure. Mixing discourses and generic understandings is not easy. Chavelita Dunne, who wrote as George Egerton in the 1890s, provides another interesting example of the issue I am discussing. In *Women and Fiction*, Patricia Stubbs writes of Dunne:

> Egerton's rejection of realism is I think significant. It has certain fundamental limitations, but is bound up with the imaginative leap she was able to make into the future. It is this vision – of new possibilities, of different ways of living – which makes her work important. It provided alternative models on which women could focus and which could act as a measure of both their achievements and their potential.

(Stubbs, 1979, p. 112)

The fact that you are likely to have heard of George Eliot but not of George Egerton no doubt has a good deal to do with the fact that Mary Ann Evans published more, but it has also to do with the form each chose – Dunne worked particularly with the less common short story – and the conventions within which they worked. Representations operating within the realistic mode have been more acceptable than non-realistic representations; even the idealized happenings of romantic or historical fiction are usually anchored within realism. In the history of women's writing, radical or utopian representations of women seem difficult to achieve.[8]

CREATIVITY

When we – or in the light of what I have said above, should I say 'when I' – analyse representations of and by women, I want to add an awareness of the difficulty of using the single category 'women' to an understanding of genre. Women with different languages work within different representational frameworks, as do women of different social classes. A difference of colour also implies a difference in generic understandings and conventions. Women of colour in the USA are different from women in Asia or Africa. The level at which you define a gender-based group in analysing representation is far more to do with how you want to place your analysis than with any fixed gender structure; you may want to stress sisterhood and use 'women's' in a wide sense (e.g. as in 'women's fiction'), or you may want to identify the very specific and particular nature of a cultural practice.

In the course of a discussion of Maya Angelou in the collection *Black Women Writers*, Sondra O'Neale pitches her analysis at a level which groups black women in the USA and assumes a crossover from literary genres to life in general in making the following point:

> The Black woman is America's favourite unconfessed symbol. She is the nation's archetype for unwed mothers, welfare checks, and food stamps. Her round, smiling face bordered by the proverbial red bandanna is the requisite sales image for synthetic pancakes and frozen waffles 'just like Mammy use to make.' Only her knowledgeable smile of expertise can authenticate the flavour of corporately fried chicken.
>
> (O'Neale, 1985, p. 25)

Elsewhere in the collection, Barbara Christian explores Alice Walker's attempts to rediscover generic meanings and forms suited to represent the specificity of Black American women's experience, aspirations and creativity. Genre boundaries again seem to be blurred. Radicalism takes a different form again, avoiding avant-garde conventions of formlessness and irrationality:

> Walker is drawn to the integral and economical process of quilt making as a model for her craft. For through it, one can create out of seemingly disparate everyday materials patterns of clarity, imagination and beauty . . .
>
> What did some slave women or Black women of this century do with the creativity that might have, in a less restrictive society, expressed itself in paint, words, clay? Walker reflects on a truth so obvious it is seldom acknowledged: they used the few media left them by a society that labelled them lowly, menial. Some, like Walker's mother, expressed it in the growing of magnificent gardens; some in cooking; others in quilts of imagination and passion like the one Walker saw at the Smithsonian Institution. Walker's description of that quilt's impact on her brings together essential elements of her more recent work . . . her transformation despite opposition of the bits and pieces allowed her by society into a work of functional beauty.
>
> (Christian, 1985, pp. 461–2)[9]

The focus on the individual writer brings in another kind of radicalism here – individual women from oppressed groups can gain special status as that kind of special person we call an artist. In this last phrase I want to draw attention to the need again to look at something familiar in an unfamiliar light: like the 'we', the label 'artist' is bound by conventions. *Conventionally* if art is valued (along with the creativity we attribute to the artist), part of that value lies in the freedom we ascribe to the originator of it. Art then has a special place in feminism because it demonstrates feminist creativity and the bringing of new light and truth. Paradoxes soon begin to appear. The feminist artist rebels against orthodoxy but shares in the long-standing conventional association in western culture that the author or artist is the originator and sole proprietor of her or his work. On the other hand, everything tells us that writers and artists cannot be entirely free; the conventions of language and imagery, as well as the forms that have been used in the past, bear upon them as they bear upon their readers. The notion that the representations and meanings they create are liberated knowledge seems vitally important and yet adopting it aligns the feminist with older more conservative views of art as entirely autonomous. Adopting a radical stance, however, aligns her with those like Raymond Williams who have argued that everything to do with a work of art, including the mind of the artist, is socially produced and complexly determined.[10]

We seem caught between a view which sees the artist as entirely free on the one hand, and one who is completely determined on the other. To see the artist as having that degree of freedom seems unreal, but it seems too limiting to see her compelled only to shuffle preprinted cards. There is no easy way of resolving this problem at a theoretical level, but the comment about Alice Walker above may help us think it through on a practical level.

The visit to the Smithsonian Institute appears as the key which enabled her to move into using new forms; a completely chance encounter which she of her own accord seizes upon and which produces an unpredictable outcome. But such new experiences and such sets of conventions do not await our visits like stations arranged by the side of a railway line where we might stop by choice or by accident and suddenly change trains. To describe the moment in a different way might then involve our saying that the meaning and conventions of the representation Walker created for herself as a black woman writer in the USA included a sense of history which was conventionally understood in terms of the Smithsonian Institute. But within that building the balance of determinations shifted and a new understanding was formed by a rejection of conventional and white meanings. As I write such sentences they seem immeasurably crude as a way of describing a complex and dynamic moment; they also stress, again, differences. As a white man living in the UK, my ability to understand how a black woman's moment in the USA was formed is very limited. But there is meaning for me, and that is formed within my own conventional and generic understandings of representations of black women, quilts, the Smithsonian Museum and so on.

REPRESENTATIONS AND POWER

These examples from black women's work in the USA emphasize the co-existence in culture of both complex understandings and the inevitably political nature of representation. The process is summed up by Griselda Pollock and Rozsika Parker in *Framing Feminism* as follows:

> ... meanings depend on the relationships between a single image and its total cultural environment of images and social belief systems ... For any viewer to understand any image she must carry a whole baggage of social knowledges, assumptions, values ... What secures which connotations prevail as a preferred meaning is ideology, understood as a complex of meanings and practices which form the dominant order of sense, a regime of truth for a particular culture or social group. Therefore notions of images whose meanings derive from the conscious intentions of their maker gave way to an understanding of the social and ideological networks within which meanings are socially produced and secured.
>
> *(Parker and Pollock, 1987, pp. 125–6)*

Stereotypical conventions and established genres which privilege the male viewpoint are here highlighted as 'a regime of truth' which bears down on women's work in creating and engaging with representations. The regime can seem almost omnipotent, the most basic means of expression being male. As Cora Kaplan puts it:

> ... the very condition of [women's] accession to their own subjectivity, to the consciousness of a self which is both personal and public is the unwitting acceptance of the law which limits their speech. This condition places them in a special relation to language which becomes theirs as a consequence of becoming human, and at the same time not theirs as a consequence of becoming female.
>
> *(Kaplan, 1986, p. 85)[11]*

Such trains of thought can rapidly lead to pessimism; to imagine some kind of free conventionless representations would provide a way out, but how could this be achieved? The act of abandonment seems too great.

One possibility, whereby pessimism may be limited, power and inequality acknowledged and creativity re-emphasized, might begin from thinking through the meaning of power in relation to discourse and the artist and reader/viewer. The models offered by Michel Foucault in his historical analyses of social forms, particularly sexuality, are helpful here. In his analysis of sexuality, two aspects seem to be particularly relevant here: first, the way sexuality has become 'the privileged place where our deepest "truth" is read and expressed' (Foucault, 1988, pp. 111);[12] second, sexuality has been used as a means of exerting control within society, particularly via the practice of medicine. Towards the eighteenth century 'the female body became a medical object *par excellence*' (ibid., p. 115).

Representations of women which dress them only in their sexuality (like 'Le Déjeuner' perhaps) in a parallel way say, 'You are nothing but your sex, you are always the object of the artist's gaze, never the artist'. The clothed doctor or artist and the naked patient or model becomes the image of gender relations in western culture.

How can we move on from here? First we can emphasize that the self cannot have a single neutral form. In an interview Foucault has said:

> . . . the political analysis of power which was offered did not seem to me to account for the finer, more detailed phenomena I wish to evoke when I pose the question of telling the truth about oneself. If I tell the truth about myself, . . . it is in part that I am constituted as a subject across a number of power relations *which are exerted over me and which I exert over others*.
>
> (*Ibid., p. 39, my italics*)

Power needs also to be separated from force:

> Power is only a certain type of relation between individuals. . . . The characteristic feature of power is that some men can more or less entirely determine other men's conduct – but never exhaustively or coercively. A man who is chained up and beaten is subject to force being exerted over him. Not power. But if he can be induced to speak, when his ultimate recourse could have been to hold his tongue, preferring death, then he has been caused to behave in a certain way. His freedom has been subjected to power. He has been submitted to government. If an individual can remain free, however little his freedom may be, power can subject him to government. There is no power without potential refusal or revolt.
>
> (*Ibid., pp. 83–4*)[13]

Some representations do subject women to 'force' by entirely silencing them – for example, hard-core pornography – but more often what we see are representations marked by power. A picture of a woman as a Madonna submits her to government by showing not a range of possible different subjectivities but a single 'true' one. But the potential revolt is there in the creativity of the female. The virgin birth which lies at the heart of Christianity may seem to entirely divorce women from sexuality and condemn them to regard man as a God, but it can be reconstructed as a kind of creativity without the inconvenience of a man.

In *The Subversive Stitch*, Rozsika Parker describes a number of examples of women's work which embody this kind of refusal and revolt:

> Beryl Weaver embroiders bouquets of flowers, ladies in crinolines amongst the hollyhocks, rustic cottages . . . [but] . . . she subverts these images: 'I was never encouraged to create disturbing images, so my anger comes through in the pretty pictures I was brought up with.'
>
> The picturesque cottage casement is embroidered with the words 'shattered and shuttered' – Beryl Weaver's feelings about the solitary confinement of a life dedicated to domestic femininity and nothing else.
>
> Kate Walker's attitude is characteristic of contemporary feminists' determination not to reject femininity but to empty the term of its negative connotations, to reclaim and refashion the category . . .
>
> She takes the format of the sampler, but the stitched sayings are defiant not compliant, most unladylike: 'Wife is a four-letter word', 'This is a present to me', both declaring her rejection of the self-repression and submission encouraged by traditional sampler-making.

(Parker, 1984, pp. 205–7)

IDEOLOGY AND POWER

Ideology gives us a way of understanding the nature of 'government' and refusal. But it is important to stress from the beginning that using the term in this singular and unitary way is as dangerous as using 'self' in a single and simple way. Rather, we should think in terms of ideologies or perhaps of an ideological process operating within society. Adopting this kind of formulation, Terry Lovell writes in *Pictures of Reality*:

> Beliefs or bodies of ideas which are ideological are in some sense inadequate, partial or distorted. This alone is not . . . enough to define ideologies . . .
>
> . . . to this first criterion must be added a second, that the inadequacies of ideology in terms of the claim to knowledge are socially motivated in relation to the class struggle . . . But again, this second criterion on its own would not serve to identify ideologies. For there are bona fide bodies of knowledge which are developed and institutionalised in such a way that they serve the interests of domination. Any dominant class will . . . attempt to ensure that that knowledge is produced

and disseminated in a manner which serves its class interests ... Ideology, then, may be defined as the production and dissemination of erroneous beliefs whose inadequacies are socially motivated ...

It follows that to speak of ideas as ideological is always to make some claims about their effects as well as about their validity.

(Lovell, 1983, pp. 51–2)

Lovell stresses that while certain conventional knowledge is 'erroneous' – for example, it is wrong not to question that women figure naked in pictures so much more than men, or that men seem to have written so much more poetry than women – there is knowledge which is bona fide; for example, that women are biologically different from men. However, since she then goes on to say that this knowledge will be used by the dominant class, one is, perhaps, entitled to ask how we could ever encounter such knowledge in a free, pure form. In this respect the notion of 'error' seems inappropriate since it also seems to suppose an 'error-free' – and thus ideology-free – knowledge. Given the way understanding in its widest sense is bound up with conventions and genres, etc., it seems better to allow that all representation is ideological; that is, that it expresses a 'partial' truth in the service of some social group. The danger of this position, in turn, is that different ideologies come to seem to be competing on equal terms within some common area. Such an understanding can hardly be sustained for these partial truths are inextricably bound up with effects, with inequality and the suppression of points of view. As Michèle Barrett puts its, 'Ideology – as the work of constructing meaning – cannot be divorced from its material conditions in a given historical period' (Barrett, 1980, p. 112), and thus cannot be divorced from class and gender relations. To speak of established art as reflecting the interests of the dominant class or gender now seems too crude. It is more useful to think of it as being involved in the authorizing of a particular partial truth as the sole truth in the interests of a particular class. A concept which can be used to describe this process is 'hegemony' which Barrett describes as follows: 'The concept of "hegemony" refers to the organisation of popular consent to the ideology of the dominant group and for "hegemony" to be secured everyone must accept, at the level of "common-sense" knowledge, the view of the dominant class' (Barrett, 1980, p. 123).

In British culture, then, representations of the heterosexual family as the natural form of social organization can be defined as part of the organizing of popular consent. Women are, in Foucault's terms, 'induced to speak' and to consent to this partial truth. Through realism too, it can be argued, popular consent is given a voice; women writers register their experience in society as different but that difference and inequality is perpetuated. Thus the notion of a single dominant ideology corresponding to a single class position can then be transformed into a model whereby power includes the ability to incorporate the interests of other groups. Realism as a literary convention works in this way for women; it appears to give women writers a means of registering their difference in society from men but becomes a means whereby that difference and equality can be perpetuated within society.

If ideology enables us to formulate ideas about power relations within the processes of representation, can an understanding of ideology enable us to see how things might change? At the simplest level one might speak of new ideological practices being opposed to conventional ones, as in the example of Anita Steckel's nudes, or men in the West wearing skirts and make-up. But such shifts can be assimilated within the ideological hegemony – Steckel's paintings can be absorbed into the mainstream art market, while perfume can be worn by men as a sign of masculinity rather than rejection of power.

Terry Lovell offers a fruitful alternative to my pessimism here and an interesting critique of the nature of realism as I have described it so far. She begins from the idea that the 'novel' form was appropriate in the eighteenth century to convey the idea of 'capitalism's own preferred self-image'. A character in a realistic novel, like a good worker, is:

> ... a unified subject who inhabits a sober, predictable world, and has a stable self-identity; who clocks on and off with a certain degree of predictable reality ...
>
> But capitalism equally needs a different kind of subject in those moments of leisure/pleasure which punctuate the working life. The self most open to infatuation with the wares of the capitalist market place is not the unified self modelled on the protestant ethic ... It is a self which feels at home and comfortable in a world in which 'all that is solid melts into air' ... The nineteenth-century realist novel had its face turned towards both poles. It produced, as it had to under conditions of commodity capitalism, narratives which entertained, and which in entertaining, opened up attractive and even frightening prospects outside of the ordered regularity of a mundane bourgeois world.
>
> (Lovell, 1983, pp. 15–16)

Representations have here been linked to the social ground from which they emerge but space has also been found for a degree of freedom, for pleasure, and for the imagination.

THE POWER OF THE READER

To some, seeking the origins and meanings of ideology and representations only in the period when the text was written is inadequate. Such a model assumes that a text has a particular meaning which it acquires when it is written and which we must recover, but can we ever 'reclaim' the past in this way? In making history, do we not construct a representation of the past? If this is so, any 'history' of an event or a period must be subject to the same kind of analysis as a novel or painting dealing with the same topic. Facts have their part to play but dates in history have the same reality as the class relationships which may be 'imagined' in a novel. From this point of view, meaning – and with it ideology – arises from representation not in the authoritative moment of its first construction, but on all the many occasions when it is read or looked at afterwards. And on each occasion a different meaning can arise. Roland Barthes has been influential in exploring these ideas; in 'The Death of the Author' he writes:

> ... a text consists not of a line of words, releasing a single ... meaning ... but of a multidimensional space in which are married and contested several writings, none of them original: the text is a fabric of quotations, resulting from a thousand sources of culture ... [it] consists of multiple writings, proceeding from several cultures and entering into dialogue, into parody, into contestation; but there is a site where this multiplicity is collected, and this site is not the author, as has hitherto been claimed, but the reader: the reader is the very space in which are inscribed ... all the citations out of which a writing is made ...
>
> The reader is a man [sic] without history, without biography, without psychology; he is only that *someone* who holds collected into one and the same field all the traces from which writing is constituted.
>
> (Barthes, 1986, pp. 52–4)

The freedom here envisaged may remind you of the possibilities of subverting conventional images to which I have already referred. The death of the author carries with it the death of authority and perhaps even the death of repressive patriarchy. Perhaps pessimism can be pushed aside, perhaps representation need not repress. If, as Mary Jacobus writes, putting the ideas within a feminist context, all readers and all readings are in some way 'different' and 'without history', then each reading can exist free. When I read I assemble the 'citations' in a unique way in the present. In this moment, selecting from the whole range of possibilities, like a shopper in a fabulous market place, I can release all my repressed desires. In more coldly abstract terms: 'though necessarily working within "male" discourse, women's writing ... would work ceaselessly to deconstruct it: to write what cannot be written' (Jacobus, 1979, pp. 12–13).

Such views chime with the notion of reading 'against the grain' of traditional or conventional interpretations of established art, writing and so on to which I have already referred. The strength of Jacobus's phrase 'to write what cannot be written' is, however, that it avoids the binary ('with the grain' or 'against the grain') to stress the creation of an individual meaning. It also avoids setting up the idea of texts having new single 'truer' meanings for feminism since this confines you as much within the idea of a limited text as an acceptance of an old 'authorized' version. Rather, each individual is creator, let loose in multi-dimensional space.

Such an idea simultaneously attracts and repels. On the one hand, it is attractive to think that one can escape from the coercion that resides in ideologically loaded and stereotypical representations; there is also a well-established notion that art involves subjective judgements rather than objective values. On the other hand, the idea offends against the sense that, though there are not fixed meanings in artworks, we can usually find some broadly shared meanings. Against the strong pressure to speak of 'different' meanings which are produced in what the introduction to this book refers to as a 'multiple subject' is the pressure to identify oneself as part of a unitary category – to write as a *woman* the history of *women's* artistic work and record *women's* creativity. Reading in the present may liberate us from the weight of history, but are we ready to give up the idea that we can understand the past and write a history of gender which is relatively stable?

Representations of self by the self (i.e. self-portraits, autobio-graphies by women), which are the subject of later essays in the book, throw the paradox into relief. When we read, is the meaning we individually create the representation of a subjectivity unified by gender, or do we construct a multiple subject in which gender is probably the main part? When we try to understand ourselves do we exclude history from that understanding?

This issue touches me personally, for the position of a man in a volume on women's studies must be problematic. Any man who is convinced of the extraordinarily valuable insights that feminist work has brought to the study of all art forms is tempted to join with the movement and believe that he can share in the meanings of representations. Yet he must immediately acknowledge that he cannot innocently cross the gender divide for his subjectivity is, in multiple and shifting ways, situated as masculine. He may rebel against the over-simplification which forces people into two gender categories (masculine or feminine) because there are two sex categories (male or female), claiming a special affinity between gay men, gay women, and women 'in general'. The alienation and repression constructed as part of gay subjectivity within European culture may allow, it might be said, a shared subjectivity with women, or at least common elements within the multiple subject. Men who are not gay may wish to feel that same sense of commonality. Such commonalities might allow a shared sense of meaning to occur, but they must equally be confronted and contradicted by the irreducible and historical fact of difference.

My share in this book must then be a temporary one. Pausing as I finished this essay, I glanced at an article on the work of the American photographer Lee Friedlander. On the one side was a photograph called 'Nude, Phoenix, Arizona – 1978' showing a naked woman asleep in a chair; on the other, 'Self-Portrait, Haverstraw – 1966' showed the artist grimly staring out over the steering wheel of a big car. I cannot shirk my voyeuristic looking at the woman but my focus must also be on the man and my aim the study of men's representation of masculinity. There as a critic I must, to borrow Jacobus's words, work ceaselessly to deconstruct what I find: to write what cannot be written.

Notes

1   In fact her husband was also a soldier and had been posted to the Gulf.

2   See Article 2.6 by Nicole Ward Jouve, Article 2.7 by Wendy Webster and Article 3.3 by Felicity Edholm.

3   On this topic see also J. Spence and P. Holland's *Family Snaps* (1991).

4   Richardson is quoting an account by Antonin Proust. Couture was an art teacher, Giorgione an Italian painter.

5   Clark's account perhaps sees feminine beauty as originating from a pagan kind of virgin birth.

6   The use of the term 'language' here contrasts with the more particularly linguistic meaning employed by Joan Swann in Article 1.4.

7   The word 'genre' is used in a shifting fashion, sometimes to refer to the larger forms like literature, art, or film, but also sometimes to refer to groupings within these larger forms such as, in film, the western as distinct from the film noir. In art history a particular kind of painting is known as a 'genre painting' so that one may speak of the genre of genre painting. For me, the term 'generic' has definite advantages in that it emphasizes the process of grouping works, and indicates that this process is a changing one.

8   For further discussion of utopian fiction, see Frances Bonner's article in Chapter 2. On the potential radicalism of the short story see Lizbeth Goodman's article, also in Chapter 2.

9   Christian is referring to an article by Alice Walker which we have included as the final article in this book.

10   See R. Williams (1977), *Marxism and Literature*, Section III, for a discussion of this issue.

11   'Representation' or 'discourse' could replace 'language' in this last sentence.

12   I have used this collection of interviews with Foucault as my source here because it seems to me to offer a very accessible introduction to his work. His own ideas on sexuality are worked out in much greater detail in the volumes of his *History of Sexuality*.

13   The pronouns here are those of Foucault or his translator.

Article 1.3
GENDER AND GENRE

Dinah Birch

The essays collected in this book show how different areas of cultural activity – television, literature, painting, film – are shaped according to the constructions of gendered identity. But those broad divisions are broken up into more specific fields of production, or genres – soap opera, science fiction, tragedy, the Western, autobiography, romance – all of which express their own complex interaction with concepts of gender. The consequences are often unexpected, ambivalent, or even contradictory. Looking at the constantly evolving forms of genre can tell us a great deal about the part that gender has to play in cultural representation.

The categories of genre are loosely defined, and often overlap. I have just called science fiction a genre, and Frances Bonner's essay on science fiction (Article 2.3) asserts its right to be seen in that light. But science fiction might also be seen as a sub-genre within the novel, or the short story – both of which are often themselves defined as 'genres'. And science fiction is more than just a literary genre: it spills over into television (*Doctor Who* has proved a peculiarly persistent example) and into film. Something comparable might be said of the Western. As a genre, it includes innumerable works of fiction, as well as the huge contribution it has made to the development of film and television.

Nor do the patterns of genre confine themselves to any single level of cultural production. Think, for instance, of the short story as a genre, including as it does both the uncompromising Modernist experiments of Virginia Woolf and the traditionally anodyne fiction of women's magazines. Given its widely ranging and often ambiguous definitions, there is no point in puzzling over precisely how we might pin the word down. Many kinds of diverse cultural practices, with distinct sets of conventional procedures and expectations recognized by both producer (writer, painter, director) and consumer (reader, audience), might be termed genres. From our point of view, a more interesting exercise is to try to trace the connections between the idea of 'gender' and that of 'genre'.

The fact that the two words sound a bit like each other is not a coincidence. They have the same root in the Latin word 'genus', meaning kind, sort, or class. Genre is a means of classifying cultural production, sorting it into kinds, just as gender is a means of sorting people into kinds. You have already encountered some comments about the association between gender and genre in the field of literature in the previous article (1.2) by Richard Allen; and I want to begin by looking at these links. In literature – as in other areas of cultural production – some genres have associated themselves with women much more readily than others. Richard Allen reminds us that it is a commonplace that the genre which has been of most service to women as writers has been the novel and that the rise of the woman fiction writer coincided with the development of what we know as the novel in the eighteenth and nineteenth centuries. It is as novelists that women have achieved something approaching critical parity with men.

Ask yourself where the most widely known, most admired and most read women authors are, and with very few exceptions the answer will be that they are in the field of fiction. Jane Austen, George Eliot, the Brontë sisters, Virginia Woolf, or Iris Murdoch, all educated middle-class women, have earned a literary prestige that has been crucial to the development of 'English Literature' as an academic subject. Sometimes this scholarly status has been accompanied by political content. Virginia Woolf has been important as a feminist as well as a novelist. The black American writer Alice Walker, whose novel *The Color Purple* has been much read in schools, has made a significant contribution to approaches to racial issues within the study of fiction. Other women novelists have played different cultural roles, earning commercial and popular success rather than scholarly approval. Barbara Cartland, Jackie Collins or Catherine Cookson rarely figure in educational syllabuses, but they are none the less household names. No doubt you can think of many more celebrated women novelists, academic or popular – Shirley Conran, Barbara Pym, Muriel Spark, Jilly Cooper . . .

But when it comes to compiling a list of women poets, you might find the going harder. What women poets have achieved the kind of popular currency of, say, Milton or Tennyson or Yeats or Eliot? The kind of currency that goes beyond the setting of lecture theatre and seminar room? Elizabeth Barrett Browning, maybe. Sylvia Plath, certainly. But even those exceptions are partial in some ways. For every reader who has looked carefully at their work, a dozen would recognize the outlines of lives that have become myths – Elizabeth Barrett's elopement with her still more celebrated poet husband Robert Browning, the suicide of Sylvia Plath, who is also, perhaps not by chance, remembered as the wife of a celebrated poet. In an American context, the same could be said of the nineteenth-century poet Emily Dickinson, where the biography is commonly more familiar than the work. Largely as a result of critics who have studied the work of women poets with a new degree of seriousness and attention, that situation is beginning to change. The writing of women poets like Hilda Doolittle, usually known as H.D. (1886–1961), who began her career as the Imagist protégée of Ezra Pound but went on to create a feminist poetic voice that was very much her own, or Elizabeth Bishop (1911–1979), another prolific and robustly independent American poet, or Stevie Smith (1902–1972), English poet and novelist, is now very much more widely known and widely respected than it was a decade ago.

Despite these changing critical perspectives, it remains true that women seem to have found poetry an order of discourse in which general acknowledgement has been harder to come by than it has in fiction. And when we come to drama, things get more difficult still. How many women playwrights can you name? Aphra Behn (1640–1689), perhaps – another woman writer brought to a new prominence through the work of feminist scholars. Joanna Baillie (1762–1851)? Lillian Hellmann (1905–1984)? Caryl Churchill (b. 1938)? You might be able to think of more. If you can, congratulate yourself on being part of a particularly well-informed minority. Many full-time students of English Literature would not be able to get that far.

Why are women in such a minority in the business of writing plays? The fact that it is a business, and a very commercial one at that, provides part of the answer. The same may be said of novel-writing, and in a different sense of poetry. But the production and consumption of novels and poems remains by and large a solitary occupation, despite the mercantile operations of the publisher who mediates between writer and reader. The theatre, on the other hand, is an unremittingly public place, and plays have very often concerned themselves with public action. All but a very few women have for centuries been confined to the domestic sphere. Only with the Restoration in 1660 were women allowed to take parts on the public stage, and it was not until around that time that they first began to write for the commercial theatre. Aphra Behn's first play, *The Forced Marriage*, was written in 1670. Only middle-class women had an education that would have allowed them to write at all, for the theatre or for any other purpose, and the status of middle-class women was very much bound up with their chastity. And a chaste woman could risk no association with the theatre. In her brief classic of feminist criticism, *A Room of One's Own* (first published in 1929), Virginia Woolf famously speculates as to what might have happened to any sister of Shakespeare venturing on to a career in the Renaissance theatre. She imagines the girl asking for an opportunity to act, and what the response would have been:

> The manager – a fat, loose-lipped man – guffawed. He bellowed something about poodles dancing and women acting – no woman, he said, could possibly be an actress. He hinted – you can imagine what. She could get no training in her craft. Could she even seek her dinner in a tavern or roam the streets at midnight?

(Woolf, 1978, p. 72)

Only in the twentieth century have these cultural barriers begun to lift, though roaming the streets at midnight is still something that women are expected not to do. What has not changed is the public situation of the theatre. Writing plays – or, more to the point, getting them performed – is still not something that you can attempt privately, sheltered within the home. You must have access to a theatre, to actors and producers, above all to communal funds. And women are, now as in the past, likely to find such access harder to come by than their male counterparts.

But these cultural and economic barriers would seem not to apply to the production of poetry. You don't need all the demanding paraphernalia of theatre and stage and actors to produce a poem. All you need – or so it might seem – is a piece of blank paper and a pen to write with. So why shouldn't women be poets as easily as men? What's to stop them?

In attempting to answer that apparently innocuous question, feminist criticism has pursued two main lines of enquiry. The first has been a largely historical one, concerned with placing women within social and economic developments in western culture. Some of these factors have a bearing on all women's activities – domestic and political, as well as cultural. Women have, for centuries, most often been economically dependent on men – fathers, husbands, brothers, sons. They have not had incomes of their own, or time of their own, or rooms of their own. Even now, in our supposedly more enlightened and egalitarian age, the average working woman is paid substantially less than the salary of the average working man. The burdens of child care and housework have always fallen more heavily on women than on men, and they still do. There are many good reasons for its having been harder for women to achieve the kind of independence and confidence that make any sort of independent cultural production possible – including literary production.

But poetry is a very particular kind of literary production. Poetry has had, as feminists and others have pointed out, a privileged and prestigious position within western literary tradition. It is the oldest literary form, and the most venerated. And its power has been closely bound up with the continuity of its traditions. The evolution of western poetry is inextricably bound up with its origins in classical culture. Homer, Theocritus, Virgil and Horace have cast a long shadow. And Homer, Theocritus, Virgil and Horace were all male. The only female classical poet of a remotely comparable stature is Sappho, but little more than fragments of her work survives – certainly nothing with the substance to compare with the *Iliad* or the *Aeneid*. So the first point to make here is that there was no cultural expectation that a major poet could be female, because in the most revered models for poetry, rooted in the ancient past, the poets that mattered had always been male.

But the story did not end there. Aspiring western poets, whether male or female, were not born with the empowering knowledge of Homer and Virgil. They needed to acquire it, slowly and laboriously. But only male poets, with very few exceptions, were in a position to do so. The schools and universities that guarded and imparted its secrets permitted no entry to women. It is important to realize that this is one area of literary history where the issues of gender intersect with those of class. Not only did you almost always have to be male to be initiated into the difficult mysteries of classical poetry, you had to be – with few exceptions – reasonably affluent. The schools and universities where Greek and Latin were taught were inaccessible to all but the most gifted and fortunate of those without the means to pay (a minority of poor boys were always allowed in), just as they were to women of all classes. And if the doors were shut on the poor, they were double-locked against black people. Black writers, male or female, with both the means and the inclination to draw on the heritage of European classical literature alongside their own cultural traditions, are rare in the twentieth century, though not non-existent: Toni Morrison and Derek Walcott are distinguished examples of such writers. Before the twentieth century, they can scarcely be said to have occurred at all.

What were the results of that? At the simplest level, it meant that when women (or working-class or black) writers did produce poetry, they were unlikely to be in a position to give their work the prestigious resonance of the classical traditions that supported the major European poets. It is not an accident that the name I first thought of when listing famous women poets was that of Elizabeth Barrett Browning, a woman who had, exceptionally, acquired from her father a confident grasp of classical scholarship. She published a translation of Aeschylus's *Prometheus Bound* in 1833, before ever she achieved fame as a poet in her own right. Her classical learning established her credentials in a masculine world. And, of course, there have always been women who found the means to do that, against all the odds. The title of Sylvia Plath's first volume of poetry, which came out in 1960, was *The Colossus* – a reference to the classical myth of a giant statue of Apollo, Greek god of poetry and music, that was said to have straddled the entrance to the ancient port of Rhodes. Plath, like Barrett Browning, was careful to establish her right of entry to a cultural territory guarded by a divinity she saw as broken but still formidable. But women with access to the scholarly education that formed Barrett Browning and, more than a century later, the academically ambitious Sylvia Plath, have been exceptional. For most women, even well-to-do women, with the will to write, the classics were usually forbidden territory. And that made an enormous difference to their confidence, their sense of being worthy to write. Furthermore, it defined the ways in which their writings were judged.

You might well feel that that barrier must have been much higher in the seventeenth, eighteenth, or nineteenth centuries, than in the twentieth. After all, hasn't the example of classical literature relinquished much of its hold over the literary production in our own century? Plenty of celebrated male poets in the twentieth century have been without a classical education. True: but only up to a point. The sense that the majesty and authority of the classics are a man's business has proved surprisingly persistent in our own times – even in situations where the knowledge of the classics has not. T.S. Eliot – one of the most eminent of the voices who have formed our sense of what is seminal in modern poetry – insisted on the authority of the classics, though his definition of what might be said to comprise classical literature extended far beyond Latin and Greek texts. Like Pound, his American friend and supporter, Eliot had a knowledge of classical literature that was more or less adequate, but by no means encyclopaedic. Nevertheless, he felt able to quote it with confidence. He felt, as very few women have felt, that his vocation as a poet entitled him to use it as it suited his own purposes. Did he not, after all, stand in the same masculine tradition as Homer and Horace? Virginia Woolf, on the other hand, of the same generation as Eliot, has much to say on the subject of not knowing Greek. And if a woman doesn't know Greek, or whatever body of classical literature might be invested with the authority of Greek, what might she substitute for it? Ballads? Nursery rhymes? After all, women had always been allowed in the nursery. Or hymns? They had been allowed into congregations (though not usually pulpits) too. Many women poets have in fact used such forms as models, with diverse and interesting consequences.

In their essay prefacing a collection of essays on women poets, entitled *Shakespeare's Sisters*, the American critics Sandra Gilbert and Susan Gubar comment on what male critics have made of these models. They quote the prominent critic John Crowe Ransom talking about the poetry of Emily Dickinson. Here is what Gilbert and Gubar have to say:

> On the one hand, the woman poet who learns a 'just esteem' for Homer is ignored or even mocked – as, say, the eighteenth-century 'Blue Stockings' were. On the other hand, the woman poet who does not (because she is not allowed to) study Homer is held in contempt. On the third hand however, whatever alternative tradition the woman poet attempts to substitute for 'ancient rules' is subtly devalued. Ransom, for instance, asserts that Dickinson's meters, learned from 'her father's hymnbook',

are all based upon 'Folk Line, the popular form of verse and
the oldest in our language,' adding that 'the great classics of
this meter are the English ballads and Mother Goose.' Our
instinctive sense that this is a back-handed compliment is
confirmed when he remarks that 'Folk Line is disadvantageous
... if it denies to the poet the use of English Pentameter,'
which is 'the staple what we may call the studied or "university"
poetry, and ... is capable of containing and formalizing many
kinds of substantive content which would be too complex for
Folk Line. Emily Dickinson appears never to have tried it.' If
we read 'pentameter' here as a substitute for 'ancient rules,'
then we can see that once again 'woman' and 'poet' are being
defined as contradictory terms.
(Gilbert and Gubar, 1986, pp. 106–12)

The wide-ranging work of Gilbert and Gubar has made a cogent
contribution to the first, historical line of enquiry into the connection
between gender and literary genre, focusing on the means by which
the construction of western poetic traditions has tended either to
exclude or to denigrate the achievement of women, in various ways
and for various reasons. It is partly that the central poets in the
tradition have always been men, thus implying that maleness in
poets is a natural and inevitable state of affairs. A further reason is
that women were so long denied full access to the social and cultural
prestige invested in the perpetuation of the classics in exclusive
educational establishments like grammar schools, public schools
and universities. Added to that is the fact that verbal skills which
are associated with women – like the singing of hymns, ballads,
or nursery rhymes – have been seen as relatively low-status
preoccupations. But clearly, these are all matters that could change,
and to some extent have changed. Women are no longer denied
access to educational institutions that used to debar them, and in
terms of numbers at least, have come to dominate many areas of
higher education in the arts. Even the Yale critic Harold Bloom, the
celebrated high priest of the sacred continuity guaranteed by the
Oedipal rivalry between the strong male poet and his aspiring son,
has conceded that the masculine mould of poetry is one that women
might break. Here is Bloom, writing in *The Map of Misreading* in
1975:

The first true breach with literary continuity will be brought
about in generations to come if the burgeoning religion of
Liberated Woman spreads from its clusters of enthusiasts to
dominate the West. Homer will cease to be the inevitable
precursor and the rhetoric and forms of our literature then
may break at last from tradition.
(Bloom, 1975, p. 33, quoted in Gilbert and Gubar, 1988, p. 131)

Whether Bloom considers that a cheering possibility is open to debate. But the point I want to make here is that this first line of enquiry, concentrating as it does by and large on external cultural, social and educational factors tending to work against the possibility of women achieving distinction as poets, will as a result also focus on the removal of those external factors as the way forward.

Few feminists would want to argue with that. But there are those who would contend that these externally applied constraints are not the only ones that we ought to consider; that there are other, internalized factors that we have to take into account to arrive at a full understanding of why women have found it hard to establish themselves in the field of poetry. This second line of enquiry, with its origins in French philosophy, has focused on psychoanalysis as the primary tool of analysis. Feminists interested in psychoanalysis have been ready to accept that social and economic factors such as women's limited educational opportunities, or their financial dependence on fathers and husbands, do indeed make it harder for them to succeed as poets. But they also claim that the nature of women's access to language itself is the first and most significant impediment. They claim, in fact, that women as writers are alienated from the language of poetry at the very deepest levels of their identity, the levels in which they are constructed as speaking subjects. It is to this second line of investigation that I now want to turn.

This is an argument that has been built on the work of the French psychoanalyst Jacques Lacan, the Freudian revisionist whose work has proved fertile for feminists in many different ways. Rosalind Minsky's article in *Knowing Women* (Crowley and Himmelweit, 1992: a companion book in this series) introduces some of the complexities of Lacan's thought. From the perspective of psychoanalytic literary criticism, the most important point is that Lacan's school of psychoanalytic thought focuses on language. The unconscious, Lacan famously asserts, is structured like a language. It is within language that our identity is constructed. It follows that Lacan's model for the acquisition of language is also a model for the production of identity. Lacan's conception of this process turns on the idea that the child must enter into the 'symbolic order', in which the structures of language, law and the social community are defined. But this 'symbolic order' is, within patriarchal societies, pervasively masculine. An identification with femininity therefore causes a girl to experience the entry into language differently. And this difference will be felt particularly acutely in areas of formal public discourse – making speeches, speaking in committees or even in seminars – and in the production of poetry, that most prestigious of all discourses. So feminist history and psychoanalytic theory here combine to point to a continuing barrier between women and the exalted forms of public discourse. The novel, most often concerned with domestic rather than public affairs, is seen as a partial exception to this rule, its primary location within the home making it the genre easiest of access to women. Other literary discourses, including poetry, remain problematic.

Lacan claims that the child must reject the maternal presence and accept the intervention of the father, representing the symbolic order, if a satisfactory social identity is to be achieved. His argument suggests that if the destiny of a girl is to become a mother, she must be identified with what all children must learn to repudiate in order to acquire the status of a speaking adult. In taking on the culturally defined role of a woman, therefore, the growing girl can only claim the power of public speech at the expense of fracturing the internalized process that gives her a position within her society. Such speech becomes difficult for most women, impossible for many. In a famous essay called 'The Laugh of the Medusa' (first published in 1975), the French psychoanalytic critic and playwright Hélène Cixous evokes what it feels like to be caught up in this predicament:

> Every woman knows the torment of getting up to speak. Her heart racing, at times entirely lost for words, ground and language slipping away – that's how daring a feat, how great a transgression it is for a woman to speak – even just open her mouth – in public. A double distress, for even if she transgresses, her words fall almost always upon the deaf male ear, which hears in language only that which speaks in the masculine.
>
> (Cixous, 1981a, p. 251)

This line of thinking might shed light on why many of the women who have, against the odds, become poets, have devoted so much of their creative energy to writing about the process of writing; their need and their entitlement to the rich cultural resources of poetry. It might also shed light on why fragmentation, hysteria and madness have so often been associated with women's identity as poets. For if the process by which women's subjectivity is constructed makes their access to public language so complicated and difficult, those who claim that access must be prepared to pay a high price.

But fragmentation, hysteria and madness are not, of course, conditions confined to women, no matter how firmly they might be marked by an association with femininity. A Lacanian analysis is not, in fact, at all a straightforward matter when it comes to the analysis of the role of gender in poetic language. It is true that poetry, with its formalized rhythms, its rhyme schemes, its homage to a resonant patriarchal tradition, is in some ways quintessentially an expression of the symbolic order. But it is equally true that poets have – and this too is an ancient concept – persistently been perceived as wild and subversive, emotional, unstable, if not from time to time quite lunatic. These are hardly characteristics of the Lacanian concept of the symbolic order. The implications of gender in relation to poetic genre are not, after all, quite as simple as they might look.

Furthermore, it is not altogether the case, in the uncomplicated way I have so far suggested, that writing poetry is generally seen – in the post-Romantic western world at least – as a wholeheartedly masculine pursuit. Far from it. Talking about cultural constructions of gender in 'Sorties', Cixous posits a list of opposed concepts:

> *Where is she?*
>
> Activity/passivity,
> Sun/Moon,
> Culture/Nature,
> Day/Night,
>
> Father/Mother,
> Head/heart,
> Intelligible/sensitive,
> Logos/Pathos.
>
> *(Cixous, 1981b, p. 90)*

If we add a second question to Cixous's 'Where is she?', and ask ourselves where poetry is, it becomes clear that the poet and the woman will often find themselves on the same side of this great cultural divide. The moon, nature, night, sensitivity and the heart – Cixous's feminine concepts have a striking association with poetry. Would a self-respecting macho dominant aggressive man's man write poetry? *Poetry*?

There is a contradiction here that has far-reaching consequences for the whole issue of the relation between gender and genre within the arts. In terms of the coded structures of gendered identity that organize so many aspects of our life, the associations of music, literature, dancing, painting or drama, tend to be with the feminine rather than the masculine. The arts are perceived as having to do with feeling, with beauty, with complex forms of resistance to the triumph of hard-edged law and logic. They are also often associated, from the point of view of the sexual identity of the men who participate in the arts, with homosexuality. A high proportion of the men who have been central in the development of the arts in the twentieth century have been gay. No man who has unquestioningly accepted the exacting codes of western cultural constructions of masculinity is going to choose a career as a ballet dancer. Or a violinist, or an actor, or even a poet. Poetry, like many other cultural genres, is in some ways at least feminine. But the poets who win the highest critical reputations are, as we have seen, for the most part male. Such contradictions have given rise to a good deal of cultural uneasiness. And perhaps this is yet another reason for women's access to poetry being a complex matter. The dominant masculine order feels peculiarly challenged by the woman poet, since her very existence confirms a deep anxiety among the male poets of our twentieth-century patriarchal culture. Despite all those centuries of masculine cultural authority, could it be that poetry will, after all, turn out to be a woman's business? And if that's the case, where does it leave the men?

The response to the complex gender identity of men who are drawn to the arts often leads to an exaggerated assertion of the masculinity that might seem to be undermined. As far as poetry is concerned, this is a response with a long history. The ancient tradition of the female Muse who bestows her favours on the fortunate poet may be seen as part of this phenomenon. The concept of a Muse externalizes what is female in the poet, enabling him to underline his difference, his masculine identity. This is yet another of the factors that problematized poetry as a genre for women: for in no simple sense could a woman poet evoke the semi-erotic relation between the suppliant poet and creatively capricious Muse, as so many generations of male poets have done. And yet it does not follow that this emphatically proclaimed masculinity led them to relate to cultural concepts of gender in a straightforward way. For centuries, the most celebrated poets in the European tradition have expressed a range of rich and subtle critiques of the assumptions of masculinity. At the same time, they have again and again insisted on the distance between themselves and the feminine. The poet John Donne (1572–1631) is an example – his writing repeatedly explores the uncertain limits of reason, the life of the body, the inward complexities of faith and desire. He is deeply interested in what western culture has defined as the feminine pole of human experience. Yet he also proclaims his 'words masculine perswasive force' ('On his Mistris', 1.4, *Elegies*), his unchallengeable superiority to the feminine and to women. So too does Milton (1608–1674), who was nicknamed, while a student at Christ's College at Cambridge, 'the Lady of Christ's'. Milton accompanies his notoriously disparaging reflections on the shortcomings of women with poetry whose subversive implications could be read (as his Romantic admirers perceived) as a wholesale repudiation of the rigid patriarchal institutions of his day.

This kind of doubleness pervades western culture, giving rise to many familiar phenomena – the hard-drinking misogynistic novelist; painters and sculptors who seemed to feel an entitlement almost amounting to compulsion to treat their wives, mistresses and female models with cavalier contempt; and the swaggering and sexually predatory actor. One result of this reaction, as far as genres are concerned, has been a tendency for its conventions to polarize into oppositional frameworks of gender. Certain areas of cultural territory were marked out as the province of women, while others have been colonized by men. Professional male artists were expected to paint female nudes, while amateur women produced delicate watercolours of landscapes or flowers; men composed symphonies, women songs; men wrote epics, women novels.

But here again, things are by no means as simple as they might seem. Science fiction is an example of an apparently masculine form which turns out to have feminist elements, elements which have become more prominent and more open in recent works by women. Similarly, masculine treatments of the female nude may be used and subverted by women painters. No single gender identity can lay claim to a cultural genre in an unqualified way.

Romance provides an example of a genre which might seem, perhaps more than any other, to support culturally sanctioned representations of femininity. Yet here too the situation turns out to be more complex than it looks. Romance takes different forms in different media, and is not always produced or consumed exclusively by women. As a recurrent and significant element in widely disseminated cultural forms – film, television, advertising – its audiences and its authors include men. But as the commercial staple of a variety of teenage magazines, Mills and Boon novels, or photo-stories, it is aimed very specifically at a female audience. Its narrative conventions are familiar. A single woman meets a dominant and successful man: they find themselves, often reluctantly, attracted to each other. After a series of mishaps and misunderstandings, the two central characters acknowledge their passion and are united in marital happiness.

The basic story of romance might seem to have little to recommend itself to feminists. Yet generations of eager consumers have shown that it has something important to offer women. Feminist cultural theorists need to ask themselves why. Are the women who relish romance, particularly as it appears in popular fiction of the kind exuded by Barbara Cartland, simply dupes? 'Feminists must baulk at any such conclusion which implies that the vast audience of romance readers (with the exception of a few up-front intellectuals) are either masochistic or inherently stupid. Both text and reader are more complicated than that' (Light, 1986).

Some version of pleasurable escapism is clearly involved in women's motives for reading romance. What they are escaping from is an experienced heterosexuality which they find less satisfying than its idealized reflection in the pages of their paperback romances. Romance fiction, almost always written by women, allows both author and reader an imaginative participation in a different version of heterosexuality. In the conventional world of romance, women take the foremost place, and the values of femininity are seen to confront and in part to defeat those of a masculine society. The heroine of romance is, as feminists have pointed out, frail and passive. Nevertheless, she emerges victorious. A transport of sexual surrender allows her to impose the values of femininity (emotion, tenderness, sensitivity) on a man who initially resists them, and she ends the novel with what used to be called a 'catch': a well-funded marriage fired by passion.

But the codes of the genre allow her to achieve this desirable end without transgressing cultural expectations of idealized gender identities. The heroine may be powerful, but she is not dominant. She gets her own way because her womanliness makes her irresistible, not because she forgets her femininity in order to scheme or fight for what she wants. The masterful hero is seen to lose some of his hard-edged aggression, but only in terms of his relation with his lover. As far as the rest of the world is concerned, he retains the virile air of command that was such an essential feature of his sexual magnetism in the first place. This is the stuff of fantasy, of course, well removed from the dynamics of the heterosexual relationships that most women experience. But it is as much a fantasy of power as of dependence, and its ambiguities allow it to satisfy a felt need in women's lives.

The ambivalence of romance as a cultural form is a reminder that neither gender nor genre function within closed parameters. They are variable concepts, and they shift according to the pressures of differing and changing contexts. But their instability does not mean that they are peripheral. Reflecting on the relation between gender and genre shows how both have persistently moulded the forms of our cultural life.

Article 1.4
WAYS OF SPEAKING

Joan Swann

On the sofa, a woman is speaking, her body inclined forward, her hands raised and slightly cupped. Three women listen intently, their faces directed towards the speaker. Two more seem less avid, but still they listen carefully. The sofa has round edges, and so do the women. Their roundness is echoed by lightly curved lines patterning the wall behind. In this picture there are no sharp edges and no hard angles.

The picture is apt. It illustrates the front cover of a book – one of a whole set of feminist books on women's language, in which women study women speaking. Many studies constitute a rescue operation: a rescue from academic neglect, and also a rescue from the stigma with which women's speech has traditionally been associated. Speech genres often thought to be 'typical' of women, such as gossip and chat, have been revisited and re-evaluated.

In this article I want to look at some examples of women speaking – to examine the respects in which, and the extent to which women can be said to have distinct ways of speaking. But I need to situate this within a broader context, which is the somewhat problematical nature of the relationship between women and language in its various guises. I shall focus on the English language – principally the varieties of English spoken in the UK and the USA – because these are the varieties that have been most heavily researched, and with which I am most familiar.

WOMEN AND LANGUAGE

Women have an ambivalent relationship with language. On the one hand, they are regarded as highly verbal: girls often score higher than boys on tests of 'verbal reasoning'; girls do well at language activities at school; and much of women's work requires them to be competent language users. On the other hand, language is one of the means through which women have been oppressed: language structures discriminate against women; women's use of language is disparaged; girls' and women's linguistic competence does not lead to their achieving high social or professional status as language users.[1]

A major feminist concern about language has been its inherent sexism. The words and meanings made available to talk about people tend to marginalize women. The best known example of this must be the use, in English, of 'generic' *he* and *man* to represent both women and men, but feminists have also identified several 'lexical gaps' – an absence of words to refer to women's experiences. Many of these relate to women's sexuality: the absence of a feminine equivalent to *virility*, for instance; the dearth of terms to represent women's active participation in the sex act. When women get into the language, they are often portrayed negatively, or in relation to men. Sometimes words for women are derived from words for men by the addition of a suffix: *duchess, manageress, usherette* – a linguistic equivalent to the social 'male as norm' phenomenon. Feminists have also documented the historical accretion, to words for women, of negative and often sexually derogatory meanings: *mistress* used to be a parallel term to *master*, for instance; *wench* once meant simply a young girl; *hussy* has the same root as *housewife* – it referred to the mistress of a house.[2]

As well as documenting difference and discrimination in the way women and men are represented in language, feminists have been concerned with how women and men use language as speakers and writers. Striking parallels have emerged from these two avenues of study. Just as women's experiences have frequently been hidden or disparaged in language, so women's access to language as speakers and writers has been restricted, and their speech has been said to render them powerless.

SPEAKING AND SILENCE

> Sir, a woman's preaching is like a dog's walking on his hinder legs. It is not done well; but you are surprised to find it done at all.
>
> (*Samuel Johnson, 31 July 1763*)

Dinah Birch, in Article 1.3, considers women's writing at the level of genre – she discusses the ways in which women have become associated with certain types of writing, such as the novel, and have found it hard to achieve serious recognition as playwrights or poets. Similar concerns have been raised about women's speech. Women have, historically, made few contributions to certain speech genres – particularly genres that are relatively public, or that have high prestige. This does not mean that women do not speak in public, or that they cannot speak skilfully. But there have been relatively few well-known woman orators, and many women find it nerve-racking to stand up and speak in front of a large audience.

Similar explanations have been advanced for women's relatively limited participation in public, and prestigious, genres of speech and writing. Women's unease at 'speaking out' has been taken as symptomatic of their alienation from (patriarchal) language itself. Dinah Birch cites Hélène Cixous, a French feminist writer influenced by Lacanian psychoanalytical theory, who describes the physical 'torment' experienced by women who 'transgress' by speaking in public – though Cixous does exhort women to 'break out of the snare of silence' and take up their own means of self-expression (Cixous 1981a, p. 251).

But there are also social explanations for women's public silence. Women have simply not held positions that have allowed, or required, them to speak. They have been absent from high office in industry, trade unions, politics, the established church, and other institutions that give people access to a public floor. Sometimes their speech has been formally proscribed. On other occasions, less formal mechanisms come into play to prevent or inhibit women from speaking.

One of the best known formal injunctions against women speaking in church comes from St Paul: 'Let your women keep silence in the churches: for it is not permitted unto them to speak ... if they will learn anything, let them ask their husbands at home: for it is a shame for women to speak in the church' (The first epistle of St Paul to the Corinthians, XIV, 34, 35). And women who have dared speak in public have been greeted with ridicule. Satirical jibes at the early Quakers sometimes focused on their practice of allowing everyone to speak, including women, as Plate 2 illustrates.

Such negative evaluations have proved remarkably resilient through history, and up to the present day. They have been a continuing force militating against women's acceptance as speakers in public, particularly in serious contexts. Ann Every, the first woman to read the news on the BBC World Service (in 1976), has commented that several arguments were advanced for women's unsuitability as newsreaders – including technical problems with recording equipment that somehow didn't apply to women in light entertainment. In the end, though, it all boiled down to women's credibility as speakers. As Ann Every has commented: 'There was always a thought that women didn't carry the authority in their voice that a man did, and this was the important part when it came to reading news'.[3]

Deborah Cameron (1985) lists several institutional constraints that have acted as 'regulatory mechanisms', inhibiting women's access to public and powerful genres. She argues that, historically, men have controlled access to literacy, and to education in learned languages – Latin, classical Arabic and Sanskrit. In contemporary urban communities, they control access to bureaucracies such as health, education, employment and tax services. They maintain the conventions and norms of certain genres of speech and writing – for instance, those associated with legal documents, religion, news reporting, lexicography – that may represent women as marginal or inferior. There are also certain customs and practices that distribute speaking roles unequally between women and men: Cameron gives the example of a wedding reception where the father of the bride proposes a toast to the bride and groom, which is replied to by the groom; he in turn proposes a toast to the bridesmaids, replied to by the best man. Finally, there are value judgements of the sort I've mentioned above. Speaking out is seen as inconsistent with conventional notions of femininity, and there is a whole set of terms used to belittle women's speech and castigate those who speak too much (*gossip, nag, tittle tattle, strident*, etc.).

These social and institutional factors impede women's access to certain forms of knowledge and to certain ways of speaking; they also affect how women are perceived when they speak. Cameron argues that these practices should be the focus of feminist attention; there is no need to look to more esoteric forms of male control of, and women's alienation from, language. She makes two further important points: that restrictions on women's speech have to be considered as part of more general social restrictions imposed on women, and that similar factors inhibit the access of working-class and black speakers to influential and prestigious ways of speaking. The issue is one of social and economic power as much as gender (ibid.).

So far, I have discussed problems of women's access to various types of public speech. Restrictions placed upon women speaking in public are consistent with the fact that, historically, women have been relegated to the private and domestic sphere, while men operate in the public domain. But this is not to suggest that women, in private, have been able to speak freely. For men to be master in their own home, restrictions need to be placed on women – and these have included restrictions on their speech. Terms such as *gossip* and *nag*, while they belittle women's speech and make it seem inappropriate for serious contexts, also serve as a reminder that women talk too much in any context if not kept in check. Checks have included punishment and physical restraint, as well as 'advice' in manuals for women and jokes about nagging wives and mothers-in-law:[4] '. . . let fewe se her and none at all here her. [. . .] There is nothynge that so sone casteth the mynde of the husbande from his wife as dothe moche scoldynge and chidyng, and her mischeuous tonge' (Vives, 1523, *De Institutione Christianae Feminae*).

WOMEN AND MEN SPEAKING

The woman who has a receptive ear not only can provide great comfort and release for her husband – she possesses a priceless social asset as well. The quiet, unpretentious woman who is fascinated by another's conversation, who asks questions which show she is digesting every word, is the girl most likely to succeed socially, not only with the menfolk, but also with her fellow females.

(*Mrs Dale Carnegie, 1957*, How to Help Your Husband Get Ahead)

Speech may be viewed, not just as the product of social and institutional constraints, or of women's and men's gendered identities, but also as the means by which relations between women and men are worked out. This involves delving into the linguistic minutiae of everyday life – looking at the expressions women and men use, and the way conversations are put together. It involves seeing speech as a form of social practice, in which gender is routinely constructed on a day-to-day level, and where gendered relations may also be subverted. This is not an entirely separate point from those I made earlier. Many characteristics of women's speech are bound up with their tendency to remain silent or be silenced.

One claim that is frequently made about women's speech is that it is more hesitant or uncertain than men's. Women's uncertainty has long been part of folklinguistic mythology, but it was also posited by the linguist Robin Lakoff. Lakoff identified several features that she claimed constituted 'women's language'. They included: 'empty' adjectives such as *divine, charming* and *cute*; question intonation in statements: 'What's your name, dear?' – 'Mary Smith?'; tag-questions ('She knows that, *doesn't she?*'); and hedges such as *sort of, kinda, you know, I guess*. These features, argued Lakoff, gave the impression that female speakers were tactful and polite but also hesitant and lacking in authority.[5]

Lakoff's claims were based on her own intuitions as a member of a middle-class US speech community. Researchers who have looked at how women and men actually speak have found things are rather more complicated than she suggested. Some research supports Lakoff's claim that women are more tentative; other research has found Lakoff's features in the speech of people with relatively little social power – and has dubbed the style 'powerless language' rather than 'women's language'. More recent research suggests Lakoff's features are quite variable in meaning, and that women and men may use the same features to different effect. This is a point I shall return to below.

Several researchers who have studied women's speech have argued that it is more supportive than men's. Pamela Fishman, for instance, found that women, speaking with their (male) partners, made frequent use of 'minimal responses': expressions such as *mmh* and *yeah* that showed they were paying attention. Men, on the other hand, gave minimal responses only at the end of a (lengthy) speaking turn by their partner. Women tried to counteract this by using attention-seeking devices of the sort also associated with children ('Do you know what?', etc.). In this context, many more men's than women's topics were successful: they were developed over several speaking turns, rather than being allowed to fizzle out. Fishman has referred to women's conversational support as 'interactional shitwork' – it supports a (male) conversational partner's topic, but does not enable women to put across their own point of view.[6]

In contrast to women's supportive speech, men's speech has been seen as competitive. There is evidence that, in many contexts, men use features such as interruptions that allow them to take more than their fair share of speech. The example below comes from a series of recordings made by Candace West and Don Zimmerman in public places around a university – drug stores, coffee shops etc.:

Female: So you really can't bitch when you've got all those on the same day (. .) but I uh asked my physics professor if I couldn't change that

Male: {Don't touch that (. .)

Female: What? (.)

Male: I've got everything jus' how I want it in that notebook (.) you'll screw it up leafin' through it like that

(Adapted from West and Zimmerman, 1977, p. 527. (.) indicates a brief pause and (. .) a longer pause; { indicates the start of overlapping speech)

In this case, the man begins to speak before the woman has finished, stops her from finishing and uses the turn to make his own point.

West and Zimmerman have provided evidence from different contexts, showing that, in talk between women and men, interruptions virtually always come from men. They argue that male/female talk is similar to adult/child talk, in that adults interrupt children but children are not meant to interrupt adults.[7]

There are one or two general points to bear in mind when thinking about women's and men's speech. First, in English, differences between women's and men's speech are always average ones: not all women, or men, speak the same. Women do not speak simply *as* women: they are also teachers or students, black or white, intimate friends or distant acquaintances; they speak to others in a variety of contexts and for a variety of purposes, purposes that sometimes overlap or shift during the course of a conversation. All these factors will affect not just what women say, but also how they say it.

Language use itself also poses certain problems of interpretation. Many claims about women's language have involved attributing fixed meanings (hesitancy, supportiveness) to linguistic forms. But it is a linguistic commonplace that formal features of a language have to be interpreted in context. The meanings of tag questions, minimal responses, simultaneous speech and so on will vary quite crucially depending on how they are uttered and in what context. The situation is complicated by the fact that we have different expectations of female and male speakers: we may interpret the same feature differently, depending on whether it is uttered by a woman or a man, to fit in with our preconceptions of female and male speech. Janet Holmes has commented: 'one (female) person's feeble hedging may well be perceived as another (male) person's perspicacious qualification' (Holmes, 1986, p. 18). Gender and language use are interrelated in a highly complex way. There is considerable evidence of differences in women's and men's speech, but the actual differences observed are context specific, and their meanings are neither precise nor unambiguous.

In so far as particular features of language become associated with female speakers, they may serve as indicators of femininity and women may use them to sound feminine. But these features will have other connotations. In sounding feminine, a woman may also sound tentative. Women also need to signal many other things as well as gender (e.g. friendliness, professional status) and they need to signal many of these things simultaneously. All speakers have to balance different aspects of their identity – what is salient in one context may be played down in another. In these various ways, women's ways of speaking will play their part alongside other communication systems (dress, gesture, posture) in the daily reproduction of the feminine as a social category.

But differences in ways of speaking do not just act as signallers of social meanings: they are also the means by which the interaction itself is accomplished. Speakers use interactions to get things done – to put forward a view, and have a say in what is talked about; to support someone else's point or contest this; to challenge another speaker or give way. The way speakers 'manage' an interaction will affect its outcomes. In many contexts the difference in women's and men's interactional styles tends to operate to women's disadvantage: it allows men to 'dominate' talk, whereas women 'give away power'. Zimmerman and West, for instance, characterize the types of interruptions they observed as 'small insults', and argue that they are one of the means by which (unequal) relations between women and men are routinely maintained.

Research that focuses on women and men interacting together has been invaluable in suggesting the intricate and complex ways in which such interactions (re)construct unequal power relations. But, inevitably, this has led to a rather negative evaluation of women's speech. Some feminist researchers have become unhappy with this evaluation, and have sought to revalue women's speech – to see it as having strengths rather than weaknesses.

THE VALUE OF WOMEN'S SPEECH

Those who wish to look at more positive aspects of women's speech have tended to focus on talk in all-female groups. I don't, here, mean groups that are *incidentally* all-female, but groups in which women meet for the purpose of talking to other women. Such talk often takes place in the private domain, in domestic or other relatively intimate settings. It has been chosen deliberately to contrast with public and/or mixed-sex talk. Sometimes, talk in these contexts seems to be seen as quintessentially female.

In a recent British study, Jennifer Coates investigated the talk of a group of women of which she was a member (Coates, 1988). The group had met together for several years, originally as a support group for mothers with young children, but extending its functions as the women's needs changed over the years. The women met in one another's houses. They talked about a variety of topics, but these tended to fall within the realm of people and feelings. A main goal of the talk, according to Coates, was the establishment and maintenance of (equal) relationships, rather than the exchange of information.

Coates' analysis of the talk in this group shows it to be highly co-operative. Topics are developed jointly between speakers. There is little competition for the floor. Many features associated with women's speech in other contexts are also found here. The women use frequent and well-placed minimal responses. They also use some of the features identified by Robin Lakoff as indicating uncertainty (*sort of, kind of,* etc.). Coates argues that such features are particularly useful in conversation that is concerned with people and feelings – in this context they allow a speaker to step back from what she is saying if it looks as if she may cause offence. By mitigating what the speaker is saying, these features are also likely to prevent conflict, which is important if a main aim of the talk is to maintain friendly relations.

The women's talk also contains a great deal of overlapping speech, but Coates argues that, here, this contributes to the joint production of a topic – it does not constitute an interruption. Here are two brief examples from Coates' work:

A: and I imagine that my two far-flung sibs
     will actually make the journey
   ⌈ I'm just (.) I'm (almost) yes I'm sure they will
E: ⌊ what (.) to your parents? to your mothers?

A: but it'll be because it'll become a public statement

E: is his father still alive?   ⌈ because that would

B: I don't know ⟨

C: ⌊ I don't think they had

E: ⌈ have a very big bearing on it
C: ⌊ a funeral either

(*Adapted from Coates, 1988, p. 110 and p. 111. { indicates when speech begins to overlap*)

In both cases the women are discussing whether it is taboo not to attend your mother's funeral. In the first example, speaker E breaks into A's turn to ask a question. Speaker A answers this question ('Yes') before continuing with the rest of her turn. In the second example, speakers E and C come in to speak at the same time and have two complete overlapping speaking turns. Coates comments on examples such as these:

> Without providing an audio tape, it is hard to describe the quality of such passages: crucially, there is no sense of competition, or of vying for turns. Speakers do not become aggrieved when others join in. The feel of the conversation is that all the participants are familiar with each other and with the way the interaction is constructed. It is very much a joint effort, with individual speakers concerned to contribute to a jointly negotiated whole.
>
> (*Coates, 1988, p. 112*)

Coates' study is of interest because it provides evidence of the formal and functional characteristics of talk in close female groups – only one or two other studies have looked at all-female talk in quite such detail.[8] There is a danger, however, of slipping from the notion of 'women's talk in certain kinds of groups', to 'women's talk' *per se*. In the desire to revalue women's talk, some people have come to regard this as inevitably (maybe inherently) co-operative. There is no evidence for such a strong claim. Women, even interacting with other women, will speak differently, and to different effect, in different contexts.

SPEAKING CHOICES

If one important characteristic of speech is its inherent variability, another is that it is constantly subject to change. Women's speech will change as part and parcel of the renegotiation of relationships between women, and between women and men. But sometimes change is initiated deliberately. As women, we may actively seek to extend the ways of speaking that are available to us – for instance, to participate effectively in mixed-sex, or more public talk.

Assertiveness training has become popular as a means of enabling women to speak out, but there have been some criticisms of this approach. It seems to see any communication problems as residing in the individual, rather than acknowledging social and contextual constraints on women's speech. Nor is it straightforward to change the way we speak. For instance, it is not sufficient simply to adopt alternative speech forms. Listeners will have certain expectations of a female speaker – of how women ought to speak in particular contexts. Confounding such expectations may produce discomfort or even outright hostility. Anna Hordyk, a teacher who carried out assertiveness training with young women students in a secondary school, recognized that social constraints – and even fear of physical violence – might prevent women from simply asking for what they want or need: she acknowledges that there are occasions when 'the best course of action is silence' (Hordyk, 1986, p. 69).

An alternative approach may be to change conventions of speaking: many types of talk associated with female speakers and private contexts have begun to 'go public'. Teachers have given increasing recognition to the value of small group talk in the classroom and this, at least in its ideal form, bears many of the hallmarks of 'female' speech: it is meant to be co-operative and to give each person the chance to contribute. In some conferences, there has been a move away from the standard format of presentation followed by the cut and thrust of question and answer sessions. Alternative sessions may be offered based on workshops (joint exploration of a problem) or group discussions reporting back to a plenary. Sometimes this is done explicitly to make sure all speakers have the chance to be heard – it is an attempt not just to favour women, but also others who might not get the chance to speak.

These alternative arrangements are often beneficial, but instituting change is never a straightforward matter. Small group talk is not always co-operative. Certain speakers may dominate in workshops as in other contexts. And talk that looks co-operative is not necessarily equal – speakers may collaborate perfectly to maintain existing power relations.

Notes

1   Diane Halpern discusses differences in verbal abilities between girls and boys in *Sex Differences in Cognitive Abilities* (1986). Janet White, in her article 'The Writing on the Wall: Beginning or End of a Girl's Career?', argues that the way 'English' is taught in schools contributes both to girls' early success and their later disadvantage (White, 1986). For general accounts of the relationship between gender and language use, see, for instance, Coates (1986) and Graddol and Swann (1989). An annotated bibliography of research studies is included in Thorne *et al.* (1983).

2   Muriel Schultz, in her article 'The Semantic Derogation of Women', documents the historical decline in words referring to women (Schultz, 1975). Dick Leith discusses similar processes at work in words for other relatively powerless social groups, in *A Social History of English*, 1983).

3   Ann Every made this comment in an interview recorded for a BBC/Open University radio programme called 'Men, Women and Language', produced by Meg Sheffield and first transmitted in 1981.

4   For a historical account of prescriptions about women's speech, see Bornstein (1978).

5   Robin Lakoff's claims were made in 1975 in a book that became something of an early classic: *Language and Woman's Place* (1975). The publication of this book stimulated a wave of empirical studies designed to test Lakoff's hypothesis. See, for instance, Dubois and Crouch (1975); Baumann (1979); O'Barr and Atkins (1980); Preisler (1986); Cameron *et al.* (1988).

6   Pamela Fishman has written several articles based on her work. See, for instance, 'Interaction: The Work Women Do' in *Language, Gender and Society*, edited by Thorne *et al.* (Fishman, 1983).

7   Candace West and Don Zimmerman have carried out several studies of interruptions. See, for instance, West and Zimmerman (1977, 1983).

8   An earlier study of gossip, which provides part of the stimulus for Coates' work, was done by Deborah Jones (1980), but this is not an empirical study. S. Kalcik (1975) describes supportive features in the interactions of women in consciousness-raising groups; and Marjorie Harness Goodwin (1980) studied groups of working-class black children playing in single-sex groups, and found that girls used fewer direct commands than boys.

2
LITERARY REPRESENTATIONS: SELF AS SUBJECT

> We are the subjects of our own narrative, witnesses to and participants in our own experience, and, in no way coincidentally, in the experiences of those with whom we have come in contact. . . . And to read imaginative literature by and about us is to choose to examine centers of the self and to have the opportunity to compare these centers with the 'raceless' one with which we are, all of us, most familiar.
>
> (*Toni Morrison, 1989, 'Unspeakable Things Unspoken: the Afro–American Presence in American Literature'*)[1]

These words were written in 1989 by Toni Morrison. In reading this quotation – if this paragraph or the endnote is not read first – it would be natural enough to assume that the 'we' refers to writers *per se*. It might also be inferred that the 'we' refers to women, as women are, after all, the subject of this book. In fact, the 'we' refers specifically to black women writers. This is Morrison's context: her position. More specifically, the 'we' refers to black women writers who speak, write and read English, and probably to middle-class writers, who would be the most likely readers of the academic journal which published the piece.

The reader's relationship with Morrison's 'we' is important: it designates the positionality of the reader in relation to the writer and thereby provides a sense of context, or a measure of perspective. But the pronoun 'we' must be considered in another sense as well. I (the author of this introduction) use 'we' to refer to the writers and readers of this book, who have certain similarities in terms of their motives for being involved in this particular project, yet who will inevitably have significant differences as well. In this sense, 'we' as writers, readers and critics of this book are also engaged in the act of reading imaginative literature by and about us. Culture, race, age, sexual orientation, ability, and class privilege may influence our readings by placing us in certain positions in relation to any given narrative. We all read, and write, and argue, and interpret, from our own positions.

Writing is always a creative act, and is often a self-conscious means of self representation. Yet women writers work within a literary tradition which has tended to depict women as passive objects rather than as the active creators or subjects of their own stories. Perhaps it is for this reason that writers like Morrison are so careful to position themselves in relation to their work. Morrison, like many writers, and women writers in particular, uses writing as a liberating tool, a political act, a subversive strategy, as well as an art form and 'platform', or means of expressing self.

This chapter offers a range of work which approaches women's creative writing in one or more of these complicated ways: that is, not only as a product (literature: criticism, prose fiction, poetry, autobiography), but also as the means of implementing political action and subversion of traditional expectations of 'what women are' and 'what should women do'. This same kind of approach will be used in the next chapter on women's visual art. Here, the particular and unique aspects of creative writing are considered.

One of the main themes in all the work in this part of the book – in literary criticism as well as in stories, poems and autobiography – is that of women's personal experience as the material of creative work. The relationship between women's experience, women's roles and women's views of self as portrayed in their writing all contribute to the literary construction of self as subject. All the essays and poems included in this part are concerned with women as the subjects of their own narratives; all incorporate – whether implicitly or explicitly – some positioning of the writer or artist in relation to her work, the context of the writing (whether it be patriarchal culture in the abstract or a particular relationship), and her intended audience.

The first article, an edited version of Elaine Showalter's 'The Feminist Critical Revolution', serves as an introduction to the history (or herstory) of feminist criticism and literature. It describes the impact of feminist criticism on academia, literature and culture since the 1970s. One aspect of 'the feminist critical revolution' which informed and complicated the choice of readings in this chapter, and in the book as a whole, is the ambiguous distinction between 'feminist literature' and 'women's literature'. This distinction has become a key point for discussion in feminist criticism of other genres as well. The questions which are raised by the distinction are complex. Two such questions are whether writing by women is *necessarily* feminist; and whether the re-evaluation of women's work since the 'feminist critical revolution' tended at times to valorize some women's writing because it is by women, rather than because of other criteria.

In 'Seizing Time and Making New: Feminist Criticism, Politics and Contemporary Feminist Fiction', a critical essay which addresses both these questions, Maria Lauret (1989) points to the tendency in some feminist criticism to privilege feminist politics over aesthetic

Pollacks

'standards'. In other words, Lauret argues, some feminist criticism is not critical enough; it celebrates women's literature because it is by women, rather than because it is necessarily 'good' literature. This is an important point, and one which can be clarified with reference to the work of another critic: Sally Minogue. Minogue has written at length on the subject of women's literary 'silences' as products of patriarchal structures. She writes:

> The remarkable way in which those silences have been filled in the last decade or two almost masks the magnitude of the achievement. Women's Studies is now a force and a market: publishers such as Virago and the Women's Press are commercially successful and feminist criticism is an academic force carrying with it career possibilities.
>
> . . . It is important to realize that, underpinning this change, . . . is the belief, not always fully stated, that writing by women is important and to be valued for that very reason, that it is by and about women. . . . And this is where the real business of feminist criticism, and the difficulties, begin. For at what stage do we begin to say that a writer is bad because he or she is misogynist (in whatever terms that misogyny is critically described)? At what stage do we demote certain works and elevate others? It is no good disclaiming that task, since that is part of what feminist criticism is about: the revaluation of the worth of texts.
>
> (Minogue, 1990, pp. 4–5)

The problem of separating feminist politics from standards of 'literary worth' cannot be easily 'solved'. The problem of valuing women's work is raised as one which complicates and enriches the reading of this (and other) feminist textbooks. One way of approaching this question is to read carefully for the situated perspective of the authors: whether it be a creative writer such as Toni Morrison or a critic such as Showalter, Lauret or Minogue. But as the introduction to this book points out, one of the hallmarks of 'academic' writing is a certain claim to 'objectivity' and a third-person voice. It is sometimes more difficult to situate the author of feminist criticism and theory than it is to situate the author of fiction. That is not to say that fiction writers can be trusted when they 'state their positions'. It is one of the advantages of fiction, and indeed of autobiography, that perspectives can be created and tampered with; details can be rearranged; facts can be altered by arrangement, ordering and the implication of the speaker's or narrator's voice and context.

In the second article, the short story is discussed as an example of one literary form in which women have been successful in subverting expectation and stereotype, in both aesthetically valid and politically liberating ways. Of course, the novel is also a fictional prose form in which women's work has played an important role, as is poetry. In study of a selection of short stories, it is possible to compare a range of 'voices' created by authors representing different class, race, cultural and generational perspectives. The stories discussed in 'Supply and Demand: Women's Short Stories', are included in Angela Carter's anthology *Wayward Girls and Wicked Women* (Carter, 1986). These stories, and indeed the anthology itself, benefit from critical reading informed by the questions of situated perspectives, and those raised by Lauret and Minogue about the valuing of women's writing.

The third article is also 'about' prose fiction, but the genre addressed is feminist science fiction. Frances Bonner's piece provides a detailed analysis of science fiction as a form which plays with and subverts 'norms' of prose fiction. Feminist science fiction, as Bonner points out, is a form of literary representation known for its particularly imaginative and self-consciously feminist body of writers and readers. Within some of the fiction, there is the suggestion that there may be 'better ways of being' imagined and imaginable by women, which might have important ramifications in our ways of thinking about the future, and about our own lives.

The next two articles focus on poetry rather than on prose fiction, and both deal with the conflicting roles of mothering and creative writing. This kind of comparison between writing and giving birth is a common theme in much women's poetry, and is one accessible way into thinking about different kinds of creativity (though it is by no means the only way in). Article 2.4 is Alicia Ostriker's 'A Wild Surmise: Motherhood and Poetry'. Ostriker describes a choice to be made between the traditional women's 'roles' of lover, wife and mother, and a creative 'act' such as writing poetry, which involves taking on the 'role' of poet. Similarly, Article 2.5, Carol Rumens's worksheets on the poem 'Moment of Faith', is a first-person personal narrative about the nature of poetry writing. The poem is about Rumens's experience of birth and mother–daughter bonding; the worksheets are about the birth pangs of writing a poem on such a personal subject. The reading of the worksheets informs reading of the poem itself, and vice versa.

The first five articles illustrate different ways in which subjectivity and representation of the 'self' are created and questioned in feminist criticism, women's fiction and poetry. The last two articles shift the ground slightly and examine the presentation of the self in women's autobiography. In writing about the self, it is possible to fictionalize in many ways (unconsciously and consciously) by either exaggerating or underestimating events and feelings. Carolyn Heilbrun has developed the idea that the process of fictionalizing, which is inherent to autobiography, has been liberated for women by the women's movement. In an essay which describes the impact of women's biography (rather than autobiography) on the public valuing of women's experience, it is significant that Heilbrun refers to the biography of a very famous woman, the anthropologist Margaret Mead, rather than to a biography of a lesser-known individual. Heilbrun writes:

> Before the current women's movement, it was difficult to find a woman's biography of an accomplished woman that was not palpably terrified of making any unseemly claims on behalf of the woman subject. Avoiding large claims was no doubt made easier by the fact that the subjects themselves were usually unable to express with full honesty the exemplary meaning of their lives . . .
>
> (Heilbrun, 1991, p. 28)

In other words, feminist criticism and developments in the women's movement in recent years have helped to revalue the lives of some women, and to position them as 'proper' literary subjects. But this does not address the question of lesser-known women. Working-class women's voices, for instance, remain relatively quiet, though no longer completely silent.

Articles 2.6 and 2.7 explore the relationships between social class, education and the accessibility of women's voices. The subject of these articles is women's autobiography (women's writing about themselves) rather than women's biography (writing about the lives of women). The extracts from Nicole Ward Jouve's 'Criticism as Autobiography' provide the critical (rather than highly personalized) views of an educated middle-class white woman, writing on the subject of subjectivity in autobiography 'as criticism'. The idea is that we recreate ourselves in our writing: that we write ourselves into being, or create images of ourselves and our lives with and through words and imagination, or, in Jouve's words: '. . . through writing the self is invented, constructed, projected' (Jouve, 1991). Jouve positions herself in her book as a critic of other critics: she observes that writing criticism is a projection of self-image, as is writing autobiography.

Wendy Webster's piece on 'Working Class Women's Auto-biography' takes a different stance on the same subject. Webster does not offer her own personal experience theorized, but rather begins with a study of the ways in which working-class women may seek to validate their senses of self and comment upon their social and domestic situations in their writing. This is autobiography as criticism, rather than criticism as autobiography. Of course, Jouve's academic perspective is heavily influenced by the personal, as Webster's is by the academic.

Similar themes emerge in all the articles in this chapter. These themes include: self in relation to both the act and the product of creative writing, representation and self-representation in fiction, a feminist use of language, and the active 'role' of the audience in reading women's fiction (whether it be a story or poem or excerpt from an autobiography). The idea that 'writing self' in autobiography is itself a fictionalizing, and can be appropriated and re-interpreted by the reader to suit her or his own 'ways of seeing' (reading as a creative act in itself), is presented in several different ways: in some of the short stories as well as in discussion of poetry and of autobiography as genre.

'We' and 'you' as readers and writers and women and men, are all the subjects of our own lives. In writing literature – essays, stories, poems and autobiography – each 'self' is defined as the subject of its own narrative. The voices and views of authors emerge in literary representations, whether they are expressed in the first person, or are diffused in other voices and presented through a multiplicity of narrative perspectives. Engaging as active readers with this part of the book may help to locate the subjects – and subject positions – of the writers. Such active reading certainly helps in discerning a certain object, or aim, in all this work: it all refers to the potential for women's writing to create alternatives and to subvert expectations. In this sense, this part of the book has an object, or objective, of its own.

Lizbeth Goodman

Note

1   This same quotation is used as the keynote in the introduction to *Changing Our Own Words: essays on criticism, theory and writing by black women*, edited by Cheryl A. Wall (London, Routledge, 1990). Morrison's article was first published in *The Michigan Quarterly Review*, vol. 38, no. 1 (Winter 1989), p. 9.

Article 2.1
THE FEMINIST CRITICAL REVOLUTION
Elaine Showalter

During the last decade [the 1970s], our academic, literary and cultural institutions have all felt the impact of a feminist critical revolution. Feminist criticism has flourished in combination with every other critical approach from formalism to semiotics, and in the literary study of every period and genre from the Middle Ages to the mass media. Since the late 1960s, when feminist criticism developed as part of the international women's movement, the assumptions of literary study have been profoundly altered. Whereas it had always been taken for granted that the representative reader, writer and critic of Western literature is male, feminist criticism has shown that women readers and critics bring different perceptions and expectations to their literary experience, and has insisted that women have also told the important stories of our culture. While literary criticism and its philosophical branch, literary theory, have always been zealously guarded bastions of male intellectual endeavor, the success of feminist criticism has opened a space for the authority of the woman critic that extends beyond the study of women's writing to the reappraisal of the whole body of texts that make up our literary heritage. Whether concerned with the literary representations of sexual difference, with the ways that literary genres have been shaped by masculine or feminine values, or with the exclusion of the female voice from the institutions of literature, criticism and theory, feminist criticism has established gender as a fundamental category of literary analysis.

[· · ·]

Women generated feminist criticism, fought for its importance and often suffered in their careers for being identified with a radical critical movement. It is in the writing of women, moreover, that we find the fullest expression of the problematic of a feminist criticism: how to combine the theoretical and the personal. Feminist criticism reveals in its own history and form many of the patterns of influence and rebellion that mark the female literary tradition as a whole. Here too women writers searched for a language of their own, a style, a voice and a structure with which they could enter a discipline previously dominated by men. The raw intensity of feeling and the insistence on the relationship of literature to personal experience that accompanied these early phases often expressed itself in an autobiographical or even confessional criticism shocking to those trained in the impersonal conventions of most academic critical writing. Sometimes angry and denunciatory, sometimes lyrical and emotional, feminist criticism flaunted its politics and its feelings. While feminist criticism neither must nor should be the exclusive province of women, it is important to understand that its history and expression were determined by issues of gender and sexual difference.

[· · ·]

In its earliest years, feminist criticism concentrated on exposing the misogyny of literary practice: the stereotyped images of women in literature as angels or monsters, the literary abuse or textual harassment[1] of women in classic and popular male literature, and the exclusion of women from literary history. Feminist critics reinforced the importance of their enterprise by emphasizing the connections between the literary and the social mistreatment of women, in pornography, say, or rape. Over the past fifteen years, these efforts to make readers question the innocence, insignificance or humour of antifeminist characterizations have succeeded in changing the atmosphere of literary response. Male critics too have noted that in the atmosphere of the 1980s, with its heightened sensitivity to questions of sexism and gender, literary misogyny can no longer be overlooked or excused. For this reason, as Lawrence Lipking observes, 'Something peculiar has been happening lately to the classics. Some of them now seem less heroic, and some of them less funny' (1983, p. 79). We may expect that the next decade will see even more vigorous feminist questioning of our criteria of aesthetic value, and even more drastic re-estimations of the old masters.

The second phase of feminist criticism was the discovery that women writers had a literature of their own, whose historical and thematic coherence, as well as artistic importance, had been obscured by the patriarchal values that dominate our culture. Although critics and writers had talked for centuries about women's writing, when feminist criticism set out to map the territory of the female imagination and the structures of the female plot, it was doing something completely new. The focus on women's writing as a specific field of inquiry, moreover, led to a massive recovery and re-reading of literature by women from all nations and historical periods. As hundreds of lost women writers were rediscovered, as letters and journals were brought to light, as new literary biographies explored the relationship between the individual female talent and the literary tradition, the continuities in women's writing became clear for the first time.

The books that first began to define women's writing in feminist terms were Patricia Meyer Spacks's *The Female Imagination* (1975) and the late Ellen Moers's *Literary Women* (1976). My book, *A Literature of Their Own* [Showalter, 1977], outlined a literary history of English women writers in the nineteenth and twentieth centuries. In 1979, Sandra Gilbert and Susan Gubar's monumental study, *The Madwoman in the Attic*, offered a full theoretical account of the situation of the nineteenth-century woman writer, her anxieties about authorship as a monstrous and unwomanly activity that transgressed cultural boundaries, and her rewriting of male mythologies in her own texts. Since 1979, these insights have been tested, supplemented and extended so that we now have a coherent, if still incomplete, narrative of female literary history, which describes the evolutionary stages of women's writing during the last 250 years from imitation through protest to self-definition, and defines and traces the connections throughout history and across national boundaries of the recurring images, themes and plots that emerge from women's social, psychological and aesthetic experience in male-dominated cultures.

The concept of a female aesthetic logically emerged from the recognition of such connections in women's writing. As the black aesthetic of the 1970s celebrated a black consciousness in literature, so too the female aesthetic celebrated a uniquely female literary consciousness. Supported by such feminist writers, artists and poets as Adrienne Rich, Marge Piercy, Judy Chicago, Susan Griffin and Alice Walker, the female aesthetic spoke of a women's culture that had been neglected and had to be revived, of a 'women's language', and of literary styles and forms that came out of a specific female psychology.

The precise nature of the female aesthetic, however, has been the subject of continuing controversy. In feminist writing of the early 1970s, it was frequently identified with lesbian consciousness and with the politics of lesbian separatism. The Amazon was repeatedly invoked as the emblem of female creative autonomy, from the muse of the poetry journal *Amazon Quarterly* to Ti-Grace Atkinson's feminist manifesto, *Amazon Odyssey*. In 'Toward a Feminist Aesthetic', published in 1977 in the women's-culture journal *Chrysalis*, Julia Penelope Stanley and Susan Wolfe equated the flowing, conjunctive, non-linear style of such avant-garde lesbian writers as Gertrude Stein with 'women's style' in general. In a paper read at the MLA in 1976, Adrienne Rich identified lesbian identity with creative and imaginative autonomy: 'It is the lesbian in every woman who is compelled by female energy, who gravitates towards strong women, who seeks a literature that will express that energy and strength. It is the lesbian in us who drives us to feel imaginatively, render in language, grasp, the full connection between woman and woman. It is the lesbian in us who is creative, for the dutiful daughter of the fathers is only a hack' (Rich, 1979a).

Many feminist critics, however, opposed both the concept of an essential female identity that expressed itself through only one literary style, and the privileging of lesbian creative identity. By the

1980s, the lesbian aesthetic had differentiated itself from the female aesthetic. As lesbian feminist criticism became more specialized, feminist critics turned their attention to the analysis of mother–daughter relations, and the figure of the mother replaced that of the Amazon for theorists of the female aesthetic. Some critics studied metaphors of childbirth in art and creativity. Others asked whether women's writing is characterized by what Joan Lidoff calls a 'female poetics of affiliation', dependent on the daughter's relation to the mother. This transition to a focus on the mother coincided with important research on maternity in other fields of women's studies. Among the most influential works were the historian Carroll Smith-Rosenberg's classic essay, 'The Female World of Love and Ritual' (1975), which demonstrated that in nineteenth-century America a strong woman's culture had produced idyllically close mother–daughter relationships; Adrienne Rich's *Of Woman Born: motherhood as experience and institution* (1976)[1977]; and Nancy Chodorow's psychological study *The Reproduction of Mothering* (1978), which argued that the relationship of the infant to the female parent was the key factor in the construction of gender identity.

Yet while feminist criticism was one of the daughters of the women's movement, its other parent was the old patriarchal institution of literary criticism and theory; and it has had to come to terms with the meaning of its mixed origins. Our efforts to define the difference of women's writing as the expression of a female aesthetic led us to a renewed interest in theories from psychoanalysis and aesthetics. The process of studying women's writing, furthermore, led us to challenge the fundamental theoretical assumptions of traditional literary history and criticism, from periodic divisions (such as 'the American Renaissance') that were exclusively based on male literary landmarks to the underlying ideas about genre, the literary career and the role of the critic. Finally, the project of creating a criticism of our own led us to think about the structure of other critical revolutions and our relationship to them. In its third phase, therefore, feminist criticism demanded not just the recognition of women's writing but a radical rethinking of the conceptual grounds of literary study, a revision of the accepted theoretical assumptions about reading and writing that have been based entirely on male literary experiences.

Another reason for the increased prominence of theoretical questions in feminist criticism since the mid-1970s is the influence of radical critical thought from other countries. As American feminist criticism has circulated abroad, so too work by English and French feminist critics has been made available in the United States. Several leading European theoreticians have come to speak at American conferences, or to teach in American universities. As a result, the different currents of English and French feminist criticism have influenced the direction of American critical theory.

American feminist criticism has always had its strongest institutional base in the academic community, both in departments of literature and in women's studies; and most of the American contributors to this book[2] are connected with the university. They are concerned with the immediate impact of feminist ideas about literature on the classroom, the curriculum and the literary canon. In Great Britain, however, where women's studies courses and programmes are less established than in American universities and colleges, the institutional bases for feminist criticism have been outside the universities, in radical politics, journalism and publishing. The English contributions to international feminist criticism have been an analysis of the connection between gender and class, an emphasis on popular culture, and a feminist critique of Marxist literary theory. There are historical and social reasons for this difference. According to Olive Banks, a sociologist who has studied the English feminist movement, 'The main difference between the United States and Britain . . . is the closer link in Britain between socialism or Marxism and feminism . . . There was never the deep rift between radical men and women that occurred, and indeed persisted, in the United States and kept the two groups not only apart but hostile to each other' (1981, p. 238). It is striking that the leading English feminist critics such as Mary Jacobus, Rosalind Coward, Michèle Barrett, Juliet Mitchell and Cora Kaplan combine Marxist theoretical interest in the production and ideology of literature with feminist concerns for women's writing.

Whereas Anglo-American feminist criticism, for all its internal differences, tries to recover women's historical experiences as readers and writers, French feminist theory looks at the ways that 'the feminine' has been defined, represented or repressed in the symbolic systems of language, metaphysics, psychoanalysis and art. French feminist theory had its base in the institutes and seminars of the Neo-Freudian psychoanalyst Jacques Lacan, the deconstructionist philosopher Jacques Derrida, and the structuralist critic Roland Barthes. All of these theoreticians played an important role in directing feminist concern to the study of language.

Taking up questions of women's relation to language, French feminists have described *l'écriture féminine*, a practice of writing 'in the feminine' which undermines the linguistic, syntactical and metaphysical conventions of Western narrative. *L'écriture féminine* is not necessarily writing *by* women; it is an avant-garde writing style like that of Joyce, Bataille, Artaud, Mallarmé or Lautréamont. However, the most radical French feminist theorists also believe that *écriture féminine* is connected to the rhythms of the female body and to sexual pleasure (*jouissance*), and that women have an advantage in producing this radically disruptive and subversive kind of writing. They urge the woman writer to ally herself with everything in the culture which is muted, silenced or unrepresented, in order to subvert the existing systems that repress feminine difference. For Julia Kristeva, female discourse that breaks with tradition is a political act of dissidence, a form of feminist action. For Hélène Cixous, the best-known and most widely translated theorist of *l'écriture féminine*, women's writing has genuinely revolutionary force. As she writes in her manifesto, 'The Laugh of the Medusa', 'when the repressed of their culture and their society return, it is an explosive, utterly destructive, staggering return, with a force never yet unleashed' (1980, p. 256).

Over the past ten years, French feminist critics have themselves attempted to make criticism a mode of *écriture féminine*, emphasizing textual pleasure and making extensive use of puns, neologisms, coded allusions, typographical breaks and other devices of surrealist and avant-garde writing. Whether these revolutionary critical styles alone can ever have revolutionary social impact is a question much debated by more empirical and activist American feminists. None the less, while at first the orientation of the French theorists seems very different from the Anglo-American tradition, it also bears many similarities to considerations of the female aesthetic and women's writing. Monique Wittig, for example, has been the French champion of the Amazon, or *guérillère*, the lesbian who eludes sexual, political and linguistic categories. Cixous and Kristeva, among others, have been involved in the process of 'rethinking the maternal' on the level of language and writing (see Burke, 1980). The influence of their work on Anglo-American feminist criticism is likely to be significant in the next decade; and its initial impact will be seen in many of the essays [in Showalter, 1985].

All of these influences – the women's liberation movement, the development of women's studies and the impact of European theory – have shaped the feminist criticism of the 1980s. The intellectual trajectory of feminist criticism has taken us from a concentration on women's literary subordination, mistreatment and exclusion, to the study of women's separate literary traditions, to an analysis of the symbolic construction of gender and sexuality within literary discourse. It is now clear that what we are demanding is a new universal literary history and criticism that combines the literary experiences of both women and men, a complete revolution in the understanding of our literary heritage.

[· · ·]

Notes

1   The term 'textual harassment' is from Mary Jacobus (1982).

2   That is, in which this article originally appeared.

Article 2.2
SUPPLY AND DEMAND: WOMEN'S SHORT STORIES

Lizbeth Goodman

IMAGES OF WOMEN

Stereotypical images of women are not uncommon in literature, nor indeed in cultural representations of any kind. Creating unstereotypical images of women in fiction is a challenge for male as well as female writers. Yet this challenge has been taken up primarily by women writers, and most powerfully by feminist writers. Some women's fiction, including feminist fiction, offers images of women which seem at first to be negative or to support existing stereotypes, yet which can be re-viewed as subversions of these stereotypes if read with an awareness of context. As Adrienne Rich has argued, it is possible to interpret writing as re-vision and thereby to re-view images of women in positive ways (Rich, 1979b). In this way negative images of women may be read and interpreted as potentially positive.

The process of re-vision requires active participation on the part of the reader. First it is necessary to consider the images themselves. It could be said that there is a 'demand' for stereotypical and dualistic images of women: that they are marketable and are rewarded by mass sales and film and television adaptations. In fact, it is sometimes those stories which offer the most evil women characters which are rewarded with adaptation.

For instance, when Stephen King's thriller *Misery* (dir. Rob Reiner, 1990), was filmed, the Oscar for 'Best Actress' went to Kathy Bates, the woman who played the psychotic 'number one fan' of the male fiction writer (played by James Caan) who is the story's hero. The hero is a writer of fiction, injured in an accident and 'rescued' by a nurse who lives in a conveniently isolated cottage. She is his fan, and his saviour, and also his jailer: she uses her power over his physical condition to keep him captive until he writes a sequel to her favourite series of romance novels. She will not accept the death of the heroine of those novels (he had killed her off in the last book, hoping to move on to a different kind of fiction writing). She threatens the writer with death unless he will bring the character back to life. Both sides of the traditional dualistic representation are depicted: the angelic woman is the fictional heroine within the hero's romance novels, and the monster is the nurse (a nurturing figure) who begins by identifying with the fictional heroine, and ends by preying on both the romance and its author. The caring nurse becomes a psychotic monster, and wins an Oscar. In this stranger than fiction scenario, it is not clear whether the judges were rewarding the performance or the character, the presentation or the image.

This paradox might also be read between the lines of a popular film 'thriller' like *Fatal Attraction* (dir. Adrian Lyne, 1987) wherein the unmarried woman (played by Glenn Close) is depicted as evil and the married man who was her partner in an adulterous affair (played by Michael Douglas) is depicted as the heroic survivor of her evil actions. The injured wife is portrayed as all-forgiving and loving. The protagonist is trapped between two extremes: the perfect wife he has betrayed and the evil woman who, when betrayed, threatens him. In both *Misery* and *Fatal Attraction*, these stereotypical images of women are both created and condemned by men. The *Misery* example is particularly interesting because it is a film about a story about fiction.

In analysing the success of *Misery*, it is tempting to consider what might have happened if the roles had been reversed; if a female writer had been hounded and tortured by a male 'fan'. That would have been both more and less typical: more so in the sense that women are often depicted in fiction and film as the survivors of male violence; but less so in the sense that women are not often cast as the *writers* of stories (even within stories). Nor are women often cast as 'heroes'. Reclaiming and valorizing images of women contradicts literary and social expectation. It is, therefore, a doubly subversive strategy and – not coincidentally – one of the most common techniques of contemporary feminist fiction writing.

WOMEN'S FICTION AND THE SHORT STORY

Of the various forms of fiction, women have contributed most substantially to the development of the novel as genre. Novels (and especially 'Romance' novels) have tended to focus on the domestic sphere: a suitably 'feminine' topic for 'women writers'. Thus, a great deal of early feminist literary criticism looked to writers like Virginia Woolf, primarily known as novelists, who subverted the form of the novel in terms of style and of content, yet who did not often break away from their largely middle-class white perspectives in the representation of female (or male) characters. Heather McVane has argued, in her critical study of *Women Writers of the Short Story*, that the attention paid to Woolf and other female modernists may be displaced: that they may deserve attention, not so much for innovations in style – which can be interpreted as interventions in the male-dominated strategy of modernist writing – but rather for their focus on women characters and female experiences as of primary importance within narratives. She contends that it is more interesting to ask: 'how do these women seem to relate to the received tradition: do they identify with it, adapt it to their needs, reject it, or ignore it?' (McVane, 1980, p. 3). In some contemporary fictional forms – for instance, feminist science fiction and feminist detective fiction – elements of the 'received tradition' may be alternately identified with, adapted, rejected *and* ignored, in varying degrees by different authors. The options are not mutually exclusive.

This article focuses neither on 'women's fiction' in general nor on the novel, but on women's short stories; that is, short stories written by and about women. It is significant that in many collections of short stories by women, the unifying factor is the gender of the authors, rather than theme or subject matter, though theme, when it is shared, is often 'feminine' to some extent: for example, it may be a focus on mother–daughter relationships, or on 'female experience'. The idea that women's writing is unique because it is by women is potentially problematic, in that it both celebrates and runs the risk of marginalizing or 'ghettoizing' women's voices. One anthology – Angela Carter's *Wayward Girls and Wicked Women* – is unified by the gender of the authors and by a theme: the subversion of the feminine stereotype (Carter, 1986).[1] One of the strengths of this anthology is its inclusion of stories by women of many different cultural, racial and generational backgrounds. The biographical details which Carter includes reveal a significant tendency of migration among the authors: cultural influences are complicated and intertwined.

The diversity of authorship is one of the strengths of Carter's anthology, but it also raises a potential problem of ideology and interpretation. The stories in this, as in most anthologies, were collected by an editor and grouped together after the fact. Their function as examples supporting the editor's chosen theme says more about the editor's careful choice in choosing examples than it does about the authors' individual (much less collective) intentions. This is not to deny the validity of the theme, nor to argue against theme-led groupings of stories; it is, rather, to problematize the assumption of intention of individual authors in any collection of stories, or of essays for that matter. Because the anthology includes stories by many different authors but does not include individual introductions by those authors, any intention which can be read into the choice of stories must be attributed to the editor alone. This is a particularly important point for the reader or critic of women's fiction, since feminist criticism may be applied to both the stories and the theme or politics of the anthology.

There is a difference between a feminist collection of short stories (like Carter's) and a collection of feminist short stories. The first refers to the feminist politics (and theme) of the anthology and its editor; the second refers to the feminist intent and content of individual stories, and thereby of individual authors. One collection may be both. But it is important to note the distinction. The multiplicity of voices in any given anthology complicates the notion that there might be *one* feminist politic, or position, running throughout. If a collection is organized around a certain theme, such as 'mothers and daughters' or 'wicked women', the phrase 'a feminist collection of short stories' will tend to be the more accurate label. There are, of course, exceptions. When short stories are written by self-consciously feminist women specifically for inclusion in a feminist anthology, as were the stories in the collection called *Tales I Tell My Mother* (and its two sequels), then it is more accurate to use the phrase which is that book's subtitle: 'a collection of feminist short stories' (Fairbairns *et al.*, 1978). The difference is subtle and important. The feminism is located in the editor's politics and feminist position, which the authors might or might not understand, much less agree with or feel included in. In reading any collection of stories, then, feminist intent and political perspectives will be easier to locate and identify in the editor's voice and position than in those of individual authors.

Positioning of an editor's feminist politics does not under-value the awareness of short story writers; it rather calls attention to the vast differences in cultural and generational backgrounds which may be represented in any given collection. The example of *Wayward Girls and Wicked Women* is illustrative in this regard. To assume that a deceased New Zealand woman (Katherine Mansfield) and a contemporary British feminist writer and critic (Angela Carter) and a number of women from Africa and Asia should all share one understanding of a term like 'feminism' is ludicrous, as is the assumption that they might possibly agree with one notion of what a 'feminine woman' is. Thus an anthology like Carter's, which includes stories organized on the premise that all the female characters share a common subversion of the feminine stereotype is – at one level – misleading. But it can also be seen as an extension of the theme of 'subversion' through feminist re-viewing and re-vision: the extent to which any reader will 'buy' Carter's organiz-ational premise depends very much upon the readers' positions and ways of reading. It also depends on making the distinction between Carter's position, which is stated, and those of the authors, which are not.

Carter's anthology differs in an important respect from other collections of women's short stories, many of which are organized around a theme connected to a personal political position. For instance, Ann Oosthuizen's *Stepping Out* is one of several prominent anthologies organized around the theme of lesbian relationships. Other collections are designed to include representative stories from women of certain generations or cultures: for instance Ellen Kuzwayo's collection of short stories by South African women and

Paula Gunn Allen's collection of stories by native American Indian women (Oosthuizen, 1986; Kuzwayo, 1990; Allen, 1990). Collections such as these are valuable not only for the stories they include, but also for their potential to establish a 'tradition' or cultural perspective within a single volume. For the same reason, they may be misleading: it is tempting to read such collections as *definitive* statements about cultures, rather than as individualized ways of representing cultures and traditions, filtered through the lens of one editor's situated perspective. That said, the value of such collections is immense: they have made images of women, created by women, available from culture to culture, generation to generation, in fictionalized form.

The short story as form has produced a very wide range of fictions – written and read by women all over the world, about women from all over the world, as well as by individual feminist writers from England, the USA and Canada. Collections of stories by writers such as Fay Weldon, Lorrie Moore, Marianne Wiggins, Alice Walker, Emily Prager, Margaret Atwood and others have been influential as well as popular. Collections of stories by individual writers such as these can be called 'feminist' with less hesitation, both because western definitions of feminism are known to the authors (though they will vary in meaning and interpretation in each case) and because the positions and intentions of the authors are clearly situated in book introductions as well as in public interviews and other media spaces. Of course, the 'feminist' status of a collection of stories is rarely what sells the book, unless it is adopted for educational purposes or featured as part of 'Feminist Book Fortnight', in which case the book's feminist politics will be used as one of the main selling points.

The form of the short story is itself important, and is located in a particular place in the literary market. The short story differs from the novel in several ways, most of which are related to length. It takes less time to read a short story, which may make the form popular with readers for the same reason that some readers prefer magazine articles to other (longer and possibly more demanding) forms of literature. An element of valuing comes into play here as well: the status assigned to the short story will tend to be higher than that assigned to magazine articles, depending upon the intended audience and relative fame or status of the authors. Similarly, a story by Katherine Mansfield may be seen to be more 'serious' than one by a less established and canonized author.

The form of the short story has literary implications as well; in McVane's words: 'The short story, like the lyric poem, embodies the completed moment: immediate, self-contained, isolated from causal chains of events . . . ' (McVane, 1980, p. 2). Ideology and politics, as well as positionality of authors and their working contexts, inform the content of any author's representation of a 'completed moment' in a short story. While stories may be separated from 'causal chains of events' in terms of content, their *intent* – the intentions and contexts of both authors and readers – will inform the value of any given story in any given culture, at the time of the reading. When stories are collected in anthologies, the ideology of the editor(s) is made explicit.

SUPPLY AND DEMAND

The subversive potential of the short story is related to its cultural valuation or status in a larger sense as well: because it is generally seen to be less influential than the novel, it is paid less attention by the mainstream and can, as a result, sometimes 'get away with more'. But collections of short stories tend to sell less than novels, and particularly less than the block-buster novels which are sold in bins in supermarkets and airports. Collections of stories, while they may be equivalent to novels in terms of length, will also tend to be directed at a different market than novels. And of course, different kinds of novels are also directed at different markets, from the 'academic' novels of A.S. Byatt and Anita Brookner to the mainstream 'pulp' fiction of the Mills and Boon Romance series and individual best-sellers like Shirley Conran's *Lace* (these later examples are discussed as examples of 'mass-market pornography' in Chapter 5).

What is at issue in all these examples is the principle of 'supply and demand': a concept which has implications for content as well as marketing strategies. Short stories are only occasionally made into films, with the notable exception of Elizabeth Jolley's *The Last Crop* (dir. Sue Clayton, 1990): a story which is self-consciously aware of the power of the market-place not only in selling images of women in fiction, but also in establishing and reinforcing certain images of stereotypical 'femininity'. This extract from *The Last Crop* links the two issues, through an exchange between mother and daughter about 'supply and demand':

> 'Yes, I'm going to write this book,' she said. 'I want it brought out in paperjacks.'
> 'Paperbacks you mean.'
> 'Yes, like I said, paperjacks, with a picture on the front of a girl with her dress ripped off and her tied to a post in the desert and all the stories will have expensive wines in them and countries in Europe and the names of famous pictures and buildings and there will be wealthy people with expensive clothes and lovely jewels very elegant you know but doing and saying terrible things, the public will snap it up. I'll have scenes with people eating and making love at the same time. Maybe they'll want to make a film of it, it's what people want. It's called supply and demand.'

'That's a good title.'

She thought a moment. 'I hadn't thought of a title.'

(Jolley, 1986, p. 11)

Supply and demand is not the title, but the principle: images of women formed and rewarded by the dominant culture are saleable commodities: marketable books and fodder for popular film treatments.

Jolley's story is included in *Wayward Girls and Wicked Women* and fits the anthology well, in that it can be seen to illustrate Carter's thematic vision, which is intricately related to – is indeed the flipside of – the supply and demand idea. What the anthology 'supplies' is a host of negative images of women who are abused, exploited, emotionally and physically oppressed, and even killed. But in all the stories, stereotypical representations of 'the feminine' are subverted, are reclaimed as 'positive' images of sorts. What is demanded of the reader is a willingness to play along: to problematize and question these stereotypes in the act of reading.

The stories which Carter includes are about women who are considered 'wayward' or 'wicked' by the standards of cultural norms of 'what women should be', but not necessarily by feminist perspectives on women's possibilities and potential. In Carter's words:

> . . . the title of this collection is, of course, ironic. Very few of the women in these stories are guilty of criminal acts, although all of them have spirit and one or two of them, to my mind, are, or have the potential to be, *really* evil. . . . Most of the variously characterized girls and women who inhabit these stories, however, would seem much, much worse if men had invented them.
>
> *(Carter, 1986, p. ix)*

Women are the writers and the protagonists of all the stories in *Wayward Girls and Wicked Women*: a collection which offers a myriad of different female characters, all variations on the feminine stereotype in radically subverted form. All of the stories can be viewed through the lens of a feminist perspective. But that is not to say that all the stories claim a unified perspective. The positions of the writers are vastly different, and not necessarily feminist. It is Carter who occupies the self-consciously feminist territory. Different readers will take different positions in relation to Carter's feminist approach, according to their own particular political position(s). Selective readers may focus on some stories rather than others – perhaps those which support, or contradict, their own ideologies and positions; while other readers will prefer to look less selectively at different stories with conflicting ideologies and perspectives.

That women from so many different cultures and generations should all have written stories about women who actively revolt against cultural expectations of 'what women should be' (mothers, wives, nurturers . . .) may in itself be indicative of a certain cross-cultural dynamic of 'supply and demand'. The norms for each writer are different. Therefore, the characters who deviate from those norms will tend to do so in different, culturally specific ways.

THEMES: WAYWARD GIRLS, WICKED WOMEN, MONSTERS AND SHE-DEVILS

One of the stories in the anthology is by Carter herself: *The Loves of Lady Purple*. The story has several overlapping themes, all of which are informed by Carter's self-proclaimed interest in redefining the criteria by which 'wicked women' may be recognized and judged. Like the female character in *Misery* (played by Kathy Bates), Carter's Lady Purple has a murderous streak. Also like the Bates character in *Misery*, Lady Purple is a product of the male imagination superimposed on a woman's sense of self. In *Misery*, the nurse identifies with the heroine of the male-created romance novel; in *The Loves of Lady Purple*, the title character is a puppet who embodies the physical attributes of 'desirability' valued by the puppet-maker. Both female characters seek revenge on the male creators of the images they embody, embrace and despise. Both female characters subvert the power relations between themselves and their male creators; they become powerful figures who are 'monstrous' in their unfeminine behaviour, and whose power is achieved *through* this 'monstrous' lack of 'femininity'. In fact, the same might be said of the Glenn Close character in *Fatal Attraction*, who becomes – or is seen to be – evil when she seeks revenge on the man who is the hero and focus of that story.

Carter's *The Loves of Lady Purple* is interesting in stylistic as well as thematic terms. The story reads like a grotesque fairy tale or an old wives' tale with an implicit warning for men, rather than for women. The story is told through a third person voice, as if by an omniscient narrator (all-knowing other), rather than by any of the characters in the story. This lends to the fairy-tale effect. The same could be said of another story in the collection: Suniti Namjoshi's *Three Feminist Fables*.

Namjoshi's story is really three stories, each of which is a succinct re-vision of a well-known fable. Namjoshi's feminist versions are told in a complicated voice: a mixed journalistic/narrative third person style. Her stories all share a moral: women's experience has to be double-thought or viewed from the outside in, in order to make it conform to the values of patriarchal society. But Namjoshi provides this moral indirectly and eloquently. She teaches by example: her little Red Riding Hood only needs a 'shrink' to convince her that 'wolves on the whole are extremely nice'. Bluebeard pleads 'provocation' (and presumably wins his case) when on trial for the murder of his wife, who *refused* to take an interest in his secrets. The She-Monster is dragged out of the sea by a group of (male) scientists, killed though she is pregnant, dissected, displayed in skeletal form with a plaque bearing these words: 'The Dreaded She-Monster. The Fumes of this Creature are Noxious to Men'.

Namjoshi's She-Monster is a 'monster' because she exists, and is guilty because she lets off a stench when she is slaughtered. The men who killed her are not punished or even implicated, but rather celebrated and martyred: 'Inscribed underneath are the names of the scientists who gave their lives to find this out'. The men who kill the She-Monster receive the same treatment as the Michael Douglas figure who stands by while his devoted wife kills the 'evil' temptress figure in *Fatal Attraction*. The differences are significant: in Namjoshi's version, the She-Monster provides no provocation yet is killed by men. In *Fatal Attraction*, the Glenn Close character is involved in an affair (provocation of sorts) but is landed with all the blame. She is the scapegoat for the man's sexual desire and betrayal. She is killed not by the man, but by another woman, his wife. It is not difficult to guess the genders of the authors of these two scenarios.

Namjoshi's She-Monster can be fruitfully compared with another woman-created monster in fiction: Fay Weldon's She-Devil (a character whose story might well have been included in Carter's anthology, were it a short story rather than a novel).[2] The She-Devil, whose name is Ruth, is caught up in the conflicting expectations of patriarchal conceptions of 'femininity' and 'beauty'. The cultural image of the feminine ideal is encapsulated in the character of Ruth's rival: Mary Fisher, a writer of pulp romance. Ruth ingests too much of the stuff, and nearly kills herself in her grotesque effort to become 'feminine' and 'beautiful' like Mary Fisher.

In the end, Ruth literally – through radical cosmetic surgery – *becomes* Mary Fisher. She even writes a successful romance novel. Only once the She-Devil proves herself capable of being (or appearing to be) both 'feminine' and a successful writer of 'romance' does she feel free to let go of the idealized image and to allow her own voice to come through. This may seem like a contradiction, as the story is told in the first person, in Ruth's (the She-Devil's) voice throughout. But for most of the story, the voice is that of a woman trying to be like someone else. In the end, Ruth decides to see, and be herself. She says:

> I tried my hand at writing a novel, and sent it to Mary Fisher's publishers. They wanted to buy it and publish it, but I wouldn't let them. Enough to know I can do it, if I want. It was not so

difficult after all; nor she so special.

I am a lady of six foot two, who had tucks taken in her legs. A comic turn, turned serious.

(Weldon, 1984, p. 240)

A 'comic turn' which is not very funny and all too real; or rather, which has very real implications in terms of the pressure on women to conform to culturally imposed images of 'femininity' and 'beauty'.

In her critical writing on 'Narrative Practice and Feminist Theory', Paulina Palmer (1989) argues that Weldon's She-Devil is 'enlivened by a strongly radical feminist spirit' and supports the claim with reference to a passage from a polemical essay entitled 'Fashion as Violence Against Women' by the British Women Against Violence Against Women (WAVAW) group. This is the passage:

> Under male supremacy women's status depends greatly on male approval. If we don't conform we pay heavy penalties. It means that many women mutilate and injure themselves, spending an enormous amount of time, energy and resources in the process. Fashion divides us into angels, whores, dolly-birds, and hags. This is important in the maintenance of male power. It prevents us seeing each other as allies, but sets us up as enemies, always in competition.
>
> *(Palmer, 1989, pp. 33–4)*[3]

These words from Carter's introduction to *Wayward Girls* make a similar point:

> ... morality as regards woman has nothing to do with ethics; it means sexual morality and nothing but sexual morality. To be a wayward girl usually has something to do with pre-marital sex; to be a wicked woman has something to do with adultery. This means it is far easier for a woman to lead a blameless life than it is for a man; all she has to do is avoid sexual intercourse like the plague. What hypocrisy!
>
> *(Carter, 1986, p. x)*

In both cases, it is the loaded words of the title which are inverted and subverted by the intentions of the authors: Carter's 'wayward girls and wicked women' and Weldon's 'She-Devil' are versions of the same beast: a male-created monster, who is a rather unremarkable – and usually likeable – woman underneath.

MORE THEMES AND STRATEGIES: IRONY, SUBVERSION, POINT OF VIEW

Both Carter and Weldon use irony within their fictions. Carter uses irony in framing her anthology as well. The first words of her introduction (quoted earlier) signal the ironic use of the phrase 'wayward girls and wicked women'. The strategy which both Carter and Weldon employ is one of revaluing the power of the label. This, Palmer argues, is a long-standing feminist strategy, used by the radical feminist Joreen in her 'Bitch Manifesto' of the early 1970s, in which the word 'bitch' is inverted and valorized by identification with 'feminist strength, independence, and rebelliousness'. (The same strategy of 'reclamation' of potentially negative words was employed in the choice of titles for several radical and Marxist feminist journals of the period, including *Shrew* and *Red Rag*.) In 'The Bitch Manifesto', the possibility of reclaiming negative words and images for feminist purposes was celebrated (Joreen, in Koedt *et al.*, 1973). But there is another side to the same technique which surfaces in relation to cultural reception of feminist ideas and images: it is the rebirth of the evil woman, the 'number one fan' who is the hero's worst nightmare but Stephen King's best friend, as she makes him a tremendous amount of money at the box office.

Here again, the gender and intentions of authors must be considered. If feminist women create 'evil' women, the intention is likely to be ironic and the effect subversive. By depicting women caught up and influenced by society's double standards for women, female fiction writers have been able to subvert even the most extreme stereotype: the ideal mother (a version of the Virgin Mary) and the whore with a heart of gold (a version of Mary Magdalene): two of the oldest surviving and most pervasive female archetypes. All of Carter's collected 'girls and women' face the same double standard. Many of the stories included in the anthology deal with the themes of mother–daughter relationships and of sexuality. Most of the stories can be re-viewed as literary representations created by women which depict and subvert stereotypical images of women. Elizabeth Jolley's story *The Last Crop* is particularly interesting in this regard.

The 'wicked woman' in Elizabeth Jolley's *The Last Crop* is a working-class mother trying to provide for her children. She works as a cleaner in luxury apartment buildings and she invites working-class friends in when the wealthy owners are out so that they may share, temporarily, in a taste of the rich life. In this sense, the mother can be seen to be a 'conwoman' in that she takes advantage of her privileged access to the apartments by extending it to her friends; she subverts the system by using her privilege (access) for other ends. In Carter's words, 'The mother in Elizabeth Jolley's *The Last Crop* is one of the few female con-men in fiction' (Carter, 1986, p. xi).

The mother–daughter theme is central to this story, and the narrative unfolds through the daughter's first-person voice. This technique effectively positions Jolley (the author) with the daughter, just as the reader is positioned – through the first-person narrative

– with Jolley. This is the first mention of the mother in the story:

> I took some bread and spread the butter thick, Mother never minded how much butter we had even when we were short of things. Mother was sitting at the kitchen table when I got home, she was wondering what to get my brother for his tea and she didn't say anything . . .
>
> (Jolley, 1986, p. 1)

And this is the last mention of the mother (also the closing words of the story):

> We heard her drive down the track and, as she turned onto the road, we heard her crash the gears. My brother winced, he couldn't bear machinery to be abused but he agreed with me that she probably couldn't help it as it's been quite a while since she had anything to drive.
>
> (Ibid., p. 21)

In both cases, mention of the mother is framed by a reference to the daughter ('I') and the son ('my brother' or 'we'). In both cases the mother is occupied with finding food for her children (in the closing scene, she is driving down the road to get them some chips).

In between, the relationship between mother and daughter is revealed more through actions than through words, more through implication than statement. One example can be found in the exchange about 'supply and demand' quoted earlier. That exchange reveals a great deal about the mother's awareness of gender and class-based power relations in cultural representations. She has obviously been influenced by images reflected in advertising and film; in fact, her description reads like a scenario for a James Bond film. But while the mother is aware of cultural representations of women, she is not limited by them. She is capable of subverting them as well. Told that she and her family may live in her deceased father's house long enough to see out the last crop in the adjacent fields, the mother searches through agricultural catalogues before choosing her crop. She sends off for the seedlings and when they arrive they are a surprise to the children:

> 'What are they?'
> 'They're our crop. The last crop.'
> 'Yes I know but what are they?'
> 'Them? Oh they're a jarrah forest,' Mother said.
> We looked at her.
> 'But that will take years and years to mature,' my brother said.
> 'I know,' . . .
>
> (Ibid., p. 21)

Here, the mother's ability to turn the 'gentleman's agreement' to her children's advantage can be seen as opportunistic, 'unfeminine' and – in Carter's terms – even 'wicked'. Yet there is another way of reading the mother's character as well. In order to be a 'good mother', Jolley's character acts as a 'bad woman'. But the power of the character lends such strength to her actions that she cannot possibly be seen as 'bad' in the same way that Carter's Lady Purple can. Jolley's characters are not 'wicked' in a sexual sense, and can be seen as 'wayward' only if the term is interpreted as a compliment.

Where the reader's imagination is engaged in Jolley's story is in characterization and motivation: the reader is (implicitly) asked to identify with both the daughter and the mother; to see the story through the eyes of the daughter, in order to understand the mother. Though it seems to be the daughter's narrative, there are aspects of the story which the daughter does not understand or which are not controlled – or told – by her. For instance, in the phrase 'I know' from the extract above, the triumph of the mother is expressed in an understated way. Jolley's authorial voice comes through as well. The reader is not controlled through this positioning: the point of view is diffused, and the reader is free to change position with or in opposition to the narrative voice.

In the end, the narrator's status shifts from her original omniscient position to that of a fictional character: the subject of the story, rather than an active subject telling the story. At the same time, Jolley effectively steps out of the narrative and becomes a person: a person who is a writer, and a woman who writes on the subject of women's means of subverting stereotypes through writing.

RE-VISION AND RE-EVALUATION

In re-viewing Jolley's, Namjoshi's and Carter's stories, it is important to note that none of the characters have individualizing names; they all have descriptive names, or no names at all. Jolley's characters are labelled in relation to their familial relationships. The narrator (the daughter, a girl who seems to be in her early teens) is 'I'; the mother is called Mother; the brother is called 'my brother' by the narrator and 'your brother' by the mother. One of the rich neighbours is called 'Mrs Lady'. Only the lawyer and the landowner are called by their proper names preceded by the obligatory 'Mr'. What is revealed in this naming system – aside from the influence of the first-person voice – is an inbred set of class distinctions, expressed in titles and forms of familiar address. Carter's character is exotically and descriptively named Lady Purple; while the heroines of Namjoshi's three fables are called 'Little R', 'the woman', and the 'She-monster'. Ironically, in the last of Namjoshi's fables, it is the men who are given names (though they are not shared with the readers), signalling an individuation of the men contrasted with the representative identity assigned to the female monster.

These 'wayward girls and wicked women' (if they are that) are all depicted by their authors as representatives of something more than individual characters; they are girls and women; daughters and mothers; prostitutes and wives and friends and lovers. They are not 'real women'. In this sense, the female characters are representatives, just as was Virginia Woolf's character, Mrs Ramsay, who went without a first name in *To The Lighthouse* (mentioned in the introduction to this book) in order to highlight both the treatment of female images and characters in male-created fictions, and the 'real life' subsuming of women's birthnames in the cultural tradition of taking the husband's name in marriage. Carter's narrative strategy in her own story, as well as her choice of stories for inclusion in the anthology, seem to encourage a creative re-viewing of the feminine stereotype, and possibly also a reclamation of women's active opposition to male norms as a positive and creative enterprise. The stories, and the anthology, can be read in this way.

Reading this anthology, then, involves active engagement with a set of images and ideas. The thematic organization of the anthology, as well as the feminist intent of the organization and of some of the stories, require a certain kind of engagement from the reader. Just as it is possible – and perhaps necessary – to question the values of a cultural market-place which demands, supplies and rewards the perpetuation of extreme and falsely dualistic female stereotypes in evaluation of films such as *Misery* and *Fatal Attraction*, so it is possible – and perhaps necessary – to question such values as they are expressed in short stories and in fiction of all kinds.

CONCLUSION

At the outset of this piece, Angela Carter was quoted as saying that the characters in the *Wayward Girls and Wicked Women* anthology would 'seem much, much worse if men had invented them'. True enough. But there is another point to be made: it is unlikely that male writers *would* have invented them, or presented them in the same way. The most radical element of the anthology is its refusal to offer images which could be pigeon-holed or slotted into any of the dominant dualities such as angel/whore. The characters in the stories in this collection tend to fit both sides of the dualistic vision of the 'feminine'. They can, therefore, be seen to question the value of that duality, and of many and varied ways of representing women in images created and rewarded by men. The 'value' of each of the short stories in *Wayward Girls and Wicked Women* must be measured separately. But the value of the anthology can be valued in accordance with the sum total of 'subversion' which the stories offer. The value of the anthology is more in its potential for creative and positive interpretation by readers, than in the words or images of any particular writer. The rules of supply and demand cannot operate without an active consuming public.

Notes

1   See also Angela Carter's anthology of feminist fairy tales (Carter, 1990).

2   This story was filmed twice: *The Life and Loves of a She-Devil* was filmed for television by BBC Drama in 1986 (directed by Philip Saville, from a screenplay adapted by Ted Whitehead); and *She-Devil* was filmed for screen release in 1990 (directed by Susan Seidelman, starring Roseanne Barr as the She-Devil and Meryl Streep as the Mary Fisher character).

3   From Joreen, 'The Bitch Manifesto', published in full in Koedt *et al.* (1973).

Article 2.3
TOWARDS A BETTER WAY OF BEING: FEMINIST SCIENCE FICTION
Frances Bonner

In the study of 'serious', as opposed to 'popular', literature, the term 'genre' refers primarily to a form, like the novel or the short story,[1] and only secondarily to a particular version of that form – a tragic drama or an epic poem. In popular fiction, as in popular film and television, 'genre' is used slightly differently, referring to a varying collection of characteristics – narrative patterns, character types, iconography, settings – recognized by writers and anticipated by readers, that function above all as marketing categories, ensuring that a reader (or viewer) can find more of the 'same kind of thing', and reducing a publisher's risk of providing a product that may not be bought.

None the less, there are certain problems involved in defining a genre. To begin with, no one sits down, defines a genre and then creates the first example. Genres are recognized retrospectively, when it becomes apparent (to members of the audience, creators, disseminators and/or critics) that several texts share a similar form and characteristics. Secondly, genres change over time as certain characteristics become overly clichéd and sub-genres develop to vary the 'formula'.

A definition of the science fiction (SF) genre is particularly difficult to provide. Ordinary commonsense beliefs about what constitutes the SF genre tend to focus on its inclusion of weird technologies like time machines and bug-eyed monsters (BEMs), although these are by no means necessary. In serious SF criticism, a time machine or a BEM is an example of what the theorist Darko Suvin calls a *novum* and is often referred to by other writers as an SF 'prop' – something as yet non-existent, an imaginary object. It need not, however, be a thing, nor alien, nor even technological. In feminist SF, for example, it is often a changed form of social organization.

Suvin and Vivian Sobchack provide the two most satisfactory definitions of the genre in terms of describing the field and attempting to place boundaries that work to distinguish SF from related genres, especially the closest ones – fantasy and horror. Sobchack writes of SF film, but claims more generally that: 'SF has always taken as its distinctive generic task the cognitive mapping and poetic figuration of social relations as they are constituted and changed by new technological modes of "being-in-the-world"' (Sobchack, 1987, pp. 224–5).

The insistence on technology is more strongly characteristic of SF film than literature, especially feminist SF literature, but can still be seen generally to hold true. Even when the principal *novum* is a transformed society, it has commonly involved technological change (not necessarily involving the introduction of bigger and better hi-tech objects, but perhaps new forms of reproductive technology or the decay of a previously advanced technological society). A total absence of technology tends rather to characterize feminist fantasy or SF-fantasy hybrids.

The most influential definition is that of Darko Suvin who relies heavily on the presence of the *novum*. He claims that: 'SF is distinguished by the narrative dominance or hegemony of a fictional "novum" (novelty, innovation) validated by cognitive logic' (Suvin, 1979, p. 63). Suvin's is a normative definition; he writes of what he considers good SF. The emphasis here on 'cognitive logic' relates to his other definition of SF as 'the literature of cognitive estrangement' (Suvin, 1979, p. 20). 'Cognitive' refers to rationality (as opposed to fantastic imagining), while 'estrangement' refers in this instance to the distancing involved in considering new and different possibilities or worlds. Together they privilege SF which acts as social criticism, which aims to mobilize dissatisfaction with the present and direct it towards bringing about a better situation. This is very precisely what feminist SF tries to do.

Recently, Suvin has extended his qualifications for good SF by adopting Marc Angenot's concept of the 'absent paradigm'. When in reading an SF text we encounter something unfamiliar like a fictive word or an imaginary artefact, we create or assume the existence of a wider group of words or artefacts of which the example encountered is just one instance. This wider group is the absent paradigm and Angenot suggests that it is in conjecturing the fictional universe that pleasure is generated by SF (Angenot, 1979, p. 10). Suvin uses the concept as the basis of his 'world-creating proposition' – those cues in the text which readers use to create an idea of the world being described (Suvin, 1988, p. 205). Again, this describes the political project of feminist SF – the creation of worlds which embody feminist thought.

It is thus within the very character of the genre at its best that its potential for feminist use is to be found. A better world can be imagined and written about; the consequences of developing philosophies or debates can be explored;[2] theory can rapidly be put (imaginatively) into practice; and, possibly most importantly, we as feminist readers can gain pleasure from reading, thinking and talking about it all. It is not totally without drawbacks however. Most popular fiction genres are castigated as trivial and worthless, but the SF genre is particularly derided and its devotees dismissed as strange. Feminist SF then risks being doubly marginalized, as few SF readers are feminists and few feminists read SF. Or so it may be thought.

There are often difficulties in identifying the original text in a genre. There are certainly arguments over this in SF criticism, but the most frequently cited 'first SF book' is by a woman – Mary Shelley's *Frankenstein*. There are two major points of interest in this: first, in the light of the female creation of what subsequently came to be perceived as a particularly male genre; second, it is possible to read the story as at least in part about the dangers of male creation – Frankenstein's creature only turns against him when he is unable to love it and also refuses to create someone who will. It would, however, be an overstatement to claim this as the first feminist SF novel, since women are not particularly important to its plot, nor is patriarchy questioned.

During the late nineteenth century there were many pieces of what are more correctly termed 'scientific romances' written (and read) by both female and male writers, published primarily in magazines. Despite the dominant male gendering of science, scientific romance was not seen as overwhelmingly a male genre. Nor was another overlapping form which can be seen as an even older precursor to modern SF – the utopian story or novel.

The term 'utopia' was coined in 1516 by Sir Thomas More to describe a place that was simultaneously nowhere (i.e. imagined) and good, both an impractical dream and a part of practical politics. Ruth Levitas has attempted to overcome this contradiction (and problems that arise from using utopia to describe a range of texts from theology to SF) by devising a new definition: '[u]topia is the expression of the desire for a better way of being' (Levitas, 1990, p. 8). No wonder women were attracted to the form. Some theorists argue that the utopian urge is part of the human condition; Levitas more cautiously acknowledges merely that utopias are widespread.

One of the earliest explicitly feminist utopias was written in 1905 by Rokeya Sakhawat Hossain, a Bengali Muslim campaigner for women's education, who also opposed the practice of *purdah*. In her story, 'Sultana's Dream', the heroine dreams herself into a land in which men rather than women are kept in purdah. The new world has no war, no crime, no transport problems and no poverty thanks to the seclusion of men and to particular scientific discoveries made at women's universities (Hossain, 1988).[3] *Herland* (1915), by the American feminist-socialist Charlotte Perkins Gilman, is a much better known early feminist utopian novel. In it three male explorers discover an all-women society where reproduction is by parthenogenesis. Again war, criminality and poverty do not exist.

A variant of utopian fiction is the dystopia, in which a worse world is created by extrapolation from particular characteristics of the present. While the best known of these – Yevgeny Zamyatin's *We* (English translation 1924), Aldous Huxley's *Brave New World*

(1932) or George Orwell's *1984* (1948) – are by men, women have long written them too. Charlotte Haldane's *Man's World* (1926) has been described as utopian, but the critic Elizabeth Russell argues that it is a feminist dystopia since it is premised on men's scientific control of women's reproductive capacities and the narrative includes the revelation of a plan to reduce the number of mothers, and perhaps thereby women, in the society to one. Russell refers to Haldane's description of herself as having been a feminist since the age of sixteen to suggest that she would have then been unlikely to regard the depicted society as a good one (Russell, 1991, p. 27, n. 7).

Utopian fiction was not, however, necessarily regarded as science fiction. SF had become formalized as a popular lightweight gendered genre, particularly in the USA, following the success of Hugo Gernsback's SF 'pulp' magazines, beginning in 1926 with *Amazing Stories*. It was Gernsback who coined the term 'science fiction'. His magazines and the market they developed were aimed directly at juvenile males, as is indicated by the tendencies of the covers to feature voluptuous women and the stories to feature omnicompetent men.

None the less, women continued to read SF and, usually under pseudonyms, initials or non-gender specific names,[4] to write it, but they were very much in the minority and by no means necessarily feminist. The situation was very different from that in the field of popular detective fiction where writers and readers were as likely to be female as male and a significant proportion of the leading writers (like Agatha Christie, Margery Allingham or Dorothy L. Sayers) were women.

In the fifties, more women began to get published without dissimulation, though the numbers were still tiny. Naomi Mitchison's *Memoirs of a Spacewoman* (1957) was an oddity in being centred on, and overtly written by, a woman, but even more because she was British. Even before the emergence of second wave feminism in the 1960s, women were increasingly becoming involved in the field. The most famous female writer of SF, Ursula K. Le Guin, began publishing then. Although not explicitly, and certainly not initially, a feminist writer, Le Guin's books explore much the same range – gender (*The Left Hand of Darkness*), critical utopias (*The Dispossessed*) and living in harmony with nature (*The Word for World is Forest, Always Coming Home*).

As it did with other areas of cultural practice, feminism influenced the world of SF with, in the early 1970s, the characteristic result – an eruption of amazing new feminist works, concurrent with the reclamation and recognition of forgotten works by women. Most of the reclaimed works were short stories. The reasons for this are a combination of those that apply to women and short stories whatever the genre (for example, both composition and reading are more easily encompassed in time 'stolen' from domestic and salaried employment; and the size is less intimidating for people who may not have the confidence to consider themselves 'real' writers) and the prevalence of magazine fiction within the field as a whole. The short story also proved a useful form in which to explore developing feminist tenets, as in James Tiptree Jnr's (Alice Sheldon) 'The Women Men Don't See' or 'Houston, Houston, Do You Read?' in which the crew of a spaceship returning after a very prolonged journey find that Earth is inhabited only by (cloned) women. Tiptree, who also published as Raccoona Sheldon, was a very equivocal feminist. Sarah Lefanu argues that though Tiptree's male narrators have hard-boiled personae and 'many of the descriptions of women, and their effects on men, correspond so convincingly with an objectifying macho view that it is hard to believe that they are written by a woman. [. . .] there is always an element of ridicule' (Lefanu, 1988, p. 107). None the less the ridicule is not always evident. Her masculine identity was unquestioned for the first eight years of her publishing life, during which time not only did she participate as a man in a (written) symposium on women in science fiction, but was asked to leave because the women found 'him' so annoying (ibid., p. 105).

The major new works were, however, novels. The most frequently cited are, with first publication date: Joanna Russ' *The Female Man* (1975), Marge Piercy's *Woman on the Edge of Time* (1976), Sally Miller Gearhart's *The Wanderground* (1979), Suzy McKee Charnas' *Walk to the End of the World* (1974) and its sequel *Motherlines* (1978). All of these can be described both as SF and as utopian but they are more diverse than their forbears, usually including dystopic as well as utopian sections. They are thus, to use Samuel Delany's term, 'heterotopian' (Delany, 1976) or, in Tom Moylan's phrase, 'critical utopias' (Moylan, 1986). As well as presenting an either/or vision, heterotopias provide greater narrative possibilities, avoiding the tendency of utopian fiction to be static: after all, if the depicted world is good, even ideal, what can happen there apart from its discovery and description?

Moylan says that Russ finished *The Female Man* in 1971, which makes it a very immediate response to the debates of the early Women's Liberation Movement. The novel's complex and fragmented narrative interweaves stories of four women, Janet, Jael, Jeannine and Joanna, from four different possible times. Janet comes from Whileaway, the all-female future utopian society where she is a Safety and Peace Officer, married and with a daughter; Jael is an assassin from a world in which men and women are fighting a desperate war; Jeannine from a 1969 America which has not emerged from the Depression, in a world which did not have a Second World

War and in which women are even more circumscribed than in Joanna's 1969 America-as-Russ-knows-it. The shifting between characters, times and worlds, the appearances and disappearances of the author as a character in her text and the various inserted injunctions to the reader, even the *envoi* addressed to the book itself are designed to unsettle the reader's expectations (and thus be contrary to popular genre conventions) and to reflect the diffuse character of the female psyche. Lefanu says that, like the other feminist utopian novels mentioned earlier, this 'relies to a certain extent for its feminism on an essentialist, unitary view of women. The French feminist philosopher Julia Kristeva ... describes this as a reflection of what she calls the "second stage" of feminism: the rejection of the male symbolic order in the name of difference' (Lefanu, 1988, p. 175).

The American novelist Marge Piercy has only written one piece of SF, but it too confronted a woman of the present with one utopian and one dystopian view of the future. The utopian future of Mattapoisett is a development of the feminist polemic of Shulamith Firestone's *Dialectic of Sex* which saw women's liberation predicated on technological methods of reproduction. In Mattapoisett, babies are grown in brooders and men can breastfeed.

Both men and women inhabit Piercy's utopia, but all-female societies are more common – they figure in both Gearhart's and Charnas's works, for example. The implications of this require examination. To some readers, particularly male ones, they reveal the hatred of men that is caricatured as the 'real' message of feminism: such readers understand these works as saying that feminists want to get rid of men. It is also possible to read the books pessimistically as saying that there is no hope for a better world, since men will inevitably oppress women. Both these responses are too simple. Utopian fiction does not operate by one-to-one paralleling of the present. Because part of the meaning of the word 'utopia' is 'nowhere', its creators can bring about the good world by improbable devices. Perhaps the tension between SF and utopian fiction may lie in this.

Certainly some of the appeal of feminist single-sex utopian SF lies in their representations of separatist ideals taken to the utmost and it is possible to enjoy them on this basis alone. Equally, the presentation of sexual relations in single-sex worlds can make them pleasurable entertainments validating lesbian experience. None the less, the primary function of the removal of men from the fictional societies is to allow the rapid, uncomplicated depiction of a non-patriarchal world. However resistantly, we are readers whose subjectivity has been constructed at least in part under patriarchy. We are quite capable of reading patriarchal assumptions back into a representation carefully created to show an egalitarian society.

Indeed, it might be argued that we are incapable of not doing so, nor are writers capable of removing all such traces. Removing men from the depicted societies makes this 'reading back in' harder. Men are not, however, usually altogether absent from the fictions. Patriarchy can only be challenged by being represented and its adherents confronted by an operative alternative. Thus even in the simplest narratives, like *Herland* or 'Houston, Houston, Do You Read?', men visit the utopia (and try to destroy it). In the novels that depict only a single possible future, like those of Gearhart and Charnas, the all-women societies exist separate from, and usually in conflict with, societies run by men.

Lefanu's comment about the essentialist nature of these early second wave feminist works is perhaps seen at its strongest in Gearhart's *The Wanderground* where women living outside the technological cities of men are shown establishing a 'natural' rapport with the earth, developing their spiritual selves in ways which the depicted men are absolutely incapable of doing. The essentialist tendency continues in some of the more recent works – Joan Slonczewski's *A Door Into Ocean* contrasts the hierarchical, military, domineering male society attempting to colonize the planet Ocean, with the peaceful female society inhabiting its seas and living in harmony with its other marine life. Yet this is a more nuanced essentialism, for these women are sophisticated genetic engineers and are represented as acting by choice, according to their will.

Essentialism is rarely characteristic of feminist dystopias. Margaret Atwood's *The Handmaid's Tale* (1985) and Zoë Fairbairns' *Benefits* (1979) are both dystopias written by authors who do not normally write SF. In fact, Atwood dislikes having her novel identified in this way, believing the label both trivializing and ghettoizing. In the UK, most feminist SF is published by The Women's Press, which has a separate SF imprint; Atwood and Fairbairns, however, are both published by Virago, which, while it has followed Women's Press in developing a feminist crime list, has not done so for SF – another indication that the feminist SF market is small.

Atwood's book is also noteworthy in being the only work of feminist SF or utopian fiction to have been filmed and the only one to be involved in the world of non-SF literary prizes (it was short-listed for the Booker Prize). Perhaps dystopias appeal to more 'serious' writers because they relate more closely to the present; the extrapolations through which they derive seem more credible than the discoveries or happenstances that bring about the better worlds. Atwood's future society is premised on an increase in religious fundamentalism and a decrease in fertility caused by environmental pollution. The few remaining fertile women are reproductive chattels of the men in power (and their wives).

Regardless of whether they are utopian, dystopian or heterotopian, most such stories now are also ecotopian. Again the term comes from a male writer's book title, Ernest Callenbach's *Ecotopia* (1975). While the tendency for feminist writers to link feminism, the pastoral and environmental sensitivity on the one hand and masculinity, cities and environmental exploitation on the other is pervasive, utopian writing since William Morris' *News From Nowhere* (1890), whatever the character of its sexual politics, has tended to incorporate ecological concerns.

This points to the general use of utopia fiction by social movements. Feminists, environmentalists, lesbian and gay activists have all deployed the form. Its use in struggles based on race or colonialism is less common. Samuel R. Delany's fiction is informed by both black and gay politics and is also identified by Russ as feminist SF. Lefanu questions this identification, although she appears willing to credit him with a non-cynical pro-feminism (Lefanu, 1988, p. 15, p. 55). Octavia Butler is the only woman using SF to write about race at any length at present. Her particular interest is in exploring conditions of slavery rather than feminist issues, but her *Xenogenesis* trilogy, comprising *Dawn* (1987), *Adulthood Rites* (1988) and *Imago* (1989), explores both, asking how possible it is to love the oppressor – as to varying extents do all her books.

Butler does not write utopian SF or any variant of it. Her work is a reminder that not all feminist SF can be categorized in utopian terms, nor does it all operate by essentialist principles, however nuanced. Suzette Haden Elgin's *Native Tongue* (1984) and its sequel *The Judas Rose* (1987) provide an example more far-reaching than most. Both books tell of the resistance of a group of women on an Earth which has discovered interstellar trade with other species, but has also barred women from all positions of power. As in *The Handmaid's Tale*, the basis for this renewed oppression of women is religious. The books focus on a group of families who monopolize communication with aliens. All members of these families, men and women, adults and children, must work as linguists. The women use their skills to devise a language to express their experiences and to work towards gaining freedom. Their language is the medium of their resistance. These novels progress slowly and, despite the second's surprise ending, resist closure. Their plots, however, are linear (few since Russ and Piercy have used more fragmentary forms, although Le Guin's *Always Coming Home* does so brilliantly). Extratextually, the books are extraordinary. An academic linguist, Elgin has developed her language, Láadan, beyond the few words used in the novels. She has published *A First Dictionary and Grammar of Láadan* and made an associated teaching tape, with the result that there are now speakers of this 'fictional' women's language.

Elgin's sequel was written almost immediately after her first, but another such duo – Josephine Saxton's *The Travails of Jane Saint* and *Jane Saint and the Backlash* – were written more than ten years apart and reflect changes in the women's movement and the societies in which it operates. Saxton is another to object to being categorized as an SF writer, disliking the marginalization involved, but also believing that the label is inaccurate. Certainly these books do not fit the definitions of SF given earlier. They are predicated on Jungian psychoanalytic theory, and are Quests. The heroine searches through the Collective Unconscious, in neither book being certain of what the object of her Quest is, except that it will explain and perhaps ameliorate men's oppression of women. She encounters archetypes, witches, devils and members of her family. Events follow a dream-like logic. Perhaps reflecting their confusion over 'appropriate' generic classification, The Women's Press published the first volume as SF and the second as general fiction.

Saxton has claimed that she is classed as an SF writer because her books do not fit any other category and publishers are happier handling genre fiction. She also argues that there is a problem in an initial identification as an SF writer. Fay Weldon and Angela Carter can write books with devices no less SF than hers, but escape marginalization because they are already identified as another kind of writer (Saxton, 1991, p. 212). The same case can be made for Marge Piercy and Margaret Atwood.

Feminist SF is a valuable political form for women writers to use to explore the implications of feminist arguments. It is an enjoyable, provocative, stimulating, infuriating sub-genre for those readers who are aware of it and not deterred by the 'boys stuff' aura of the genre as a whole. Unfortunately, for the wider dissemination of feminist ideas, it must be admitted that it is indeed sadly marginal.

Notes

1   See also Article 1.3 by Dinah Birch and Article 2.2 by Lizbeth Goodman, in this volume.

2   *Benefits* is an example of a piece of feminist science fiction acknowledged by its author, Zoë Fairbairns, to have been written out of a desire to explore a debate within feminism – the question of wages for housework.

3   A slightly abridged version is included in Kirkup and Keller (1992) (companion volume to this book).

4   For example, Katherine Burdekin published the anti-fascist dystopia *Swastika Night* under the name of Murray Constantine; Catherine L. Moore published a large number of short stories in the 1930s, but only as C.L. Moore; Leigh Brackett, who started publishing short stories in the 1940s and wrote the screenplay to *The Empire Strikes Back*, had an ambiguous first name; Mary Alice Norton legally changed her first name to Andre in 1938 (and also wrote as Andrew North).

Article 2.4
A WILD SURMISE: MOTHERHOOD AND POETRY
Alicia Ostriker

That women should have babies rather than books is the considered opinion of Western civilization. That women should have books rather than babies is a variation on that theme. Is it possible, or desirable, for a woman to have both? What follows here consists of some autobiographical remarks, offered on the assumption that my history as a writer has something in common with others of my generation; and a bit of exhortation addressed to younger writers.

My initiation as a woman poet occurred when I was in my first year of graduate school at the University of Wisconsin in 1960, writing poems as nearly resembling those of Keats, Hopkins and W.H. Auden as I could. We were visited that year by a distinguished gentleman poet, to whom students were invited to submit work for scrutiny and commentary. I went for my conference hoping, of course, that he would tell me I was the most brilliant young thing he had seen in twenty years. Instead, he leafed through my slender sheaf and stopped at a tame little poem in which, however, my husband and I were lying in bed together, probably nude. 'You women poets are very graphic, aren't you', he said, with a slight shiver of disgust.

Not having previously encountered this idea, I reacted in a complex way. Certainly I was hurt and disappointed. At the same time, something in me was drawing itself up, distending its nostrils, thinking: 'You're goddamned right, we are graphic.' I had not seen myself as a 'we' until that moment. Like Huck Finn deciding, 'All right, then, I'll *go* to hell,' I had just decided 'All right, then, I'll *be* a woman poet,' which meant I would write about the body.

A year out of graduate school, in 1965, I found myself in Cambridge, England, composing a poem about pregnancy and birth called 'Once More Out of Darkness', later informally dubbed by my colleague Elaine Showalter, 'A Poem in Nine Parts and a Post-Partum'. The work was drawing from the experiences of two pregnancies, during which I had written numerous bits and scraps without intending anything so ambitious as a 'long' poem, and it was thickening like soup. One morning when it was about two-thirds done, I realized that I had never in my life read a poem about pregnancy and birth. Why not? I had read hundreds of poems about love, hundreds of poems about death. These were, of course, universal themes. But wasn't birth universal? Wasn't pregnancy profound? During pregnancy, for example, I believed from time to time that I understood the continuity of life and death, that my body was a city and a landscape, and that I had personally discovered the moral equivalent of war. During the final stage of labour I felt like a hero, an Olympic athlete, a figure out of Pindar, at whom a stadium should be heaving garlands. At times, again, I was overwhelmed with loathing for the ugliness of my flesh, the obscenity of life itself, all this ooze, these fluids, the grossness of it. Trying to discover a poetic form which could express such opposite revelations simultaneously, and convey the extraordinary sensation of transformation from being a private individual self to being a portion of something else, I had the sense of being below the surface, where the islands are attached to each other. Other women knew what I knew. Of course they did, they always had. In that case, where were the poems?

At this time I had not read Sylvia Plath's 'Three Women', a radio play consisting of three intertwined monologues in a maternity ward. Nor in fact had I heard of Plath. I had neither read nor heard of Rich's *Snapshots of a Daughter-in-Law* (1963), Sexton's *To Bedlam and Part Way Back* (1960) and *All My Pretty Ones* (1962), Diane Wakoski's *Inside the Blood Factory* (1962) or Carolyn Kizer's 'Pro Femina' (1963), in which the poet wisecracks that women writers are 'the custodians of the world's best-kept secret,/Merely the private lives of one-half of humanity'. Though I had read *The Feminine Mystique* [Friedan, 1963], I had not read Simone de Beauvoir. My field was nineteenth century, my dissertation on William Blake. Consequently I did not know that I had the good fortune to exist in a historical moment when certain women writers – mostly in utter isolation, unaware of each other's existence, twisted with shame, pain, fear of madness or the fact of it, and one of them already dead by her own hand – were for the first time writing directly and at large from female experience. The early grassblade slips through some crack in the dirt. It enters the cold alone, as Williams tells us in 'Spring and All'. It cannot guess how the ground will soon be covered with green fire. What I concluded, ignorant that this 'we' existed, was that no poems had been written on the subject of pregnancy and childbirth, first because men could not write them. Love and death *sí*, pregnancy *no*. Second, women had not written the poems because we all reproduce the themes of previous poetry. One doesn't need a conspiracy theory here, just inertia. But third, pregnancy and birth were, I suddenly realized, subjects far more severely taboo than, for example, sex. One did not discuss pregnancy or birth in mixed groups. It was embarrassing. Threatening. Taboo because men were jealous of us, did not know they were, and we had to protect them from the knowledge. Threatening because we have a society which in many ways adores death and considers life disgusting. (In the same year that I wrote this poem, Lyndon B. Johnson was sworn in as President of the United States, having campaigned as the peace candidate committed to ending our involvement in Vietnam, against Barry Goldwater, who wanted to bomb North Vietnam back into the Stone Age.)

'Once More Out of Darkness' was published in 1970, and has since generated other poems. On one occasion when I read it to a graduate class in Women and Literature at Rutgers, arguing that writing and motherhood were not necessarily mutually exclusive enterprises, someone remarked that it was one thing to write about pregnancy, where you could be symbolic and spiritual, but quite impossible to use the squalling brats as poetic material after you had them, messing around underfoot, killing your schedule. This seemed a gauntlet flung down, which I had to seize in order to defend my opinion that you can write poetry about anything; that night I wrote 'Babyshit Serenade', a poem in which I complain among other things that men don't do diapers, one happy result of which was that a man I know wrote a fine and funny poem called 'Finding the Masculine Principle in Babyshit'.

On another occasion, a group of students who had absorbed a certain line of militant feminist doctrine popular at the time greeted 'Once More Out of Darkness' with an overt hostility I had not met before (male audiences and readers when hostile to women's writing either feign indifference or ladle condescension onto you – my dear, what a wonderful natural poem you've written, they say, meaning they think it required no intelligence or craftsmanship). My suggestion to this group that motherhood for me was like sex, a peck of trouble but I wouldn't want to go through life without it, was intended to produce laughter and illumination. Instead it produced outrage – motherhood to them was a burden imposed on women by patriarchy – which I took personally and defensively. The poem I wrote in what must be called rebuttal is titled 'Propaganda'. All these poems, I might mention, are formally experimental: a result of emotional involvement combined with intellectual tension, and a feeling of stumbling from shadow into hot sunlight. Often my poems on mothering and children come from more normal, less intense states, and are more conventional poetically; for example, 'The Wolves', in my first book, which I think is a nice thing but not a discovery.

I began my most recent work on motherhood, *The Mother/Child Papers*, in 1970, when my third child and only son was born just after we invaded Cambodia and shot the four students at Kent State University. It was impossible at that time to avoid meditating on the meaning of having a boy child in time of war, or to avoid knowing that 'time of war' means all of human history. Adrienne Rich in *Of Woman Born* quotes a Frenchwoman declaring to her, when her son was born, 'Madame, vous travaillez pour l'armée'.

Lady, you're working for the army. I had the despairing sense that this baby was born to be among the killed, or among the killers. What was I going to do about that, I who had been a pacifist since childhood, was then, and is now, a question. *The Mother/Child Papers* is, again, an experimental work for me, in the sense of posing formal problems correlative to moral ones. It begins with a section of prose about the Cambodian invasion paralleled with the delivery of my son in a situation of normal, that is to say exploitative, American medicine. A second section is a sequence of poems alternating between the consciousness of a mother and that of an infant, as the single fabric they are made of wears away and divides in two. Here a good deal of the excitement and difficulty lay in the attempt to imagine the changes in a newborn mind and invent a music for them. A third section consists of individual poems and prose-poems composed over the last ten years: a few scraps salvaged from the gullet of devouring Time, an enemy familiar to all mothers.

This brings me to the question raised by the activist and writer Alta, when she calls her book *Momma* 'a start on all the untold stories'. For women as artists, the most obvious truth is that the decision to have children is irrevocable. Having made it you are stuck with it forever; existence is never the same afterward, when you have put yourself, as de Beauvoir correctly says, in the service of the species. You no longer belong to yourself. Your time, energy, body, spirit and freedom are drained. You do not, however, lack what W.B. Yeats prayed for: an interesting life. In practical terms, you may ask yourself, 'How can I ever write when I am involved with this *child*?' This is a real and desperate question. But can you imagine Petrarch, Dante, Keats, bemoaning their lot – 'God, I'm so involved with this *woman*, how can I write?'

The advantage of motherhood for a woman artist is that it puts her in immediate and inescapable contact with the sources of life, death, beauty, growth, corruption. If she is a theoretician it teaches her things she could not learn otherwise; if she is a moralist it engages her in serious and useful work; if she is a romantic it constitutes an adventure which cannot be duplicated by any other, and which is guaranteed to supply her with experiences of utter joy and utter misery; if she is a classicist it will nicely illustrate the vanity of human wishes. If the woman artist has been trained to believe that the activities of motherhood are trivial, tangential to main issues of life, irrelevant to the great themes of literature, she should untrain herself. The training is misogynist, it protects and perpetuates systems of thought and feeling which prefer violence and death to love and birth, and it is a lie.

As writers like Rich, Dorothy Dinnerstein, Tillie Olsen, Phyllis Chesler and Nancy Chodorow already demonstrate, it would be difficult to locate a subject at once more unexplored and more rich in social and political implication. Among the poets who have begun the exploration I would cite Plath, Sexton, Alta, Susan Griffin, Maxine Kumin, Lucille Clifton, Gwendolyn Brooks, Robin Morgan, Lisel Mueller, Sharon Olds, Patricia Dienstfrey, Alice Mattison, Marilyn Krysl – a beginning, a scratching of our surface.

The writer who is a mother should, I think, record everything she can: make notes, keep journals, take photographs, use a tape recorder, and remind herself that there is a subject of incalculably vast significance to humanity, about which virtually nothing is known because writers have not been mothers. 'We think back through our mothers, if we are women', declares Woolf, but through whom can those who are themselves mothers, when they want to know what this endeavour in their lives means, do their thinking? We should all be looking at each other with a wild surmise, it seems to me, because we all need data, we need information, not only of the sort provided by doctors, psychologists, sociologists examining a phenomenon from the outside, but the sort provided by poets, novelists, artists, from within. As our knowledge begins to accumulate, we can imagine what it would signify to all women, and men, to live in a culture where childbirth and mothering occupied the kind of position that sex and romantic love have occupied in literature and art for the last five hundred years, or the kind of position that warfare has occupied since literature began.

Article 2.5
'MOMENT OF FAITH': WORKSHEETS

Carol Rumens

I was asked by Birthright, a charity researching into safer childbirth, to write a poem for an exhibition on the theme of Mother and Child. I decided to interpret the theme literally, because I have long felt I wanted to write more about the birth of my first child, and particularly the moment of 'bonding' which I remember extremely well. She had been washed and wrapped and put in my arms; she was crying lustily and one of her little hands stuck out of the shawl. I stroked the palm with my own finger and this tiny hand shut round it and the crying stopped! It was the most magical thing that had ever happened to me. I'd hardly ever *seen* a baby before, and didn't have a clue how to look after one. But at that moment I felt I was a mother.

I realised this would be a risky thing to write about, so never did. (Most of my earlier birth poems are bad imitations of Sylvia Plath.) Having the commission decided me: I'd write that poem which has been waiting for twenty-one years! The first four drafts show its gestation from the time of the commission to the publication – about three months. I should add that, eventually, a sequence of ten birth poems sprang up around it. Some of these are still work-in-progress.

First draft (longhand):

It was the crying hand
that stuck out tense, fully opened
like the sudden appearance of a star

it was the way the palm
and each of the little jointed wands
was waxed for its own protection

that made her think
that this had somehow all been planned
and when she touched it

it was the way the hand folded
shut round her stroking finger
and the crying died away

that made her begin to dream
that somehow it had all been planned
and the plan was matchless.

When I got to the last stanza, I realized that this was where the material originally put in the third stanza should go, so my next step was to erase stanza three.
The next draft was typed:

It was the crying hand
Thrust from the shawl, wide-opened:
a celandine in cold March grass

It was the way the palm
And each little jointed wand
had been carefully waxed like a swimmer

It was the way it clammed
Tight round her probing finger
And the crying shivered into stillness

That made her begin to imagine
This had somehow all been planned
and the plan was matchless.

It will be obvious what seemed to me OK from the first draft and what did not. The basic structure seemed right: the first and last lines seemed right. I was specially pleased with 'matchless' because it echoes that mediaeval carol, 'I sing of a mayden who is makeles'. I had not heard it for a long time but I'm sure it was a shaping force behind the poem. At school I learned the Britten setting, and I can still sing it. I like vigorous, colloquial language, but 'stuck out' seemed clumsy, so I substituted 'thrust'. The main problem was describing the hand and what happened when I touched it. Should I talk about the hand or the fingers? I couldn't talk directly about the baby's fingers, because then I'd have a repetition when I spoke about 'her' finger. 'Wands' is a pretty feeble metaphor. I feel I want to do something more with the idea of the swimmers. Supposing I make each finger a swimmer? Is it too 'Martian'? I have always thought of fingers as a miniature people, so I'm not simply copying a manner. Let's try . . .

It was the crying hand
Thrust from the shawl, a sharp-petalled
Celandine in cold March grass:

It was the five little swimmers,
Sea-wearied, bent at the waist,
Waxed still in each hair-fine crease:

It was the sealed fortress
They built round her terrified finger
As the crying shivered into stillness

That made her think that the seeming
Shambles of it all was planned
And that the plan was matchless.

As usual, I made changes as I typed: 'fully-opened' became 'sharp-petalled', and I added some descriptive detail about the finger-swimmers. A new idea came into the third stanza – that of the child somehow comforting and protecting the mother. I finally lost that: a pity, but in such a short, lyric form there is only room for so many ideas. I tried 'wall' instead of 'sealed fortress', then pencilled in 'stronghold' but crossed it out.

MOMENT OF FAITH

It was the crying hand
Thrust from the shawl, a sharp-petalled
Celandine in cold March grass:

It was the five little swimmers,
Sea-wearied, bent at the waist,
Still waxed in each wrinkle and seam:

It was the stronghold they closed
Round her probing finger, the way
The crying shivered into stillness,

That made her think that the teeming
Shambles of it all was planned,
And the plan was matchless.

This was the version I considered finished enough to submit: it is the version framed and printed in the Birthright Exhibition catalogue. As soon as I saw it in print my eye flew to the repetition of 'Still' (1.6) and 'stillness' (1.9). Damn and blast! The more I look at it and say it to myself the uglier it becomes. I can't just get rid of that first 'still', not only because it locates the swimmers in time, i.e. they've now finished swimming but only just, but because if I do I've got a horrid repetition of Ws ('waist' and 'waxed'). The other obvious device, to change 'stillness' to 'silence', also offends my ear: anyway, 'stillness' in the context has a much richer meaning than 'silence'. At the moment the problem seems insurmountable and it might even be better to leave it unsolved.

There are other worries. If the celandine is taken literally as a metaphor for the baby's hand it's clearly not right. What I meant to convey was suddenness: the celandine is always the first flower I see after winter, and the sight of it, so clean and bright on some ghastly grey March day, always moves me. I can't help if this sounds pseudo-Wordsworth. It's what I genuinely feel. I wonder if I should change 'sharp-petalled' to 'astonishing' or even 'sudden'. 'As sudden/as a celandine in cold March grass?' 'Abrupt' is better. But it doesn't convey the thrill, or the 'thereness' of the flower. I want to see the flower as well as the hand, but separate. I want the feel of utter newness, that is what they have in common.

The 'Martian' flavour of the 'swimmers' stanza still worries me, but I refuse to be intimidated by categories. I shall let it stand.

On the whole I like the poem. I like its sound, and the faint bits of rhyme ('hand' and 'planned', for example. Those words are far apart but I still think the echo can be heard. 'Distant rhyming' is something I'd like to explore further). I feel a strong emotion in the poem, I am moved by it. I think I've avoided sentimentality. I've certainly managed to avoid rhetoric, something I find very difficult when strong feelings are involved. My most deeply-felt poems always sound my most fake. I feel it's a very English poem. I just hope the scepticism comes through sufficiently. (A very English wish, that!)

MOMENT OF FAITH

It was the crying hand
Thrust from the shawl, unannounced
Celandine in cold March grass:

It was the five little swimmers,
Waxed in each wrinkle and seam,
Bent at waist, sea-wearied.

It was the stronghold they closed
Round her probing finger, the way
The crying shivered into stillness,

That made her think that the teeming
Shambles of it all was planned,
And the plan was matchless.

'Unannounced' now worries me because although it's true – or
seems true – of the flower, it's not really true of the baby, which
has been announcing its advent for the last nine months. I'm
reasonably pleased with stanza two now, having got rid of the 'still'
and indicating the time-factor by making the line-order more logical
as narrative.

On reappraisal, 'unannounced' seems OK: after all, it's the
baby's hand I'm referring to, not the whole baby! I miss the 'still'
(still), and prefer the previous arrangement of stanza two after all,
but I shan't change back, as the repetition ('still' and 'stillness')
seems to me the greater of two evils.

I *still* feel I may re-work it! I went on being dissatisfied with
version 5, and feeling that 4 was better, provided I got rid of 'sharp-
petalled' and the 'still/stillness' repeats. I decided to try it with a
simile instead of a full metaphor in the first verse and deleting
'stillness'.

It was the crying hand
Thrust from the shawl, unannounced
As celandines in March grass.

It was the five little swimmers,
Sea-wearied, bent at the waist,
Still waxed in each wrinkle and seam.

It was the stronghold they closed
Round her probing finger, the way
The crying shivered, and ceased,

That made her think that the teeming
Shambles of it all was planned,
And the plan was matchless.

Is that it? God, I hope so!

Article 2.6
CRITICISM AS AUTOBIOGRAPHY
Nicole Ward Jouve

It is odd. There is now a massive and sophisticated body of criticism on autobiography. Autobiography as practice as well as theory. How pervasive it is. How through writing the self is invented, constructed, projected. Or remains poised on the threshold. Yet it never seems to occur to the critics who say such wise things that they themselves, through writing, may be in the process of inventing or projecting their own selves. The critical genre, it seems, makes its adepts feel that they are being miraculously transported on a magic carpet from which they can survey, or peer into, the operations of the rest of humankind, the common herd of writers as it were. They themselves are removed from the obligation of having to bother with the self that writes. They inhabit a secure, objectified, third-person mode that protects them from having to be self-aware.

[· · ·]

Contemporary theory has problematized the subject in manifold ways, ways that preclude the search for the self that you propose. Psychoanalysis would demonstrate to you, through Lacan in particular, that 'I' is always another, first grasped as an imago. And what about the unconscious, the divided self and all that? Self-knowledge is a mirage, a hang-over oasis from the Greeks. And you speak about the autobiographical voice as if there was such a thing, as if the prodigious wealth of recent studies on autobiography, first male then female, hadn't endlessly questioned its existence as a genre. Is it form? Is it content? A mixed genre? An inferior genre? Necessarily ruptured and discontinuous? Does it involve a contract with the name of the author? Is it meant to make a fallacious whole of the disparate elements of the personality? To separate, or to connect, private and public self? How can you so glibly assume that by saying 'I' you will somehow make everything add up?

I take the point. It is no easier to say 'I' than to make theory. The construction of relations, of sense, is infinitely hard, whichever way you go at it. Yes, 'I', today, is perhaps more problematical than it has ever been. I say 'perhaps' thinking of Montaigne, who has always been a great love and a source of strength to me. Here is a man who went from a third-person voice and would-be philosophical debates and critical commentaries on the texts of others to his own script. A fall from his horse, making loss of consciousness totally painless; seeing the natural stoicism with which country people all around him were dying of the plague, changed his whole manner of thinking about death, made years of meditations on philosophy at one remove irrelevant. He no longer thought all the forces of the mind should be deployed to learn to die, be it stoically or through growing accustomed to a sceptical view of things. 'M'est avis que c'est le bout, non le but, de la vie.' Death as the end, not the aim, of life. 'Essaying' his faculties, directly relating what he was, found himself to be, what he perceived and discovered, to the great texts he had become familiar with, became his object. Or his subject.

An exercise. The creation of self through process and relationship.

In any case, as I have tried to show at the outset, any writing constructs and betrays a subject. It is not a question of choice. One might as well make something of the process. It is not because consciousness can never be full, never more than fragments or a patchwork, that the enterprise is fallacious.

Indeed, it is because subjecthood has become so difficult, has been so deconstructed, that there is need to work towards it. This is particularly so for women. It has often been pointed out in recent years that women's autobiographies carry a sense of their being somehow 'unfinished' human beings. The awareness of being 'different', pain arising from that sense of being somehow incomplete, unable to add up, to see your existence as related to, let alone symbolic of, the world at large.[1] Just as the writing of autobiography has been, for many women, the road towards selfhood, so writing criticism as autobiography may be the way to a fuller, more relevant voice. If, as bilingual or trilingual or transcultural being, you are never all in one place – if you are, of necessity, as women, split – you have to say 'and'. You have to say 'both', or all three, or yes and yes and yes. You cannot say 'either/or', for that would mean banning part of yourself. Perhaps you have to learn to say 'as'. You can only be genuinely at home in relations. Relations are never more than relations: metaphors, for instance, like my 'white woman speaks with forked tongue', which enables me to hold for a while, and to relate, various aspects of myself to politics and history and interpretation, yet remains an image and a relation. None the less true for that. Relations never amount to identity, never are fixed. They exist as movement, they enable. But then, life is movement. And if you wish for balance, the contemplative life, this too has to be reached through a relation, an equilibrium.

But isn't this desperately predictable? Don't women always go for the autobiographical, as Colette made an imaginary 'man' blame her for in *The Break of Day*? Am I not just reinforcing another cliché? Are women, yet again, to produce 'body', autobiography, metaphors, for men to do the serious thing with, that is, analyse and theorize?

'Patience', Colette replied. 'I am not making my portrait. This is only my model.' Spell it out: I am not giving you anything fixed, present or past, to theorize. If you think you can theorize what I've given you, you're a simpleton. I am creating something ahead of me, something I can work towards, something that may help you work towards your own model. It's a praxis, a process. Not a static thing.

It is white women's paradoxical advantage that in the past few hundred years and in the nineteenth century in particular they have been 'relegated' to the realm of the so-called personal, put in charge of the emotions, the ethical. It is white women's further advantage that twenty years of feminism have made them question everything radically, and primarily themselves. For white women who care to think, the idea of crisis is very much alive. The way the world is going, as well as the new awareness of the limitations of their, so bizarrely called, whiteness, ensures that it will remain alive. We have not lost touch with ourselves, or not so radically that we cannot still think in the full sense of the word.

Note

1   The field of studies of autobiography in general and women's autobiography in particular is now so rich it is impossible to represent even minimally here. I refer the reader to the bibliographies in Lejeune's books, *Je Est un Autre* and *Le Moi Autobiographique*, or to the useful summary in the introduction by Estelle Jelinek (1986) or to Shari Benstock (ed.) (1988).

Article 2.7
OUR LIFE: WORKING-CLASS WOMEN'S AUTOBIOGRAPHY IN BRITAIN

Wendy Webster

Some of the earliest autobiographies by working-class women were written in the eighteenth and early nineteenth centuries. Poets like Mary Collier, Elizabeth Bentley and Ann Candler included short accounts of their lives as prefaces to published volumes of poetry, to authenticate their claims to be labouring women against those who doubted that women of their class could have written poetry (Landry, 1990, p. 12). The belief that working-class women cannot and should not write has proved remarkably persistent. Evelyn Haythorne, author of *On Earth To Make The Numbers Up*, interviewed about her work on a local radio station in 1991, was introduced as 'the lady who can't spell', and asked during the interview to spell 'liaison' and 'university'.[1]

Since the eighteenth century when labouring women like Mary Collier and Ann Yearsley wrote poetry, autobiography has been the major genre in which working-class women have written. It occupies a low place in the hierarchy of genres, so that it offered working-class women a form which did not involve claims to high artistic aspiration, and was often seen for that reason as appropriate for them to work in, in so far as writing was regarded as appropriate work at all. While it also offered a form which could be private or semi-private, written for family or a religious/local community, avoiding fears of entering any kind of public discourse, for those who did have educational and literary aspirations, there was often disappointment. Autobiography has seldom secured working-class authors any sort of literary reputation. A very few works have acquired the status of minor classics, like Flora Thompson's *Lark Rise*, reprinted many times since 1939, and particularly with its sequels as *Lark Rise to Candleford* since 1945. Some post-war works have attracted commercial publication and a wide readership. Winifred Foley's *A Child In The Forest*, which was broadcast on BBC Radio's 'Woman's Hour' in 1973, has been reprinted a number of times, and so has Margaret Powell's *Below Stairs*, and Molly Weir's *Shoes Were For Sunday*. Autobiographical writing by working-class women seems to have been most well received when it records a vanishing way of life, particularly a rural childhood, with its associations of innocence and simplicity, as in the work of Flora Thompson and Winifred Foley.

The low status of autobiography may have contributed to its being seen as an appropriate genre for working-class women but the low social status of its authors sometimes had the opposite effect. Few could assume that their selves or their lives were of any interest to others or that they were marked out in any way from others, and many consequently felt a need to justify writing about such 'ordinary' lives. 'Ordinary people do not consider their lives of sufficient importance to spend time in writing them down, even if they have a flair for scribbling', Florence White writes at the beginning of her autobiography. 'And', she adds, 'they are probably right' (White, 1938, p. ix).

One justification that was often provided was that however uninteresting a working-class woman might be as an individual, the record that she might offer of a way of life, a community, the times through which she had lived, was of historical interest. Paradoxically, although autobiography is often seen as a particularly personal form of writing, a story of the self, a striking characteristic of much working-class autobiography, by men as well as women, is its tendency to avoid a focus on the personal. Although most write in the first person, their subject is often 'we' as much as 'I': they write of their family, street, community, or social group, often taking trouble to explain the geography of their territory and their lives, assuming a middle-class audience for whom tenements, back streets, the interiors of rural cottages, the experience of hunger and boots with holes is completely unfamiliar.

This shifting of attention away from the individual towards the group has sometimes been understood as a defect in working-class autobiography, a sign of depersonalization and psychological deprivation (Hackett, 1985, pp. 1, 37). In work by women it might also be understood as part of the process by which they have been denied individuality, their identity subsumed into that of others as daughter, wife and mother, their special responsibility for the maintenance of family life involving an expectation that they will pursue familial or communal rather than individualistic goals. But a different way of understanding it is as an affirmation of communal values against the cult of individuality evident in much autobiographical writing. On this view, working-class writers have been concerned to record and affirm the value of working-class community and culture, as well as its difficulties, against the idea that individual mobility offers the solution to class divisions, and the particular invitation to individual movement away from their class that the identity of 'writer' might suggest.

An emphasis on the communal has recently extended to the writing process itself. Autobiographies like Dolly Davey's *A Sense of Adventure* have been produced through discussion, in her case at meetings of the SE1 People's History Project where she talked about her memories (Davey, 1980). Although perhaps replicating the way in which working-class experience has often been mediated through middle-class journalists and interviewers, 'as told to' autobiographies, based on transcriptions of tapes, have become an increasingly common form over the past twenty years. They have been promoted by adult education classes and developments in oral history, as well as by the commitment of feminist historians to recording, reclaiming and reconstructing the lives of working-class women. By contrast, feminist literary critics have seldom discussed working-class women's writing, although they have produced a large body of critical work theorizing women's autobiography. Working-class women's writing is almost always read as social history rather than literature.

Any selection which is used to illustrate a discussion like this is rather arbitrary, drawing on what has survived, what was published, what I can get hold of. I have chosen the three texts here to show how gender and class have been bound up differently at different times, both with processes of literary production and with ways in which working-class women have constructed versions of their selves and their lives.

JANE JOWITT: DEFERENCE AND DISPOSSESSION

The *Memoirs of Jane Jowitt, The Poor Poetess* were published at her own expense in 1844 in Sheffield where two of the few surviving copies are now owned by Sheffield City Library. In them she records earning a living at times through literacy, first through writing letters for her local community in Sheffield – 'reading love letters that were brought to me to read and answer . . . I knew almost half the secrets and love affairs in the town' – and later through writing poetry which she sold (Jowitt, 1844, pp. 28–9).[2]

Both the autobiography and the poetry were addressed to the local nobility and gentry, and are imitative of the language of this audience, including literary references and quotations from Shakespeare. Both too are deferential, and in the *Memoirs* Jane Jowitt constructs an identity which emphasizes her respectability and piety while making herself an object of pathos as she relates 'my sorrowful history' (ibid., p. 16).

A main theme of her autobiography is charity. She writes extensively in praise of the benevolence of the nobility and gentry towards the poor, and also towards herself, tracing a particular pattern of female philanthropy, from the ladies in Sheffield who hastened to relieve her after her first husband's death, to Mrs Greaves who gave her half a guinea and a new blanket, to Mrs Cotterill who gave her a guinea and a gown. She writes also of her gratitude to those, especially amongst the nobility, who purchased her poetry, which was often written to commemorate the deaths of individual gentry (ibid., pp. 27–8, 31).

One way of reading Jane Jowitt's *Memoirs* then is as a 'pretty tribute of respect' (as she describes one of her poems) to her social superiors, where she constructs an identity both as an object of pity and at the same time a worthy object – the deserving rather than the undeserving poor. But another identity conflicts with this for her respectability is presented not only as moral worth, but also as independence. Stories of 'men who take liberties', and of her second husband who abuses her verbally and physically, are told in the context of her own successful resistance in challenging and reproving them. The emphasis on paying her debts and making a living stresses her independence. There are the rudiments of a more picaresque story here, as she tells of leaving Ireland to 'try my fortune in England', of walking from Liverpool to London and then from London to Dover, hawking goods, and of wanting to 'shift about continually' since 'I . . . had such a desire for travelling and seeing strange places' (ibid., pp. 17, 19).

The conflict between deference and assertion, dependence and independence is partly a conflict between 'poor poetess' – the occupational identity she chooses for her title – and the record in the *Memoirs* of a much more disrupted and precarious pattern of work, as she moves from lodging-house keeper to hawker of goods to needlewoman to cook to letter-writer, and only begins writing poetry for sale when she is left destitute after her second husband sells all her furniture and drinks the money. A pattern of part-time, casual, seasonal, insecure and poorly paid employment has been characteristic for working-class women in the twentieth century as well as in the nineteenth, but Jane Jowitt, in choosing from these varied occupations the writing of poetry, lays claim to an identity which has associations with gentility and education. This claim is further enforced by what she reveals about her origins – an identity as 'daughter of an Irish barrister' which she has previously kept secret. But in singling out one particular occupational identity, she delineates it more exactly – not 'poet' but 'poor poetess' – an identity to do with class and gender, announcing her inferior status and her deference.

The story that she tells is, in this way, not only about a geographical but also a social journey – of downward mobility. As Jane Jowitt tells it, it is a story of dispossession and disinheritance, always by men, particularly her 'wild and dissipated' father, who squanders his money on an actress and is last seen in a debtor's prison – a dispossession which forms a contrast to the pattern of female philanthropy and protection that she traces.

On the last journey Jane Jowitt records, walking from Doncaster to York selling her poetry, she is so destitute that, falling in with an old Irish man, she can only relieve him with a dry crust she finds at the bottom of her basket. The story of individual enterprise in all her journeys and occupations cannot be told either as adventure or success. Any protest is confined to the individual men who dispossessed her – there is none against a society that, despite all her efforts, has afforded her only the most precarious subsistence and survival. The story of enterprise is for pressing reasons subsumed into a narrative of deference. The purpose of the autobiography is to advertise her present condition as 'a Distrest Widow', who can no longer travel to sell her poetry for a living, since she has suffered a stroke. Addressing her patrons, those who have purchased her poetry, she makes clear her present needs: 'It is now my only wish that I may be provided for in some Asylum where I can end my days in peace' (ibid., p. 49).

HANNAH MITCHELL:
POLITICS AND THE PERSONAL

Hannah Mitchell wrote a century after Jane Jowitt and at the same age – seventy-four – and she records a life spent in socialist and feminist activity. She was a young woman when the Independent Labour Party (ILP) was founded, and thirty-two when the suffragette movement began in 1903, and she worked in both as a speaker and organizer. Where Jane Jowitt speaks of 'the poor', Hannah Mitchell speaks of 'workers', and her construction of self is within a framework of socialist and feminist ideas and a narrative of collective rather than individual endeavour. It ends with the collective 'we' of suffrage and socialist movements rather than the autobiographical 'I', expressing the hope that 'the work we began, ... the faith we held will remain to be carried on ... by abler hands than ours' (Mitchell, 1968, p. 242).

When Hannah Mitchell first sent *The Hard Way Up* to publishers after the Second World War it was rejected. I imagine a male editor, for whom it formed part of a pile of unsolicited manuscripts, dismissing it as too uninteresting, or too subversive in its treatment of domesticity, marriage and motherhood. In the mid-1960s, after Hannah Mitchell's death, the manuscript was brought to the attention of George Ewart Evans, a writer on folklore, and in 1968 it was published by Faber and Faber (who also published Ewart Evans) and edited by Geoffrey Mitchell, Hannah's grandson. The two men supplied a preface and introduction which suggested how the text should be read. Both recommended it for its depiction of old rural traditions, a theme which in the work of Flora Thompson and others was already established as interesting and acceptable.

Plate 1
Barbara Kruger, *(Untitled) We Won't Play Nature to Your Culture*, black and white
photograph, 1983, 186 x 124.46 cm. Ydessa Hendeles Art Foundation

Fluſht with Conceit (which ſhe if Spirit calls)
Upon a Tub ſee how Dame Silence bawls
Whilſt Dunghill Cocks in a moſt pious ſtrain
Liſten to heare the Cackling of the Hen

The Quakers
Meeting

In publick who can heare a Females tattle
Let me in Bed heare my kinde Miſtreſs prattle
For if their Preaching edifies the Nation
It muſt be by an uſe of Application

Plate 2

The Quakers Meeting, engraved by Egbert van Heemskirk and Marcel Lauron, after a painting by Heemskirk [late seventeenth century], satirical engraving contemptuous of women preaching. Reproduced by permission of the Library Committee of the Religious Society of Friends

Plate 3
Janine Wiedel, *The Chainmaker*, Cradley Heath,
Birmingham, photograph, 1977.
Reproduced by permission of Janine Wiedel

Plate 4
Harriet Powers, portrait photograph, *c.* 1890.
Courtesy, Museum of Fine Arts, Boston

Plate 5
Edmonia Lewis, portrait photograph, c. 1875.
Boston Atheneum, AA/5.4/Lewis e(no1)(no2)

Plate 6
Edmonia Lewis, *Forever Free*, 1867, marble,
105 cm. high. The Howard University Gallery of
Art, Washington, DC. Photograph: Jarvis Grant

Plate 7
Edmonia Lewis, *Hagar*, 1875, marble, 133.6 x 38.8 x 43.4 cm.
National Museum of American Art, Smithsonian Institution, Washington, DC.
Gift of Delta Sigma Theta Sorority, Inc.

Plate 8
Elizabeth Catlett, *Homage to My Young Black Sisters,* 1969, cedar wood, 180 cm. high.
Collection of the artist

Plate 9
Judy Chicago, *Sojourner Truth*, ceramic plate from *The Dinner Party*. Copyright Judy Chicago, 1979

Plate 10
Elizabeth Catlett, *Harriet Tubman*, 1975, linocut, 28 x 23 cm. Museum of African American Art, Los Angeles

Plate 11
Käthe Kollwitz, self portrait,
1889, aged 22,
pen, sepia, pencil, 22 cm.
signed with maiden name
Schmidt.
Kupferstich-kabinett, Staatliche
Kunstsammlungen, Dresden

Plate 12
Käthe Kollwitz, self portrait,
1910, aged 43, etching,
15.4 x 13.7 cm.
National Gallery of Art,
Washington, DC,
Rosenwald Collection

Plate 13
Käthe Kollwitz, self portrait,
1934, aged 67, lithograph, 20.8
x 18.7 cm. National Gallery of
Art, Washington, DC, Rosenwald
Collection

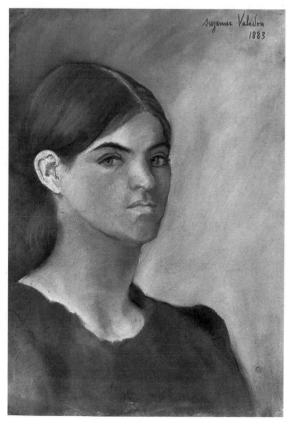

Plate 14
Suzanne Valadon, self portrait,
1883, aged 18, pastel.
Musée National d'Art Moderne,
Centre Georges Pompidou, Paris

Plate 15

Suzanne Valadon, *Family Portraits* (Portraits de famille), 1912, oil on canvas.
Private collection. Photograph by courtesy of Musée National d'Art Moderne,
Centre Georges Pompidou, Paris

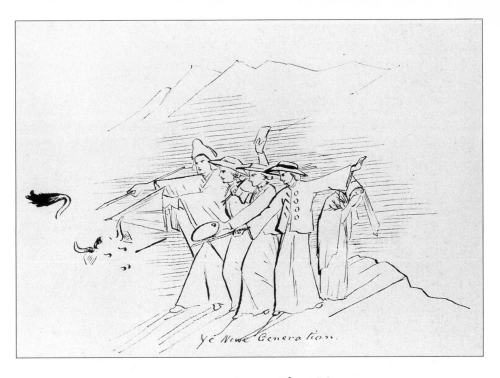

Plate 16
Barbara Leigh-Smith,
Ye Newe Generation, 1855,
pen and ink. Reproduced by
permission of the Mistress and
Fellows of Girton College,
Cambridge

Plate 17
Sojourner Truth seated with knitting,
photograph, 1864.
Sophia Smith Collection,
Smith College, Massachusetts

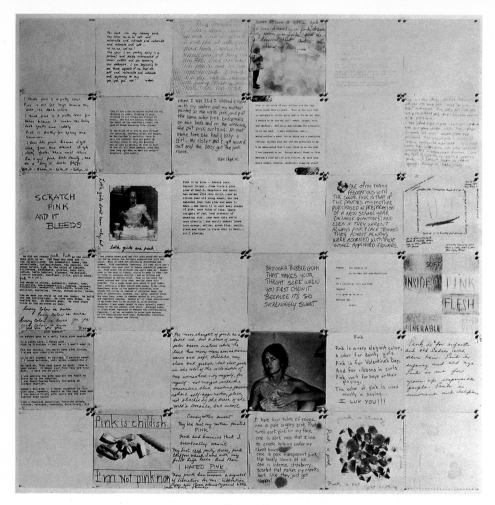

Plate 18

Sheila Levrant de Bretteville, *Pink Poster*, created in response to a request from AIGA and put up in Los Angeles, 1974. Reproduced by courtesy of the artist

Plate 19
Geneviève Bujold as Dr Susan Wheeler in
Coma, 1977, directed by Michael Crichton.
Photograph: John Kobal Collection

Plate 20
Tracy Camilla Johns as Nola Darling,
Redmond Hicks as Jamie Overstreet,
in *She's Gotta Have It*, 1985,
directed by Spike Lee.
Photograph: John Kobal Collection

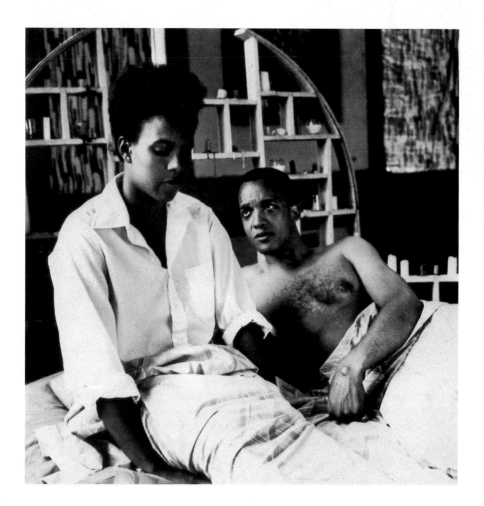

Plate 21

Lizzie Minim as Cinderella, Bridget Long as Princess '… Stay close to me, darling, stay very close …', Act II, Scene 26 of *Cinderella: The Real True Story* by Cheryl Moch. Hull University production by Jools Gilson, 1991. Photograph: John Spencer, Hull University

Plate 24
Detail from *Margaret III*. Lip Service production

But although enthusiastic champions of some aspects of her narrative, both were apologetic about others, displaying particular anxiety about the way Hannah Mitchell represents her femininity. She may come across as hard, George Ewart Evans suggested, particularly in the way she speaks of motherhood, but the reader should not be misled by surface impressions. She does not do justice to her husband, Geoffrey Mitchell claimed, when 'it was indeed he who led her into public life', and he remedied the deficiency by supplying biographical details (ibid., pp. 11, 29–30).

Hannah Mitchell writes of her involvement in the suffragette movement: 'It seems to me now, looking back, that all my previous life had been a preparation for this great experience' (Mitchell, 1984, p. 135). The identity she constructs is primarily political, an identity shaped by a coherent narrative in which the themes she traces are to do with the formation and expression of her politics. This is a story where the personal and the political cannot be separated, where the personal is political. She does not write the conventional story of woman, with its romantic and domestic plot centred on a man, and marriage and motherhood as fulfilment. Instead, she explicitly contests all these, representing her identity as wife and mother as one which conflicts with her political work.

The narrative structure of Hannah Mitchell's work neatly reflects one of its main themes by relegating the conventional life and concerns of women to a subordinate place, and treating them as sources of constraint and difficulty. Neither her husband nor her son are named, and she tells of her disappointments with the new life that marriage involved, redeemed only by 'my growing interest in the Socialist movement'. She explicitly challenges not only general ideals of marriage, but also the particular working-class version, with its emphasis on household management – making ends meet smoothly – drawing attention to her own contribution to the family income earned through dressmaking, and the impossibility of managing on her husband's wage in early marriage. Childbirth is 'twenty-four hours of intense suffering' since her baby is born in an operation she calls 'sheer barbarism', 'with instruments and without an anaesthetic', and she resolves to bring no more babies into the world. The effect of her feminist politics on her relationships with her family is generalized: 'Public disapproval could be faced and borne, but domestic unhappiness, the price many of us paid for our opinions and activities, was a very bitter thing'. But if she is silent on this unhappiness, she is eloquent on her rejection of domesticity: 'Looking back on my life', she writes, 'I feel my greatest enemy has been the cooking-stove – a sort of tyrant which has kept me in subjection . . . The cooking, preparing and clearing away of four meals a day – which I do not want – are the things I hate with an undying hatred' (ibid., pp. 97, 101–2, 130, 240).

Her cooking-stove may not dominate Hannah Mitchell's narrative as much as it threatened to dominate her life, but its demands thread their way through her story, both as a central part of the experience which made her feminist, and as a tyranny which has to be resisted to make feminist activity possible. She traces her feminist consciousness back into childhood experience, awakened by resentment at her weekly task – darning all the household stockings, while her brothers could read or play cards. Her hatred of housework she represents as a central source of conflict with her mother, and later, although less explicitly, with her husband, whose support for her political work is conditional upon his dinner being ready on time. Not only socialist husbands, but male socialists more generally expect her to cook dinners for them, she discovers – a source of tension between her socialism and feminism. At the same time she pays tribute to support for feminism from ILP men, something which makes her ambivalent about suffragette attacks on some socialist leaders.

The tension that Hannah Mitchell explores between her private and public life is a characteristic theme of many women's autobiographies where there is conflict between the conventional roles of daughter, wife, mother, and a less conventional self which is ambitious. Married life, Hannah Mitchell says, is 'fatal to ambition' and she resists its requirement to 'sink my individuality' in the lives of others. But her ambition, while occasionally prompting her to distinguish herself from her class and gender (the 'average stay-at-home woman' who, she writes, is not made of such stern stuff as 'the woman who fought the suffrage battle'), more often prompts her to identify with them, since it is an ambition to secure change for all working-class women (ibid., p. 190).

This means that she does not write her life as a success story. There is scope to do this for while she worked before marriage as a domestic servant and a shopworker, her later political work led to election as a councillor in Manchester, and she became a magistrate. A story of individual advance through career or public work is a rare story for a working-class woman to tell at any time, and she does not tell it like that. There is some sense of achievement, particularly about her appointment as City Magistrate in 1926, but this is expressed so impersonally that it is almost a surprise to realize that Hannah Mitchell is referring to herself when she writes: 'Ignorance, poverty, the disabilities of women in general and married women in particular, had all been faced in the years of service and study which had preceded this result' (ibid., p. 226). Her tone is generally self-effacing: I found to my surprise that in a small way I was regarded as a popular speaker . . . I don't pretend to have cut a brilliant figure on the City Council . . . I am not going to pretend that I added much wisdom or lustre to the magisterial bench' (ibid., pp. 121, 204, 227). Because of the emphasis of her autobiography on collective endeavour, any story of individual advance is subsumed into the story of collective achievements and failures.

If Hannah Mitchell does not construct her identity as a 'woman of achievement', she also does not present it through a narrative of adventure. Like Jane Jowitt, she traces journeys, from a rural childhood to an adult life spent mainly in different Lancashire towns, and as a suffragette, travelling to London. She tells of her speeches at large London meetings and in London parks, of her arrest, trial and imprisonment in Manchester, of mob violence, wrecked meetings, and her part in the first raid on the House of Commons. But any sense of adventure in her journeys is undercut by their aftermath: 'I knew that arrears of work, including the weekly wash, awaited my return'. Her account of involvement in suffragette activity is as much of the psychological price paid for it as of its excitement, and it ends with a short description of a nervous breakdown which she attributes in part to the strain of suffrage work, especially militant work: 'My nerves were so shaken, that whenever I was in a meeting, however orderly, I found myself trembling from fear disorder would break out' (ibid., pp. 162, 175).

There remains another ambition which is hinted at, for writing a book which constructs a political identity raises questions about a different identity: that of writer. Hannah Mitchell's characteristic image for her longing for a wider life in childhood is books. She longs passionately for books but her mother rejects them as a waste of time. She longs for education, but receives only two weeks formal schooling because her mother needs her at home to do housework. Like many working-class women autobiographers, she tells of a mother who 'bitterly resented my coming into the world', and of a relationship which is violent, both emotionally and physically, and at the centre of their conflict is her mother's contempt for her desire for culture, and her own resistance to her mother's valuation of housework.

Hannah Mitchell's autobiography could in this way be read as a movement from literature to politics. As a child she reads literature, but as an adult, politics. Cherishing 'some faint hope of becoming a writer', instead she becomes a speaker, expressing herself on soap boxes and in council chambers, even though 'I had never aspired to the platform, my secret ambition being to become a writer'. Although always a muted theme, the identity she desired, which is educated and literary, is always in conflict with the reality of a different life. That is why the personal is political – since what she desires can only be achieved by political change. At the age of seventy-four she writes: 'More intensely than ever I believe in woman's right to equality, whether married or single, the right to her own individuality, her own soul. A lifetime of drudgery is too high a price to pay for following her natural instincts, a price no man is ever called upon to pay' (ibid., pp. 121, 242).

EVELYN HAYTHORNE: OUR LIFE

In contrast to Jane Jowitt and Hannah Mitchell, Evelyn Haythorne's *On Earth To Make The Numbers Up*, focuses not on her adult life, but her childhood. Although she wrote it in her fifties, her story finishes when she is still in her teens and depicts a childhood and youth during the Second World War. The form is also different, for she writes it like an autobiographical novel, portraying characters and their speech within a realist 'slice of life' convention, where the use of the colloquial is central. Unlike Hannah Mitchell whose language is rather restrained and formal, Evelyn Haythorne's is lively and energetic and stays closer to the spoken language of the characters she depicts with no attempt to conform to an educated or literary formal or elevated style.

Within a form where dialogue is used, it is notable how little Evelyn Haythorne gives to herself. Speech in *On Earth* is the prerogative of other characters, while she represents herself as an observing and watching presence, straining to overhear what others are saying, in a world where she is prohibited from speaking very much, or hearing almost anything at all. Language conveys class divisions at times, but more often divisions between adults and children, for it is confined to adults, and is a language of whisperings, mutterings and silence, where what is said can only be divulged in lowered tones, particularly when children are present, and there is a good deal that cannot be said at all. In this way the autobiography could be read as a story of exclusion, a child's exclusion from an adult world, told literally from the margins as Evelyn Haythorne stands in doorways straining her ears to learn what's going on.

On the rare occasions when Evelyn Haythorne does give dialogue to herself, this is characteristically in the form of questions, which are answered with lies. 'Did the nurse bring it (the baby)? . . . Did you see it in the black bag?' 'Yes', her mother replies, twice (Haythorne, 1990, p. 9). But she also gives herself some dialogue which is in the form of protest, expressing tension between the autobiographical 'I' and the family and community which she portrays – the possibility of a different subjectivity. The protests are particularly against her mother: for lying about her father's illness, for her constant surveillance of Evelyn Haythorne's sexuality, and lectures and reminders of virginity, for telling her on the day she passed the 11-plus and gained a place at grammar school that 'you can't go'.

For Hannah Mitchell, her mother's attitude to education was central to the antipathy between them, something for which 'I never quite forgave her'. Evelyn Haythorne, in contrast, is 'a little resentful'.

It is at this point in the narrative that her autobiography could be read not so much as a story of the self but as her mother's story. What is described as 'my dream' – to go to grammar school – and 'one of the most exciting days of my life' – the day she learns that she has gained a place – is a short episode framed by and subordinated to the story of the strains and tensions of her mother's life. Where the story of Evelyn Haythorne's 'dream' is scarcely told at all, the story of her mother's hardships is told in detail. The strains are to do with class, for a sick husband means her finances are 'nil', that she must pawn everything and then defy the contempt of the parish men from whom she claims relief. They are also the strains of a gender role where she must nurse a dying husband while looking after three young children. But chiefly, as depicted in several episodes, they are about the tension between class and gender, where the ideal of good mother and household manager are impossible, and she must send her eldest son away in secret to get relief, and neighbours can sneer that 'you feed your kids on waggon fat' although she starves herself to feed them first, and she has all the anxiety and responsibility for managing on nothing. The tension is expressed in what could be shocking images of violence, but are undercut by comedy, as she hits her husband on the head with a dinner plate (and bits of potato and meat stick in his hair), shakes her fist close to Mrs Jessop's face (and Sidney Jessop delights in the prospect of a fight), and threatens the men from the parish with a heavy glass ashtray (ibid., pp. 45–73).

If Evelyn Haythorne's 'dream' is subordinated to the story of her mother's difficulties, the sense of tension between the autobiographical 'I' and her family and community remains. The tension focuses particularly on sexuality where she protests not only against her mother's constant lectures, but also against her elder brother's punitive regulation of her sexuality after her father's death. It is expressed characteristically in violence, as he grabs her and scrubs her face with soap and water and she flies at him 'like a mad bull' and her mother drags her off and clouts her ear (not his) (ibid., pp. 89–90). The opposition between 'decent' and 'slag' is a theme with which the autobiography begins and which runs through it, and the working-class community that she depicts is seen as 'narrow' chiefly because of the secrecy and shame that surround sexuality.

There remains too a tension between the conventional expectations of a woman, and ambition for something different. After she can't go to grammar school her father offers Evelyn Haythorne one version of what awaits her – the conventional romantic and domestic plot in which 'when you grow up and meet the man in your life that you want to marry, you'll think you're the happiest, luckiest person on earth'. But her mother offers her a different version of what it is to be on earth in this role: 'nowt but hard work . . . sometimes I think God only put me on this earth to make the numbers up' (ibid., p. 53).

On Earth To Make The Numbers Up: the title encodes the working class as 'ordinary', their lives of little interest, an undifferentiated mass. The view is expressed within *On Earth* by one of the men from the parish – 'you people are all alike' – and more comically as a southern stereotype of northerners generally: 'my mother . . . has always said it's all incest and buggery up here'. Evelyn Haythorne challenges this, writing, she says, because 'very little is known about our life'. The emphasis on 'our' rather than 'my' life is apparent in the autobiography where her theme is as much her family and community as herself. Where Jane Jowitt is deferential, Evelyn Haythorne depicts characters actively defying and resisting their conditions, not through the collective endeavour on which Hannah Mitchell focuses, but through self-help. There is her Uncle Fred who poaches, and when the family eat his spoils, clasps his hands piously and says 'God helps him who helps himself'. But it is particularly her mother who is depicted as defiant, victoriously so, worsting the men from the parish in angry confrontations, breadwinning for her family, selling pies and peas (ibid., pp. 59, 18, 4, 77).

As told by a mother to a daughter 'on earth to make the numbers up' is not just about class but also gender, a destiny of childbirth and childrearing, especially perhaps in wartime when numbers need replacing. Her mother who is depicted as active, strong and angry in resisting poverty and those who speak with contempt of her class, seems here to counsel resignation to a particular female destiny which cannot be resisted or defied. Within *On Earth*, Evelyn Haythorne prefers her father's version of this destiny which is about romance and fulfilment, but this resolution lies outside the narrative. Within the narrative the resolution is neither romance nor marriage, but the image of settlement with which the autobiography ends: 'I . . . knew, as young as I was, that Conisborough was for me and that I would never willingly leave it' (ibid., p. 117). Although within *On Earth* there is some tension between the autobiographical 'I' and her family and community, and between conventional roles and a less conventional self, the final image is of a sense of self bound up with class, community and place.

REFUSING EXCLUSION

I am conscious that in writing this I have used the term 'working-class women's autobiography' a great deal, as though it is a deviation from some norm called 'autobiography' which is written by people who are neither. Lizbeth Goodman, in the introduction to this chapter, draws attention to the way in which feminist politics may value writing simply because it is by women. In 1991, while I was writing this, Ros de Lanerolle, the managing director of the Women's Press, was sacked. The reason given was that the Press had been losing money, and Naim Attallah who sacked her claimed that it had been publishing too much writing by working-class and Third World women (Pallister, 1991). Gender, class and race are bound up in many different ways with the process by which writing can be produced and is valued, whether commercially or in terms of literary worth.

Exclusion, marginality and constraint are themes of the story I have told here. There is exclusion from literacy, from education, from publication. There are the constraints of poverty and space and time. There is also a fundamental constraint in the idea that a working-class woman cannot write, much less be 'a writer', an identity associated with professional rather than amateur status. Hannah Mitchell's ambition was 'secret' and she wrote her auto-biography in secret, working while her husband was out and taking care to put her papers away when anybody was around (Mitchell, 1984, p. 32). Evelyn Haythorne also wrote in secret, keeping a diary for many years which she burnt periodically when it started to pile up and 'I knew it was getting conspicuous', telling her husband that she'd written *On Earth* only when it was ready to be published. 'Really I had writing knocked out of me', she says. '"Scribble", my mother used to call it – when I used to get my pen and paper out at home my mother used to say "oh put that scribbling away". It was never looked at as writing'.[3] For working-class women writing has been seen, and remains seen, as an illegitimate activity. In writing their autobiographies they have been actively engaged in refusing that exclusion.

Notes

1   Information from Evelyn Haythorne, interview with Wendy Webster, 7 March 1991.

2   I am grateful to Dr Jane Rendall for telling me about this autobiography.

3   Evelyn Haythorne, interview with Wendy Webster, 7 March 1991.

3
VISUAL IMAGES: TAKING THE MASTERY OUT OF ART

In the earliest phases of feminist historiography in art, in the 1850s, women retrieved the history of women image-specialists[1] and they valued the feminine arts, like textiles, placing them in the history of women.[2] The next wave of feminist art history, initiated in the early 1970s, also sought out the herstories hidden from history.[3] As well as celebrating women image-specialists, they also demanded revaluation of women's arts, demoted unjustly as crafts.[4] Such crafts were arts, not counted as such, merely because they were practised by women. These historians were accused of political interest inappropriate to scholarly or critical judgements and sneered at for studying weak products and unimportant artists. But during the 1980s, women responded to these arguments by showing that mainstream art and design history is malestream, with his monographs for geniuses, inventive in style or technique, and is as politically interested as feminist herstory. By analysing the history of art and design in terms of 'the Great Designers and Image Specialists' as a sexist way of writing the past, we have been able to begin to put women into our rightful place in their story (Parker and Pollock, 1981).

'The Great Masters' were not producers of untouchable canonical works which have stood the test of time to dwarf the 'minor mistresses', but simply people who were privileged with training through advantage of sex at their time, and who were provided with large audiences of admirers and interpreters by the powerful institutions of publishing/education. Through the interests of such male clubs, generations were created, considering certain images and certain kinds of art prestigious and worthy (Herrnstein–Smith, 1983). A fuller history would consider the skilled making of the widest range of artefacts, which for most human societies have had, and still do have, prime meanings and use. Value is to be placed on collective, domestic and amateur products, and on traditional things (not solely on the individual, professional creation for fame and money, of ever newer technologically and stylistically different objects). In an open history, the making of the family photo album, say, will be of interest[5] or, perhaps, the making of their homes by young women in the 1950s new city of Harlow.[6] Women's works in the home, in the factory, in the art gallery are to be celebrated and considered, in their segregations, as produced by and producing ideologies of gender difference.[7] Where masculinist art history has focused largely on making art, a new art history wants to study also the audiences and buyers of artefacts, and the way figurative images present women and men too (Buckley, 1986).

The business of image-making is interesting not because it is the field in which mankind has expressed his highest aspirations in works of genius, but because figurative images, especially in the media, bolstered up by traditions in Western European painting, play important rôles in making women second-class viewers: in encouraging us to act as sights rather than authors of images and in selling us definitions of femininity. As well as persuading us that we are choosing man-made womanhood, some images which show women as desirable-to-men-for-sale, in order to advertise commodities, threaten women's sense of full autonomy, and other images can frighten and humiliate.

In the last two decades, feminist viewpoints (along with the perspectives of ethnicity) have opened up the narrowed history and criticism of craft, of art and of design, to value women's works, and see how the cultural representation of gender is effected through human artefacts and visual images. Building, in this way, from the insights of the early 1970s (that women's crafts are arts, that women painters and sculptors existed and can be celebrated, and that women's use and response to things and images are distorted by male visual ideology), a feminist art history is being made.

In the first article in this chapter, I consider further some of the issues raised in a feminist account of the reproduction of femininity through visual images and objects (see Chapter 1, Articles 1.1 and 1.2). It is important to stress that gendered meanings are mapped across many constitutions of identity – of nationality, religion, class and ethnicity. In selecting the second article, by Michelle Cliff, we have chosen to focus on the specific experiences of black women creating statements of themselves, to counter white 'representations'. In the third article Felicity Edholm probes further the way women, demonstrating themselves, negotiate masculine definitions of creativity, female beauty, conventions for portrait images, and who looks at whom. In the final piece I look at the particular activities of artists with self-consciously feminist aims. How can they choose forms of representation which are fair to the objects represented, and capable of presenting a critique of dominant male imagery? How can they value skills, media, themes, and ways of working together, which promote women's works without perpetuating feminine segregation? How can they work with a masculine visual and plastic ideology to change it?

Catherine King

Notes

1   See, for example, Elizabeth Ellet's *Women Artists of All Ages and all Countries* (1859).

2   See, for example, Lina Eckenstein's *Women Under Monasticism* (1896).

3   See, for example, Isabelle Anscombe's *A Woman's Touch: women in design from 1860 to the present day* (1984), or *Women Artists: recognition and reappraisal* by Karen Petersen and J.J. Wilson (1976).

4   See, for example, Patricia Mainardi's article 'Quilts: The Great American Art' (1973).

5   See, for example, *Family Snaps*, edited by Jo Spence and Patricia Holland (1991).

6   See, for example, Judy Attfield's article 'Inside Pram Town' (1989).

7   See, for example, Roszika Parker's *The Subversive Stitch: embroidery and the making of the feminine* (1984).

Article 3.1
THE POLITICS OF REPRESENTATION: A DEMOCRACY OF THE GAZE

Catherine King

Representation can, most narrowly, refer to the creation of a convincing illusion of reality, often produced photographically, but also by painstakingly minute pictorial and sculpting techniques. Good examples would be Maud Sulter's series of photographs inventing *Nine Muses* to stand for black women's creativity in diaspora in a representationally accurate way (Col. Pl. 1). A sculpted example would be Christine Merton's *Tree Tomb* where a small tree has been virtually buried by the planks whose continual cutting threatens not only the trees themselves, but the entire planet (Col. Pl. 3). Maud Sulter used photography to make an illusion which is detached from real life (she has famous women playing the rôles of each Muse). Christine Merton does not mimic a real scene somewhere, though she refers the viewer accurately to items in the visual world. But the term 'representation' also carries the possibility that the viewer could be looking at an image evoking an ordinary slice of life. Janine Wiedel's photograph of a woman at her workbench making chains is such a representation (Pl. 3). Representation could, more generally, be used to describe statements employing more obviously symbolic and suggestive means. In *The Struggle Between Ambition and Desire*, Alexis Hunter used an invented animal (a composite of other real ones) which she called a *chimaera*, to represent, symbolically, warring desires in women's lives for fame, sex and to be protected (Col. Pl. 2). Even more abstractly, the sign for a woman (as in the abstract female figure on a lavatory door to denote 'Ladies', or the astrological sign for the planet Venus, ♀, to denote women) does not need to resemble women, in the sense of looking like women look, to represent us.

'Represents', in its widest senses, can mean 'stands for', 'states', 'announces', 'symbolizes', as well as 'suggests illusionistically', or 'gives a snapshot impression of'. Although we need to discuss various kinds of visual images in terms of their relative closeness in appearance to optical impressions, no image is other than a construction taken from a specific social and physical viewpoint, selecting one activity or instant out of vast choices to represent, and materially made out of and formed by the technical processes of the medium and its conventions. So the chainmaker is shown in a particular way as if we were close to her, from an angle which concentrates on her, rather than on her skill (we can't see how she is using her machine), uses black and white, leaves her physical

i blurred, and refers to the styles of 'realistic photography'
ring the presentation of the harsh facts of people's lives in
ultural and industrial work. These statements can be transposed
he family photo album, where notions of what should be
ebrated in photographic records, and who takes the images, for
example, warn us to use the term 'realistic' about them with extreme
caution. (They are good evidence, but only as long as we think
about who, and what, is presenting this evidence to us.) There are
no visual facts without values leading them to us by the nose. And
as there are no 'innocent images', there are no 'innocent eyes'. The
eye constructs meaning according to a person's 'mental set', in
looking, and the visual image presented to us has been made in
this way too. The politics of representation considers the changing
institutions which govern the encounters between constructed
images and constructing eyes.

The term 'realistic' is therefore best reserved for describing
whether the objects of representation are known to have existed or
to exist (the chainmaker or Sojourner Truth), might plausibly have
existed (an idealistically lovely woman 'portrayed' in the past), or
are absolutely fictional and legendary (the Muses or the *chimaera*).
Although perhaps initially startling, the term 'signifies' and the
notion of 'creating an illusion' can be more productively used to
refer to *the means of representation*, because they highlight the
constructedness of all representations, now and in the past. The
analysis of the way forms are given arbitrary meanings using the
terms 'signifier' for the 'form' chosen and 'signified' for the equally
arbitrary meaning assigned to it, was demonstrated by Barthes, in
Mythologies, to unpick visual ideologies, and taken over from the
linguistic theory of Saussure. As explained by Deborah Cameron:

> In 1916 the study of language was revolutionised when the
> collected lectures of a dead Swiss linguist, Ferdinand de
> Saussure, were published under the uninspiring title, 'A
> Course in General Linguistics'. Saussure broke with the
> nineteenth-century Darwinist approach to languages as evolv-
> ing organisms, and analysed them instead as self-contained
> systems of *signs*.
>
> Signs are produced, Saussure said, by linking a form – for
> instance the sounds c-a-t – with a meaning, 'feline domestic
> animal'. This link is not natural (there's nothing about a cat
> which means we have to call it a cat) but arbitrary and
> conventional. The sign acquires its value not from anything
> intrinsic but by contrast with other signs: a *cat* is not a *bat* or
> a *dog* . . . These systems can be treated metaphorically as
> languages. The study of them is known today as semiology or
> semiotics, from the Greek work *semeieon*, meaning a sign.

(Cameron, 1991, p. 11)

In the face of the mass of western images which employ illusion-istically convincing techniques to denote 'women' to us, it is worthwhile being ready to use the terms 'signifier' and 'signified', not 'form/colour/image' and 'represented'. The illusionism of an image and the way 'represents' can slide over onto 'is, stands for, shows', has the dangerous tendency to suggest that images tell us what sort of beings we are. This is what could happen reading the following:

> Renoir in his glowing pink iridescent curving forms represents all the sensuous warmth of womanhood.

So what Renoir represents is what women are. We can rewrite the sentence so that we avoid seeing the painting as telling us about the essence of femininity:

> Renoir's arbitrarily selected signifiers of shimmering pinks and curvaceous forms signified his dream of womanhood.

The painting/image could now be read as a sign of Renoir's notion. We can be other than what Renoir supposes.

Similarly, the prestigious traditions of representing women (the standing or reclining nudes, the mother and child) tell us about the tenacity of the visual ideologies of the men who selected the shapes, and assigned them meanings, with variations, generation after generation, and about the interests of the institutions which sustained notions of their value and interpretations:

> Feminists have a particular stake in this sort of analysis. Arguably, female subordination is part of the meaning of the nude; but by taking a semiological approach – which insists that the meaning of signs is not natural but conventional – feminist critics leave open the possibility that this meaning could be challenged and ultimately changed. This is important, because feminist cultural producers want more than just permission to write or sculpt or paint using the existing codes of meaning . . . In the light of all this, we can see that feminist art practice has a dual task; to create new languages and to try to disrupt or subvert the old, inherited ones.
>
> (Ibid.)

The consumption of visual images is dangerously asymmetrical. Most images are made by men for men, creating a closed, collusive relationship between makers and prime consumers. Men control the media through which visual images are circulated, from books and newspapers, to the museums curating them, and the galleries exhibiting them for sale. Men control the teaching of art-making, and of how to write its history and criticism. The institutionalization of this dominant masculine ideology is stated in, for instance, the poster advertising the sixth International Contemporary Art Fair: 'Art, London, 1991'. This shows a naked white female statue, with 'classical' profile, totally hairless body, handcuffed by chains to a post, and apparently smiling serenely about this. She is the female object surrounded by the heroic male subjects of art (amongst them, van Gogh), who are represented through their portraits as authors. On the same page, in the newspaper in which it appeared, we have a report of this exciting, 'international' event, with a large illustration of what we are told is the 'biggest bargain': for 'Art Line magazine is offering a free silkscreen print by Tom Phillips, worth about £500, to anyone who takes out a year's subscription – which will cost them £28, including postage' (The Independent, 18 April 1991, p. 6). The silk-screen print shows a naked woman with one eye, lying in a sort of landscape, with her legs wide open. So woman is constructed as object of art, and man as the representer. As discussed earlier in Article 1.1, women are discouraged from certain kinds of making (here the creativity of the image-specialist) by the social structures of family and education, as well as by the systems of ideas which refuse the definition of truly feminine to anyone showing the boldness, confidence and ruthless single-mindedness which has been developed to secure the masculinity of 'genius'.

We have begun to study the crushing weight of the visual images, made by men, of women in the past: the good mother; the chaste maiden; the whore; the witch; the smiling naked. These images of women have the cultural prestige of antiquity, or of being the creations of Old Masters. But they can be constructed as 'men's-imagined-women', signifying men's desire to control women's sexuality in the family, enjoy it outside it, and displace the qualities they fear in themselves (such as passivity, openness and emotionality) onto the body of the woman, where these qualities can be controlled. Equally, the modern advertising images which show woman as object for sale, as house-proud mother, or young woman desiring the gaze of men, can be read as men's-imagining-of-women. For instance, a survey of advertisements appearing in the Ladies Home Journal (1909–1980), showed that domestic appliances shown for sale were promoted not in terms of the way they worked functionally, nor in terms of labour-saving, but rather in terms of women's service to the family in housework (Fox, 1990, p. 25).

Men make images showing men as important actors and sufferers, while women are signs of their desires and requirements. As suggested by John Berger, women and men have an unequal power in looking (Berger, 1972). He characterized men as having a privileged gaze, able to look actively and critically without their look being returned with equal scrutiny by women. We can observe this mastery of the gaze being exerted in social life: when a man 'eyes up' a woman, and the way women, once outside their home space, do not look freely about. Women are second-class spectators, and 'suitably' passive, forced to concern themselves with how they look (that is, how they *appear*). This gendering of looking is pinned into place by the way male visual ideology treats women as an object of art so as to secure the artist as primarily male. Underlying the way women live as the seen rather than as a seer, is the discourse of social life (in which women are 'private', 'passive', 'body' to men's 'public', 'active', 'mind' and so on). Women's positioning as subordinate was put, long before Berger linked it to art, by Olive Schreiner in *The Story of an African Farm* (1883). Lyndall is talking, in the moonlight, to her good friend, the farmworker Waldo:

> We all enter the world little plastic beings, with so much natural force perhaps, but for the rest – blank; and the world tells us what we are to be, and shapes us by the ends it sets before us. To you it says – *Work*; and to us it says – *Seem*!
>
> (Schreiner, 1883, p. 39)

Women in visual images made by men, to quote Laura Mulvey, usually connote 'to-be-looked-at-ness' just as, in life, they are encouraged to play the rôle of 'being desirable' to the male gaze. This perversion of the human faculty of seeing is rendered in Barbara Kruger's *I Can't Look at You and Breathe at the Same Time* (1987) (see Figure 3.1.1). The woman can only be allowed to stay

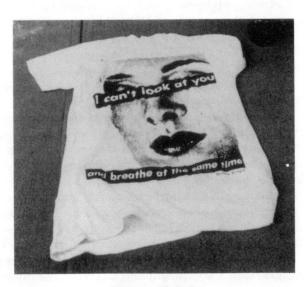

Figure 3.1.1
Barbara Kruger, *I Can't Look at You and Breathe at the Same Time*,
tee shirt, 1987

alive if she does not look back at the man. Or, if the woman looks at men's objectifications of women all around, she is as good as dead, without independent will, without subjecthood. The full right to look is male and it denotes power over the object made for his desire.

The notion of the gaze has important links with men's control of objects through ownership of capital, and it has implications, too, for the 'mastery' of nature and of science and connotations of an asymmetry in sexual relations, in which women are supposed to make themselves passively receptive, and men are supposed actively to seek out their pleasures.

In this situation women have few options as viewers. They may 'choose' to attempt to view the image from the angle of a surrogate male viewer, but are fractured in their responses if they do so because they are then denying their femininity as it has been constructed socially. Indeed, many images made for the male viewer show objectifications of women (the nude laid out only for male desire: or the woman in the advertisements who is there to signify 'what-is-a-desirable-commodity-for-sale') which will damage the woman's sense of her own worth if she tries to look at them as if she were a man. Alternatively, the woman may sacrifice any hopes of acting as prime viewer, but decide to look from the viewpoint of her socially constructed femininity – as it were, from the edges of the frame. This sort of viewing can be very productive of a powerfully critical viewing, which is able to analyse how the image works, and in whose interests. Such looking can be compared with 'reading against the grain' and provides plenty of pleasures: such as those experienced by the women who ruined the car advertisement, 'To Volvo a Son', with the withering response, 'Better Luck Next Time'.

Just as most images in masculine visual ideology are created to empower men as spectators – that is, to see themselves as endlessly important with things laid out for their desire – in advertising, multitudes of visual images are especially geared to please women and offer them objects to desire. But it seems unlikely that these images offer women first-class viewing since they provide pleasures neatly demarcated in bedroom and kitchen, subsumed to the overall requirement of looking good for, and of being good to the masculine. Such advertisements encourage the anxious self-surveillance which characterizes the inferiorized gaze – is my skin, my hair as perfect as that in the advertisement? Can I get my washing, carpet, curtains as clean as that? Advertising for cameras, cars, mortgages, sports equipment and so on, on the other hand, is spoken to men, for the most part, therefore engendering notions of sexual difference yet again. While women have been represented as vain because they have been socialized to look at themselves (to ensure they are 'attractive'), it is, actually, men who exist in the more narcissistic condition, gazing lovingly either at themselves in visual images, or at what they think desirable in their objectifications of the subordinate 'other'.

As discussed in Article 3.4, women are developing ways of making women prime viewers, by, for instance, providing women with powerful images of the female. It is the feminist project, to nurture and explore the female gaze, to construct images creating a democracy of looking and being looked upon, and to gestate an iconography which makes known experiences of birthing, suckling and bleeding, which dominant male visual ideologies have hidden away.

Although all representation entailing the indication of the human figure through tangible and visual shapes entails a form of objectification (in that the person is presented as an object for sight and touch, in some sense), it seems important to discuss the kinds of objectifications that could be dangerous for those objectified, and under which, if any, circumstances, objectification can be considered relatively safe. Objectifications which ensure that viewers realize that the one who has been represented is an individual with will, with autonomous desires and powers, with a specific personality and with rights and human dignity, would perhaps be regarded as acceptable. The test might be – would the artist be willing to represent her- or himself this way? Does this objectification render the subjecthood of this person: their ability to be the author, or representer, too? Again, all representations of this sort would have to take place in circumstances in which those objectified can have the right of reply in words and visual images themselves. The old-fashioned relationship between commissioner and artist, where the powers of the artist in objectifying were balanced by the powers of the 'matron' or patron in paying for and judging the product, is interesting to pursue. Jo Spence has created a process of portrait photography in which women make images of each other in mutual attempts to seek out their subjectivities: exploring therapeutic 'objectifications' in partnership. However, the ease with which new voyeuristic uses, or undignified meanings, can be placed upon these visual images by the viewer, means that some women will not represent/objectify anyone but themselves. And some women will not represent woman at all. In considering the politics of visual representation, we might question why we should not expect to follow the rules we insist on in legal and political representation: that representation means the fair and beneficial statement of the interests of clients and voters.

But do all feminists want to take the 'mastery' out of the gaze? Some women may want the empowered gaze at the objectified woman or man for *themselves*. Or there may be feminists willing to risk male voyeurism, as long as explorations of women's sexuality can be explicitly shown. Feminist groupings are deeply divided over the representation of women, and its censorship, so that there are no answers to what *the* feminist position should be, on the definition of the goal of equal rights of representation for woman.

Women's images are most likely to be used to stand as objects for the desirability and sale of products to male consumers. Rosalind Coward suggested how dangerous these uses of women's images are for women, and how difficult to stop, in comparison with the easier task of insisting that, in all forms of representation, women in work and at leisure are shown in their full variety and potential: 'At present, communications which foster misogyny (unlike incitements to racial hatred) are considered above the law, a realm of personal choice. But sexism, like racism, is not a private matter. Anti-woman attitudes underlie aggressive and oppressive actions' (Coward, 1980, pp. 6–7). These concerns were voiced in relation to the Williams Report (1979) which had allowed the public display of all images that would not offend 'reasonable people', and the campaigns *Reclaim the Night* and *Angry Women/WAVAW* (Women Against Violence Against Women) (1978–80).

Feminist groups are not unified on the issues of visual censorship. It has been suggested, for example, that pornography should be allowed because it will then be possible to dismantle images of violent power over women, through the analysis of how pornographic images work. As Betterton says: 'By examining the structure [of pornography] as an industry . . . and as a system of representation whose visual codes and technologies interact with others, it may be possible to demystify pornography's powers as the forbidden' (Betterton, 1987a, p. 149). Or it is felt that further forms of censorship could play into the hands of those opposing feminist self-knowledge and communication of women's sexualities (like the attempts to take *Our Bodies Our Selves* out of public libraries). Arguments against censorship – as with those of the film maker Barbara Hammer – can foreground women's sexual pleasure: 'We see the most horrible violence on screens and yet we can't look at our own sexuality: our own organs of pleasure. The main thing we've been oppressed around is our pleasure' (B. Hammer, quoted in Collis, 1988, p. 12). Further, there are those who argue that 'some women like and feel empowered by pornography. They like reading or watching it, and they like producing it' (Hunt, 1990). Such diversities of thought illustrate some of the differences that now exist *between* women within the feminist movement.

A different response to the debate is to stress that there must be equality between the kinds of people who represent and those who are represented (Kappeler, 1986), together with a democracy of the gaze. Without this, the 'freedom' of looking at and making images is too dangerous for those who are always the object of the white male gaze, never his representer, in images which represent violent power relations. Stating that freedom of representation is a middle-class illusion, Maud Sulter expressed what it feels like to be a black woman object of the dominant white female gaze:

> If my flesh is your meat, then I must make of you a vegetarian, for my flesh is not for your consumption; not if you are white, not if you are black, not if you are a woman, not if you are a man. My body is the home of my spirit, my ancestors reside with me. I may choose to share it with you. But you will not own me. Not again.
>
> *(Sulter, 1990/91, p. 42)*

This was Maud Sulter's response in a review of an anthology of lesbian erotic stories, employing a naked black woman as its front cover, in which she asked: 'Are the majority prepared to speak out in the face of an ideology which uses sexism, class bias and racism as a prime mover and shaker for a purportedly feminist sex "scene" in the name of feminism?' (ibid.). In this view, 'freedom' of visual expression is another name for the tyranny of those who hold all the means of communication.

Do women want to enter into representation as makers of images on an equal footing: to make images as men do? In my view, women must develop a politics of representing which does not produce a lot more women creating the sort of images men have made. Women could seek modes of image-making that are colloquial, giving their due to those represented and refusing exploitative methods. We could try to make images which give women the full right to the gaze, and try to empower generations of women to define their own femininities against the representation of everything from advertisements to Old Masters. We can use our scope as consumers, voters, theorists, representers, historians and critics, using both institutional change and the development of a feminist theory of representation, to give women their rights to representing and representation. What began with questions of women artists' equal representation in exhibiting, and campaigns over the stereotyping of women as 'sex objects' in advertising, or the Miss World contest, has entailed no less than a revolution in considering the work that visual images and artefacts do, and ought to do, in all human societies. Radical changes are required in the entire way representation in the widest sense is produced, and certainly not merely half shares in the established system. What will these changes be?

Article 3.2

OBJECT INTO SUBJECT:
SOME THOUGHTS ON THE WORK OF
BLACK WOMEN ARTISTS[1]

Michelle Cliff

In my room there is a postcard of a sculpture by the Venetian artist
Danese Cattaneo, done in the mid-sixteenth century – *Black Venus*.
The full-length nude figure is bronze. In one hand she holds a
hand-mirror in which she is looking at herself. On her head is a
turban, around the edges of which her curls are visible. In her other
hand she carries a cloth – or at least what appears to be a cloth.
Who was she? A slave? Perhaps in the artist's own household, or
maybe that of his patron – one of the many black women dragged
from Africa to enter the service of white Europeans. I have no idea
who she actually was: she was an object, then as now.

Around this image are other images of black women: Bernadette
Powell, who killed the man who beat her and is now in Bedford
Hills; Fannie Lou Hamer; Billie Holiday; Elizabeth Freeman, who
sued for her freedom and won it, in Massachusetts in the nineteenth
century; Josephine Baker; Harriet Tubman, portrayed in a linocut
by Elizabeth Catlett; women students making basket furniture at
the Hampton Institute; Lucy Parsons; Ida B. Wells-Barnett; Audre
Lorde; Phillis Wheatley; two women in Botswana seated around a
gourd; Sojourner Truth; women in the Black Liberation Movement
in England; Betye Saar's Aunt Sally HooDoo; a girlchild balancing
a basin on her head in southern Africa.

My moving toward the study of the work – written and visual
– of black women has been a moving toward my own wholeness.
My interest in this work is a deeply personal interest, because
through these words and images I begin to capture part of who I am.

I should begin with my title – *Object into Subject*. What does it
mean? We live in a society whose history is drenched in the
philosophy and practice of racism, the oppression of black and other
Third World peoples. This is the point at which my definition
begins. If you study racism – if you understand the history of the
United States – you will find that under racism the person who is
oppressed is turned into an object in the mind of the oppressor.

The white anti-racist southern writer Lillian Smith was among
the first to offer a metaphysical and psychological explanation of
racism as a personal and political American practice.[2]

[· · ·]

Within the rationale reason lends to racism, Smith argued, is the practice of objectification, an absolute necessity in the racist effort to oppress. (I use the word 'effort' because it is and has been so; one which has been carried on on every level of this society, against constant, historic opposition.) Through objectification – the process by which people are dehumanized, made ghostlike, given the status of Other – an image created by the oppressor replaces the actual being. The actual being is then denied speech; denied self-definition, self-realization; and over-arching all this, denied selfhood – which is after all the point of objectification. A group of human beings – a people – are denied their history, their language, their music. Their cultural values are ignored. This history, this language, this music, these values exist in the subculture, but in the dominant culture only certain elements are chosen, recast, co-opted, and made available to the definition of these people. And these elements presented by the dominant culture tend to serve the purpose of objectification and, therefore, oppression.

The practice of objectification stands between all black people and full human identity under the white supremacist system: racism requires that black people be thought different from white; and this difference is usually translated as less than. This requirement has been stated in various ways throughout the history of America. Did you know, for example, that Thomas Jefferson held the popular view that the black race was created when black women mated with orangutans (Stetson, 1981)? (I do not know where the original black women were supposed to have come from.)

[· · ·]

'Segregation', for Smith, described a phenomenon deeper than legal statute or town custom. She saw segregation as a form of dichotomizing within the white western male tradition. She observed, for example, that white women are segregated from black women and also objectified within the dominant culture:

> Another split took place . . . Somehow much in the white woman that (man) could not come to terms with, the schizophrenic split he had made in her nature – the sacred madonna and the bitch he had created of her – could now be projected, in part, onto another female: under slavery, he could keep his pure white 'madonna' and have his dark tempestuous 'prostitute' . . . Back of southern people's fear of giving up segregation is this fear of giving up the 'dark woman' who has become a symbol which the men no longer wish to attach to their own women.

(Smith, in Cliff, 1978, p. 204)

Smith's observation is important: white and black women were/are both objectified and split from one another. I feel that Smith oversimplified the split, however. For example, the sacred madonna, in order to maintain her status (and most often she was intent on maintaining her status), had to objectify the black woman according to the white male imagination. The white woman on the slave plantation knew that white men used rape against black women. She knew that black women were for the most part fieldhands, working alongside men – when they were pregnant, when they were nursing. The black woman was made into a sex object, yes, but Smith's use of the word 'prostitute', even in quotes, suggests more choice than any slave woman ever had. It also denies or glosses over the use of rapism by white men against black women as an instrument of terror, of oppression.

Black women have been doubly objectified – as black, as women; under white supremacy, under patriarchy. It has been the task of black woman artists to transform this objectification: to become the *subject* commenting on the meaning of the object, or to become the subject rejecting the object and revealing the *real* experience of being. In her essay 'In Search of Our Mothers' Gardens', Alice Walker ponders the degree of difficulty faced by a black woman with artistic ambition: 'What did it mean for a black woman to be an artist in our grandmothers' time? In our great-grandmothers' day? It is a question with an answer cruel enough to stop the blood' (Walker, 1977, p. 94) [and see the Conclusion in this volume].

In her novel *Sula*, Toni Morrison makes the following obser-vation about the seemingly destructive nature of her main character:

> In a way, her strangeness, her naiveté, her craving for the other half of her equation was the consequence of an idle imagination. Had she paints, or clay, or knew the discipline of the dance, or strings; had she anything to engage her tremendous curiosity and her gift for metaphor, she might have exchanged the restlessness and preoccupation with whim for an activity that provided her with all she yearned for. And like any artist with no art form, she became dangerous.
>
> *(Morrison, 1975, p. 105)*

Sula's tragedy, and the tragedy she represents, is 'cruel enough to stop the blood'. Because of her race, perhaps also because of her sex, she has been shut out from art and denied access to art forms. She is an intelligent, thinking woman, who ultimately has nowhere to go.

The objectification of black women has taken many forms: the Mammy, Mama – wetnurse, midwife, cook – usually large, usually dark, combining humility and capability. The temptress, sex-object, whore – sometimes mulatto (from the Latin for mule, i.e., a creature unable to reproduce herself) – misbegotten and tragic, the power of the master coursing through her powerless veins. These are but two examples which recur in white western literature and art. And these have been repeated by white women as well as white men. There is, of course, 'Mammy' in *Gone with the Wind*; and there is Julie, the woe-begone quadroon in Edna Ferber's *Showboat*. Another novel, *Imitation of Life* by Fanny Hurst, attempts to 'deal with' both Mammy and mulatto.

[···]

We know that black women – mothers and non-mothers – have been intrinsic to the activism of black history. There is the following story, for example, quoted by Angela Davis:

> She didn't work in the field. She worked at a loom. She worked so long and so often that once she went to sleep at the loom. Her master's boy saw her and told his mother. His mother told him to take a whip and wear her out. He took a stick and went out to beat her awake. He beat my mother till she woke up. When she woke up, she took a pole out of the loom and beat him nearly to death with it. He hollered, 'Don't beat me no more, and I wont let 'em whip you'.
>
> She said, 'I'm going to kill you. These black titties sucked you, and then you come out here to beat me'. And when she left him, he wasn't able to walk.
>
> And that was the last I seen of her until after freedom. She went out and got an old cow that she used to milk – Dolly, she called it. She rode away from the plantation because she knew they would kill her if she stayed.
>
> (Davis, 1971, p. 13)

This story tells of a black woman in the act of freeing herself. A selfish need for freedom, and a recognition that freedom is their right, is something usually denied to black women historically, even when they are recognized as liberators of their race. But Fannie Lou Hamer, Ida B.Wells, Mary McLeod Bethune, Sojourner Truth – and the many women whose names we do not know – all felt a personal desire for freedom, which came from a feeling of self-esteem, self-worth, and they translated this into a political commitment that their people also be free. Harriet Tubman said:

> I looked at my hands to see if I was de same person now I was free. Dere was such a glory ober eberything, de sun came like gold trou de trees, and ober de fields, and I felt like I was in heaven.
>
> I had crossed de line of which I had so long been dreaming. I was free; but dere was no one to welcome me to de land of

> freedom. I was a stranger in a strange land, and my home after all was down in de ole cabin quarter, wid de ole folks, and my brudders and sisters. But to dis solemn resolution I came; I was free, and dey should be free also; I would make a home for dem in de North, and de Lord helping me, I would bring dem all dere.
>
> *(in Bradford, 1974, pp. 30–2)*

The artist, like the liberator, must begin with herself.

Edmonia Lewis (1843–1900?) is the first woman of colour we know whose work as a visual artist was recognized by the dominant culture. During her life as a sculptor she was confronted with the objectification of herself as black and female. While her work was not ignored, it was given a secondary place of importance by most critics. Lewis was seen as a 'wonder', a work of art in herself – a curiosity [Pl. 5]. The following excerpt from an abolitionist newspaper describes the artist and her marble group *Forever Free* (1867)[Pl. 6]:

> No one . . . could look upon this piece of sculpture without profound emotion. The noble figure of the man, his very muscles seeming to swell with gratitude; the expression of the right now to protect, with which he throws his arms around his kneeling wife; the 'Praise de Lord' hovering on their lips; the broken chain – all so instinct with life, telling in the very poetry of stone the story of the last ten years. And when it is remembered who created this group, an added interest is given to it . . . Will anyone believe it was the small hand of a girl that wrought the marble and kindled the light within it? – a girl of dusky hue, mixed Indian and African, who not more than eight years ago sat down on the steps of City Hall to eat the dry crackers with which alone her empty purse allowed her to satisfy her hunger; but as she sat and thought . . . of her homeless state, something caught her eye, the hunger of the stomach ceased, but the hunger of the soul began. That quiet statue of the good old Franklin . . . kindled the latent genius which was enshrined within her, as her own group was in marble, till her chisel brought it out. For weeks she haunted that spot and the State House, where she could see Washington and Webster. She asked questions, and found that such things were first made in clay. She got a lump of hard mud, shaped her some sticks, and, her heart divided between art and the terrible need for freedom . . . she wrought out . . . an admirable bust of Col. Robert Gould Shaw, white Bostonian commander of a company of Black troops organized due to pressure from Frederick Douglass.
>
> *(in Hanaford, n.d., pp. 296–7)*

When this article was written Lewis was a well-known sculptor living in Rome, with a degree in liberal arts from Oberlin College. She had studied sculpture with Edward Brackett, a prominent neo-classical artist. She was not particularly interested in creating likenesses of Franklin, Washington or Webster – her interest in these pieces would have been purely technical, not inspirational. The only 'leader' of white America she ever depicted was Abraham Lincoln. All her other subjects were drawn from her history as the daughter of a black man and a Chippewa woman, and her consciousness of racism.

Just as the author patronizes the artist, so does he minimize the political statement of her work. For instance, he uses the word 'gratitude' rather than 'pride' or 'triumph', in his comments on the male figure; he focuses on the arm which embraces the woman, rather than on the hand which is raised, the broken chain dangling from the wrist. He cites the struggle of the last 'ten' years with typical white solipsism. In addition, his 'Praise de Lord' does not allow us knowledge of the politics of black Americans, to which religion has been historically intrinsic. Rather, it can be read in such a way that the triumph is taken from the hands of those who have won it and placed somewhere 'out there'.

It is commonly believed that the slaves were freed by white Northerners. But as W.E.B. Du Bois observed: 'In proportion to population, more Negroes than whites fought in the Civil War. These people, withdrawn from the support of the Confederacy, with the threat of the withdrawal of millions more, made the opposition of the slaveholder useless, unless they themselves freed and armed their own slaves' (in Bennett and Gibbs, 1980, pp. 14–15). The journey out of slavery was one in which black people played a dominant role. It is this that Lewis is commemorating in her work. She had earlier commemorated the slave-woman in her piece *Freedwoman on First Hearing of Her Liberty* (which has been lost to us).

In an interview with the *Lorain County News*, Lewis spoke of her childhood:

> My mother was a wild Indian and was born in Albany, of copper color and with straight black hair. There she made and sold moccasins. My father, who was a Negro, and a gentleman's servant, saw her and married her . . . Mother often left home and wandered with her people, whose habits she could not forget, and thus we were brought up in the same wild manner. Until I was twelve years old, I led this wandering life, fishing and swimming . . . and making moccasins.

(in Tufts, 1974, p. 159)

Alice Walker speaks about looking 'high – and low' for the artistic antecedents of black women; she speaks specifically of her own mother's garden – how this was the place of her mother's creative expression, the background against which Walker's own work proceeded: 'Guided by my heritage of a love of beauty and a respect for strength – in search of my mother's garden I found my own' (1977, p. 101). This statement makes me think of Lewis's mother, her independence and her craft. The fact that she trained her daughter in her art form. That she taught her strength.

Lewis's sculpture, because she chose primarily to depict subjects directly related to her own and her people's experience, has a certain power. Where her pieces lose power is in the style she adopted and the material she used: the neo-classical style, with its emphatic focus on Greek idealization, and the pristine whiteness of the marble, which supports the narrowness of the style – so that a black face must appear white and be carved according to principles of beauty which are white, 'fine' features as perfection. The nineteenth century was the century of jubilee, of a women's movement, and of a revolutionary movement in Europe. But these moral reactions need to be understood against the immorality which dominated that century: the 'white man's burden', the political/religious/economic affirmation of the supremacy of the white race. The neo-classical style arose quite naturally from all this, based as it was on the imitation of fifth-century Athens, a slave-owning, gynephobic society, but one popularly regarded as high-minded and democratic. In Lewis's *Forever Free* the limitations placed on a black and Indian artist working in this style and with this material are evident: the curly hair of the male figure and the broken chain are the only signs that these are people of colour.

Of her sculpture *Hagar* (1875), Lewis said: 'I have a strong sympathy for all women who have struggled and suffered' (in Tufts, 1974, p. 163). Again, we have to look beyond the actual figure to the story Lewis is illustrating to find the political/historical statement in her work [Pl. 7]. Hagar was an Egyptian, a woman of colour, the slave of Abraham's wife, Sarah. Hagar was 'given' to Abraham by Sarah so that he might have an heir; and she was the mother of his first-born son, Ishmael. Then Isaac was born to Abraham and Sarah. The book of Genesis continues the story:

> Sarah saw the son of Hagar the Egyptian, whom she had borne to Abraham, playing with her son Isaac. So she said to Abraham, 'Cast out this slave woman with her son; for the son of this slave woman shall not be heir with my son Isaac'. And the thing was very displeasing to Abraham on account of his son. But God said to Abraham, 'Be not displeased because of the lad and because of your slave woman; whatever

Sarah says to you, do as she tells you, for through Isaac shall your descendants be named . . .' So Abraham rose early in the morning . . . and sent (Hagar) away. And she departed, and wandered in the wilderness Beer-sheba.

(Genesis, ch. 21, verses 9–14)

It is quite impossible to read this story and not think of the black woman under slavery, raped by the white master, serving the white master's wife, bearing a child by the white master, and bearing the responsibility for that child – with no power over her own fate, or that of her child. Lewis's choice of Hagar as a symbol for black slave-women also fits into the black tradition in America, one immersed in the stories of the Bible (often the Bible was the only access slaves had to the written word), and characterized by the translation of these stories according to black history.

In reading this account from Genesis, I am also thrown back to Lillian Smith's description of the split between black and white women. It is Sarah who is made responsible for the banishment of Hagar. Her husband and his god remain blameless, even noble.

After approximately ten years of recognition, Edmonia Lewis 'disappeared'. This sort of falling out of fame is usually seen as tragic, but I wonder what happened to her? Was her disappearance by choice? Or did she disappear because she was a black woman artist who was no longer in vogue, because she was no longer seen as 'exotic'?

In contrast to Lewis's white marble sculptures, Elizabeth Catlett's figures are done in brown wood or terra cotta, or another material which suggests the colour of her subjects, or at least that her subjects are people of colour. No white western features replace the characteristics of black and other Third World people. But Catlett is a contemporary artist, one who relatively early in her career left this country and moved to a country of coloured people – Mexico.

Yet her piece *Homage to My Young Black Sisters* (1969), when we make allowances over time and across space, is not that far removed in political intent from Lewis's *Hagar* [Pl. 8]. In form the differences are enormous: Hagar's hands are clasped in front of her, in resignation, in supplication – in the wilderness she has to turn to Abraham's god to save the life of her son. The female figure of *Homage* has one arm raised in a powerful and defiant fist. The similarity between the two pieces is that both, I think, represent part of the history of black women, particularly black motherhood, in America. The mid-section of the *Homage* figure is an open space, which I take as Catlett's statement of the historical white denial of black women's right to motherhood in any self-defining way, and of the theft of the children of black women, and of what these children represent – whether through the laws of the slavocracy or those of post-industrial America.

147

Catlett uses the theme of black women and children often in her work, depicting over and again the heroism required of black women simply to survive. In her lithographs, engravings and lino-cuts, Catlett seeks to tell the history of black women, breaking away from the objectification of the dominant culture. We might, for example, look at her wood engraving of Harriet Tubman (1975), in contrast to Judy Chicago's Sojourner Truth plate in the *Dinner Party*[3] [Pls. 10 and 9]. Catlett's Harriet dominates the foreground; one powerful arm points forward, the other holds a rifle. She is tall and she is strong and she is black. In the background are the men and women she leads. What is interesting to me is the expression on Tubman's face – she is fiercely determined. This expression is repeated in the group she leads. There is no passivity here, no resignation, no impotent tears, no 'humming'. Rather, this is a portrait of the activity of a people in conflict with their oppression.

Catlett has stated that art should be obviously political, available to the people who are its subject. We have no such clear statement from Lewis, but we must wonder for whom her work was done, finally: and whether she stopped working as she did because of a distance between her art and her subjects.

Harriet Powers (1837–1911)[Pl. 4] was a quilt-maker (only two of her quilts are known to survive). She worked in appliqué, a method of needlework devised by the Fon of Dahomey, brought to this country on slave ships[4] [Col. Pl. 4]. Betye Saar is a collector; an artist who constructs images with various objects, memento[e]s, photographs, bits and pieces picked up here and there and saved; things used in another context, by other hands. Both Powers and Saar endow their work with a belief in the spiritual nature of the ordinary. Powers's quilts, constructed from the scraps saved by a poor black woman, convey a real portrait of one black woman's religion and politics. Marie Jeane Adams states: 'The more one examines the style and content of Harriet Powers's work, the more one sees that it projects a grand spiritual vision that breaks out of the confines of folk art' (n.d., p. 16).

The employment of once-used objects by these artists is one aspect of their work which needs further thought. In the history of white western art there is an obsession with the purity of materials. And also with their value. For one example: in the art of fifteenth-century Italy, and even earlier, the colour ultramarine was often used to depict the most important figure or feature in a painting or fresco. This choice was made with the knowledge that the colour was created by crushing lapis lazuli, the most expensive source of pigment after gold (Baxandall, 1972, p. 9ff). And this choice extended to the very meaning of the work produced. In the art of Powers and Saar, the sources of the artist's materials are also important, but the choice is more deeply personal. We might ask: how much does the power of a work of art consist in the material which makes up that work? What is the difference between a work of art made with things specifically employed in that work and never before? Is one more useful than the other? More magical than the other?

We know of Harriet Powers's work partly because of a white woman – Jennie Smith, herself an artist – who left an 18-page monograph on the artist. She recorded the following in 1891, when Powers finally agreed to sell her a quilt:

> I found the owner, a negro woman, who lived in the country on a little farm whereon she and her husband made a respectable living ... Last year I sent word that I would buy it if she still wanted to dispose of it. She arrived one afternoon in front of my door ... with the precious burden ... encased in a clean crocus sack.
>
> She offered it for ten dollars, but I told her I only had five to give. After going out consulting with her husband she returned and said, 'Owin' to de hardness of de times, my old man 'lows I'd better teck hit'. Not being a new woman she obeyed.
>
> After giving me a full description of each scene with great earnestness, she departed but has been back several times to visit the darling offspring of her brain.
>
> (in Bank, 1979, p. 118)

Powers's second quilt – now in the Boston Museum of Fine Arts – was commissioned in 1898 by the wives of professors at Atlanta University. This quilt, known as the second Bible quilt, consists of five columns, each divided into three frames [Col. Pl. 5]. All the frames deal with the theme of God's vengeance and redemption, illustrated through Biblical images and representations of cataclysmic events in eighteenth- and nineteenth-century America.

> This ... much-exhibited quilt portrays fifteen scenes. Ten are drawn from familiar Bible stories which concern the threat of God's judgment inextricably fused with His mercy and man's redemption, among which are the Fall, Moses in the wilderness, Job's trials, Jonah and the whale, the Baptism of Christ and the Crucifixion ... Four others depict astronomical or meteorological events, only one of which, an extremely cold spell in 1895 in the eastern United States, occurred in Mrs Powers' adult life. Given Mrs Powers' intensely religious outlook, she interpreted these events in the celestial atmosphere as messages from God to mankind about punishment, apocalypse, and salvation.
>
> (Adams, n.d., p. 14)

The one frame which does not fit into this categorization is the one which, as Marie Jeane Adams observes, is the key to the quilt. Powers left a description in her own words of all the scenes in the quilt; of this particular frame she said:

> Rich people who were taught nothing of God. Bob Johnson and Kate Bell of Virginia. They told their parents to stop the clock at one and tomorrow it would strike one and so it did. This was the signal that they had entered everlasting punishment. The independent hog which ran 500 miles from Ga. to Va. Her name was Betts.[5]

The frame has a clock in the centre, stars and a moon scattered around two human figures. At the bottom is the independent hog named Betts, the largest figure of the quilt. Metallic thread outlines the clockface and creates a tiara around the head of the white woman Kate Bell. Betts is made from grey cloth, but she is placed over a swatch of orange so that her figure unmistakably stands out.

This quilt represents a great spiritual vision, but it also represents a great political vision: as well as hope, it represents rage. It is a safe guess that Bob Johnson and Kate Bell of Virginia were a son and daughter of the slavocracy. They stand surrounded by scenes representing the punishment meted out to those who are arrogant and self-serving, and the redemption promised those who are righteous. In this particular frame it is their sin of pride which has damned them; and Powers is clear in her belief that their damnation is well-earned. In contrast is the dominating figure of Betts, who in an act of self-liberation goes free. Her 500-mile flight from Georgia to Virginia is, as Adams points out, a reference to one route travelled by runaway slaves. And Betts is undeniably female – her teats hang down from her grey-cloth body. I think of Dolly – the cow in the anecdote cited above – being ridden away by a black woman. And I think of the white idea of black women as beasts of burden, 'mules', farm animals; of the image of Harriet Tubman being forced to draw a wagon for the entertainment of white folks. I take Betts to be a metaphor for this experience. Angela Davis has quoted Frederick Law Olmstead's description of a slave crew in Mississippi returning from the fields:

> (I saw) forty of the largest and strongest women I ever saw together; they were all in a simple uniform dress of a bluish check stuff; their legs and feet were bare; they carried themselves loftily, each having a hoe over the shoulder, and walking with a free, powerful swing like chausseurs on the march.

(Davis, 1971, p. 11)

It would be very simple to romanticize this group of women. But, as Davis says, it is not slavery and the slave system that have made them strong; it is the experience of their labour and their knowledge of themselves as producers and creators. She quotes Marx: 'labour is the living, shaping fire; it represents the impermanence of things, their temporality'. Davis makes a brilliant connection here:

> ... perhaps these women had learned to extract from the oppressive circumstances of their lives the strength they needed to resist the daily dehumanization of slavery. Their awareness of their endless capacity for hard work may have imparted to them a confidence in their ability to struggle for themselves, their families and their people.
>
> (*Ibid.*)

Black women were not dehumanized under slavery; they were dehumanized in white minds. I return again and again in my own mind to the adjective 'independent', which Powers uses to describe Betts, a 'chasseur on the march'.

It is not that far a distance from Lewis's *Hagar*, to Catlett's *Homage*, to Powers's Betts, to Betye Saar's *Aunt Jemima*. Saar's construction, entitled *The Liberation of Aunt Jemima*, is perhaps the most obvious illustration of what I mean by the title of this essay: 'Object into Subject' [Col. Pl. 6]. Here is the most popularized image of the Mammy – in the centre of the piece she is a cookie jar, the source of nourishment for others; behind her are faces cut from the pancake mix. In front of the central figure is another image of Mammy, holding a white baby. And there is a broom alongside the central figure. But she also holds a pistol and a rifle; and the skirt of Mammy with the white baby forms an unmistakeable black fist. Saar's message is clear: Aunt Jemima will free herself.

In an interview in *Black Art*, Saar described the components she uses in her work:

> They are all found objects or discarded objects, so they have to be remnants. They are connected with another sensitivity so it has to be a memory of belonging to another object, or at least having another function.
>
> (*Saar, n.d., p. 9*)

Aunt Jemima has been created by another sensitivity than that of the artist who has made this portrait. Aunt Jemima has a memory of belonging to someone else, of being at the service of someone else. She exists against an image, which exists in another mind. The cookie jar is a remnant of another life: most likely she 'lived' on the kitchen counter of a white family, maybe Saar found her discarded on a white elephant table, or at a garage sale. She has appeared to me in my travels, usually turning up in rural antique stores or church basements, labelled 'collectible'. The picture of Mammy with the white baby reminds me first of old magazine advertisements, usually, as I recall, for soap or cereal or other necessities of the servant role. And I additionally recall the many films of the forties and fifties about white middle-class America, in which a large black woman who worked in the kitchen was always present but only occasionally given a line to speak. She was played by Louise Beavers, Hattie McDaniel or Ethel Waters – and she was usually characterized by her loyalty to the white family for whom she worked. She also appeared on television: *Beulah* was a programme in which she was featured. She was kind, honest, a good cook, always with a song to hum her troubles away; and, as usual, devoted to those white folks.

All but three of the elements in Saar's construction are traditional to Aunt Jemima; the two guns and the fist are not. Saar, by including these unfamiliar aspects, has changed the function of the figure she is representing. She has combined the myth with the reality of black women's historic opposition to their oppression.

This representation of Aunt Jemima is startling. All of us who have grown up with the mythical figure of Aunt Jemima and her equally mythical attributes – whether or not we recognized they were mythic – have been affected. We may not have known her, but aren't we somehow convinced that somewhere she exists, or at least has existed? The last thing we would expect would be that she would carry a gun, or raise a hand. As a child in Jamaica I was taught that the women who worked for us were to be respected and obeyed, and yet I remember my twelve-year-old, light-skinned self exercising what I felt was my authority over these women, and being quite taken aback when one of the women threatened to beat me – and my mother backed her up. Just as I was shocked to find that another houseworker had tied up my cousins and shut them on the verandah because they were interfering with her work.

So while we may know the image is an image, the expectations of black women behaving according to this image persist. As far as I can tell, Harriet Tubman carried both a carbine and a pistol. And she threatened to shoot any slave who decided to turn back on the journey north. Just as Lorraine Hansberry's slavemother armed her children and set out with them – after leaving a white man to die.

Notes

1   For the first time, this 'classic' article has been fully illustrated with the images to which Michelle Cliff refers.

2   For Lillian Smith's definition of racism, see 'The Mob and the Ghost' and 'Words That Chain Us and Words That Set Us Free', in Cliff (ed.) (1978).

3   For a brilliant analysis of the Sojourner Truth plate in Chicago's *Dinner Party*, see Walker (1981b).

4   This detail, and most of the information about Powers and her quilt, comes from Marie Jeane Adams, 'The Harriet Powers Pictorial Quilts' (n.d.).

5   Mrs Powers's description of the quilt appears in both Adams (n.d.) and Bank (1979).

Article 3.3

BEYOND THE MIRROR: WOMEN'S SELF PORTRAITS

Felicity Edholm

In this article I am going to look at some of the self portraits done by Käthe Kollwitz (1867–1945), Frida Kahlo (1907–1954) and Suzanne Valadon (1865–1938). Although the social worlds they came from were very different (Berlin, Mexico, Paris), they were all identifiably contemporary, patriarchal worlds. All three women were concerned with representing women – particularly themselves – in that world. I want to suggest ways of 'reading' these self portraits and to reflect on their significance and implications. This will involve a consideration of: (1) representations of women in contemporary western culture; (2) what is involved when a woman in such a culture looks at herself; (3) the conventions which surround the portrait; (4) the position of the female spectator/consumer of such images; and (5) the significance of women artists' attempts to represent themselves.

IMAGES OF WOMEN IN CONTEMPORARY WESTERN CULTURE

To begin to think about what is involved in a woman painting her own portrait we can start with what is involved when women look in the mirror – as nearly all of us do, quite frequently. We have an image, or images, of ourselves. We have contradictory and changing responses to our bodies and our faces (pictures of ourselves in photographs usually evoke ambivalent feelings). Most women feel, or have felt, uncomfortable, uneasy and insecure about how they look – 'the long love affair/despair between image and self image' as Laura Mulvey put it (Mulvey, 1975, p. 10). Most women spend or have spent time and emotional energy trying to 'do something' about themselves. For most women, particularly young women, self is very centrally bound up with appearance; it is difficult to be entirely disinterested. Connected to this is the way in which women are characterized as vain, preoccupied with appearance, with how they and other women look, and as judgemental and jealous of other women's looks. Female 'vanity' is itself a subject of representation: some of the most famous images of women are of them involved in self-contemplation (such as the Rokeby Venus by asquez). It is Narcissus who died for love of his own reflection it is Woman who is represented as endlessly gazing at her own age, supposedly in self love. She is seen as viewer and viewed, desiring and desired. Her gaze reinforces the idea of women's intense involvement in themselves as objects of desire and of visual contemplation. It is almost impossible to find explicit representations of men in the same rapt self-contemplation in the mirror.

Such self-consciousness among women about their own (and other women's) appearance has to be located in its cultural and social context. In dominant contemporary western culture, women's social value is crucially constructed through appearance. We ask 'How do I look?' because how we look matters to how much we are valued. Our identities as women – and therefore our feelings – are inevitably bound up with how we look, and this is itself evaluated in terms of how we are seen by others. Simone de Beauvoir expressed most painfully the relationship with self and others that this involves in her belief that old age (which she dreaded) came when you were seen by others as old (de Beauvoir, 1974); women are, in this perception, constructed, in part at least, by the gaze, by others. Women in western culture are always aware of being looked at, they are the objects of the look, and the look is essentially male. Women therefore experience their own bodies and faces from outside as well as from within – a woman must continually survey herself. A woman has, then, a split relation to her body and her face; she is both inside and outside, both self and other.

Images of women's bodies and faces are central to the construction of gender, to notions of fundamental, biological difference between the sexes and to ideas of appropriate sexuality. The contemporary western world is saturated by images of women – in advertisements, magazines, on television, film and in the press. The images are everywhere – in the street, in our homes, where we work, where we consume. We are taught to look at, respond to and appraise these images. Most follow a particular formula: the women are almost invariably non-identified or those whose personal identity is irrelevant. They have similar faces and bodies; they are overwhelmingly white, young, bland and passive. Either they do nothing or they do nurturing, caring, domestic things. Although these women are often alone, they are seldom self-sufficiently alone, independent or autonomous. The images almost invariably display considerable self-consciousness, an awareness of being looked at, of there being someone outside looking, gazing. The images, then, depict absence and lack, through the presence of an absent, significant other, the viewer, the person she is supremely conscious of, and often looks out at, for whom she is waiting, by whom she is completed; the man. In images where she is with the significant other(s) – man, children – she tends to be contained within the image and not looking or projecting outwards to the male viewer. In this way, she is represented as complete, as needing and seeking no other to give her identity. The women are, finally, always conspicuously not masculine, their difference to men is strongly signalled.

The (fewer) images of men on offer in the same way are very different. Men are seldom just presented as face and body, they are almost always represented because of who they are or what they are doing. They are seen as authorities, as having power over persons or objects, as active, autonomous, independent and in control. Even when it is an anonymized face that we see, it conveys exactly these characteristics alert, strong, looking outwards. There is no search for, or awareness of, the other, no recognizable self-consciousness, no engagement via the look with the sense of self as an object of desire and contemplation. The man is not seen as needing an Other for completion.

The women imaged are presented as the objects of desire to men, but also to other women. Men and women are offered very clear subject positions in relation to these images. For men, such a woman is the Other, his opposite (the heightening of sexual difference is crucial in this), his complement. She is something to possess, have power over, for without him she is incomplete, lacking. In this way, men are always implicated in representations of women in a way that women are not in representations of men, who are defined not by their relation to women but by their relation to the outside world. For women, the represented woman is to be identified with, emulated and measured against. She is what is seen as desired and desirable, a constant reminder of what Woman is, and the social value she is assigned. She is also the only, the essential female, the one each of us should (must) want to be. There is no possibility of difference. All women are, by implication, identical in their desires and their incompleteness. The only significant difference is the difference from men. The only significant desire is for the male other, for completion.

Women who cannot or do not make this identification are marginal and peripheral in terms of dominant cultural representations of gender. They are in a sense de-gendered. Images which represent women in different ways and offer different subject positions to women (and thus to men), find a space in dominant culture only in such marginalized or stereotyped, and often ridiculed, forms (such as the Virago) that take meaning by the implicit contrast they offer to the dominant image of Woman. They thus reinforce its homogeneity and its truth.

Even when we as individuals reject the subject positions offered in dominant images, or see them as irrelevant, it is still difficult, in the absence of many powerfully visualized alternatives, to escape their influence and impact. The process of looking at our own reflections in the mirror is some indication of this; it is at some level uncomfortable. Gaining a sense of self-worth and autonomy against these dominant images and the values they represent can be difficult. So, the image in the mirror is shadowed by these other images – 'ideals' of Woman, of desirability – and by the gaze of others.

To begin to envisage themselves, to look at and represent themselves outside the conventions of Woman this pervasive discourse prescribes, women have to challenge the kinds of subjectivity offered by the images which bombard us and assert something different. They have to be critical of, and find ways of resisting, the pressures to see and value women in particular ways. And most women do value difference and strength and independence in other women, do admire those who stand outside, do see beauty in other women in ways in which it is never sanctioned in dominant images. But we do not usually value ourselves enough to dare to claim this validation for ourselves, nor do we have the social power to assert it against the dominant image. To begin to look at, to validate and recognize faces and bodies that are in all ways different to the dominant images of women, to see women as whole and complete, is to open the possibility for women to create and claim for themselves other ways of experiencing their own bodies and faces. It is to challenge the normative assumptions embedded in the way women's faces and bodies are described and represented in dominant images and to destabilize their meanings. It is to begin to eradicate the shadow image in the mirror, to free ourselves from the dominant male gaze. To see and represent is to allow, define and celebrate difference and independence, to recognize strength and begin to explore ways of constructing 'a non-patriarchal expression of gender and the body' (Wolff, 1990, p. 138).

While the kinds of images of women that were dominant in the worlds in which Käthe Kollwitz, Frida Kahlo and Suzanne Valadon lived and painted were in some ways different to those I have just described, and not nearly so pervasive, in most fundamental respects they were the same. All three lived in patriarchal societies, dominated by the same power relations between men and women, the same notions of the importance of female beauty and appearance, the same identification of women with lack, and its corollary – the necessity for full identity and meaning to be given them by men and children. There were, moreover, far fewer spaces or possibilities available for women to construct any public representations of themselves, let alone any that challenged dominant images. I will, then, be asking how they came to represent themselves, how far what they represent can be seen as a challenge to the dominant image of women, how far they are making the invisible visible, offering alternatives, giving us ways of seeing beyond the mirror.

REPRESENTATIONS

Before we analyse these images, we need to think through some of the processes involved in doing so:

1   There is no such thing as one, definitive meaning of a text or image. The import of any representation will vary according to different readers and historical/cultural contexts.

2   Readers/viewers will read things differently according not only to where they come from and their experience, but also to the way they or aspects of them are addressed or implicated in the representation; in other words, the subject position that is offered to them by the image. For example, the image of a conventional western family offers particular kinds of positions to the viewer according to their sex and age. In family portraits, the position of the man, his wife and their children, and the way in which they are placed in relation to each other, offer very clear messages and represent a whole set of relationships or indicators of social position and power. More often than not, the man is bigger, higher, central, protective, confident, if a bit detached. The woman is dependent on him, subordinate, caring, loving; the children protected, controlled, contained by the parents with rather different relations to each of them. A woman looking at this image is offered a very particular kind of identification, a man another. If you look at Suzanne Valadon's 'Family Portraits' (Pl. 15), a rather different set of positions is on offer, which disturb and destabilize some of the meanings implicit in the first image.

3   Our individual responses to the same images are often quite contradictory, and change as we ourselves, our sense of the world and our place in it – in other words, our subjectivity – change. We see images from within the particular subject positions we occupy at particular periods in our lives.

4   What we know about what was intended by the creator of the image will, and must at some level, inform the way we look at or 'read' what they produce. Our reading will also be informed by our knowledge of the tradition from which the image comes and to which it refers, and the references made to other traditions, images, styles and meanings, which will be consciously established (for both painter and viewer).

5   No producers of images, however, can be aware of all the meanings inherent in the images they produce. All kinds of subconscious and unconscious processes will be at work, for both the producer and the viewer, making connections with and drawing upon other images and ideas of which they will not be aware.

6   What a painter paints will also be largely influenced by the audience for whom she is painting, those she is trying to reach.

Women as subjects in the portrait and self portrait tradition

The portrait and self portrait centrally address the issue(s) of identity, self and relationship to others. The western portrait tradition of the past three centuries falls into three main categories. Each approaches these issues in different ways, and has a different emphasis: (1) the subject's social position; (2) the subject's private self, the psychological truth about the individual; and (3) the subject as representing abstract absolute human attributes or qualities.

1   Such portraits are essentially concerned with the public person. They are designed to represent social position; their concern is with social identity. They stress attributes seen as appropriate for the positions the subjects occupy: country gentleman plus family, royal mistress, king or queen, judge, admiral, politician, bank manager. Such portraits effectively reinforce conventional expectations about the kinds of individuals who should occupy these positions, and draw on a range of traditions and associations which validate these expectations. The images and their associated conventions are, above all, related to class, power and gender. Women in these portraits are invariably represented in relation to a man (or men): father, husband, son, lover; they reflect the status of the men by whom they are identified. Only rarely are women seen in an independent, autonomous relation to a social position and therefore as significant in themselves.

2   The psychological portrait is essentially concerned with the private aspect of individual subjects, their relation to themselves and their world. Portraits of this kind came into their own in the nineteenth century and most self portraits tend to belong to this category. Underlying these representations are certain assumptions about individual identity. The most basic is the humanist, liberal notion that the individual has some innate, essential self, a true, ultimately realizable identity. This self is at some levels expressed in and through the body and, in particular, in the face. The face is the mirror of the soul. A portrait, then, is supposed to tell some fundamental truth about the sitter; it should see into and reveal their true self. Reading the face is our means of knowing the other and of knowing their story. For behind many portraits of this kind is an assumption of a biography, a known or knowable story, for men in particular a story of potential when young and

achievement when middle-aged. Women's lives and faces cannot tell this same story. Their stories are or should be what Carolyn Heilbrun has called 'the classic script of marriage and children and the suppression of identity in relationship to others' (Heilbrun, 1989). In terms of representation, it is beauty – or if not that, due modesty and gracefulness – when young, and the loss of beauty when old, although the contentment of a woman completed by fulfilling her ordained function can also feature. The psychological portrait also tends to focus on the individual's uniqueness and difference to others, to emphasize the isolation of the individual: the aloneness. Many such portraits seem, in effect, to problematize the individual's relation to the world, and to stress the separation between the individual and the social world. Portraits of women that fall into this category are rare. There are, moreover, very few self portraits by women prior to the nineteenth century (Nochlin, 1989).

3   Both social, public portraits and the more private concerns of the psychological portrait can fit this third category, in which individuals are seen to embody or personify abstract qualities – for example, virtue, integrity, honour, courage, resolution and so on – or states of mind/forms of consciousness. Van Gogh's intention when painting Dr Gachet, for instance, was apparently to record 'the heart-broken expression of our time' (Nochlin, 1989). It would have been impossible for him to do that by painting a woman. A woman cannot stand for Man, for 'mankind'.

Although the qualities of justice, truth and beauty in western culture are almost always represented by female figures, these figures are idealized representations, not portraits (Warner, 1987). Women as individuals in portraits represent almost exclusively the virtues and qualities attached to what have been seen as their appropriate social positions: beauty, sexual desirability, modesty, virginity, innocence, maternity, love, care/nurture, servitude and sometimes respectable old age. Women can also represent particular kinds of loss – the anguish of widowhood, the loss of children, the incapacity to nurture; they can represent sorrow in relation to the loss of life of others but seldom anything more philosophically significant than that. They could never stand in this way for the consciousness of an era, only for particular, grounded emotions.

In all this it is possible to identify some of the contradictions that are at the heart of individual portraits of women. On the one hand, women are surface, appearance, beauty: their faces can tell you nothing more because they are supposed to be nothing more. On the other hand, single portraits are to a very large extent constructed on the assumption, or indeed conviction, that they can and do reveal something significant about individual human beings, that they will tell the story of promise and achievement about what it is to be human, about the basic and fundamental emotions and values of individual existence. Women cannot be seen as sufficiently individuated, as having the kind of fully developed self, the same autonomy or problematic relationship with the world that such portraits presuppose. They supposedly have less to express and therefore less can be represented through them.

It is perhaps, then, not entirely surprising that there have been so few really great portraits of women. The few that have entered the canon tie in with the conventions which dominate representations of women, that women are only valued in so far as they are beautiful or focused on the needs of others (there have been some powerful representations of women as mothers – beginning with every Virgin and Child). On the other hand, the number of famous paintings of women is legion, but they are paintings of the unnamed (or only circumstantially named) and, almost by definition, the beautiful – and, endlessly, paintings of the nude. They are paintings which are addressed to the male viewer in which a large part of the appeal is the representation of the woman's look at and need for the absent man (the appeal that is reiterated and reinforced in contemporary photographic images of women, as we have seen above). The implications of the representations of women have been much discussed by feminists: particularly relevant in this context is work by Betterton (1987b), Mulvey (1975; 1981), Parker and Pollock (1987), Pollock (1988) and Wolff (1990).

Women and self portraiture

Issues of identity and notions of the self are specifically raised by self portraiture. Inevitably, such issues are posed rather differently for men and women. In much of the psychoanalytic literature (in particular the Lacanian), the identification of self in the mirror (however symbolic this mirror might be) is a crucial moment in the process of the formation of self, the entry into language and gendered identity. What is relevant here is that the moment the child confronts its image in the mirror is significant for the beginning of ego formation, a sense of individuality, for the child sees itself as whole, co-ordinated and complete. In its experience of itself up to this point the child has as yet not had this sense of coherence and wholeness, and indeed the crucial point about the image of completeness in the mirror is that it is a misrecognition of self as unified, whole. The seen coherence is a fantasy. The moment of the mirror is, in addition, the moment in which the child locates itself in an outside world – outside, that is, the world defined by its mother – in the world of the law of the father, and sees itself as subject to that law. The confrontation of self in the mirror is thus crucial for the child's sense of itself in the world. It is different for girls and boys, however, since the relation to that outside world – to the law of the father – has very different gender implications (Crowley and Himmelweit, 1992).

The significance of the mirror in later life is not something explored very fully in this literature, but the sense that the mirror gives of self as whole and complete is one that, it could be argued, remains important as a means of trying to maintain or regain a sense of coherence, of selfhood, of connection between inner and outer identity. Simone de Beauvoir reinforces this reading in her argument that 'all her life the woman is to find the magic of her mirror a tremendous help in her effort to project herself and then attain self identification' (de Beauvoir, 1974, p. 643). Women, she says, seek individuality in the mirror since they are denied individuality and autonomy in their lives. They are 'reduced to generality, one wife and housekeeper among millions of others . . . [a woman's] individuality is not conferred upon her by the concrete world' (ibid., p. 645). To become a woman, a girl has to renounce autonomy. De Beauvoir's position is again echoed in the discussion in the psychoanalytic literature of the different experience of differentiation and separation available to girls and boys in the Oedipal phase. While boys need to learn to separate from their mothers, to repress ties to others in order to acquire masculine identity, girls do not. Girls therefore do not develop such a strong sense of autonomy as boys, but have a stronger sense of connectedness to others. Understandings of this kind are clearly relevant to the way in which women see themselves, and therefore represent themselves in self portraiture.

Other, more concrete, issues are specific to women's self-representation. For women to choose to represent themselves, they have to face the problems outlined at the beginning of this essay, the problems posed by the reflections in the mirror and dominant representations of women. How do they negotiate around these and validate their difference from such images? The conventions of portraiture would imply that to paint themselves women have to claim that they are worth representing. They have not only to feel that what they can say of themselves has intrinsic value and interest but to demonstrate this – such problems are implicit in autobiographical accounts (Heilbrun, 1989; Webster, Article 2.7, this volume). Self portraiture, by confronting an individual woman with herself and with powerful conventions around the representation of Woman in dominant culture, is in many ways one of the most difficult subjects a woman can tackle.

The three women painters I am going to consider all chose to use themselves as one of the main subjects of their work. Their self portraits are either the central or one of the most important strands of their work.

KÄTHE KOLLWITZ, 1867–1945

Käthe Kollwitz was not strictly a painter since she worked almost entirely in black and white. She said herself that she had no talent for paint or colour and it is impossible to imagine her work in anything other than the concentrated contrast and modulation of black and white. She used a variety of different media – etching, drawing (pencil, charcoal), pen and ink, lithography, wood cuts – and is one of the greatest graphic artists of the contemporary period in Europe. Quite early in her career she was recognized in Germany as a major artist. As with all women who achieve recognition of this kind, the circumstances that enabled this have to be explained. She was not, as so many successful women painters were, the daughter of a painter, nor was she born into an aristocratic or haut bourgeois family which allowed space and training for daughters to pursue their artistic interests (Parker and Pollock, 1987). Kollwitz's father was a non-conformist political radical (rather than work as a lawyer in Bismarck's Prussia in a regime he was opposed to, he became a builder). He believed in educating his daughters and was particularly keen to encourage Käthe's painting. It is significant that one of his reasons for encouraging this was because he felt she would need to be self-sufficient since she was 'not a pretty girl' and would not be 'distracted with love affairs' (Kearns, 1976). He supported her studies at women's academies in Berlin and Munich, and encouraged her to exhibit and sell, although his ideas about the kinds of subjects and treatment she should adopt were very different from hers. Kollwitz did marry relatively young and had two sons. Her husband shared her socialist politics and values and encouraged her work as a professional artist. According to her, he gave her consistent love and support. He was a medical doctor and they lived for all their married life in a working-class district of Berlin.

Kollwitz's subject matter was working-class and peasant life: above all, the lives of working-class and peasant women – not subjects chosen by many painters. Her emphasis made her choice of subject even more unusual: she portrays women's anger, resistance, strength, energy, solidarity and activism; as well as poverty, deprivation and oppression by men. Her work is, too, unusual in that she is offering these women as standing for and representing Woman, she is claiming significance and centrality for their experiences. In many ways, then, her work defies and challenges the conventions surrounding representations of Woman. As she grew older, she concentrated more on women's relationships with, their protectiveness and defence of, children and on the devastation of war (this was particularly her concern after the death of her son in the First World War). Most of her work had an explicit political focus. She saw it as art which had some use: 'It is all right with me that my work serves a purpose. I want to have an effect on my time' (Hinz, 1981). Much of her work took the form of posters and propaganda of all kinds.

Despite the power of her portrayals of working-class life, her self portraits can in some ways be seen as her most moving and original work. She did over eighty self portraits and in fact used her own face and body as the model for many other representations of women. The three reproduced in this volume (Pls. 11, 12 and 13) give some idea of her range and the changes both in her physical self and in style and content. In Plate 11 she portrays herself, at twenty-two, quite conventionally, as a young woman looking in the mirror. The lines are, as the face itself seems to be, sure but tentative. The woman in the picture is strong, certainly not concerned to present herself as responsive to the male gaze, albeit aware of it. But there is also a sense of defensiveness, of self-consciousness. It is very clearly a depiction of a particular individual.

Her later portraits are very different. She focuses mostly just on her face, seen as close as possible; sometimes there is a hand, seldom hair of any recognizable kind. She does not pose in any way. The face she draws is totally unconcerned with appearance, with notions of the feminine. There are no markers of gender or of sexual difference. She looks at, confronts herself, serious and unflinching. There is no sense of any other outside the exploration of herself. There is certainly no male gaze: it is totally irrelevant. The shadow other in the mirror seems not to be there.

Although the portraits are of a very recognizable, specific individual, their power lies in what this face seems to express and represent and how this is conveyed. It seems to be the face of someone who has gone far beyond appearance, for whom appearance is totally irrelevant. It is the feelings that the face conveys and seems to embody – and therefore evoke – that are the real subject matter. Her face seems to convey the pain, hardship and strength of existence and the understanding of this. The lines in the drawing get stronger and blacker, as her face is seen closer and closer, and becomes more absolutely exposed and revealing. These representations unambiguously claim significance and meaning.

These later self portraits are not just private reflections, and were indeed exhibited along with her other work. And they belong with her other images of women as icons or symbols. She represents her face as her own and yet as one that conveys experiences and feelings which are shared with others and which connect her to them. Her face becomes in many ways as universal as are her images of mothers and children, of poverty and grief and anger and struggle, although in a very different way. In the images of other women, of mothers and working women, she sought, particularly in her later work, for simplicity; she tried to strip everything down to its fundamentals in order to convey general truths, to produce archetypes. In this process the figures of workers, of women and children become monumental. She uses and develops a type of face and body from which individuality is eliminated. Her later figures are given the same faces and bodies, even expressions. While many of these are indeed powerful, in some ways the simplicity can become a problem of overgeneralization – the figures become too remote. In her self portraits she seems to avoid this problem through the closeness and intimacy which is allowed to the viewer through her confrontation with her own face, her own existence. It is, though, a very particular kind of intimacy; she does not engage with the viewer. The face makes no appeals to you, is unaware of you, but allows you too to be there, to see her. She seems to be able to convey and concentrate extraordinary emotional intensity – more of the pain and struggle of existence – into the particularity and individuality of her own face. She represents herself, her own resignation and strength, her seriousness and pain, and says perhaps more than she does in one of her generalized, iconic figures. She said 'I want to do a drawing of a person who sees the suffering of the world' (Kearns, 1976). Her drawings of herself do exactly this.

The point at which the portraits become most powerful and intense is, not insignificantly, when she is older – the age at which, in the cultural world to which she belonged, women are no longer seen as objects to be looked at, when they are no longer sexualized by the look, no longer the object of the gaze. There are very few competing representations, few portraits of women of this age, because it is the moment when Woman no longer exists. There is, then, in some way, more licence to represent alternatives and, as it were, break the silence. Kollwitz asserts her existence and significance as an individual woman; one, moreover, whose experience and self can make absolute statements about life and human existence, and, in particular, about the experience and understanding of other women who have struggled and fought and suffered as women and mothers. The great power and dramatic value of her work has something perhaps to do with its uniqueness: no one else has dared do what she did.

FRIDA KAHLO, 1907–1954

Frida Kahlo was Mexican, her paintings almost exclusively self portraits, her subject her life. Kahlo came from a bourgeois background – her mother was Mexican, her father a relatively successful German émigré photographer – and was therefore part of the privileged élite in a dominated colonial world. She lived all her life in Mexico City and had, for the time and within the culture and class she came from, a relatively free and unchaperoned girlhood. When she was eighteen she was in a near fatal bus accident which broke her spine, and for the rest of her life she was disabled and in pain: she had forty-nine major operations. In 1929, she married Diego Rivera, already an internationally famous painter, muralist and communist, part of the Mexican renaissance. She remained with him (with a brief divorce and remarriage) until her death. She had three miscarriages and never bore a child. She was hailed as a surrealist by Andre Breton and exhibited in Paris and New York as well as in Mexico. She had no professional training and, although she identified as a professional painter, exhibited her work and sold it, she, like Kollwitz, did not depend on her painting to survive.

In all the portraits (see Col. Pls. 7, 8 and 9) Frida looks out at the viewer, the 'other' who is also herself. In all, she has the same direct, expressionless, almost defiant look; she presents herself as there to be looked at. Rather than reject the conventions which surround representations of women, she works with these. She makes and represents herself as decorative, she plays on herself as constructed, adorned. She is seen in this way as the subject of her own creation: her lips painted, her hair in complex and very different styles, her clothes elaborate and highly decorated. She makes herself a picture, an image, as women are seen as doing – and do – as they clothe and make themselves up, as they look in the mirror. As Laura Mulvey pointed out, she is involved in masquerade, in pretence and in artifice (Mulvey, 1981). Often she will deliberately place herself within a frame, underlining her self as image as reflected back at herself by the mirror. In a portrait she gave to Leon Trotsky, she explicitly places herself on display behind curtains parted to reveal her as though on the stage. She is quintessentially self-conscious, and the self-consciousness is deliberate, is part of the representation. She knows what she looks like and what people see, she knows that it is what they are supposed to see in a woman. She uses the woman as the object of the male gaze, the 'to-be-looked-at-ness', deliberately and provocatively. She looks at herself in that way with a male gaze. Her knowing and her control over what is represented, her production of this object figure, is a part of the power of the representation. For she is not a man, she is a woman playing the game of woman and thus to some extent exposing it. Consciously or unconsciously, she is thereby directly confronting the tensions inherent in portraits of women.

The face she paints is unchanging. Although she ages her expression, her look and her position remain virtually identical. Her face is an enigma: it is precisely not possible to tell what she is, apart from a beautiful woman, by her face. Her self portraits in this way, while conforming to conventions about the representations of women as objects of beauty and male desire, challenge one of the conventions about the portrait – that the face does tell about the person. Her face on its own tells nothing; it is a mask. In fact, one of her self portraits is just this, a painting of a mask; she is in just the position she is in in many of her paintings but her face is obscured by a mask held in her red-nailed hand. The images of intense pain are of the same face; only the conventionalized tears show the suffering. In all the images she is removed and enigmatic, looking at herself and at the viewer, mediating and defying response.

Her portraits do, in fact, tell all kinds of things about herself. She reveals and exposes herself through the context in which she puts herself in each painting, but she is absolutely in control of what she tells, of what she allows the viewer to know and assume. It is the context which changes and represents all kinds of different things: the images and symbols, the obsessions and narratives of her rich and tangled dream world, her unconscious, the events that have scarred and marked her, the crucial relationships, the ways in which she is located historically and culturally. These are the real subjects of her portraits: feelings, identity, the body, time and place. She is primarily concerned with those things which construct an identity, an individual subjectivity. As she herself wrote: 'my subjects have always been my sensations, my states of mind and the profound reactions that life has been producing in me, I have frequently objectified all this in figures of myself . . . in order to express what I felt inside and outside of myself' (Herrera, 1989, p. 288).

She does not present just one identity despite the unchanging face. Each image explores a different set of feelings, associations and experiences, a different sense of self, different subjectivities. The one link between these different selves is her physical self – her body and her face to which she constantly returns. She conveys the complexity of her (or of any) life through representing different facets of it, the webs and strands that make up its particularity and represent different experiences and significant events in it. Her portraits taken together represent a self that is constantly changing and seen as constructed by a whole set of cross-cutting and competing experiences and identities. Kahlo's constant return to her face and body, to the mirror, can perhaps also be read as a need for confirmation of identity, the search for reassurance: 'it is, I am the same person, I am there recognizable whatever the contradictions of experience, the changes in feeling, the fragmentation of self'. This constant return could also be read as a response to her damaged and devastated body. In her paintings, even when the body is exposed in its pain and damage, even when the face is in pain, she, Kahlo, is there, whole, undestroyed, unbroken, a powerful, striking, complete self.

Although Kahlo is so central in her paintings and so often portrays herself alone, a great many of her self portraits offer images of connectedness or rootedness. Sometimes she represents herself as linked by blood to parents, by milk to her nurse and Indian Mexico, by veins to herself and to Diego. In many of her solitary self portraits she is connected by roots and tendrils to the earth, to plants; tied with ribbons or plants to animals. She represents herself as intensely in relation to others, to place, to the physical world.

Kahlo's paintings are rich and complex and in many ways profoundly disturbing. The discomfort comes from a range of different things, not least the contradictions inherent in what she is doing. Her paintings can be read as both reinforcing and challenging conventions about women. The former is evident not only in the way in which she does present herself as there to be looked at, as an object of the gaze, as constructed and adorned, but in the way that she focuses so absolutely, almost narcissistically and masochistically, on herself as wounded and in pain. Furthermore, Kahlo's expression of her life, of all her experiences and feelings, as so closely tied to her body can in one way be seen as validating one of the other dominant notions about women: that they are quintessentially embodied, that they are their bodies, are reducible to and no more than their bodies. And the themes in so many of her paintings of passionate identification with and dependence on Diego Rivera, and her preoccupation with her inability to bear children, reinforce the sense that women's central identity is given by men and children. Even her style of painting – small, intimate, detailed, meticulous and seen in some ways as naïve – is seen as a very feminine style of painting and is indeed different to the grand public style of painting that is so much the preserve of acclaimed male painters and valued 'high' art.

On the other hand, her exploration of the connections between, and the absolute interdependency of, body and feeling, her validation of the personal as of central importance, her exploration of dreams and memories, of her unconscious (which is what made Breton claim her as a surrealist), challenge dominant notions of the nature of identity and subjectivity, and of the unified, rational self, the male self. The very intensity and meticulousness of her work is, too, a way of claiming the power and importance of the non-monumental, the particular. Furthermore, her representation of herself as the quintessential Woman stresses the artifice of such an identity, and thus undermines the notion of Woman as natural. Her paintings are disturbing in other ways too. There is the disconcerting sense of intimacy and distance, of revelation and boundaries, of intense emotion and non-engagement. It is the control that she exercises that is perhaps most challenging. The viewer is forced to face the complexity of the identity, experience, feelings and pain of another, a woman, in ways that are usually avoided and that challenge dominant understandings.

SUZANNE VALADON, 1865–1938

Suzanne Valadon, like Kahlo and Kollwitz, was a successful and acclaimed painter, but, unlike them, she did not concentrate on one particular theme or area. Her self portraits are only one strand in work that ranges from to nudes to still lives, portraits and some landscapes. But the self portraits are an important strand because it is in these that she takes most risks (as some of her nudes also do – see Betterton, 1987b), that she seems deliberately to confront and challenge dominant conventions around representations of women and by women.

Valadon had a very different entry into painting compared with either Kollwitz or Kahlo. She was brought up, in what must have been considerable poverty, by her mother, a single parent, in working-class Paris. Her mother was either a laundress, a seamstress or a domestic servant. Valadon became an artist's model when she was fifteen, working as such until she was in her mid-thirties. She herself had an illegitimate child when she was eighteen (who became the painter Maurice Utrillo). Valadon received no formal training. She learnt, presumably, through what she picked up as she modelled, watched and listened. She became a fully professional painter when she was in her forties.

Valadon's relation to representations of Woman was very particular. As a model she would have been intensely aware of the processes, the expectations and conventions around the production of ideals of feminine beauty and behaviour. She would, after all, have seen herself transformed into all kinds of manifestations of Woman (perhaps the most famous of these is Renoir's 'Danse a Bougival'). Her self portraits can be seen in many ways as a commentary on and a critique of representations of Woman, of which she was so endlessly the subject. In this context, her earlier portraits are themselves interesting since she depicts herself in a very different way to that of the ideal, as is evident in any comparison between her self portrait and Renoir's painting. In Plate 14 she looks out at the viewer, who is certainly not just herself, in a very direct, confrontational way; she seems aware of the viewer, of the look. In her posture, in the way she holds her head and looks out, she could be seen as challenging, defying him/it to make any assumptions about her. Although there is self-consciousness, there is certainly no passivity or obvious acceptance of the look. There is none of the deliberate artifice of Kahlo; none of the indifference and self-containedness of Kollwitz. But nevertheless, Valadon portrays herself as an attractive young woman and her defiance and challenge do not cancel this out, since they are an indication of her awareness and self-consciousness in response to a male gaze. They could, therefore, be seen as reinforcing its power, its effect. She has not, despite her resistance, dislodged the relation between represented woman and male viewer.

We can see, in her self portrait with her family (Pl. 15), how Valadon challenges notions of male–female relations within 'family' units, and firmly states her centrality and power. It is a complex and in some ways disturbing picture, which seems to challenge all kinds of conventions about family life. The three others (son, husband and mother) gaze out of the picture or into themselves. There is no obvious interaction between them – no obvious connections to each other or to Valadon. None of them is given centrality in relation to Valadon herself, as though they are all in different ways equally dependent on and important to her and only related to one another through her. Her hand on her chest recalls the gesture of many portraits of women in which it is often a gesture of modesty, almost humility – here it seems to reinforce the sense of her as self-contained. She is not explicitly dependent on any of them – though they may be dependent on her, she has an existence *in*dependent of them. There is, furthermore, a sense of tension of some kind between the individuals grouped together in this way – the avoidance of eye, of bodily contact, the discon-nectedness. This can in no sense be seen as a celebration of conventional family life.

One of the most interesting and again challenging of her later self portraits was done when she was sixty-six (Col. Pl. 10). Unlike Kollwitz, Valadon has not rejected or ignored the markers of gender but made them central in her representation of herself as an ageing woman. She is again deliberately engaging with the look, with herself as object of the look, through the way in which she represents herself as very deliberately looking at the viewer (and it is interesting that her position and expression is very similar to that in Plate 14). But she is also deliberately engaging with the notions of Woman as constructed through her made-up face, her fashionable hair cut and her necklace – as well as, through her nakedness, with the central place of the nude, of female nakedness in representations of women, with women seen as primarily body. Again, the portrait is forcing the viewer, explicitly the male viewer, to confront conventions and expectations about Woman as to-be-looked-at. Because Woman is only valued in this way when presented as sexually desirable and, by definition therefore, as young, the challenge is considerable. Through its explicit sexualization, through the nakedness, of a sixty-six-year-old woman, through the juxtaposition of her firm, smooth breasts and skin and her lined neck and face, she is disrupting a whole set of easy identifications. She is claiming her own sexuality, presenting her body as her own to inhabit and making her viewer think through ways in which she or he looks at women and their bodies, thinks about age and sexuality, sees the relationship between body and self.

Valadon makes a similar challenge and claim in her etching for a poster for a benefit for L'Aide Amicale des Artistes in 1927 (Figure 3.3.1). As Parker and Pollock argue, Valadon in this representation shows herself as active and self-absorbed in her own work and thus 'calls into question the role of the nude model as simply bystander to the male artist, object of his work, rather than agent of her own work' (Parker and Pollock, 1987, p. 123). They also argue that Valadon here is exposing the conventions at work in representations of Woman, but she is not posing any real alternatives (ibid.). But her challenge is powerful enough.

Figure 3.3.1

Suzanne Valadon, woodcut for a poster for a benefit for L'Aide Amicale des Artistes, 1927

Valadon's style was much discussed by contemporary critics, largely because the boldness and harshness of her lines, particularly her use of heavy outline, seemed to represent nothing that was feminine. The etching shown in Figure 3.3.2 is a perfect example of what was seen as her 'virile' line. Indeed, because so many of her nudes did not conform to notions of feminine beauty, she was also accused of being deeply misogynistic (Warnod, 1981). But her strength and even crudity of line convey very powerfully the strength and power she acknowledges in women and recognizes in herself.

Figure 3.3.2
Drawing by Suzanne Valadon

These three women offer, through their representations of themselves and the ways in which they challenge some of the conventions around the representations of Woman that construct gendered identity, some sense of the ways in which women can begin to assert their own identities and their own experience and thus claim themselves. By the very different ways in which they each chose to engage with self and other, with dominant images of women and sexuality, with what constitutes identity, with age and change, they reveal some of the variety and difference of women's lives, a range of lived and potential experience that is totally denied by the monotony and uniformity of dominant representations of women. By the very intimacy of the engagement with their own selves through the confrontation in the mirror, they also offer us a sense of our own individual importance and the possibilities of finding images beyond the mirror which express and validate our selves, our shared and individual experiences and values.

Article 3.4
FEMINIST ARTS

Catherine King

What constitutes a self-consciously Feminist Art? The earliest feminist images adopt strategies which recur in later times: the taking over from men of the forms of art which are most prestigiously masculine, in order to make feminist statements; and the use of women's ghettoized arts (normally used to corral the feminine in prettiness and passivity) to state a new womanhood.

A mid-nineteenth century quilt from the USA places a narrative of women's rights permanently in the home (Col. Pl. 11). It shows a woman dressed to go out, while her man wears an apron; the woman driving a trap on which is a banner proclaiming 'Women's Rights'; and her destination – a public meeting, where she is speaking to an audience. Her banner is beside her. She wears a bright red check skirt, leaning forward and waving her arms – not pretty, nor passive (Chadwick, 1990, p. 194). (This quilt was probably made soon after the first National Women's Rights Convention in the USA at Seneca Falls, in 1848.)

In the UK, women took over the masculine forms of caricature and allegory. Barbara Leigh-Smith, the founder of the first women's campaign in the UK to fight for suffrage, in 1851, was also an artist. In a drawing, entitled *Ye Newe Generation*, she showed four women facing a bull (Pl. 16). They are holding as weapons the attributes of their arts (paint-brush, palette, pen and musician's baton) and (apart from the one who has on a matador's hat) are wearing the new sensible attire which were statements of their feminism.[1] As they advance on the bull, a woman in an old-fashioned poke-bonnet and shawl turns away. As well as her other political activities, Barbara Leigh-Smith helped to organize a petition by women for entry into the Royal Academy Schools in 1859 and assisted the foundation of Girton College, Cambridge.

In this campaigning mood, Florence Claxton, a younger woman, aged only twenty-one (and who had signed the Royal Academy petition), exhibited a more developed comic allegory in a canvas she called *Woman's Work: A Medley* (Col. Pl. 12). Painting in 1861, she made bold claims in adopting oil, and in taking the arch-topped field associated with important religious, political and moral statements in figurative painting. She pirates the allegorical narrative which was the exclusive property of male artists at this period, and uses it to make her audience laugh at a world in which women worship Man as if he were the false god of the Israelites: the Golden

Calf. She tactfully did not allude to the Golden Calf, which is in the centre of her painting, when she wrote her catalogue entry for the exhibition at the National Institution in 1861:

> The four ages of man are represented: in the centre youth, middle age, and old age reposing on an ottoman, infancy being in the background; all are equally the objects of devotion from surrounding females. The 'sugar-plums' dropping from the bon-bon box represent the 'airy nothings' alone supposed to be within the mental grasp of womankind. A wide breach has been made in the ancient wall of Custom and Prejudice, by Progress – Emigration – who points across the ocean. Three governesses, seen in the foreground, apparently ignorant of the opening behind them, are quarrelling over one child. The upright female figure to the right is persuaded by Divinity, and commanded by Law, to confine her attention to legitimate objects. Another female has sunk, exhausted, against a door, of which the medical profession holds the key; its representative is amused at her impotent attempts, of perceiving that the wood is rotten and decayed in many places. An artist Rosa B[onheur] has attained the top of the wall (upon which the rank weeds of Misrepresentation and prickly thorns of Ridicule flourish) – others are following. The blossom of the 'forbidden fruit' appears in the distance.[2]

With its references to emigration as one solution to women's demands for employment beyond the family (and the service of families by governesses or maidservants) and to women's attempts to enter artistic and medical professions, this allegory is thoroughly topical. To prevent it from being recuperated by masculine visual ideology, she placed two inscriptions. Over the door leading out to the medical profession, from the rotting Bastille of patriarchy, to the right, is the inscription 'Women's noblest ? station is retreat'.[3] In the spandrels she added this fable:

> A forester meeting with a lion, a dispute arose as to who was the stronger. They happened to pass by the statue of a man strangling a lion.
>
> 'See there', said the man, 'what better proof can you have of our superiority?'
>
> 'That', said the lion, 'is your story. Let us be the sculptors and we will make the lion vanquish the man'.
>
> Moral: No one is fair witness in his own cause – *Aesop's Fables.*
>
> (*Sotheby's Sale Catalogue, London, November 1982*)

Like the quilt and the drawing, this image addresses women as primary spectators. They are the lions who can paint themselves vanquishing the man. It seems likely that this allegory is a feminist answer to the grandiose vision entitled *Work* which Ford Madox Brown was painting at this time. Whereas he presented men's physical labour as the epitome of all human work, she states that men offer images of masculine self-interest as if they were objective human truths. In *Women's Work: A Medley*, Florence Claxton pronounces the feminist claim, that women can speak their truths from their experience.[4]

Whereas the feminists of the 1970s put great stress on collective structures, those of the nineteenth, and early twentieth, century, while campaigning together too, set up leaders as sources of inspiration and devotion. Within this context should be placed the portraits of the great feminist of the USA, Sojourner Truth, taken about 1864 (Painter, 1990) (Pl. 17). Speaking both for the repeal of slavery and for the liberation of women, she made her living as a housekeeper (hence perhaps the unusual inclusion of her art as knitter in this formal portrait), and, to help her finance her lecture tours, sold copies of her autobiography and portrait photographs of herself, as mementoes. The commemorative portraits of political campaigners like Barbara Leigh-Smith or Lydia Becker, President of the Manchester Suffrage Society, can be considered in this feminist-heroic category too (Cherry, 1987, pp. 8–9).

The sustained campaigns which eventually achieved the vote moved beyond the journals, petitions, conventions and committees, with which the movement began, to mass demonstrations, attacks on property, prison and the invention of a new form of political protest – hunger-striking. To activate these events, many women, and two specific organizations (the Artists' Suffrage League, and the Suffrage Atelier) made diverse objects and visual images. Suffrage artists sustained the hero treatment accorded to leaders like Sojourner Truth, in pageants welcoming figures like the Pankhursts from prison, and in portrait photographs of other prominent women. Women employed the mass media, in designing newspapers, posters, postcards, playing-cards, covers for printed music, packaging for cigarettes, tea and soap, and in making badges, sashes and scarves. Women defied decorum by chalking on walls and on pavements. Instead of appearing passively to the male gaze, women organized spectacles in public demonstrations which actively stated their subjecthood. Women wore the suffrage colours of white, purple and green, embroidered even on their parasols: and they showed themselves, as vividly stated by Lisa Tickner, for the first time, as the female body politic (Beckett and Cherry, 1989, p. 329).

Again, we find women taking over masculine domains – such as the political processions with banners developed by trade unions, and the use of advertising goods on packaging – and also employing areas and arts demarcated as special to the gentler sex, to redefine their femininity. This is distilled in the suffrage handkerchief of Janie Terreno (Col. Pl. 13). Janie Terreno was a musician who was imprisoned in Holloway and force-fed (Parker, 1984, p. 200). The handkerchief was sewn with the suffrage colours and a pocket to hold the iconic double portrait, on a postcard, of Emmeline Pankhurst and her daughter Christabel. Violets surrounded the signature 'Worked in Holloway Prison by Janie Terreno', while the information 'arrested March 1st 1912 sentenced by Judge Laurie on Wednesday March 27th to four months', is written in thread. The handkerchief is sprigged with prison arrows and the hammers the women had used to break windows in Oxford Street. On either side at the top are the words 'Hunger-Strike', flanking 'W.S.P.U.' and 'Deeds not words'. The women called themselves, 'Mrs Pankhurst's Bold Bad Ones': 'They signed their names in the very medium which was considered proof of their frailty, and justification for their subjugation (Parker, 1984, p. 201).

When, in 1969, women began again to make feminist networks in art, they returned to the agenda of their foremothers: to change society, and to change the arts. But where activists like Barbara Leigh-Smith and Florence Claxton aimed for women's equal entry into the professions of Fine Art, without, as far as we know, satirizing the validity of the hierarchy posited in these institutions, the feminist artistic networks of the past two decades have campaigned for equal entry into the professions of image-specialism and building, *and at the same time have denied any special value to these skills.* The feminist debates in the arts have, in other words, taken the insistence on equality right into the very structuring, practice and values of making objects or visual images. A critique has been created which refuses the notion of a hierarchy of arts from 'menial' crafts, and 'mechanical' manufacture to the 'high' arts of painting, sculpture and architecture, and the segregation, by gender, of producing things. The skills which women have been able to practise have been celebrated, and women should be free to work creatively in these areas, as well as in any others, as they please (Col. Pl. 14). The demolition of the hierarchy of skills entails removing the notion of transcendent masculine genius (which is not to say that the importance of especially creative people is not valued) and giving due weight to the collectivity of making (in which personal inventiveness is embedded in process). Issues of equality are entailed in the community of making, and training, or choosing to pursue skills. And they have implications for consumers and users of the things we make: who are to be thought of as having active needs and rights with regard to products and production. The collaborative model of making and using has important consequences for image-specialists, such that those who represent, have regard for the rights of those who are represented, and so that images attempt to provide equality for gazes: an equality of spectatorships, for diversities of people. Women have pursued and developed elements in this revolutionary programme in the practice and the implications of their work in a variety of ways. What follows are samples from the great diversities of experiments women have made to explore the possibilities of such new arts.

It is important to sample the work and ideas of the founding mothers of this phase of feminist art. During 1969–1970, Faith Ringgold organized an association, Women Students and Artists for Black Art Liberation, to obtain exhibition space for women, on the occasion of a show of black art, at the School of Visual Arts in New York, purporting to address issues of racism, repression and sexism, without any women's works. She went on to help found 'Where We At' as a campaigning group for black women artists' rights (Chadwick, 1990, pp. 318–19; Gouma-Peterson and Mathews, 1987, p. 329). She announced her identity as a feminist and as a black woman in her art. For the Women's House of Detention on Rikers Island (1971), she made a huge mural painted to the inmates' specification, promising rehabilitation. She depicts women in different jobs (police officer, bus driver, basket-ball player). There is a traditional mother 'but she's reading feminist literature to her daughter' (Lippard, 1976, p. 259) and a woman being married by a woman priest and given away by her mother. Faith Ringgold also developed masks announcing her African ethnicity and, through her entitling them *Witches*, her female identity. This series presents the 'heads of weeping women, beaded and fringed and embroidered on fabric, showing the magical power attributed to women, their mouths open to denote the need for women to speak out' (ibid., p. 260). She stated that, 'art has gender, that women have their own culture and it needs to be modified, freed, to produce a new unrepressed female art' (ibid.).

The search for a 'true femaleness' imprisoned by masculine representation was being taken up in California by Judy Chicago, founder of the first Feminist Art Programme at Fresno State College (1970) and at the California Institute of the Arts (1971) with Miriam Schapiro. Both artists attempted to valorize women's sexual difference. Chicago explained:

> I was pushing at the boundaries, internalizing the idea that a woman could shape values, shape culture, upset society. To me, the flower in O'Keeffe stands for femininity, so moving through the flower is moving into some other place. With the *Through the Flower* series, I started to build on other women's work. . . . I wanted my work to be seen in relation to other women's work, historically, as men's work is seen.

(*Ibid.*, p. 219)

177

As well as producing paintings and sculptures aimed to take a female art into the highest reaches of Fine Art galleries, Judy Chicago and Miriam Schapiro were intent on producing an alternative art community. Chicago moved out of her studio and worked in a home space: 'At Fresno I found that the most natural and direct way for the women to get at their subject matter was to act it out and I worked with theatre and film' (ibid., pp. 218–19). The students remodelled a complete house (*Womanhouse* 1971–1972) – 'to violate all those preconceptions about what you're supposed to be as a woman artist' (ibid., p. 219). They used the materials that damn women's works as crafts. Schapiro employed textiles and sewn motifs. In the *Dinner Party*, Chicago orchestrated the collective activities of many women to celebrate thirty-nine heroic women. This employed womanly textiles and ceramics, but on that vast scale usually accorded male monuments. The great women are commemorated through images on a series of place-settings which counter phallic history, with vaginal herstory (Pl. 9). The upper-class hostesses' dinner party art is put into the area of the High Art gallery to claim womens' rights to be fully sexed artists. Rather than denying womanhood, and housework, in order to be the artists, women like Mierle Laderman Ukeles made the house into the gallery, for environment and performance art. In her art, cleaning floors became Maintenance Art (ibid., p. 60). Concurrently, Sheila Levrant de Bretteville was making parallel interventions in the teaching of design in her Women's Design Program at California Institute for the Arts (1970–1972):

> I found that my teaching and my graphic work shared a method: fostering dialog and reciprocity. Perhaps a clear listing of some of the methods I see inviting dialog by evoking the viewers' thoughtful response would be of use:
>
> 1. *The inclusion of several perspectives on the same subject* indicates that the viewpoint of the viewer is likewise welcome.
>
> 2. *Asking a question without providing an answer* requires a response from the viewer so that the conversation can continue.
>
> 3. *Providing evocative but not explicit views of the subject matter* involves the receiver in a quest for meaning.
>
> (McQuiston, 1988, pp. 20–1)

The way in which this method refutes the position of the artist as controlling genius expressing 'his' feelings is clear in her collective poster for the streets of Los Angeles in 1974. She had been asked by the American Institute of Graphic Arts to 'say something about color' for an exhibition at the Whitney Museum in New York. She divided the space into thirty-six equal squares and asked various women to contribute their views on the meanings of pink, in the squares. She developed a poster from this, with some clear pink squares left open, for people to write their views (Pl. 18). The commitment among feminist artists, to collective making, was rendered in numerous group productions, as for instance in the *Wall of Respect for Women* (1974–1975) painted by the women of the Lower East Side Collective, New York:

> In the *Wall of Respect* women are shown sewing, doing laundry, caring for children, working in sweatshops, and protesting against injustices. Their struggle for equality, however, is seen as part of a larger struggle. 'The symbol of the woman pointing to the globe was our way of expressing that the women's fight for equality is part of the greater struggle of all people in the world for their basic human rights' explains Tomie Arai.
>
> *(Hedges and Wendt, 1980, pp. 290–1)*

This was made by women of varied extraction – Italian, African-American, Jewish, Puerto Rican, Asian – who portrayed their diversities in their huge painting on the side of a house.

Women attempted to reverse the weakness of women in male visual ideology. By making huge effigies of *Great Goddesses*, for example, (1974), Mary Beth Edelson tried to provide a new feminist mythology, and to take women back to an ancient original and natural femininity (Lippard, 1976, p. 21, quoting the artist). Women claimed the power to represent males as desirable, but not to humiliate them as 'tit and bum', and to offer both female and male spectators equal pleasures in spectatorship. Sylvia Sleigh's oil paintings of male nudes (1973) purposely use the medium which men have used to 're-present' the Female Nude, and painted naked men as lusciously as possible for our regard: 'My idea was to do a *Turkish Bath* [Col. Pl. 15] which would be exactly the opposite of Ingres' heap of flesh. Everyone in mine would be fully individualised' (Bowman and Adrian, 1990, p. 5). Again using oil, and a large scale, Joan Semmel portrayed the naked bodies of women and men together (1974). In an attempt to elide the distancing which goes with objectification, she shows us personal, close-up viewpoints (Lippard, 1976, p. 36).

Women experimented variously with images of the female body to oppose male constructs around the female. In Performance Art women attempted to take control of representations of the female body. Rather than making images of other women (which may be malappropriated), performance artists were at least using representations of themselves. For instance, Eleanor Antin produced a performance in which over thirty-six days she lost ten pounds in weight, taking a series of 144 nude photographs documenting the work she called *Carving, A Traditional Sculpture*. Here she demonstrated the way masculine visual ideology, by its power over images of women in the media, can make women sculpt themselves for men's requiring gaze. Slimming is the art which a masculine hegemony of art allows to the subordinate other.

With knowledge of the US precedents, a 'Women's Liberation Art Group' exhibition in the UK was held in 1971 (Parker and Pollock, 1987, p. 4). The group emphasized the importance of moving out of the isolation of the individual 'woman-artist and the aim to become proud to show in company with each other' (ibid., p. 5). The very large oil depicting *God Giving Birth* (Col. Pl. 16) shown by Monica Sjoo at this exhibition, offers a sample of the images which went, in her words, towards 'beginning to acknowledge the validity of our own and others' work . . . to explore and develop our own version of a new consciousness' (ibid.). Monica Sjoo represented the most taboo image of the powerful woman – of giving birth, which conveyed her spiritual belief in a Cosmic Mother. She stated that, while abstract art is 'not entirely without purpose and interest, we feel that it is not possible as members of an oppressed group – half of the human race – and with a powerful means of communication in our hands to sit around playing games with surface reality' (ibid.). As well as being able to state ideas in complex forms, figurative art was felt by feminists to be much more communicative to wide audiences, than was the abstraction of Modernism.

During 1969–1970 in New York, Women Artists in Resistance (WAR) had been established as a splinter group from the Art Workers Coalition, because 'radical' men had no interest in female artistic equality, and women formed a committee to campaign against the Whitney Museum of American Arts' inclusion of only ten per cent women artists in its annual show. More campaigns and associations followed, and the women's movement in art began to obtain some institutional footholds giving women all-women exhibition and work spaces, as well as segments in educational institutions and bases for publishing women's art journals.[5] In the UK, women have never achieved quite this kind of institutional toehold. In 1972, women in the UK were able to influence the founding of the Artists' Union so that it contained a Women's Workshop as an integral part of the union's work – not, as in the USA, a split away from it. This Women's Workshop of the Artists' Union, for example, organized two all-women exhibitions in 1974. One item from these exhibitions emphasizes that the essentializing approach of Monico Sjoo was just one of the approaches adopted. Mary Kelly showed *Prima Para* (1973–1974) as documentation of the meanings of baby care, and generalizations based on her experience of motherhood:

'Prima para' is an attempt to document my first experience of pregnancy, childbirth and childcare. The Post Partum section includes records of childcare tasks, i.e., actual corporeal evidence as well as written and photographic material. My previous involvement with women's work outside the home showed me to what an extent women's status in the labour market is determined by the social function of reproduction. Women's unpaid work in the home not only maintains the labour force in the physical sense, but also mediates the relations of production through the ideology of the family. In fact, mother–child relationships determine the whole process of socialisation, in so far as it constitutes the dominant factor in the formation of unconscious mental life.

(*Ibid.*, *p. 161*)

Mary Kelly presented taboo materials (nappies) equated in masculine ideology with messy, emotional, private, body – and pronounced them art, and to be employed to make authoritative analyses of what mother work means.

Equally inspired by US models, in 1974 (following *Womanspace* in Los Angeles a year earlier) the Women's Art Group took over a London house and, calling it *A Woman's Place*, turned what is 'normally' the private isolation of women's crafts into the display of women working together to make art that states their oppressions and the system which creates them. Kate Walker – one of the women making this environment – commented that the rooms were 'images of mental states from unconscious basements to hot tin rooftops' (ibid., p. 200). Reviewing it, Roszika Parker described the basement as representing the instinctual, nurturing aspect of the home ('a nightmare kitchen, oppressive and cluttered. Footsteps on the floor marked an endless, persistent circle from fridge to basin to stove and back again. Out of the centre of the stove floated an enormous wedding-cake': ibid., p. 206). The ground-floor rooms treated the social and emotional expectations bound up with marriage. ('On the mantelpiece, along with a copy of the Common Prayer Book and Charles Dickens' *Great Expectations* was a long line of silver beer bottles capped with baby bottle teats': ibid.). The emphasis was on demystifying art-making and on expressing women's viewpoints. The flourishing postal collective, *Feministo*, stemming from the Bristol Women Artists' Group (1972), transposed the theme of *The Portrait of the Artist as Housewife* (as they called their resulting exhibition, in 1974) from one house to many all over the UK. The collective entailed enthusing women to begin a dialogue by sending images to one another ('a knitted picture, spaghetti sculpture, embroidered poem, what you will': ibid.). In these small things made out of feminine materials and skills, women satirized constructs of womanhood in media and forms supposedly proofs of their fitness for subjugation: exactly like some of the feminist artists of the nineteenth and early twentieth centuries (ibid.).

If *Feministo* insisted on the value of the amateur and home-made, other groups focused on paid work, exhibited as professional artists, and aimed at a gallery audience, employing overtly mechanically produced images and sounds. The *Women and Work* show created by Margaret Harrison, Mary Kelly and Kay Hunt in 1975, using film, photography, tapes, tables and charts, documented the gender segregation in one paid work location: the Metal Box factory. These women followed the method of Florence Claxton and adopted masculine stereotypical art-forms, locations and status (for this is High Art), stressing rationality, logic and documentation. This is women's art which unfixes the feminine, in taking over the qualities which are supposedly the prestigious male possession and using them to expose how femininity has been 'fixed onto' the workplace (ibid., quoting Rosalind Delmar's 1975 review, p. 201). Both the collective works situated around women's works in the house and in the factory placed emphasis on the social and cultural construction of women-as-sign: they did not trace the path of Mary Beth Edelson, or Monica Sjoo, in seeking a universal trans-cultural femaleness to which we could revert or progress.

The collectives had, for the most part, considered images of women's condition, but in 1980 an exhibition at the ICA featured *Women's Images of Men*. Like the US artists, women experimented with making images of men (Parker and Pollock, 1987, p. 36).[6] The show demonstrated, quite painfully, that women could not objectify the male in the way that male artists continually objectify the female. For no image showed the masculine as taking passive pleasure in being the desirable, submissive object of feminine desire. Men were shown with affection, with irony, or, often, distorted, deformed and even sometimes mutilated. Mandy Haver's *Framed Figure* (1980) was striking. In a life-size leather torso she showed a man as that piece of meat which women often see themselves objectified as. To *frame* him she strung him up on a metal frame, recalling the flayed ox of seventeenth-century Dutch pictorial codes (Kent and Morreau, 1985, p. 100, Plate 71). The experiments demonstrated the excessive asymmetry of the gaze against the subordinate other (Parker and Pollock, 1987, p. 51). The deformations of men proposed the kinds of mutilations naturalized in men's images of woman.

The difficulties revealed in attempting to take the male or female body away from a masculine hegemony encouraged artists to try to show up the tricks of visual communications. Such images insist upon the processes of representation, and spectator routines, evoked through constant consumption of film, photography and, especially, advertising, and draw attention to the problems of representing women within existing systems. In *Tattoo*, for example, (1981), Susan Trangmar placed veils of regular patterning preventing the pleasurable consumption of the photographic image of woman. Words are written over her skin, and multiplicities of readings are typed beneath. 'She is a battlecry . . . she is a decoration . . . she is an emblem . . .' and so on, so that we concede that she is the 'sign' woman, not 'real' woman. Such policies insist on the fluidity of the meanings of the word 'women' (ibid.).

Women in the UK had also followed US practices in employing Performance Art, to make statements about the female body which could remain somewhat in the control of the artist herself, and refused commodification. Women have dared to represent menstruation, as Catherine Elwes describes: 'By enclosing myself in a glass-fronted compartment in the corner of a Slade studio and visibly bleeding for several days, I confronted the forcible eradication of women's biology from culture' (Elwes, 1985, p. 182).

Women have demonstrated the Art of Childcare and Mother-hood (ibid., pp. 182–3). (Shirley Cameron has performed with her twins since they were three weeks old, while Tina Keane performs with her daughter Emmeline.) Performance has allowed a woman disabled by thalidomide to represent herself naked (Mary Duffy, *Stories of a Body*, 1990), emphasizing that her 'monstrosity is in your imagination':

> The presentation of her naked body was as much a comment on the general misappropriation of the female form in art history, as it was a meditation on the way people (herself in particular) are classified by their physical appearance.
>
> Turning the tables on a medical case conference scenario, Duffy commenced with her dialogue: a dialogue with her imaginary and yet all too real audience, 'I stand here for you to assess the damages'.
>
> (*Douglas, 1990, pp. 6–7*)

It is a concomitant of this art form that it is *not* easily recorded to provide other women artists with a disruptive iconography of the female body.

In the UK the 1980s was a period when many artists of cross-cultural identities were establishing the rights to image-making. Their explorations entail dual assertions of their representational domain, against notions of artists as women-of-European extraction or men. The womanly arts of the artist's ethnic origins can be used to announce her identity – as, for example, in Rita Keegan's large self-portrait (1990) painted on a canvas hanging (*not* stretched tightly onto a frame) and edged with the indigo dyed fabric which is woman's work in West Africa still. The artist may challenge western imperialist stereotypes. Lesley Sanderson (1989, *Time for a Change*) (Col. Pl. 17) contrasts the popular media representation of oriental womanhood kneeling, demure, eyes cast down, in pink and yellow silk, with a real oriental woman. Ruthlessly, she shows herself naked, hair cropped, staring straight at herself and us. She states what must be risked, for her to make her look into her gaze. During the 1980s, sensitivity about the dangers of representing the body of woman because of the ease with which images may be recuperated intensified. But, as Frederika Brooks noted, in reviewing the risk-taking images by Claudette Johnson, of herself, women of cross-cultural diversities are placed differently in this dilemma, than artists of immediately European origin:

> Claudette's work has a simplicity/unambiguity which perhaps comes out of her sifting through complex issues. There is also a kind of 'what-have-we-got-to-lose', undefensive, openness about it, taking the knocks of automatically stereotyping gazes. I'd like to compare this with a kind of cool, arrogant detaching abstraction, in the work of feminist artworld icons such as Mary Kelly, Susan Hiller, Barbara Kruger, that points to a defence of something they already have access to.
>
> *(Brooks, 1990, p. 188)*

This different positioning explains perhaps also the boldness of Lesley Sanderson's self-portrait, or, say, the sensuous body-prints covered with gold glitter made by Chila Burman. Other artists of cross-cultural diversity have turned away from self-portrayal, to represent powerful women from their own mythological heritage. Sutapa Biswas (1986) explained her painting *Housewives with Steak-knives* as showing the Hindu belief that every woman is seen as a goddess, and recalling the original matriarchy of Hinduism. Here the woman is the good goddess Kali who destroys evil. Kali has just beheaded one evil man, and already has a necklace of other ones. Said Sutapa Biswas, 'Humour and the use of satire is intrinsic to much of my work'.[7]

In the initial phases, feminist arts had turned their backs on abstraction, and favoured figurative, referential work that could communicate complex ideas. Recently, attempts have been made to integrate an abstract practice back into feminist arts. According to such arguments, feminist art which concentrates on figuration and its critiques is too monolithic. Rather, 'It is hoped that Feminism might aim to contain the work done by women, rather than control it' (Fortnum and Houghton, 1989, p. 4).

Françoise Dupré, for example, is an abstract artist who works from home. It is a situation she positively explores. It suits the fragmented life she has, like many of her contemporary women artists, and it fits her artistic and feminist strategies. For her, sculpture making should be demystified and its masculine gender challenged. Today, to make a sculpture, one does not need 'muscles', huge studio space, technical skills and equipment. She is concerned with the personal and the familiar. In her recent work, these concerns have become more pronounced and her intuitive working method more predominant. She employs the container/vessel/nest as a metaphor for personal feelings, memories. Her sculptures are 'human' in scale; they can be lifted, carried or embraced without difficulty. She chooses non-traditional methods and materials (chicken wire and paper), creating rich surfaces by trapping photocopied images in layers of paper and sawdust. The use of crochet images, sewing and mending techniques, culturally considered as feminine, are reclaimed in her work as sculpture making. In this way, an abstract art can adopt feminist methods, means and meanings.[8] Arguably it is a part of the unfixing of the feminine, for the woman artist to be found making artefacts any place in the system, and therefore dislocating critical assumptions continually. Abstract art by women which looks stereotypically 'masculine' might be especially welcome.

Media associated with 'malestream' codes, like bronze, marble, or oil, have been regarded with suspicion. Women preferred women's materials, like, say, fibre for sculptures, or evanescent art forms like installations or performances. Women favoured new media like photography and art video, because as well as *not* carrying the codes of genius, they have the edge over the women's craft groups of skills in being associated with the masculine machinery of the gaze and technological masteries. This has been especially successful for women of cross-cultural origins, who are at risk of being malappropriated as primitives by the art world and can block all such attempts by employing male, white, technologically sophisticated methods.[9] In the case of Sonia Boyce, for instance, we find that by the late 1980s she had already turned from her resonating figurative pastels to collage of mixed media on photographic paper. In her *Talking Presence* (1988) (Col. Pl. 18) she reversed the meanings of white suburbia. Where whites would sit at 'their' cosy fires, fully clothed, in rooms adorned with the decorative plunder of empire, blacks are wistfully naked and belong, dangerously, to the 'ornaments' of colonialism – the sailing ships, the exotic flowers, shells and birds – dreaming of distant shores. The wealth of London visually rests upon the bodies of these two people, whom she presents as objects for an equity of the gaze in gendered terms. Latterly, Sonia Boyce has moved even further away from any image which could be recuperated as Gauguinesque, or womanly decorativeness, towards installations.

Collective design has been encouraged, on the model announced by Sheila Levrant de Bretteville, with the idea of providing equality for commissioners and users of artefacts, through close consultation. The principles have been practised, for example, by the architects' collective, *Matrix*, founded in 1980. Collectives of image-specialists have continued to flourish too.[10] The connections between feminist arts and campaigns have been multifarious. For example, the peace movement used the corporate skill of women's weaving and its symbolism, in signifying networks, and caring, opposed to the chainmetal fences surrounding war camps: the art of peace contained the art of war. Individual artists address a diversity of campaigning issues. For example, feminist arts have been used in the opposition to the Local Government Bill: Clause 28. Rosie Martin signified her lesbian identity being wrapped up and mummified, by photographing herself bandaged, tightly, while vilifying terms had been written on her cocoon (*Unwind the Ties that Bind*, 1988). For instance, women have frequently taken themes from the defence of the environment: Christine Merton's *Tree Tomb* (1988) is an installation alerting us to the way trees are being stifled. In these pieces, the sense of representation meaning *representing the interests of women* comes over strongly.

In 1971 Linda Nochlin proposed in, 'Why Are There No Great Women Artists?', that we must work to remove the disadvantages of women so that they can attain true greatness (Gouma-Peterson and Mathews, 1987, p. 326). By 1990, at the American Art Historian's Conference, she revised her view and stated, 'The cannon ought to be fired'. But if values are agreed to be historically contingent, this does not prevent us from discussing the guide-lines for making critical judgements about what counts as good feminist arts now: for feminist artists and spectators make value judgements every second, in the choices of creating and perceiving. I want to end by considering three feminist images which in different ways meet the criteria that feminist art should make women prime viewers, and be impossible for the dominant ideology to recuperate.

In the exhibition *The Subversive Stitch* (1988), Lyn Malcolm showed the installation *Why Have We So Few Great Women Artists?* which she had made in 1982 (Col. Pl. 19). Each word is made of items signifying the trivial pursuits of women. But, recalling the Emancipation quilt, and the Suffragette silk handkerchief, unfeminine meanings have been structured into the pretty piece: the challenging question recalls the text of Linda Nochlin. 'So' is made from a knitted bootee. 'Artists' is a rug. Words *and* the use of scorned women's crafts refuse recuperation absolutely. The other strategy practised by Claxton in 1860, of capturing male High Art forms and reversing them in meaning, has not been available in the 1970s and 1980s, because it presupposed one type of High Art topping the pile. Feminism helped to destroy the primacy of the modernist High Art – that is to say, Abstraction – and helped create a situation where there is now a plurality of styles. In this cluster of post-modernist styles, Barbara Kruger has made representations which expose the ploys of advertising and other mass media in reproducing notions of gender difference and has given primacy of spectatorship to women viewers. (Arguably, the real bastion of male visual ideology is what Kruger calls the *mediacracy*.) She pronounces her aim as ruining representation. In her 'We Won't Play Nature To Your Culture' (see Article 1.1), for example, the female artist speaks to a male audience, but the privileged viewers are women, who share the assumption, and the full subjecthood, of the female artist as we look. Leaves blind the woman in the picture: but we can see how men's representations of women to 'stand for' Nature, take away women's ability to see in their own right. These brilliant images reverse the advertising tricks used in designs aimed at the woman consumer. Kruger has given these incisive analyses the prestige of gallery art, but she has also given them wide circulation, printing them on tee-shirts and on advertisement hoardings. As Malcolm's piece slides from craft to art, so Kruger's designs are happy on a piece of cloth.[11]

The collusive pleasures of Barbara Kruger's images work best for women of European extraction, because the mediacracy is saturated in pale-skinned representations. Lubaina Himid has provided refusals of black woman stereotypes of a different kind (Himid, 1989, pp. 78–81, 122–4, 145). In her *We Will Be* (1983), she made a large, one-dimensional hardboard cut-out of the racist stereotype of black woman as household servant (Col. Pl. 20). True to white sign of black woman, her arms are folded protectively across her body and she looks modestly away from us. But her skirt is made of images of black civil rights leaders and black fighters. And her apron tells us 'we will be who we want, where we want, with whom we want, in the way that we want, when we want and the time is now, and the place is here, and there'. On her apron pocket is the word NO fifteen times. Following the example of Bettye Saar (see Article 3.2), Lubaina Himid defies the stereotype of the passive black servant as if to say, 'cut-out' racist stereotypes.

During the last two decades, feminist artistic experiments have been diverse. But it seems that, as in previous phases of feminist arts, the images which are strongest against hegemonic reframing are objects with words on them, and performances where speech is possible. Granted the advantages of images-with-some-meanings-attached, perhaps the metaphor of the Guerrilla Girls could still be followed, and women artists be urged to keep shifting the ground and to attack phallocentric images in *all ways* they think best, even if sometimes the effects are short-lived and can slip from control. And in any case, being all words, the Guerrilla Girls should have the last words.

THE ADVANTAGES OF BEING A WOMAN ARTIST:

Working without the pressure of success.

Not having to be in shows with men.

Having an escape from the art world in your 4 free-lance jobs.

Knowing your career might pick up after you're eighty.

Being reassured that whatever kind of art you make
it will be labeled feminine.

Not being stuck in a tenured teaching position.

Seeing your ideas live on in the work of others.

Having the opportunity to choose between career and motherhood.

Not having to choke on those big cigars or paint in Italian suits.

Having more time to work after your mate dumps you
for someone younger.

Being included in revised versions of art history.

Not having to undergo the embarrassment of being called a genius.

Getting your picture in the art magazines wearing a gorilla suit.

Guerrilla Girls CONSCIENCE OF THE ART WORLD

Notes

1   *Barbara Bodichon (1827–91): Centenary Exhibition*, Cambridge, 1991 (Catalogue, pp. 5–18).

2   Florence Claxton, *Catalogue to the National Exhibition*, 1861, quoted by Pamela Gerrish Nunn in unpublished material kindly made available to me.

3   I am grateful to Charlotte Yeldham for sending me this information.

4   All this information derives from Pamela Gerrish Nunn, except the connection with Ford Madox Brown's work (see *The Pre-*

Raphaelites, 1984, pp. 163–5) dated 1852–63. The painting was made for the Leeds stockbroker, Plint, and Claxton came from Leeds. I can also add that the Aesop's Fable might have been intended to call to mind for the Victorian audience, the reference to it in Chaucer's *Canterbury Tales* (C.T., iii, 669–96), by the Wife of Bath. Furious because her husband glories in reading a book villifying women, the Wife tears up his book and knocks him down. These are her words:

Who peyntede the leon, tel me who?
By God! If wommen hadde written stories,
As Clerkes han withinne hire oratories,
They wolde han writen of men more
Than al the mark of Adam may redresse.

See Priscilla Martin, *Chaucer's Women* (1990, pp. 1–13) for discussion of this moral, and its re-use in the 1970s by feminist literary critics: Sandra M. Gilbert and Susan Gubar, *The Madwoman in the Attic* (1979, p. 11).

5   The Feminist Art programmes in California; the Woman's Interart Center in New York (1971); Air Gallery, New York (1972); the So Ho Gallery in New York (1973); the Artemisia and Arc Galleries in Chicago (1973); Feminist Art Institute, New York (1973); Woman Space, Los Angeles and the Los Angeles Woman's Building (1973).

6   The event was achieved through the campaigns of the Women's Art Alliance, petitioning the ICA for 'the right of reply' following an exhibition of the fetishist 'sculptures' of women by Allen Jones. (Earlier, in 1978, similar campaigns had succeeded in obtaining a Hayward Annual Show chosen by women, and including more than half women exhibitors.)

7   Sutapa Biswas, interviewed by Yasmin Kureishi in *Spare Rib*, no. 173, December 1986 (reprinted in Robinson, 1987, pp. 37–42).

8   Taken from a statement given by the artist.

9   I owe all understanding of the 'primitivist' categorizations of black women's art and their effects on artists to conversations with Rita Keegan, 1990–91, and hearing her lectures.

10   For example, the Brixton Art Gallery Women's Collective described in *Women's Work: two years in the life of the Women Artists Group*, London, 1986.

11   Kate Linker, *Barbara Kruger* (1990, p. 14), 'I learned to deal with an economy of image and text which beckoned and fixed the spectator. I learned to think about a kind of quickened effectivity, an accelerated seeing and reading which reaches a near apotheosis in television.'

4
NEGOTIATING MEANINGS FROM POPULAR TELEVISION AND FILM

Feminists' initial interest in film and television was part of a general concern with the under-representation and misrepresentation of women in the media. It identified not only a paucity of roles for women in fiction and a limited range of those that did exist (basic variations on the madonna and whore, or, according to the title of Molly Haskell's early feminist study, *From Reverence to Rape*), but also a similar situation in non-fictional media like television documentary and news. The practical aim of this research was to seek to redress the situation by drawing attention to women's absence and calling for an increase in the number of women employed at all levels of the industry. There was little concern with the nature of representation itself and none with the contribution of the culture industries to situating women and constructing their subjectivity. The theories used were those dealing with role models and the beliefs that women's subordinate positions were due in part to a lack of models of powerful (or even particularly competent) women.

To a considerable extent, early feminist work on film and television reflected the bifurcation of the field in the non-feminist world (film studies, media and cultural studies are all interdisciplinary areas, not disciplines of themselves). Film or cinema studies had developed from literary studies and was concerned to situate the cinema as 'art', while television was studied as part of the (mass) media, where the parent disciplines were politics, sociology and psychology, and the issues were ones of control, uses and effects. While these, with the exception of 'effects', were not major feminist concerns, the separation meant that film and television were rarely considered together. Though the articles in this section do not fully exhibit this separation, it still tends to operate.

The transformation of the area of feminist film criticism can be attributed in large part to the Women's Event at the 1972 Edinburgh Film Festival from which came the publication *Notes on Women's Cinema*, including the important article 'Women's Cinema as Counter-cinema' by one of the organizers, Claire Johnston (Johnston, 1973). In 1975, another organizer, Laura Mulvey, published one of the most influential articles on film (feminist or not) – the much anthologized 'Visual Pleasure and Narrative Cinema', already referred to in the introduction to this book. In this polemical article, Mulvey explicitly attempted to destroy the spectator's pleasure in narrative cinema, by exposing how dependent it was on patriarchal ideology. The article's influence, however, has not rested on this but on its exposition of the male gaze. Christine Gledhill's article in this section refers to this, and the work arising from it, as 'cine-psychoanalysis'.

The emphasis on the need to challenge the pleasures offered by narrative cinema because of their role in maintaining patriarchal ideologies and social formations continued, though in a modified form. Teresa de Lauretis explains: '[t]he project of feminist cinema therefore is not so much "to make visible the invisible," as the saying goes, or to destroy vision altogether, as to construct another (object of) vision and the conditions of visibility for a different social subject' (de Lauretis, 1984, pp. 67–8).

From the mid-1970s on, most feminist film theory and criticism was involved with psychoanalytic theory. So was mainstream film theory; the distinction between it and feminist work is less severe than is the case in more traditional disciplinary areas – perhaps because the area is a recent one for academic study.

Psychoanalytic theory has been less influential in the study of television – though by no means negligible. Again, because of the recency of the subject area, feminist theory and practice has had a substantial influence on the mainstream. This has been more the case in investigations of the fictional material and (latterly) the audience, than in studies of news or of communication policy.

The articles in this section continue the book's concern with representation but focus more on the relationship between audience and texts. In the first article, Christine Gledhill suggests that 'negotiation' is a particularly useful tool for feminist textual analysis since it notes the instability of identity of those reading and also the unfixed meanings of texts, while acknowledging the political need to seek a certain amount of consistency.

In the second article, Felly Nkweto Simmonds examines the representation of black women in a much praised piece of black film making – Spike Lee's *She's Gotta Have It*. Lee's films have been important in Hollywood's recognizing the desirability (i.e. profitability) of addressing black audiences, but Simmonds argues that there are definite problems with their gender politics.

One of the major areas of feminist televisual investigation has been the much maligned female genre of the soap opera. This has overlapped with studies of the romance genre in popular fiction, and melodrama in film. In all three the concentration on emotions and various stylistic devices, particularly those associated with excess, have been seen as productive of particular pleasures for a female audience. In the period since the publication of early feminist work in this area, such as Tania Modleski's *Loving with a Vengeance* (Modleski, 1982a), not only has academic work proliferated, but the genre itself has expanded its occupancy of prime time television and infiltrated other genres – even highly masculine ones like crime shows.

The third article by Christine Geraghty examines the pleasures women get from watching and talking about soaps, and the depiction within the programmes of woman's involvement in both public and private spheres. The soaps she considers are all broadcast in prime time, making them, in American terms, not soaps but prime time dramas.

Finally, Frances Bonner's article on game shows examines a (critically) neglected area of popular culture that inhabits the boundaries between the fictional and non-fictional, the scripted and the spontaneous. She demonstrates how these programmes provide spaces for self-representation, but serve also as sites for the monitoring of sexuality.

There are two major constraints on the articles in this section. First, they are concerned only with mainstream media. This means that the substantial amount of feminist film and the lesser amount of feminist television are not treated here. Women, feminists or not, do make films and television programmes, but these do not comprise a major part of what women consume. We decided in this section to concentrate on women's imagining as members of the audience rather than, as was the case in the previous sections, on women as creators.

Secondly, the articles only consider film or television from a limited range of the English-speaking world. This is not because alternative articles do not exist, but because of difficulties of access to the texts being considered. Non-English language material of any kind is very rare on British television, particularly if it is television programmes rather than films that are being considered. We do not want to deny the many interesting developments in foreign language films – from comparatively mainstream phenomena like the international success of the female director Mira Nair's *Salaam Bombay* and Nobuko Miyamoto's wonderful portrayal of the independent middle-aged Japanese professional woman in Juzo Itami's *Taxing Woman* duo, to alternative feminist works like Ulrike Öttinger's various films. We urge readers to seek out work like this. But, equally, we cannot assume that it will be easily encountered.

Frances Bonner

PLEASURABLE NEGOTIATIONS
Christine Gledhill

This essay takes as its starting-point the recent renewal of feminist interest in mainstream popular culture. Whereas the ideological analysis of the late 1970s and early 1980s, influenced by post-structuralism and cine-psychoanalysis, had rejected mainstream cinema for its production of patriarchal/bourgeois spectatorship and simultaneous repression of femininity, other approaches, developing in parallel, and sometimes in opposition to, psychoanalytic theories argued for socio-culturally differentiated modes of meaning production and reading. Feminist analysis has focused in particular on forms directed at women; . . . feminist work on film and television has particularly explored the woman's film, melodrama and soap opera.[1] A frequent aim of this enterprise, which relates commonly derided popular forms to the conditions of their consumption in the lives of socio-historically constituted audiences, is to elucidate women's cultural forms, and thereby to challenge the male canon of cultural worth . . .

CINE-PSYCHOANALYSIS AND FEMINISM
The theoretical convergence of psychoanalysis and cinema has been problematic for feminism in that it has been theorized largely from the perspective of masculinity and its constructions. Notions of cinematic voyeurism and fetishism serve as norms for the analysis of classic narrative cinema, and early cine-psychoanalysis found it difficult to theorize the feminine as anything other than 'lack', 'absence', 'otherness'. Underpinning these concepts lay the homology uncovered between certain features of cinematic spectatorship and textual organization, and the Oedipal psycho-linguistic scenario theorized by Jacques Lacan in which the child simultaneously acquires identity, language and the Unconscious[2]. . .

According to cine-psychoanalysis, classic narrative cinema reproduces . . . psycho-linguistic and ideological structures, offering the surface illusion of unity, plenitude and identity as compensation for the underlying realities of separation and difference.[3] The subject of mainstream narrative is the patriarchal, bourgeois individual: that unified, centred point from which the world is organized and given meaning. Narrative organization hierarchizes the different aesthetic, and ideological discourses which intersect in the processes of the text, to produce a unifying, authoritative voice or viewpoint. This is the position – constructed outside the processes of contradiction, difference and meaning production – which the spectator must occupy in order to participate in the pleasures and meaning of the text.

Since in this argument narrative organization is patriarchal, the spectator constructed by the text is masculine. Pleasure is largely organized to flatter or console the patriarchal ego and its Unconscious. . . . In particular the 'look' of the camera – mediated through the 'gaze' of a generally male hero – has been identified as male.[4] While these arguments have attracted feminists for their power to explain the alternative misogyny and idealization of cinema's female representations, they offer largely negative accounts of female spectatorship, suggesting colonized, alienated or masochistic positions of identification. Moreover, given the absorption of class struggle within patriarchal narrative structures – the textual spectator is a trans-class construct – this perspective has difficulty in dealing with the female image or spectator in terms of class difference.

While the theoretical gap between textual and social subject may seem unproblematic when considering male spectatorship – perhaps because the account of the male spectator fits our experience of the social subject – this distinction is crucial for feminist criticism, with its investment in cultural and political change for women in society. . .

Recent initiatives in feminist film theory – drawing on the work of feminist psychoanalysts and social psychologists such as Luce Irigary, Julia Kristeva, Nancy Chodorow and Dorothy Dinnerstein – have made possible considerable revisions to the cine-psychoanalytic construction of the classic narrative text, facilitating attempts to take account of the 'female spectator' (for example Modleski, 1982b, 1987; and Williams, 1987). However, as Annette Kuhn points out, this work draws on theoretically divergent analytical approaches. 'Female spectatorship' elides conceptually distinct notions: the 'feminine spectator', constructed by the text, and the female audience, constructed by the socio-historical categories of gender, class, race and so on (Kuhn, 1984). The question now confronting feminist theory is how to conceive their relationship.

One approach to the problem of their elision is to question the identification of mainstream narrative structures with patriarchal/bourgeois ideology on which it is based . . . [R]ecent work suggests that the textual possibilities of resistant or deconstructive reading exist in the processes of the mainstream text. To pursue this avenue, however, we require a theory of texts which can also accommodate the historical existence of social audiences. For 'femininity' is not simply an abstract textual position; and what women's history tells us about femininity lived as a socio-culturally, as well as a psychically differentiated category, must have consequences for our understanding of the formation of feminine subjectivity, of the feminine textual spectator and the viewing/reading of female audiences. Work on women's cultural forms, female audiences and female spectatorship poses this problem in acute form.

CULTURE AS NEGOTIATION

Arguments which support the notion of a specific, socio-historically constructed female cultural space come from diverse intellectual contexts and traditions and do not yet form a coherent theory. A range of concepts have been drawn on, including sub-cultural reading, cultural competence, decoding position and so on. A notion frequently deployed in various contexts is that of 'negotiation' (for example, Hall, 1980; Morley, 1980; and Dyer, 1980). It is the purpose of this [article] to suggest that this concept might take a central place in rethinking the relations between media products, ideologies and audiences – perhaps bridging the gap between textual and social subject. The value of this notion lies in its avoidance of an overly deterministic view of cultural production, whether economistic (the media product reflects dominant economic interests outside the text) or cine-psychoanalytic (the text constructs spectators through the psycho-linguistic mechanisms of the patriarchal Unconscious). For the term 'negotiation' implies the holding together of opposite sides in an ongoing process of give-and-take. As a model of meaning production, negotiation conceives cultural exchange as the intersection of processes of production and reception, in which overlapping but non-matching determinations operate. Meaning is neither imposed, nor passively imbibed, but arises out of a struggle or negotiation between competing frames of reference, motivation and experience. This can be analysed at three different levels: institutions, texts and audiences – although distinctions between levels are ones of emphasis, rather than of rigid separation.

A theory of 'negotiation' as a tool for analysing meaning production would draw on a number of tenets of neo-Marxism, semiotics and psychoanalysis, while at the same time challenging the textual determinism and formalism of these approaches in the ideological analyses of the 1970s. In place of 'dominant ideology' – with its suggestion either of conspiratorial imposition or of unconscious interpellation – the concept of 'hegemony', as developed by Antonio Gramsci, underpins the model of negotiation.[5] According to Gramsci, since ideological power in bourgeois society is as much a matter of persuasion as of force, it is never secured once and for all, but has continually to be re-established in a constant to and fro between contesting groups. 'Hegemony' describes the ever shifting, ever negotiating play of ideological, social and political forces through which power is maintained and contested. The culture industries of bourgeois democracy can be conceptualized in a similar way: ideologies are not simply imposed – although this possibility always remains an institutional option through mechanisms such as censorship – but are subject to continuous (re-)negotiation.

INSTITUTIONAL NEGOTIATIONS

The economics and ideologies of the 'free market' produce a contradictory situation which lays capitalist production open to the necessity of negotiation. Terry Lovell argues that the search for new markets requires new products, exchanged for a range of ever extending use-values.[6] But these values vary according to particular groups of users and contexts of use . . . If this is true of consumer products, then the use values of media texts (which lie in a complex of pleasures and meanings operating at different levels – aesthetic, emotional, ideological, intellectual) are far less easily predicted and controlled. Thus the use-value to a particular group of a profitable (in the short term) media product may be in contradiction with the ideologies which in the long term maintain capitalism. An obvious example of this is the publishing industry, for certain branches of which Marxist and feminist books make profitable commodities.

Negotiation at the point of production is not, however, simply a matter of potential contradiction between the needs of the media industries and user groups. Within media institutions, the professional and aesthetic practices of 'creative' personnel operate within different frameworks from, and often in conflict with, the economic or ideological purposes of companies and shareholders. Such conflict is, indeed, part of the ideology of creativity itself. Aesthetic practice includes, as well as formal and generic traditions, codes of professional and technical performance, of cultural value and, moreover, must satisfy the pressure towards contemporary renewal and innovation. These traditions, codes and pressures produce their own conflicts which media professionals must attempt to solve.

An example of the kind of negotiation provoked by the inherent contradictoriness of the media industries is offered in Julie D'Acci's (1987) chronicle of struggles over the American television series, *Cagney and Lacey*, between CBS network executives and their advertisers, its independent writing/producing team (two women friends, plus a husband) and sections of the American women's movement. According to D'Acci, the series would not have originated without the public spread of ideas circulated by the women's movement – with which the producing trio identified and which could be called on in times of trouble to support the programme. What made the series saleable was not its incipient 'feminism', but the innovation of a female buddy pairing in the cop show – an idea inspired by Molly Haskell's [1975] critique of the 1960s–1970s male buddy movie for its displacement of good female roles. The series, however, despite successful ratings and an Emmy award, had been under frequent threat of cancellation from CBS, in large part, D'Acci argues, because of the problematic definitions of 'woman' and female sexuality that it invokes, particularly in relation to the unmarried Christine Cagney, whose fierce independence and intense relation to another woman has led to three changes of actress in an effort to bring the series under control and reduce the charge of lesbianism – something such strategies have singularly failed to do.

TEXTUAL NEGOTIATIONS

The example of *Cagney and Lacey* suggests how the product itself becomes a site of textual negotiation. Contradictory pressures towards programming that is both recognizably familiar (that conforms to tradition, to formal or generic convention) and also innovative and realistic (offering a twist on, or modernizing, traditional genres) leads to complex technical, formal and ideological negotiations in mainstream media texts. For example, the decision by the makers of *Cagney and Lacey* to put a female buddy pair inside a cop series, as well as using gender reversal to breathe new life into an established genre, immediately raises aesthetic and ideological problems. Conflicting codes of recognition are demanded by the different generic motifs and stereotypes drawn into the series: the cop show, the buddy relationship, the woman's film, the independent heroine. Moreover, the female 'buddy' relationship can be 'realistically' constructed only by drawing on the sub-cultural codes of women's social intercourse and culture. Inside a soap opera, such codes are taken for granted. Inside a police series, however, they have a range of consequences for both genre and ideology. When female protagonists have to operate in a fictional world organized by male authority and criminality, gender conflict is inevitable. But the series could not evoke such gender conflict with any credibility if it did not acknowledge discourses about sexism already made public by the women's movement in America. Such discourses in their turn become an inevitable source of drama and ideological explanation. The plotting of *Cagney and Lacey* is itself made out of a negotiation, or series of negotiations, around definitions of gender roles and sexuality, definitions of heterosexual relations and female friendships, as well as around the nature of the law and policing.

[· · ·]

RECEPTION AS NEGOTIATION

To the institutional and aesthetic vagaries of production is added the frequent diminution of textual control at the third level of media analysis – reception. The viewing or reading situation affects the meanings and pleasures of a work by introducing into the cultural exchange a range of determinations, potentially resistant or contradictory, arising from the differential social and cultural constitution of readers or viewers – by class, gender, race, age, personal history and so on. This is potentially the most radical moment of negotiation, because the most variable and unpredictable. Moreover we are not dealing with solitary viewers or readers. Ien Ang and Janice Radway, writing respectively on soap opera viewing and romance reading, discuss viewing and reading as a social practice, which differs between groups and historical periods and shapes the meanings which audiences derive from cultural products. This line of argument points beyond textual analysis, to the field of anthropological and ethnographic work with 'real' audiences (Ang, 1985; Radway, 1987).

A frequent aim of this research is to rescue the female sub-cultural activity, resistance and pleasure that may be embedded in popular, mainstream culture. However, to start from the perspective of audiences and their putative pleasures is not without problems of its own. Such an approach is open to charges of relativism – in other words, there is no point to ideological analysis because meaning is so dependent on variable contexts. Or it may be accused of populism – a media product cannot be critiqued if audiences demonstrably enjoy it [see, for example, Williamson, 1986] ... [C]oncern with the pleasures or identifications of actual audiences seems to ignore the long-term task of overthrowing dominant structures, within which resistant or emergent voices struggle on unequal terms. In any case, it is often argued, capitalism cannot ignore the potential market represented by groups emerging into new public self-identity and its processes invariably turn alternative life-styles and identities into commodities, through which they are subtly modified and thereby recuperated for the status quo. Thus the media appropriate images and ideas circulating within the women's movement to supply a necessary aura of novelty and contemporaneity. In this process, bourgeois society adapts to new pressures, while at the same time bringing them under control[7] ...

To characterize cultural exchange between text and reader as one of negotiation, however, does not necessitate a return to an economistic view of language and cultural form as transparent instruments of subjective expression. The concept of negotiation allows space to the play of unconscious processes in cultural forms, but refuses them an undue determination. For if ideologies operate on an unconscious level through the forms of language, the role of the 'other' in these processes is not passively suffered. The everyday working of argument and misunderstanding – in which contesting parties are positioned by, and struggle to resist, the unarticulated, 'unconscious' meanings running through their opponents' words, tones and gestures – demonstrates the extent to which 'otherness' may be negotiated. In this process, such constraints may become available to conscious understanding. A similar struggle can be posited of cultural exchange. Language and cultural forms are sites in which different subjectivities struggle to impose or challenge, to confirm, negotiate or displace, definitions and identities. In this respect, the figure of woman, the look of the camera, the gestures and signs of human interaction, are not given over once and for all to a particular ideology – unconscious or otherwise. They are cultural signs and therefore sites of struggle; struggle between male and female voices, between class voices, ethnic voices, and so on.

NEGOTIATION AND CULTURAL ANALYSIS

The value of 'negotiation', then, as an analytical concept is that it allows space to the subjectivities, identities and pleasures of audiences ... [I]f arguments about the non-identity of self and language, words and meaning, desire and its objects challenge bourgeois notions of the centrality and stability of the ego and the transparency of language, the political consequence is not to abandon the search for identity. As has been frequently noted, social out-groups seeking to identify themselves against dominant represen-tations – the working class, women, blacks, gays – need clearly articulated, recognizable and self-respecting self-images. To adopt a political position is of necessity to assume for the moment a consistent and answerable identity. The object of attack should not be identity as such but its dominant construction as total, non-contradictory and unchanging. We need representations that take account of identities – representations that work with a degree of fluidity and contradiction – and we need to forge different identities – ones that help us to make productive use of the contradictions of our lives. This means entering socio-economic, cultural and linguistic struggle to define and establish them in the media, which function as centres for the production and circulation of identity.

However, knowledge of the instability of identity, its continual process of construction and reconstruction, warns the cultural critic not to look for final and achieved models of representation ... Too frequently, cine-psychoanalytic analyses suggest that to read a mainstream text, to 'submit' to its pleasures, is to take a single position from which it can be read or enjoyed – that of the textual (patriarchal) subject, bound into ideological submission. However, such analysis relies on a complete reading, on tracing the play of narrative processes through to narrative closure, which it is assumed conclusively ties up any ambiguity or enigmatic 'false' trails generated by the processes of the text. Such textual analysis depends on total consumption of the cultural product and merges with the economistic critique of the spectator as passive consumer ... The

199

notion of 'process' suggests flux, discontinuities, digressions, rather than fixed positions. It suggests that a range of positions of identification may exist within any text; and that, within the social situation of their viewing, audiences may shift subject positions as they interact with the text. Such processes ... are a crucial source of cultural and formal regeneration, without which the culture industries would dry up.

[· · ·]

FEMINIST FILM ANALYSIS

A problem for feminist analysis is that it enters critical negotiation from a specific political position, often beginning with the aim of distinguishing 'progressive' from 'reactionary' texts. Yet ... any attempt to fix meaning is illusory. Moreover, the feminist project seeks to open up definitions and identities, not to diminish them. While the attempt to define the ideological status of texts may stimulate debate, such judgements also threaten to foreclose prematurely on critical and textual negotiation. It is necessary, then, for feminist criticism to perform a dual operation. In the first instance, the critic uses textual and contextual analysis to determine the conditions and possibilities of gendered readings. The critic opens up the negotiations of the text in order to animate the contradictions in play. But the feminist critic is also interested in some readings more than others. She enters into the polemics of negotiation, exploiting textual contradiction to put into circulation readings that draw the text into a female and/or feminist orbit. For example, *Coma* (Michael Crichton, 1977) was conceived, publicized and discussed critically as a futuristic thriller exploiting public concern about organ transplants. But the film also makes the central investigative protagonist a woman doctor. This produces a series of textual negotiations which are both ideologically interesting to feminists and a considerable source of the film's generic pleasure. My analysis of the film is partisan to the extent that it focuses on these considerations at the expense of the issues of medical science.

CONDITIONS AND POSSIBILITIES OF TEXTUAL NEGOTIATION

A major issue for the analysis of textual negotiations is how 'textual' and 'social' subjects intersect in a cultural product; how the aesthetic and fictional practices engaged by a particular text meet and negotiate with extra-textual social practices; and, more specifically, how we can distinguish the patriarchal *symbol* of 'woman' from those discourses which speak from and to the historical socio-cultural experience of 'women'.

It is my argument that a considerable source of textual negotiation lies in the use by many mainstream film and television genres of both melodramatic and realist modes (Gledhill, 1987). This dual constitution enables a text to work both on a symbolic, 'imaginary' level, internal to fictional production and on a 'realist' level, referring to the socio-historical world outside the text. Thus two aesthetic projects may co-exist in the same work. Popular culture draws on a melodramatic framework to provide archetypal and atavistic symbolic enactments; for the focus of melodrama is a moral order constructed out of the conflict of . . . polar opposites – a struggle between good and evil, personified in the conflicts of villain, heroine and hero. At the same time such conflicts have power only on the premiss of a recognizable, socially constructed world; the pressure towards realism and contemporaneity means that a popular text must also conform to ever shifting criteria of relevance and credibility.

If, however, melodramatic conflicts still have imaginative resonance in twentieth-century culture, melodrama as a category is rejected for its association with a discarded Victorianism – for its simplistically polarized personifications of good and evil and 'feminized' sentimentalism. In order, therefore, to find credible articulations of such conflict, which will re-solicit the recognition of continually shifting audiences, current melodramatic forms draw on those contemporary discourses which apportion responsibility, guilt and innocence in 'modern' terms – psychoanalysis, for example, marriage guidance, medical ethics, politics, even feminism. The modern popular drama, then, exists as a negotiation between the terms of melodrama's . . . moral frameworks and conflicts and those contemporary discourses which will ground the drama in a recognizable verisimilitude. These conditions of aesthetic existence ensure the continuing renewal of popular forms, the generation of renewed use values that will bring audiences back to the screen.

Gender representation is at the heart of such cultural nego-tiation. For during a period of active feminism . . . gender and sexual definitions themselves become the focus of intense cultural negotiation. Central to such negotiation is the figure of woman, which has long served as a powerful and ambivalent patriarchal symbol, heavily over-determined as expression of the male psyche. But while film theory suggests how narrative, visual and melodram-atic pleasures are organized round this symbol, feminist cultural history also shows that the figure of woman cannot be fixed in her function as patriarchal value. The 'image of woman' has also been a site of gendered discourse, drawn from the specific socio-cultural experiences of women and shared by women, which negotiates a space within, and sometimes resists, patriarchal domination. At the same time new definitions of gender and sexuality circulated by the women's movement contest the value and meaning of the female image, struggling for different, female recognitions and identifications. When popular cultural forms, operating within a melodramatic framework, attempt to engage contemporary discourses about women or draw on women's cultural forms in order to renew their gender verisimilitude and solicit the recognition of a female audience, the negotiation between 'woman' as patriarchal symbol and woman as generator of women's discourse is intensified.

COMA: WOMAN-AS-VICTIM VERSUS INDEPENDENT HEROINE

The generic base of *Coma* is the suspense thriller, a melodramatic subgenre which involves a race against time between 'villain' and 'hero' – the one to conceal and get away with, the other to solve and expose, a criminal plot. In this case, a hospital provides the context for a futuristic crime in which selected patients are deliberately put into and maintained in coma, so that their organs can be auctioned to the highest bidder. The villain, George Harrison, Chief of Surgery (Richard Widmark), has so far got away with turning a public good into something sinister and evil – not simply because of his power and cunning, but because the medical world is shot through with ambition, careerism, politics and cynicism. Read as melodrama, such a world requires a heroic protagonist who can embody medical innocence and thereby confront and unseat the villain through the force of natural ethical conviction. Given the function of 'woman' as symbol of moral value in melodrama, the film supports a female rather than male doctor for this central role. For Dr Susan Wheeler (Geneviève Bujold), helping people and the pursuit of medical truth comes before any careerist or political consideration. In this respect she occupies the typical role of the melodramatic heroine/victim – whose perseverence to the end, against danger and public opinion, leads to public recognition of the truth.[8] Correspondingly, in order to create narrative space for the heroine's activity, the 'good' male doctor, Mark Bellows (Michael Douglas), is cast in a role typical of the Victorian melodramatic hero: supportive but imperceptient and therefore a hindrance rather than a help – until everything is explained and he leaps in for the last-minute rescue.

In terms of textual negotiation, the issue is how this atavistic melodramatic framework will renew itself as the basis of recognizable contemporary conflict. In the first instance, *Coma* successfully regenerates and disguises this format in contemporary and controversial terms by recourse to public debate about the ethics of organ transplants ... However, the deployment of a central female protagonist as upholder of 'truth', while conforming to the demands of melodrama, produces problems on the level of 'authentication'. In generic terms, the film must draw on the 'independent heroine' stereotype, established in screwball and romantic comedies of the 1930s. However, 'independence' is not just a formal attribute, but must be established in relation to current social definitions. For an American movie, made in the late 1970s, and seeking to address a white, middle-class, professional audience, contemporary reference is inevitably supplied by the discourses on sexism and medical practice, made publicly visible by the activity of the American women's movement. At the same time, however, such reference, while giving the film a 'controversial' dimension, makes it also the subject of feminist debate – giving rise to claims and counter-claims as to the film's progressiveness or sexism . . .

MEDICAL PRACTICE AND SEXISM

. . . The film opens in a teasingly ambiguous fashion. The establishment of Dr Susan Wheeler/Geneviève Bujold attempts to suggest a female protagonist who combines aspects of the typically 'feminine' with an equally recognizable 'new' independence. Bujold's physique and performance style is crucial here: petite features and soft voice, combined with an obstinate lower jaw and fractious manner [Pl. 19]. The characterization she offers is of a woman both vulnerable and tough.

Our first encounter with Dr Wheeler is constructed to disturb expectation both of the conventional and the feminist image of woman. She offers an impersonal and mechanistically efficient rundown on the condition of a middle-aged, visibly bewildered and abashed female patient to a group of male students and their tutor . . . Our next encounter with Susan introduces her private life: here the film must engineer a second ambivalence around Susan's heterosexuality, in order to confirm Susan's 'femininity' and at the same time motivate the marginalized role of the hero in the coming drama. For this, the film draws on the estrangement produced by Susan's struggle against sexism, both in her personal and institutional relationships. In the scene which introduces Mark Bellows/Michael Douglas, convention is once more disturbed, as Susan ungraciously resists – in phrases of women's movement discourse – her lover's claim that the burdens of his day entitle him to first call on her attention and the shower . . .

This context of struggle, defined by sexism, is continued the following day when . . . Susan insists that her aerobics class take precedence over [Mark's] hopes for a conciliatory lunch. A further element in the struggle is introduced here, in that she attends an all-woman class with her closest friend, Nancy, with whom she shares a brief exchange about the difficulties of relating to Mark . . .

The needs of contemporaneity and melodrama are drawn together in the following parallel sequences, during which Nancy undergoes the abortion that will put her into a fatal coma, while Susan reassures a child about his imminent kidney transplant . . . For the hospital plot, the choice of abortion as the exemplary coma-inducing operation introduces an ethical and futuristic dimension – medicine's power over life and death – which will found the coming melodrama. However, for feminism abortion is a highly resonant, politicized choice . . . The film gains credibility for its modern 'independent heroine' by touching on controversial issues raised by the women's movement . . . At the same time, the film's melodramatic premises require of the hospital a credibly villainous ambiance and a female sacrificial victim. In this respect, Nancy's abortion . . . serve[s] melodramatic plotting as well as the need for contemporary reference, diverting ultimate sacrifice from the 'independent heroine', while motivating Susan's pursuit of the truth against the advice of her male colleagues and lover. Ideologically, because Susan is melodrama's innocent heroine, the abortion that motivates her heroic action must also be perceived as innocent for the melodrama to work.

THE MELODRAMATIC SCENARIO: MISRECOGNITION AND SEXISM

Nancy's unexplained coma and subsequent death open out on to a melodramatic scenario, which starts with a simple desire on Susan's part to understand what has caused her friend's death . . . Susan's function as a melodramatic heroine is to hang on to, and keep asserting, her demand for truth and its public recognition, despite unknown and intensifying dangers, both physical and moral, which she must undergo alone . . .

Susan's role as independent heroine, however, complicates her melodramatic construction as victim. She is both insightful in her unravelling of the medical mystery and resourceful in dealing with physical danger. Why then does no one believe her? In its search for answers which will be consonant with 'the changing position of women', the film draws women's movement discourses into its plotting. For the Chief of Surgery engineers misrecognition of Susan's questions, insights and intentions by recourse to sexism. Susan is a victim not only because there is a hired assassin roaming the hospital seeking to eliminate her, but because of the hold that gendered (mis)definitions have over what counts as knowledge, reason and emotion, over who has which and in what circumstances. Thus the success of the villain's designs is not simply a matter of personal evil, but is due to the range of male misconceptions, ambitions, desires and fears he can rely on or motivate in his colleagues, including the hero.

[· · ·]

SUSPENSE AND THE INDEPENDENT HEROINE

Blockage and misrecognition are the source of two melodramatic narrative strategies – *suspense* and *pathos* – through which the symbolic and referential roles played by Susan are further negotiated. As *Coma* is a suspense thriller, *suspense* is the stronger of the two . . .

. . .[S]uspense is created out of the conditions of subjectivity. Susan's identity and what she thinks she knows shifts from encounter to encounter. She is, by turns and according to whose perception is operative, female hysteric, cool professional, needy lover and a woman struggling with patriarchy . . .

. . . Because the suspense thriller depends on a play with the giving and withholding of knowledge, potential guilt is distributed between nearly all the film's male protagonists, and the misrecognition to which Susan is subjected and which founds the pathos is shared or perpetrated – we are not sure which till the film's end – by her superiors, colleagues and lover. In the world constructed by *Coma*, men are dangerous; even Mark may be part of the plot against the heroine. We see Susan in battle with a 'male' other who appears in many guises; lover, boss, father, assassin . . . In the swings between normality, security and comfort on the one hand, and futuristic medical crime, nightmare and danger on the other, the melodrama throws up images from the underside of conventional wisdoms about the 'caring professions' and protective paternalism. The lover becomes an assassin, doctors become murderers, the preservation of life a financial racket, and – given the rows of male cadavers in the dissection room, or stored in the deep-freeze – the male body itself an image of death.

Susan's persistent pursuit of knowledge, despite dangers within and without, uncovers what the crime is, and how and why it is being committed. But she makes a near-fatal mistake about the *who*, taking her newly found solution of the plot to the principal villain himself. For the melodrama this is less a mistake than a rendering of her innocence – it is her trust that is abused by a corrupt paternalism . . .

NEGOTIATIONAL PLEASURES

Negotiation between symbolic and referential roles in *Coma* is not only a critical means of generic renewal; it is also a source of aesthetic pleasure. Some of the film's pleasures have been identified as patriarchal constructions, thereby denying the space of negotiation. Most readily critiqued are early moments in the construction of Bujold as heroine – the shower and aerobics episodes – which focus on her body as an object of desire. However, these moments are potentially under negotiation as the film struggles to align woman as melodramatic symbol with the independent heroine's reference to women's struggles in the real world. Moreover, to deny the spectacle of the body is to deny not only male desire for the female body but women's too. In these particular instances this critique also ignores their narrative placement at moments of female resistance. Susan both grabs the shower first and offers us the pleasure of the female body. If the look of the camera at Susan's blurred outline through the shower screen is already and only male, negotiation ends here. However, the camera remains with the disconsolate hero, left outside, on the losing end of this particular argument. To identify with the male look here opens up a position of desire, rejection, frustration and annoyance with the woman. For a woman, however, following the line of the hero's gaze may offer an identification with Susan's resistance, ungraciously claiming rights to the shower and the body's comfort . . . To identify with Susan offers a stake in a female claim to the body and its image, of resistance to male demand or amusement in his frustration . . .

The aerobics class – another instance of Susan's resistance to Mark's demands – similarly puts at issue the gendering and possession of the 'look'. As well as pleasure in looking at women's bodies, the session also suggests a different order of being from heterosexual strife: women together, pleasure in physical being, intimate friendship. These are 'moments' from the subculture of women in the social spaces where they meet and talk, made publicly recognizable through the cultural forms of the women's movement which are increasingly, as here, brought into wider circulation in the mainstream media. The Bujold character is offered as a woman caught in the contradictory demands of independence, of professional practice, of female community, of heterosexual intimacy and, later, dependence. In Susan's continuing arguments with Mark, male and female perspectives and priorities conflict as they each struggle to define the other. It is, however, impossible to say that the image is claimed either for patriarchy or for feminism. The struggle continues because each character continues to desire the other, while not giving up their positions – until perhaps at the film's end. What I am suggesting for the moment is that the intermeshing of symbolizing and referential modes constructs the female image as an object of contest, of negotiation, for the characters and for the audience.

A second pleasure is offered by the suspense structure's negotiations between the melodramatic need for woman as victim and *Coma's* deployment of the 'independent heroine'. Indeed the film cannot work for audiences not prepared to enter into the world of the suspense thriller. It assumes we take pleasure in certain kinds of dramatic enactments, emotional situations, aesthetic frissons – the chase, off-screen threats, suspense, shock cuts. Deploying a woman doctor protagonist regenerates these enactments, by bringing pressure to bear on and renegotiating many of the assumptions involved in them. For instance, the intersection of suspense with the independent heroine raises the question, how will a woman deal with the tough action and physical violence which are the hallmark of the thriller? . . .

THE LAST-MINUTE RESCUE

Such negotiational play is taken to extremes at the end of the film, when identification of the villain leads into the suspenseful coda of the last-minute rescue. For some, this ending represents the putting into patriarchal place of the would-be independent heroine: Susan becomes the ultimate victim, drugged and supine on the operating table, while Mark tracks down the carbon monoxide inlet and calls the police. Analysed in terms of negotiation, however, the attempt to bring to conclusion such a strongly generic film, that also engages discourses running counter to the ideological balance of gender roles in our society, leads to an almost frantic intensification of its textual processes. Susan, drugged, knows that she is herself, under guise of an appendectomy, being taken to the operating theatre where comas are induced, while Mark continues blandly reassuring her. By the time he understands what Susan is telling him, he is trapped into assisting at the operation. It is the female victim who, by pressing his beeper, provides him with the excuse to leave the operating theatre. And it is Susan's earlier investigation which guides him in voice-over to the lethal gas input. Susan may be supine, while Mark breathlessly charges about the hospital engineering plant, but without her earlier calm, logical tracing of pipelines, she could not be saved now. Mark finds nothing for himself, but depends on memories of her recounting her discoveries and a clue which that investigation left behind – her tights abandoned during her climb of the hospital works. All is safe at the end, when Mark, holding Susan's hand, quiets her attempts to continue her self-justification with an acknowledgement of the truth she has discovered: 'I know, baby' – hardly the feminist last word. She is not given the recognition the melodrama owes her, perhaps because it cannot – given its embrace of women's movement discourse – find the terms to produce the image of a loving heterosexual couple and an accepting, united community such as closes traditional melodrama, though it attempts to do so with a close-up of a 'clenched' hand-clasp. Instead, the film closes on the recognition by a public apparatus, the law, of the villain who earlier has been explicitly identified with paternalism and misogyny, and who now puts out the lights of the operating theatre and the film. This ending is perhaps symptomatic of the state of gender conflict in our culture. The culture can acknowledge what we don't want; rejection and contestation produces drama. Imagining the new future in popular images is more difficult.

Clearly the ambivalence of textual negotiation produces a wider address – more serviceable to a capitalist industry – than a more purely feminist text, or counter-text, could. If for many – not necessarily feminist – women, Susan's struggles with sexism at home and at work, and the formal negotiations of the woman-as-victim role, produce echoes of recognition and pleasure, viewers who support sexist attitudes have a route through the film in the humorous exasperation of Mark – 'what you want is a wife, not a lover!' – and can take comfort in the fact that identification of the culprit expels both male and medical villainy: Mark is exonerated. On the other hand, if we accept the role of the mass media in making cultural definitions – and also post-structural theory's exposure of the ideologically 'pure' and full representation, whether feminist or dominant, as an illusory goal – perhaps we may take a more positive stance towards the spaces of negotiation in mainstream production. For into dominant typifications and aesthetic structures are locked both atavistic and utopian desires; archetypal and futuristic motifs; sensibility and reason; melodrama and realism. The productivity of popular culture lies in its capacity to bring these different dimensions into contact and contest; their negotiations contribute to its pleasures. We need to attend to such pleasures if we are to appreciate what holds us back as well as what impels us forward, and if cultural struggle is to take place at the centre of cultural production as well as on the margins. Thus critical readings made under the rubric of negotiation offer not so much resistant readings, made against the grain, as animations of possibilities arising from the negotiations into which the text enters. Such readings work with the pleasures of the text, rather than suppressing or deconstructing them. The pleasures *Coma* offers feminism are in many ways gruesome ... There are of course other pleasures of various ideological complexions in play in the film: of gender role reversal, of the victimization of women, and so on. No doubt these pleasures, too, can be read in their double-sidedness; but the point of a feminist reading is to pull the symbolic enactments of popular fictions into frameworks which interpret the psychic, emotional and social forces at work in women's lives.

Notes

1   For examples of feminist analysis of women's film, melodrama and soap opera, see Modleski (1982a), Ang (1985), LaPlace (1987) and Williams (1987).

2   For an account of Lacanian psychoanalysis, see Burniston *et al.* (1978).

3   The psychoanalytic underpinnings of classic narrative cinema were first signalled in a special issue of *Screen*, vol. 14, no. 1/2 (Spring/Summer 1973), dealing with semiotics and cinema and were developed by Colin McCabe (1974) and by Stephen Heath (1974), also in *Screen*. *Screen* (vol. 16, no. 2) translated Christine Metz's 'The imaginary signifier' in a special issue on psychoanalysis and the cinema.

4   Kuhn's (1982) book, *Women's Pictures*, offers a succinct and critical introduction to feminist cine-psychoanalysis, and Kaplan (1983), *Women and Film*, a distinctive development of it, dealing in particular with the notion of the 'male gaze' in classic narrative cinema. See also Gledhill (1984) for an account of feminist engagement with psychoanalysis.

5   See Antonio Gramsci (1971). For discussion and application of the notion of hegemony to cultural products, see Lovell (1981).

6   See Lovell (1980), pp. 56–63. She defines the 'use-value' of a commodity as 'the ability of the commodity to satisfy some human want', which according to Marx, 'may spring from the stomach or from the fancy'. 'The use-value of a commodity is realized only when it is consumed, or used' (p. 57).

7   For examples of fully developed textual analysis of the 'recuperative' strategies of mainstream cinema, see Steven (1985).

8   This account of melodramatic narrative structure is drawn from Brooks (1976) and Elsaesser (1972).

Article 4.2
SHE'S GOTTA HAVE IT:
THE REPRESENTATION OF BLACK
FEMALE SEXUALITY ON FILM

Felly Nkweto Simmonds

The black man . . . particularly since the Black Movement has been in a position to define the black woman. He is the one who tells her whether or not she is a woman and what it is to be a woman. And therefore, whether he wishes it or not, he determines her destiny as well as his own.

(*M. Wallace, 1979,* Black Macho and the Myth of the Superwoman, *p. 14*)

I think this film should be the antidote to how the black male is perceived in *The Colour Purple* . . . the film's black men . . . are just one-dimensional animals . . . because if you read Alice Walkr, that's the way she feels about black men. She really has problems with them . . . To me, it's justifying everything they say about black people and black men in general that we are animals.

(*S. Lee, 1986,* Film Comment, *p. 48*)

INTRODUCTION

She's Gotta Have It (SGHI) has been hailed as the new face of black American cinema by critics both in America and Europe. Its writer and director, Spike Lee, young, gifted and black, has been dubbed the black Woody Allen and, in 1986, *SGHI* won the Prix de Jeunesse at Cannes. *Film and Filming* concluded its review of the film with the words:

Only time will tell if he is going to make it as a mainstream American film-maker. But if he does, and can do it without compromising, then he won't only become the first important Black film-maker America has produced, but the first of any colour, to tell it as it really is in Black America.

(*Film and Filming, 1987 pp. 42–3*)

Spare Rib, while acknowledging some of the film's more obvious limitations, called it a:

well observed and humorous film ... about a sexually liberated woman ... [which] offers a refreshing alternative to the stereotyped and peripheral roles and concerns which have become the domain of Black people.

(Alexander, 1987 p. 32)

My concern in this article is not primarily with the film narrative, nor with the question of whether the character Nola Darling represents a realistic image of a black American woman. I am more concerned with the messages and definitions that accumulate in the film around black sexuality and, in particular, black female sexuality. The analysis will therefore examine not only the totality of the film, its construction and method, but also the political context in which the film has been made and in which it will be viewed. This will include the examination, not only of who constructs film, and for whom, but also who is excluded from such a framework. Finally, the article examines the construction of women in the narrative and asks whose interests are served by such a construction.

THE FILM

The focus of the film is the sexual life of a young black American woman, Nola Darling. She is economically independent and works as a graphic artist. She has her own apartment in Brooklyn. Nola Darling wishes to remain a sexually free woman. She has three male lovers: Jamie Overstreet, Mars Blackmon (played by Spike Lee) and Greer Childs. There is also a woman, Opal Gilstrap, who would like to have Nola Darling as her lover.

In various ways – its use of black and white photography, direct address to camera and so on – the film departs in form from the conventional feature. This, combined with the fact that it has an all-black cast, gives *SGHI* the air of being a different, and more acceptable film about black experience in America.

Throughout, *SGHI* is a humorous film. An early sequence, for example, shows a series of stereotyped male figures making direct, comical sexual advances to women. The same play on sexual behaviour as a source of humour is returned to throughout the film, especially by Mars Blackmon. The characters use humour to maximum advantage, since each is given the opportunity directly to address the camera, and thus the audience. We are invited to laugh with them.

Nola Darling's three male lovers spend most of the film trying to convince her, and us, why each is best for Nola, and why she should give up her other lovers. In defence of their own positions, they spend much time telling us what they think is wrong with her because she refuses to choose between them. Nola is presented to us as odd because she chooses to have more than one lover. Even her father agrees she is odd.

Most of the time, the lovers' attempts to persuade Nola to give up their rivals are light and playful. Towards the end, however, one of Nola's lovers rapes her, to teach her a lesson.

The majority of the scenes are shot in Nola's apartment, where her lovers come to her. The central feature in her apartment is her bed. It is from here that she addresses the camera at the beginning of the film. In the opening sequence, Nola states what for her is the purpose of the film. She wants to clear her name. Her position, however, has already been undermined by the title of the film, *She's Gotta Have It*, which frames our subsequent perceptions of Nola. The 'it' that she has to have is sex. Lots of it. Spike Lee as the writer and director defines Nola's sexuality, exercising what Andrea Dworkin defines as the male power of naming:

> Men have the power of naming, a great and sublime power. This power of naming enables men to define experience, to articulate boundaries and values, to designate to each thing its realm and qualities, to determine perception itself.
>
> (*Dworkin, 1981, p. 17*)

By naming the film in the way that he has, the writer invites the viewer – even if she is a black woman herself – to view Nola Darling from the outside. The title is value-laden, for the word 'it' carries male-defined sexual meaning:

> Commonly referred to as 'it', sex is defined in action only by what the male does with his penis. Fucking – the penis thrusting – is the magical, hidden meaning of 'it', the reason for sex, the expansive experience through which the male realizes his sexual power.
>
> (*Ibid., p. 23*)

Spike Lee's use of 'it' in his title demonstrates his assent to the notion that all a woman really needs is a man who can fuck her. *SGHI*, then, is not a woman-centred film, and it is a mistake to classify it, as *City Limit*'s Saskia Baron has done, as a 'feminist sex-comedy' (*Baron, 1987, p. 15*).

Spike Lee is quite specific in his reasons for making the film. In the summer of 1985 he had failed to make a different film, *The Messenger*, and, in his own words, 'out of that devastation and disaster . . . out of desperation . . . we came up with the idea to do *SGHI*. I was determined to do another film for as little money as possible' (Lee, 1986, p. 47) He therefore needed to make a film that would guarantee some return. Sex, it seemed, was not a bad place to start. He also wanted to make a film that would appeal to black men, and counter what he saw as the exploitation of black men by black women writers such as Alice Walker and Ntozake Shange:

Within recent years, the quickest way for a black playwright, novelist or poet to get published had been to say that black men are shit. If you say that, then you are definitely going to get media, your book published, your play done . . . that's why they put Alice Walker out there. That's why she won the Pulitzer Prize. That's why Hollywood leaped the pond to seize this book and had it made.

(Lee, 1986 p. 47)

Thirdly, Spike Lee wanted to make a film about black sexuality:

I think a lot of people, particularly black Americans, have been waiting for a film like this for a long time. They never saw black people kissing on the screen or making love.

(Lee, 1987)

Spike Lee, as a black film director, wanted to challenge the notion that white film directors, such as Spielberg, could define the black experience on film. He used down-to-earth Brooklyn humour to make his audience accept the sexual experiences of a black woman and her three male lovers at face value.

The use of an all-black cast is significant. It releases the film from the race issues that surface in any film with a black and white cast. The lack of racial tension in *SGHI*, and the humour of the film, give it a fresh, relaxed air, and help us to swallow what would otherwise be bitter and painful messages about black sexual politics.

Spike Lee alone created the film. He wrote, directed and edited it. It is exactly as he labels it in the humorous credits: a 'Spike Lee Joint'. It is therefore safe to assume that the views and messages of the film are predominantly his. Yet, he admits himself that, as a black man, he can never be a spokesperson for black women: 'To me this film is about various men's views on this type of woman . . . [it is] not meant to represent every single black woman in the United States' (Lee, 1987). As he (alias Mars Blackmon) would have said, it is mighty black of him to acknowledge that he can neither speak for, nor represent, black female experience. And yet, the very expression 'this type of woman' starts to define categories of women. The film explicitly defines one particular woman and classifies her experience as unnatural. The words 'freak', 'nympho' and 'bogus' are all used in the film to define and categorize. Whether or not it was so intended, the film has been received as a film about a sexually promiscuous black woman, and this is what brings the crowds to the cinemas. Spike Lee could not have been unaware of the attraction a black woman on the screen, presented as an erotic being, would have for an American audience. This is why he makes Nola the central figure. It is around Nola, not around male sexuality, and certainly not around black women's views on sexually promiscuous young men, that the film revolves.

To understand the attraction of *SGHI*, we have to move beyond the image of Nola Darling on screen, and examine the combination of black + woman + sex in the context of the politics of gender and race, both in the historical and current political context. These, then, are the questions on which the following section focuses.

THE BLACK WOMAN AND SEXUALITY

Black sexuality has historically been defined by white racism to justify its perception of the inferiority of black people. That perception has always been explicit. Blacks, considered lower on the evolutionary ladder, have always been considered more sexually active than whites. In the United States that notion of black sexuality has its roots in the history of slavery. Black sexuality was used to the economic advantage of white slavers, particularly after the banning of direct importation of enslaved Africans, when the reproduction of an enslaved workforce had to be ensured. The image of the black woman as breeder played a crucial role in the reproduction of the workforce. As T.F. Gossett suggests:

> The market required that a brutal emphasis be placed upon the stud capabilities of the black man and upon the black woman's fertility . . . she was labeled sexually promiscuous because it was important that her womb supply the labor force.
>
> (*Gossett, 1965 p. 48*)

Black women were, therefore, subjected to ruthless exploitation of their sexuality. The rape of black women by white slavers was one of the more acute manifestations of this exploitation. The perception of a black woman's sexuality was damaged for all time, and out of this exploitation grew the image of a black woman as 'not only emotionally callous but physically invulnerable' (Wallace, 1979, p. 138).

Through history, the image of the black female as breeder has remained dominant. Even black resistance movements have failed to address, let alone unseat, this view. In the 1960s the black power movement never challenged dominant images of black female sexuality. Black power was explicitly expressed as the pursuit of black manhood. The manhood that black male activists like Malcolm X proclaimed was black patriarchy, and the black woman had only one place in it – on her back. Even the young George Jackson wrote from his prison cell: 'Black Mama, you're going to have to stop making cowards . . . Black Mama, your overriding concern with the survival of our sons is mistaken if it is a survival at the cost of their manhood' (Jackson, 1971, p. 220). He talked of a manhood that excluded women, for he too had heard Malcolm X, Stokely Carmichael and Eldrige Cleaver all proclaim black manhood as the essence of black power. The black woman was asked not to do anything that would stand in his way and, more importantly, not to threaten his manhood. As Michelle Wallace points out:

> The message of the Black Movement was that I was being watched, on probation as a Black Woman, that any signs of aggressiveness, intelligence or independence would mean I'd be denied even the one role still left open to me – my man's woman ... Black men were threatening me with being deserted, with being alone.
>
> *(Wallace, 1979, p. 138)*

This message produced its own antagonisms, within black sexual politics, between black men and black women. This position remains largely unchanged in the 1980s. It is, however, a position that has started to change as black women, influenced by feminist politics, are trying to define their own reality as black women. A reality that can be uncomfortable for black men and which requires a re-examination of black sexual politics, a task which the black power movement of the 1960s singularly failed to address. Women were defined then as men's possessions and 'as a possession, the black woman was of little use to the revolution except as a performer of drudgery' [Hull *et al.*, 1981, p. 7].

Today, black women such as Alice Walker are trying to redefine black sexual politics, and it is in this context that the film *SGHI* has been made, in an attempt once again to restrict a black woman's ability to assert her independence. Nola Darling, beautiful, independent and black, is the very embodiment of a black woman's threat to black manhood. Spike Lee speaks of his film as being 'an antidote' to Alice Walker, and it is on this basis that he justifies making *SGHI*.

THE CONSTRUCTION OF WOMAN

Nola Darling is constructed as a sensuous body. She is, in fact, what Spike Lee condemns others for creating: a one-dimensional animal. She only seems to be able to make relationships through her sexuality. Her three male lovers, the stable Jamie Overstreet, the narcissistic Greer Childs and the humorous Mars Blackmon, all want her body. Each of them tries to persuade us – and Nola – that he is the best lover for her. The film is structured so that we hear more of the men's voices, reasoning and pleading, than Nola's reasons for being a sexually free woman. The male voice is given more actual time in the film. Even when Nola invites all three men together to her apartment for Thanksgiving, it is the men who are given space to express their feelings.

215

Throughout most of the film, Spike Lee presents Nola to us on the bed. It is from here that she addresses us, both at the start and the end of the film. In her own bed she is at ease. Outside it she feels awkward. It is the only bed in which she makes love. 'I can only do it in my bed,' she tells Jamie. The bed is constructed as an altar, illuminated by scented candles, to which the lovers come to worship the sex goddess herself. We are encouraged to view these acts of worship, not only as outsiders, but as male observers [Pl. 20]. The lovemaking scenes are shown in a context where they are part of the men's stories. We too are thus forced into the position of trying to work out which man is the best for Nola. We are invited to look at Nola's body through male eyes. The voyeuristic, erotic scenes, the lingering camera shots over Nola's naked body, Nola making love and the slowing down of the film to make the moment last longer, are constructed to excite the (male) audience.

Nola seems obsessed with men. She spends most of her time with them. Even when alone in her apartment (which is not very often) she works on a collage of male political figures. She shares a birthday with Malcolm X, to whom the collage is dedicated. The images also include that supreme male patriarch, Jesse Jackson. Even Nola's politics cannot include women. In fact, the only image of a woman is from an advertisement that she is working on. The caption proclaims: 'She is fresh!'.

Nola is curiously isolated, not only from other aspects of her life – her job, her family – but also from genuine female friendships. Her independence excludes female solidarity and female politics. The film does not allow us to establish why she chooses not to have female friendships. What comes through, however, is that she cannot handle female friendships because they threaten her relationships with men. It is not from a very secure position that she defends her independence. Both her position as a woman and her independence are isolated. The film only allows the men to define her relationships with other women.

One relationship is made particularly pathological. 'It was bad enough with Nola and her male friends, but there was one particular female friend' states Jamie Overstreet as the film's way of introducing Opal Gilstrap. We, as the observers (male?), are expected to sympathize with him. What ensues is a male fantasy of what a lesbian relationship is like. Opal is portrayed in the same way as Nola's male lovers, in active pursuit of Nola's body, like a lioness about to pounce on her prey. The very words she uses to introduce herself confirm this image: 'From an early age I knew what my preference was, and I pursued it'. Opal is also portrayed as more sexually threatening to Nola. Nola is more uncomfortable with her and feels that this is a situation that she might not be able to control. This threat is never extended to her male lovers. Even when Jamie rapes her, the threat and danger are minimized by the way the scene is constructed.

All Nola's relationships with other women are underscored with mistrust. Opal threatens her sexuality. Her room-mate, Clorinda Bradford, threatens her independence. The men's other lovers (real and imagined) also threaten her sexual independence. Nola rejects even the one woman who can help her understand her sexuality – the analyst, Dr Jamison, who tries to make Nola realize that whatever her male lovers tell her, her sexuality is not warped. She offers her the potential to recognize that sexuality is only one dimension of her life. 'The beautiful sex organ is between your ears, not between your legs', she advises Nola.

Conveniently for the film, Nola has no sisters (or brothers) and even her mother is absent. This allows us to relate to Nola in isolation from other women and only in relation to men. The film denies Nola women friends, because male language and meaning devalues female friendship and emphasizes sexual relationships with men . . .

It is men who occupy the privileged position in the film, silencing women's voices. Nola is a lonely woman. By constructing Nola Darling as a woman, free and independent, yes, but one who has no need for female friendship and solidarity, the film forces us to view all the other women in terms of the positions they occupy in relation to men. It is this isolation that undermines Nola's professed independence. It also makes her vulnerable to male violence.

THE RAPE

Without the rape scene, the film could have remained what most reviewers have chosen to see it as, an erotic sex comedy. The rape, however, is the climax of the film. It cuts through the comedy and exposes the very meaning of the film, which justifies rape as a legitimate tool that a man can use to punish a woman. Nola Darling is punished for trying to define her own sexuality. She is punished not only because one man, Jamie, rapes her, but because the structure of the scene allows him to punish her for the other men, as he subjects her not only to physical but also to psychological rape. The scene must also have taken considerable time to film. All three main male characters had to be filmed acting out the rape to make the sequence of Jamie's fantasy. In a low-budget film it is a curious decision to make since the scene could have been made much more cheaply if filmed in other ways. Why then does the director make the decision to capture male sexual fantasy so elaborately? It is easier to understand this decision if we examine how rape functions for some men. It is the ultimate tool, not only for female subjugation, but also over women's sexuality. It is used to punish Nola and to excite other men, the spectators. The very positioning of Nola, on her knees, evokes an air of punishment and submission for her, and power and domination for Jamie. The very words he uses – 'Is this how you like it?' – confirms what Andrea Dworkin classifies as one of the most enduring sexual 'truths' in pornography, that 'sexual violence is desired by the normal female, needed by her, suggested and demanded by her' (Dworkin, 1981, p. 166). The preceding scenes in the film illustrate and confirm this 'truth'. Nola Darling, in need of sex, rings up Jamie and asks him to come over. 'I need you,' she says to him. Jamie, angry at having to leave his other lover, is even more angry when he finds out that nothing is wrong and that what she wants is sex. He rapes her, not just to teach her an immediate lesson, but also for all the times he has been trying to get her to reject other men. Throughout the film, he has tried to reason with her, offering her love and protection which she had rejected. Finally, as he rapes her, he says, 'Is this what you want?' and concludes, 'I am trying to "dog" you as best as I can and what bothers me is that I enjoyed it!' What are we meant to understand by this ending? Is it that she has made him rape her? Is it what she has really been asking for? What makes her especially vulnerable at this point is that we know she is sexually promiscuous and likes sex. The underlying message is that a woman who needs so much sex and, as the title suggests 'has gotta have it', deserves whatever she gets from men.

Spike Lee, as a black director, is treading dangerous ground by using his first film to be the teller of this 'truth' about black women's sexuality. He has joined the ranks of men, themselves products of white racist views of a black woman's sexuality, who have contributed to this myth about black women. More important, since it is a black man who articulates this 'truth', his word will be taken more seriously. The black woman is silenced and there is no place for her to express anger, or she will be accused of undermining all black men. She must accept this violence at the hand of a black man in silence and alone. Nola Darling is made to do just this. She cannot even admit that anger, even to herself. When she goes to her old room-mate, she actually says, 'I think I have fucked up this time . . . Jamie hates me.' Why is she not angry with him? She is supposed to be an independent person, in control of her body. Why does she return to Jamie and, in fact, goes to look for him, not to challenge him, but to justify to him what she intends to do next? Towards the end of the film, she tells Jamie that she intends to give up all her lovers and stay celibate. Significantly, she fails to keep her word and Jamie persuades her to return to him without too much trouble. The fact that he is the man who raped her makes no difference to her. When in the final scene of the film she starts by saying 'that celibacy thing didn't last long' it is the final undermining of the character Nola by her creator. Whatever she says subsequently from her bed in the last scene sounds hollow to us as spectators, for we have seen her humiliated and beaten. We are left with a lingering doubt about the strength of her intention to stay an independent woman. Even the final words, 'I am not a one-man woman, there you have it', do not leave much room for a positive future for Nola Darling unless she can define more clearly what she means by being a sexually liberated woman.

CONCLUSION
A CHALLENGE FOR BLACK WOMEN:
REDEFINING FEMALE SEXUALITY FOR OURSELVES

She's Gotta Have It chooses to leave black women silent in a discussion about sexuality, by omission (the absent mother), by isolation (Nola is isolated from Opal and from her room-mate Clorinda) and by over-emphasizing competition for men as one of the most important factors in black female sexuality (the men's other lovers). Our sexuality continues to be defined by others. Spike Lee labels Nola 'that kind of woman' and even more negatively, Opal Gilstrap, the lesbian, as a 'freak'. Yet no one needs to have their sexuality labelled by, or justified to, other people. Any valid discussion needs to hear what black women have to say about themselves. A position has to be found that gets strength from both black politics and women's politics, for we are *black women*. That position has been identified and used by many women – Alice Walker, Bell Hooks, Michelle Wallace and many more – to articulate black women's priorities. It is not only a feminist position but a black feminist position; Alice Walker has specifically named it a 'womanist' position. It is not a comfortable position because it has to identify both gender and race as primary sources of oppression for black women. It means we have to recognize the limitations of both black male politics and white female politics, since we are neither black men nor white women. We have to recognize that although we share common oppressions with both, as black people and as women, we constitute another quite specific group of people as black women. To do this effectively, we need to find and talk to each other. We need to transform both black politics and female politics if we are to define black female sexuality for ourselves. As long as men like Spike Lee continue to define it for us, the emphasis will be on phallic sex. We need a wider definition of sexuality and its relationship to other aspects of our lives. As Molly Haskell says:

> It is a mistake in any event, and an oversimplification that does great injustice to female sensibility to isolate orgasmic

sexual fulfilment as the supreme . . . it excludes a wide range of effective feelings and behaviour.

(Haskell, 1975, p. 340)

We cannot allow sexual promiscuity to be the sole defining factor in our liberation. In fact, it pinpoints the basic contradiction for women in over-emphasis on sex. By treating sex as the supreme, defining quality of the self, we trap ourselves in male-dominated society's moral stance, that classifies sexual freedom as pathological. It traps us into positions where this freedom becomes the ultimate symbol of control and independence, and leaves us vulnerable to society's sanctioned punishments for such behaviour – verbal and physical abuse. It also simplifies and belittles the struggle for women's total liberation – sexual, political and economic: 'if we are to accept the screen version . . . there is only sexual liberation or non-liberation, either/or' (Haskell, 1975, p. 340). However, we have learnt with hindsight that the 1960s sexual revolution only gave men more access to women's bodies, while women continued to be responsible for contraception and taking care of unwanted babies. Women have decided that the sexual revolution has to go beyond sex as defined by men. We also have to recognize that 'the closer women come to claiming their rights and achieving independence in real life, the more loudly and stridently films tell us it's a man's world' (Haskell, 1975, p. 363). To change the meaning of sexual liberation, or any other liberation, women have to challenge the very language of film – the narrative and the meanings. The woman's voice has to be heard, and it is only in the context of female-defined liberation that the control of our bodies and minds can be explored. Film has to get away from evoking only male pleasure in looking at women on film, whatever the message of the film, and especially if the film is trying to establish woman as in control of her body. This is the challenge for black women. In the words of Martina Attille and Maureen Blackwood, we need

> . . . to establish an ongoing forum for discussion around the social and political implications of the fragmentation of black women in film . . . as well as a forum to talk about the kind of images we want to construct ourselves, in an attempt to offer a more complete picture of our lives/politics.
>
> (Attille and Blackwood, 1986, p. 203)

The need for such a forum becomes even more urgent as black film-making begins to grow. If the black woman's voice is silent once more, we cannot ensure that the new image is not just the same old one, but without its racist overtones.

Article 4.3
A WOMAN'S SPACE: WOMEN AND SOAP OPERA
Christine Geraghty

'I'm glad you're with me.'
(*Pam to Sue Ellen*, Dallas)

'Men are lucky. They get women. Women just get men.'
(*Debbie Lancaster*, Crossroads)

'No one knows women, mate. And if you think you do,
you're sadly mistaken.'
(*Den*, EastEnders)

The assumption that soaps are for women is widely held and the
interest shown in soaps by both feminist critics and the more
traditional women's magazines stems from this appeal to a predominantly female audience.[1] This chapter attempts to explore the way
in which the programmes offer particular enjoyment to female
viewers and to point to the ways in which they differ in this respect
from other TV programmes ... [While] the prime time soaps I am
examining have changed in their attempts to attract a less specifically
female-dominated audience, ... it is still possible to map out the
traditional framework which had been established by programmes
like *Coronation Street* and *Crossroads* over many years and to examine
the nature of the appeal of more recent soaps like *Dallas* and *Dynasty*
to women. This is a complex area in which we need to distinguish
between the position offered to the woman viewer by the programmes; the social subject positioned through race, gender and
class; and the responses of individual viewers. As Charlotte
Brunsdon (1981) has argued, a distinction needs to be made 'between
the subject positions that a text constructs, and the social subject
who may or may not take these positions up'.[2] A particular view
on abortion, for instance, may be proposed by a soap but it may
not be adopted by women in the audience. The individual woman
viewer may reject the positions and pleasures offered by soaps, as
David Morley (1986, p. 164) found in interviewing women in South
London who saw themselves as different from other women because
they did not like or watch soaps. Even those who accept the
invitation may do so for different reasons than those implied by
the programmes, taking pleasure in the spectacle of *Dallas* for
instance but refusing its emotional demands. Enjoyment will be

affected by the way in which the woman viewer is herself positioned within the home as mother/wife/daughter, for instance, and her activities outside it ... So in assuming an audience in which women predominate neither programme-maker nor critic can assume that women are a consistent or unchanging category. Nevertheless, the importance of soaps in western culture as one of the litmus tests of the 'feminine' still needs to be considered. What is it about soaps that makes a male viewer assert, 'it's not manly to talk about soaps'?[3]

THE PERSONAL SPHERE

The concerns of soaps have traditionally been based on the commonly perceived split between the public and the personal, between work and leisure, reason and emotion, action and contemplation. This tradition not only offers a set of oppositions but consistently values what are seen to be the more active modes – those of the public sphere – over those whose terrain is the personal and hence deemed to be less effective and more passive ... The ultimate pair of oppositions, on which such differences rest, is masculine and feminine and it is feminists who in different ways have been questioning the naturalness of such dichotomies. In some cases, the task has been to bring the personal into the public sphere and thus to repair the split (the introduction of child care and sexuality issues into trade union activity, for example); in others, it has been to celebrate the specificity of women's pleasures and to re-evaluate them against the grain of male denigration.

In this context, it becomes possible to see why soaps are not merely seen as silly but positively irritating and even unmanly. Soaps overturn the deeply entrenched value structure which is based on the traditional oppositions of masculinity and femininity. Compared with other TV programmes, such as police series or the news, the actions in soaps, while heavily marked, lack physical weight. Bobby's periodic punch-ups with JR hardly compare with the regular confrontations even in *Hill Street Blues* let alone *Miami Vice*. Instead, the essence of soaps is the reflection on personal problems and the emphasis is on talk not on action, on slow development rather than the immediate response, on delayed retribution rather than instant effect. All television relies on the repetition of familiar characters and stories but soaps more than other genres offer a particular type of repetition in which certain emotional situations are tested out through variations in age, character, social milieu and class. Personal relationships are the backbone of soaps. They provide the dramatic moments – marriage, birth, divorce, death – and the more day-to-day exchanges of quarrels, alliances and dilemmas which make up the fabric of the narrative. The very repetition of soap opera plots allows them to offer a paradigm of emotional relationships in which only one element needs to be changed for the effect to be different. Soaps offer a continually shifting kaleidoscope of emotional relationships which allow the audience to test out how particular emotional variations can or should be handled.

On a broad level, soap stories may seem to be repetitive and over-familiar. One set of stories, for example, deals with the relationships between men and women, offering a recognizable scenario of courtship, marriage and separation through quarrels, divorce or death. At the micro level, however, the differences become crucial since the testing-out process depends on the repetition of a number of elements but with one significantly changed. The audience is engaged by the question 'What would happen if . . .?' and given the opportunity to try out a set of variants. *Coronation Street* offers a good example of this process in its handling of the courtship/marriage scenario. It invites the audience to consider a number of pairings as if to test out which is the most satisfying and durable. What happens to a marriage, it asks, if the husband is the local liberal conscience of the community and the wife lively, sociable and previously married to a ne'er-do-well (Ken and Deirdre Barlow) . . . if 'one of the lads' marries a woman who is more mature and sensible than he is (Brian and Gail Tilsley); if 'one of the lads' marries an irresponsible but determined young girl with a mind of her own (Kevin and Sally Webster).[4] The same stories yield a rich vein of plots in which the differences in age, character and status are minutely explored. The same variety can be seen in other general plots – those concerned with parent–child relationships for example or with the parameters of community and friendship. This testing-out process is, of course, carried out within the serial by the commentary of the characters, some of whom achieve an almost chorus-like function, underlining the nuances of the changing situation . . . [The] role of audience discussion about soaps [is crucial] and . . . 'gossip' between episodes serves not only the narrative function of engaging the viewer but also provides the means by which the paradigms provided by the programmes can be tested. Viewing soaps with friends or family is often accompanied by a commentary of informed advice to the characters – 'she shouldn't trust him,' 'if he hadn't said that, it would have been alright,' 'how could she forget?' When the popular press asked their agony aunts whether Deirdre Barlow in *Coronation Street* should remain with her husband or leave him for her lover, they were making concrete (and using one of the sources chosen for support by women themselves) the conversations which were taking place in homes and workplaces all over the country[5] . . .

. . . [I]t is still women who are deemed to carry the responsibility for emotional relationships in our society – who keep the home, look after the children, write the letters or make the phone calls to absent friends, seek advice on how to solve problems, consult magazines on how to respond 'better' to the demands made on them. It is this engagement with the personal which is central to women's involvement with soaps but it is important to be precise about how that involvement works. It is not just that soap operas have a domestic setting. Much of television takes place either in home settings or leisure venues. Nor is it that social problems are made personal or manageable in soaps. It could be argued that many different types of TV programmes, including police series and the news, use the same mode. Nor is it just the fact that soaps feature strong women in major roles though the pleasures of that are certainly substantial. It is the process which is important, the way in which soaps recognize and value the emotional work which women undertake in the personal sphere. Soaps rehearse to their female audience the process of handling personal relationships – the balancing of each individual's needs, the attention paid to every word and gesture so as to understand its emotional meaning, the recognition of competing demands for attention.

This engagement of the audience in a constant rehearsal of emotional dilemmas has been articulated in a number of ways. Two of the most important contributors to the debate, Tania Modleski and Charlotte Brunsdon, have specifically looked at the structures by which soap operas address their female audience in a way which chimes with the construction outside the programmes of women as the emotional centre of the home and family. Modleski, in her influential study of US daytime soaps, argues that 'the formal properties of daytime television . . . accord closely with the rhythms of women's work in the home' (1982a, p. 102). She describes two different kinds of women's work, to be both 'moral and spiritual guides and household drudges' (p. 101) and sees the daytime soaps as permitting and indeed supporting both roles. For the household drudge, the soap operas, with their slow pace, repetition, dislocated and overlapping story lines and their emphasis on the ordinary rather than the glamorous, provide a narrative which can be understood without the concentration required by prime time television. 'Unlike most workers in the labour force,' Modleski suggests, 'the housewife must beware of concentrating her energies too exclusively on any one task – otherwise, the dinner could burn or the baby could crack its skull' (ibid., p. 100). The soap opera form replicates this fragmented and distracted approach and makes it pleasurable. Modleski argues that the housewife's 'duties are split among a variety of domestic and familial tasks, and her television programmes keep her from desiring a focused existence by involving her in the pleasures of a fragmented life' (ibid., p. 101). In doing so, the soap opera 'reflects and cultivates the "proper" psychological disposition of the woman in the home' (ibid., p. 98).

On the moral and emotional front, Modleski ascribes to soaps a similar function of reinforcing the work ascribed to women of nurturing relationships and holding the family together. Again, she adroitly links the formal properties of the genre with its subject matter and proposes that 'soap operas invest exquisite pleasure in the central condition of a woman's life; waiting – whether for her phone to ring, for the baby to take its nap, or for the family to be reunited after the day's final soap opera has left its family still struggling against dissolution' (ibid., p. 88). It is important to Modleski's argument that soaps do not, as they are sometimes accused, present ideal families able to achieve harmony and resolution. Instead, the literally endless tales with their variety of insoluble dilemmas offer reassurance that the woman viewer is not alone in her inability to reconcile and hold together the family unit. What is demanded by the soaps is the tolerance of the good mother who is able to see that there is no right answer and who is understanding and sympathetic to 'both the sinner and the victim' (ibid., p. 93). 'Soap operas convince women that their highest goal is to see their families united and happy, while consoling them for their inability to realize this ideal and bring about familial harmony' (ibid., p. 92). And indeed the goal is unrealizable in more ways than one since Modleski points out that the soap opera does not offer a mirror image of the viewer's own family but 'a kind of *extended* family, the direct opposite of her own isolated nuclear family' (ibid., p. 108). What the housewife experiences is an isolation rooted in her real experience for which soap operas offer a form of consolation.

[· · ·]

Loving with a Vengeance deals with US daytime soaps which in their scheduling and format are different from the soaps discussed in [the book from which this article is taken]. Nevertheless, there is much here which rings true, particularly in Modleski's account of the way in which soaps encourage the viewer to take into account a number of viewpoints on the same story and provide, over a period of time, explanations (or perhaps excuses) for ill-advised or even wrong actions. It is sometime unclear, however, whether Modleski is analysing the position of the good mother which soaps encourage their viewers to adopt or is describing the housewife/viewer as a social subject, formed by her own social and economic circumstances. This is, as we have seen, a difficult distinction but in either case the female viewer seems curiously passive and isolated. Despite her argument that soap opera is in the vanguard of all popular narrative art and her appeal to feminists to build on rather than reject the fantasy of community offered by soaps, Modleski's viewer comes close to the model offered by less sympathetic critics. She is distracted, lonely, unable to make judgements or to discriminate; her anger is internalized, directed at her own scarcely expressed desire for greater power. She waits for the non-existent family to return so that she can perform her role as ideal mother but is denied even 'this extremely flattering illusion of her power' (ibid., p. 92) by the genre's insistence on the insolubility of the problems it is the mother's task to solve. Almost despite herself, Modleski seems to share the doubts which feminists and others have expressed that soap operas, like other forms of women's fiction, serve only to keep women in their place. The depressing nature of this place seems to come about not merely because of the low economic status of 'the housewife' but also because her very pleasure in soap opera is based on a masochistic acknowledgement of her powerlessness and the uselessness of her own skills.

Other feminist critics have taken a more positive approach which, while not doubting the oppression imposed on women in and outside the home, has argued that it is important not to underrate women's role in the personal sphere. Charlotte Brunsdon, in her article on *Crossroads*, examines the notion of a gendered audience in an attempt to come to terms with the pleasures offered to the female viewer. Brunsdon argues that the scheduling of the programme in the late afternoon/early evening and the advertising and spin-offs surrounding it – interview material, cookbooks, knitting patterns – are addressed to the feminine consumer, the viewer who is constructed in her gender-based role of wife, mother, housewife, and that these extratextual factors 'suggest that women are the target audience for *Crossroads*' (1981, p. 34). Drawing attention to the distinction made between public and personal life, Brunsdon defines 'the ideological problematic of soap opera' as that of 'personal life in its everyday realization through personal relationships' and argues that 'it is within this realm of the domestic, the personal, the private, that feminine competence is recognized' (ibid., p. 34). She acknowledges the incoherence of *Crossroads* in terms of its spatial and temporal organization, its narrative interruptions and repetitions and its dramatic irresolution but argues that its coherence, for those (feminine) viewers who know how to read it, is articulated through the moral and ideological frameworks which the programme explores; '*Crossroads* is in the business not of creating narrative excitement, suspense, delay and resolution, but of constructing moral consensus about the conduct of personal life' (ibid., p. 35). The competent viewer needs to be skilled in three areas – that of generic knowledge (familiarity with soap opera as a genre), that of serial-specific knowledge (knowledge of narrative and character in *Crossroads*) and that of cultural knowledge of the way in which one's personal life is (or should be) conducted. It is this last competence to which Brunsdon draws particular attention for it is the basis of her argument that *Crossroads* as a text (rather than through its extratextual factors) implies a gendered audience; 'it is the culturally constructed skills of femininity – sensitivity, perception, intuition and the necessary privileging of the concerns of personal life – which are both called on and practised in the genre' (ibid., p. 36). *Crossroads* requires skilled readers to make it pleasurable and the competencies necessary for that process are the very ones which are valued in the soaps themselves.

The process of testing out emotional situations which I described earlier clearly owes much to Brunsdon's notion of competence in personal life. Brunsdon does not take up Modleski's suggestion of the viewer as the 'ideal mother' possessed of endless tolerance, although she agrees that *Crossroads*, like the US daytime soaps, offers a 'range of different opinions and understandings' and 'a consistent holding off of *denouement* and knowledge' (ibid., p. 35). Nevertheless, the article does imply that the viewer is called on to make judgements about characters even while recognizing that events next week might change the basis of that judgement once more. Brunsdon emphasizes the importance of stories which centre on lies and deceit when the audience knows more than the characters involved and 'can see clearly what and who is "right"' (ibid., pp. 35–6). She adds that the question determining a soap opera narrative is not 'What will happen next?' but 'What kind of person is this?' – a question which both acknowledges the importance of the individual character and implies a moral/social judgement about that character. I emphasize this, perhaps against the grain of other parts of the article, because it seems to me that it is this acknowledgement of the capacity to judge which enables Brunsdon, unlike Modleski, to value the process she describes. The judgements may not be firm or final; certainly the moral framework is not fixed – two similar actions (the breaking off of an engagement, for example) may require different decisions and the viewer may indeed decide to postpone judgement until a more suitable time, in itself an active decision rather than a passive one. But until we replace the model of the tolerant viewer accepting everything with that of Brunsdon's competent viewer weighing the emotional dilemmas put before her, we are always going to underestimate the position offered to the female viewer of soap operas.

The question of judgement is the more important because it is tied in with one of the most consistent pleasures offered to women by soaps – that of being on our side. Again this is not just a question of a domestic setting or an emphasis on a particular type of story, both of which could apply to situation comedies without the same kind of effect. It is more that soap operas, not always, not continuously, but at key points, offer an understanding from the woman's viewpoint that affects the judgements that the viewer is invited to make. This sense of being 'down among the women' is crucial to the pleasures of recognition which soaps offer women – a slightly secretive, sometimes unspoken understanding developed through the endless analysis of emotional dilemmas which Modleski and Brunsdon describe. This effect is achieved in a number of ways but essential to it is the soap's basic premise that women are understandable and rational, a premise that flies in the face of much TV drama.

Because soaps are rooted in the personal sphere, the actions of the women in them become explicable and often, though not always, correct. In itself this runs counter to much television drama in which women's association with the personal is deemed to be a disadvantage because it clouds their judgement. In soaps, competence in the personal sphere is valued and women are able to handle difficult decisions well because of it . . .

. . . [C]onsistent recognition is given to the emotional situations which women are deemed to share. At its most obvious, this sense of a common feeling marks major events such as birth, marriage, the death of a child or the development of a romance. When such a moment occurs for a female character, the other women are seen to understand it even while they might not welcome it. Thus, Pam in *Dallas* was sympathetic to Miss Ellie's fears when the 'new' Jock Ewing appeared and encouraged her to talk about her sexual and emotional feelings . . . Similarly, Deirdre Barlow in *Coronation Street* supported her step-daughter's decision to have an abortion and argued with Mike Baldwin that he should be looking to his wife Susan's needs rather than his own desire to have a child. Even when the women are at odds with each other they share a common sense of what is at stake. When Nicola in *Crossroads* tried to explain to her long-lost daughter why she had given her away at birth, Tracy was angry and upset. But she and Nicola were able to conduct a dialogue from which the men were excluded either because of ignorance or from a desire to rush to hasty judgement . . .

. . . Traditionally, soaps value this sense of female solidarity and have worked on the assumption that women have common attitudes and problems, are 'sisters under the skin' as the respectable Annie Walker once acknowledged to the rather less respectable Elsie Tanner in *Coronation Street*. Women in soaps define themselves as different from men and pride themselves on the difference, a position which the programmes endorse. 'Despite everything,' says Angie in *EastEnders*, 'I'm still glad I'm not a man.' 'You've got to remember they're like children,' Lou Beale tells her granddaughter Michelle in the same programme, voicing another common feeling shared by women characters in soaps. In addition, the women frequently console each other at the end of a romance, as Bet Lynch did with Jenny in *Coronation Street*, with a variation on 'There's not one of them worth it.' This expression of an underlying solidarity based on a shared position persists even when the women appear to be on opposite sides . . .

A further factor in establishing a shared female viewpoint is indeed the range of emotional relationships in which the women characters are involved. It is too often assumed that soaps emphasize male–female relationships at the expense of others. In fact, because the central husband–wife relationship is such hard work for the women characters, they need to be supported by other friendships which are more reliably sustaining. The relationship between mother and daughter, for instance, is central to many soaps, providing an irresistible combination of female solidarity and family intimacy. *Brookside* has movingly presented the love and impatience, passion and reticence, which marked Sheila Grant's engagements with her daughter, Karen, while in *EastEnders* Pauline and Michelle seem to be fighting their way through an oppressive relationship to one which acknowledges what they share. In both *Dallas* and *Dynasty*, Miss Ellie and Krystle offer patient affection and support to a variety of surrogate daughters and receive from them a reciprocal understanding. Equally important, perhaps, is the emphasis placed on female friendship . . . The programmes continually show women talking to each other, sometimes in moments of high drama, sometimes in a routine way as if it were an everyday occurrence that needed no emphasis. When *EastEnders* devoted a whole episode to Ethel and Dot, reminiscing, quarrelling, spilling secrets, making tea, it was unusual only in that it was drawing specific attention to the fact that female conversation is the backbone of the traditional soap.

The centrality of women in soaps has the effect of making them the norm by which the programmes are understood. They are not peripheral to the stories; they are not mysterious, enigmatic or threatening as they so often are in thrillers or crime stories. They handle the complex web of relationships which make up a soap opera with a care and intensity which makes the men seem clumsy and uncomprehending. Even when the women are wrong they are transparent and understandable, an unusual characteristic for women in a culture in which they are deemed most desirable when they are most opaque and enigmatic. This is not to say that soaps present women more realistically as feminists sometimes demand of representations of women. Neither Sue Ellen nor Angie Watts would be deemed particularly realistic representations and in some ways their characters are presented as particularly and conventionally feminine. Married to men who emotionally abuse them, apparently irrational and sometimes devious, volatile, brittle and soft-hearted, Angie and Sue Ellen, it could be argued, represent gender stereotyping of a high degree. Yet it is also important that the audience is not only consistently presented with information and comment on what these women do but is also continually implicated in their actions by being drawn into their logic. The baffled assertion of commonsense in the face of women's emotions still permeates much of TV fiction as it did mainstream film genres like film noir. In soaps, such a lack of understanding is impossible for the male as well as the female viewer because we have been led through every step of the woman character's way.

This shift is accompanied by a move away from the male figure as the agent of the action. TV fiction took over from mainstream film the narrative structure in which 'the man's role' is 'the active one of forwarding the story, making things happen' (Mulvey, 1975, p. 12). Even in *Hill Street Blues*, for example, the stories are initiated by men making things happen or by women having things happen to them. But in soap operas, not only do women take action but the audience is led through that process with them. In *EastEnders*, for instance, the traditional triangle of Den manoeuvring between his wife Angie and his mistress Jan might have given the impression that it was the man who was, if not in control of the situation, at least the active agent. Nothing could be further from the truth because the audience was aware not merely of Angie's plans to fight for her marriage through her lies about her illness, for instance, but also of Jan's determination to push for her own needs. Only the man remained baffled, frustrated and incoherent in the centre of an emotional maelstrom. What is important here is not so much the outcome of the action (Angie's strategems failed in this instance) but the fact that the audience was prevented from sharing Den's bafflement. Whatever judgements are made about the women's behaviour, the reasons for their actions are laid out in detail to the audience and are meticulously worked over as the triangle of relationships shifts . . .

It would be overstating the case to assert that, in prime time soaps, the position of men as narratively active, women as passive, is reversed. The action of male characters is crucial and often provokes, as in the examples above, the action taken by the women. Nevertheless, the position of engagement with the women characters which the audience is encouraged to adopt is based on the transparency of the women's behaviour; our understanding is invoked by the process of going through the narrative with them. Surprisingly often in soaps men are caught in a position of baffled impotence. 'Women,' they say to each [other] with resigned incomprehension 'who can understand them?' If this were said in a thriller or a police series, the male characters would be speaking from a position of ignorance, allowing the female viewer the satisfaction of knowing more and understanding more than these enraged and frustrated men. This is one of the central pleasures offered to women by soaps, a recognition based not so much on a realistic representation of women's everyday lives but on what it feels like to have so much invested in the personal sphere, while men are unable to live up to or even be aware of its demands – Den and JR, the apparently powerful, caught in close-up at the end of the episode, floored once again by their inability to keep up with the women's ability to operate in the personal sphere.

THE PUBLIC SPHERE

While soaps are traditionally associated with the domestic and the personal, account needs to be taken of the way in which they handle issues raised in the public sphere of work and politics. Soaps, in fact, range more widely in their settings than many other TV genres and the distinction between public and personal space is crucial to their structure. Clearly, the US prime time soaps have made a feature of business and the wheelings and dealings of the oil industry, in particular, figure strongly in their stories. In the British soaps, business is likely to be more down-market – a small motel, a one-man clothing factory or building firm. Most characteristically, British soaps feature a variety of small businesses – cafés, pubs, shops – in which one or two individuals make a precarious living and contribute to the life of the community.

Issues concerned with business and politics do get raised in soaps. In the US programmes, battles over the control of the business are central to the plot and the audience is given a plethora of detail of shares, interest rates, loans and takeover battles . . . In both *Dallas* and *Dynasty*, some reference is made to the fate of the workers who rely on the decisions of the Ewings and the Carringtons to keep them in employment . . . In British soaps, too, although on a different scale, business and work have provided stories and settings. Mike Baldwin's clothing factory in *Coronation Street* was over the years the scene of a number of strikes and industrial disputes . . . *Brookside* has shown its characters at work and used a variety of work locations as a base for stories about pay, health and safety, youth employment and the experiences of women at work. *EastEnders* has emphasized the financial pressures on small businesses such as the building firm, the café and the hairdressing salon.

Nevertheless, it would be misleading to pretend that soaps deal with work and business relations in any depth or with particular political insight. A common complaint is that by concentrating on the personal sphere of marriage, family and friendship, soaps ignore or glamorize the public sphere of work, unemployment, trade unions and business. 'Ugly social issues are *reduced* to a level of private, family melodrama,' wrote one left-wing critic of the way in which *Coronation Street* was tackling unemployment (Gardner, n.d.). In itself, this comment seems to exemplify the split between the personal and the public as if ugly social issues do not have deeply felt personal consequences . . . Nevertheless, it is important to look at the process by which soaps colonize the public sphere and claim it for the personal and to assess the consequences of this approach.

The settings of the programmes provide a useful starting point for an analysis of soaps' handling of the public sphere. As we have seen, soaps do feature locations which are connected with business and work, whether it be an office, a factory floor or a corner shop. In British soaps, these locations are used not because of a particular concern with the work done there but because in general they provide a public place in which people can meet and the gossip which fuels the narrative can be exchanged. The launderette, the pub, the office provide public spaces for comment on what has occurred in the private space of the characters' homes. This function helps to determine the nature of the public locations which can be deployed in the programmes.

Soaps find it virtually impossible to use work settings which deny or suppress the emotional needs of individual characters or locations in which conversations cannot take place. Here, the advantage of a corner shop or café is clear over a large factory or office where noise levels of machinery or typewriters are high and routine work prevents conversation. Even in the *Coronation Street* factory, the women characters are more likely to be featured at break times or when they are clocking in or out. Public space also needs to be widely accessible, free-for-all areas where no one can be prevented from joining in a conversation even when their views are not wanted. Characters like Hilda Ogden in *Coronation Street* and Dot Cotton in *EastEnders* are marked by their ability to lurk in public places, popping up every now and then to provide a pointed comment. Such behaviour is generally accepted until it intrudes into the personal space of the characters' homes at which point it becomes unwarranted. Mary Smith, for instance, in *EastEnders*, had to endure or try to avoid the chorus of comments on her failure to care properly for her child when they were made in the pub or launderette, but she was able literally to eject those who ventured into her room and the audience was invited to share her outrage at the anonymous letter which was slipped under her door in a clear breach of the public/personal boundary.

The distinction between public and personal space and the use of the public space as the accepted site for commentary applies even in *Dallas* and *Dynasty* where the distinction between the home and the office is much more blurred; Alexis frequently conducts her business affairs from her home and the Ewing wives regularly visit their husband's offices. Even here though, the establishment of personal space in the home is still important. The office, the club and the hotel are locations where information is exchanged, deals are done and actions subjected to public scrutiny. The home provides a retreat from that world and the entry of business characters into Southfork or the Carrington mansion is always represented as something of a violation. In *Dallas*, it is Miss Ellie in particular who preserves and values that distinction. She it is who complains when business is brought to the dinner table or when JR's colleagues interrupt the family's evening. Conscious of her own role in the family, only a serious crisis takes Miss Ellie to the Ewing office . . .

It is clear, then, that while the public and private locations in soaps are well defined, they are not watertight and that the most dramatic moments occur when behaviour appropriate to the private space, be it a love affair or a marital quarrel, occurs in public. This is reinforced by soaps' strong tendency both to bring personal relationships into the work arena and to deal with relationships at work as if they were personal. Soaps are of course marked by the intermingling of family and business relationships. Innumerable husbands and wives work in businesses together, whether it be a pub like Angie and Den in *EastEnders* or an oil company like Pam and Bobby Ewing. Children work with their parents in *Dynasty* and *Crossroads*, siblings do business together in *EastEnders* as in *Dallas*. In *Coronation Street*, Rita Fairclough managed the shop her husband owned and in *Brookside* even Annabelle Collins has had her husband help out on occasions with her small catering business. Even when no family relationship is involved, business relationships are based on friendship rather than on the usual employer/employee arrangements. Rita Fairclough is Mavis's boss but she is also one of her closest friends; Terry and Pat in *Brookside* ran their removal business on the basis of being mates and the business collapsed when their friendship faltered. In their case, as in so many others, relations in the public sphere depended on relations in the private and we need to note the way in which soaps tend to provide characters with emotional reasons for business decisions and link business success with personal motivation. Thus, Alexis's pursuit of Blake Carrington makes her a powerful and successful businesswoman; her success, however, is not based on good business reasons but is rooted in her hatred of her ex-husband and her desire to wreak emotional vengeance . . . In *EastEnders*, the decline of the Queen Vic and Den's financial crisis was entirely dependent on the crisis in his marriage and then the success of all the other small businesses in soaps hinges on the relationships between those running them.

Within the businesses themselves, working relationships are conceived of as an extension of family feelings or friendships. Individual bosses run their institutions in a way that expresses their personal characteristics whether it be JR's devious deals over shares in the company or Mike Baldwin's semi-ironic demands for better productivity. The relationship between boss and worker is frequently presented even in the US prime time soaps as one of direct communication and personal knowledge. With his empire crumbling, Blake Carrington is seen to win over the workers on the potential gas field which might save him through personal charisma . . . Even more common in British soaps, however, are the situations where there is no evident boss, where employer/employee relationships are blurred or non-existent. This is clearly the case in husband and wife partnerships where the business relationship operates as an extension of the marriage. But it is also true of other businesses where the emotional ties are less obvious. The launderette in *EastEnders*, for instance, has no visible owner so the working relationships hinge on the friendships (or otherwise) of the women who work in it – Pauline Fowler, Dot Cotton, Mary Smith – as they try to juggle the demands of this work with their other commitments . . .

The question of external power relations in prime time soaps is nearly always, then, either ignored altogether or translated into personal relationships. This may seem obvious and a further confirmation of the split between the personal and the public sphere and soap's inability to deal with the latter. Certainly, the soaps make little attempt to express the abstractions of modern capitalism and the alienation of workers from their labour in ways acceptable to their left-wing critics. Alvarado, Gutch and Wollen (1987, p. 163) are right to argue that *Dallas* and *Dynasty* 'mystify the actual process of multinational wealth creation'. Yet this treatment of the public sphere of work, business and employment as if it were the private sphere repays further examination rather than being dismissed as unrealistic or exploitative. By adopting this strategy, soaps are attempting to explain the incomprehensible – the economy and business – through what is known and understood by their audience – the intricate wheeling and dealing in the personal sphere. The programmes play to the competencies of their audiences as Brunsdon has described them and encourages them to use those competencies in judging the public as well as the private sphere. Clearly such an approach cannot deal with the impersonality, the repetition and exploitation of work which may be the direct experience of many viewers, nor with the way in which effective decisions are institutional rather than individual. Nevertheless, the strategy has more positive consequences than may at first be realized.

For a start, it ensures that women, because of their capabilities in the personal sphere, are also seen to be capable in the business world in a way that is still unusual in TV fiction. Meg Richardson could run the Crossroads Motel successfully precisely because she knew the personal foibles and circumstances of all her staff . . . In businesses which are based on marriage, the woman is likely to be seen as a more equal partner at work because the soap gives her (at least) equal weight in the marriage. Thus, Kathy Beale in *EastEnders* succeeds in her wish to run her own market stall because she refuses to defer to her husband in her marriage. The soaps' need for independent women who can be involved in stories about personal relationships thus has the side-effect of presenting an unusually large number of economically self-sufficient women who are out at work ... Even in the factory set-up, in *Coronation Street*, the women asserted themselves with humour and vigour in their working environment because their leading representatives, Ivy and Vera, were characters in their own right outside the factory. In an important sense, then, women are more active at work in soaps than they are in other kinds of TV drama, precisely because the working situation is presented as an extension of the personal – if work is marriage by other means, soaps seem to say, then women are more likely to be engaged with it.

As well as giving a larger than usual role to women in this way, the soap strategy also invites us to make judgements about work and business outside their own terms. Such an approach cannot begin to tackle the complexities of modern capitalism but it can mean that values other than those of business itself are brought to bear on such issues. The judgements are never, of course, unambiguous ... From its beginning ... *Dallas*'s central tension was between JR's gleeful relish of capitalism and Pam's sustained critique of the way in which her brother-in-law regularly put family relationships at risk by his pursuit of more money and power. On an obviously smaller scale, the factory in *Coronation Street* was the site for a number of stories in which the interests and values of Mike Baldwin and the women workers were seen to be different. Traditionally, in dealing with stories of strikes, disputes and difficulties at work, *Coronation Street* heads for the middle ground – yes, Mike Baldwin did push them too hard – yes, the women were wrong not to see that industrial unrest puts jobs at risk.[6] Nevertheless, there have been moments when Ivy Tilsley's clear statement as a union steward of her opposition to Baldwin has provided him with an effective challenge and it could be argued that many of the scenes in the factory represented Baldwin's failure to turn the women who work for him into the quiet, compliant, hard-working automatons he would like. While stories such as these refer to the importance of increased productivity and higher profits, what they show is that the values of the personal sphere – whether it be Ivy upset over a family drama or Vera's urge to disrupt everything with a laugh – consistently take precedence.

Soaps, then, can take up public issues around work and power but they do so by bringing such matters onto their own terrain. The only soap which has recently tried to extend its own space has been *Brookside*, which gave itself the task not only of taking up social and political questions but of changing the context in which they are normally dealt with in soaps. This led *Brookside* literally into the public terrain – scenes took place not merely in the home or the street but in the factory, the picket line, the trade union meeting, the working men's club. In early episodes, Bobby Grant led a strike at the factory and the scenes on the picket line made it quite clear that this was no small family business in the back streets but a large firm with international connections where decisions were made by directors who certainly had no personal relationships with their employees . . .

It has to be said, however, that *Brookside* has found it difficult to move into the public sphere. The factory setting appeared intermittently even before Bobby's disappearance from the programme and none of the characters now has Bobby's fierce commitment to principle outside the family . . . Heather Haversham's work as an accountant did involve her visiting large businesses and enabled *Brookside* to take up . . . issues around sex discrimination and sexual harassment, but her romance with the millionaire Tom and her marriage to heroin addict Nick were in the end more central to the stories built around her . . . [T]he changes in *Brookside* have led it to concentrate more on the Close and the people in it so that public issues around work are brought back into the home. It has proved more difficult than might have been expected to break out of the 'natural' soap terrain of the family and the community.

Notes

1   Although soaps are still derided by television critics and by many in the TV industry, the work of Brunsdon, Ang and Modleski, among others, has, rather ironically, given soaps a higher status in the academic world of cultural studies and media theory.

2   For a more extensive discussion of work in this area, see Kuhn (1984).

3   Male viewer in ITV's *Watching Us, Watching You*, 6 April 1987.

4   For a fuller discussion of the way narrative variants are organized in soaps, see Geraghty (1981) and Paterson and Stewart (1981), both in Dyer (ed.) *Coronation Street*.

5   *The Sun* (28 January 1983), for instance, ran contrasting articles on Deirdre's dilemma – 'Yes, why not have a fling?' by the Women's Editor Wendy Henry, and 'No, don't fall for Mike's charms' by the Problems Columnist, Deirdre Sanders.

6   For an analysis of how a strike story was handled in *Coronation Street*, see Paterson and Stewart (1981).

Colour Plate 1
Maud Sulter, Alice Walker as
Thalia, One of The Muses,
from Zabat series 1989.
Reproduced by courtesy of the
artist

Colour Plate 2
Alexis Hunter, *Struggle
Between Ambition and Desire,*
1983, oil on canvas,
171 x 190 cm.
Collection of the artist

Colour Plate 3
Christine Merton, *Tree Tomb*, 1988, wood and earth, 305 cm. high. Private collection.
Photograph by courtesy of the Women Artists Slide Library

Colour Plate 4

Harriet Powers, *The First Bible Quilt*,
c. 1886, pieced cotton with cotton
and metallic thread.
National Museum of American
History, Smithsonian Institution,
Washington, DC

Colour Plate 5

Harriet Powers, *Pictorial Quilt*, 1895–1898, 175 x 267 cm., pieced and appliquéd cotton and printed cotton embroidered with plain and metallic yarns. Bequest of Maxim Karolik, courtesy, Museum of Fine Arts, Boston

Colour Plate 6
Betye Saar, *The Liberation of Aunt Jemima*,
1972, mixed media, 30 cm. high.
University Art Museum/Pacific Film
Archive, University of California at
Berkeley. Purchased with funds from the
National Endowment for the Arts

Colour Plate 7
Frida Kahlo, self portrait with
thorn necklace and humming
bird, 1940, oil on canvas,
63.5 x 49.5 cm.
Harry Ransom Humanities
Research Center,
University of Texas at Austin.
Reproduction authorized by
Instituto Nacional de Bellas
Artes y Literatura

Colour Plate 8
Frida Kahlo, *My Nurse and I* (Mi nana y yo), 1937, oil on sheet metal,
30 x 37 cm. Collection of Fundacion Dolores Olmedo.
Photograph: Archivio CENIDIAP-INBA. Reproduction authorized by Instituto
Nacional de Bellas Artes y Literatura

Colour Plate 9
Frida Kahlo, *Roots*, 1943, oil on sheet metal, 30.5 x 49.9 cm.
Collection of Fundacion Dolores Olmedo.
Photograph: Archivio CENIDIAP-INBA. Reproduction authorized by Instituto
Nacional de Bellas Artes y Literatura

Colour Plate 10

Suzanne Valadon, self portrait with the necklace in maturity, 1931, oil on canvas. Private collection. Photograph by courtesy of Gilbert Petrides

Colour Plate 11
Detail from *Women's Rights Quilt*,
c. 1850, cotton, 177 x 176 cm.
From *Heart and Hands: the influence of
women and quilts on American Society* by
Pat Ferrero, Elaine Hedges and Julie
Silber. Quilt from the collection of Dr and
Mrs John Livingston and Mrs Elizabeth
Livingston Jaeger

Colour Plate 12 *(below)*
Florence Claxton, *Women's Work:
A Medley*, 1861, oil on panel,
51 x 61 cm. Private collection.
Photograph: A.C. Cooper

Colour Plate 13

Janie Terreno, Suffragette Handkerchief, worked in Holloway, showing Mrs Pankhurst and Christabel, 1912, silk, 51 x 45.5 cm. Museum of London

Colour Plate 14
Sally Ranson (1870–1956) of New Seaham, border patterned cotton quilt, *c.* 1890.
The North of England Open Air Museum, Beamish

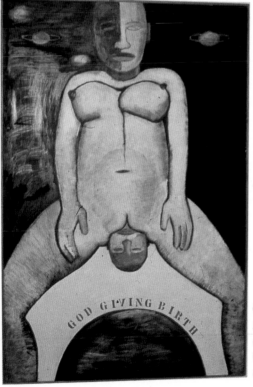

Colour Plate 15
Sylvia Sleigh, *Turkish Bath*, portraying the art critics Paul Rosano, Laurence Alloway, Scott Burton, John Perrault and Carter Ratcliff, 1973, oil on canvas, 193 x 259 cm. Reproduced by courtesy of the artist

Colour Plate 16
Monica Sjoo, *God Giving Birth*, 1969, oil on hardboard, 183 x 122 cm. Collection of the artist. Photograph by courtesy of Women Artists Slide Library

Colour Plate 17

Lesley Sanderson, *Time for Change*, 1989, oil on canvas, 240 x 350 cm.
Reproduced by courtesy of the artist

Colour Plate 18

Sonia Boyce, *Talking Presence*, 1988,
mixed media on photographic paper,
165 x 120 cm.

Reproduced by courtesy of the artist

Colour Plate 19
Lyn Malcolm, *Why Have We So Few Great Women Artists?*, mixed media installation, 1982, life-size. Detail: inset top right. Courtesy of the artist. Photograph by Paul Guest

The text visible within the artwork reads:

WE WILL BE
WHO WE WANT
WHERE WE WANT
WITH WHOM WE WANT
IN THE WAY THAT WE WANT
WHEN WE WANT
AND THE TIME IS NOW
AND THE PLACE IS HERE
+ THERE AND
HERE + THERE
+ HERE
NOW NOW
NOW NOW
NOW NOW
HERE   HERE   HERE NOW
HERE IS NOW + NOW HERE
NOW NOW

Colour Plate 20
Lubaina Himid, *We Will Be*, 1983, hardboard cutout, larger than life-size.
Installation photograph by courtesy of the artist

Article 4.4
CONFESSION TIME: WOMEN AND GAME SHOWS

Frances Bonner

Television programmes are gendered in several ways. It may be that, as in the soap operas, they depict a world in which women and their concerns are central and the private and emotional are more important than the public and economic (see Article 4.1); or it may be that only men are shown and they are engaged in what is marked as an overwhelmingly male activity, like motor racing. Beverle Houston even argues that the institution and apparatus of television itself creates a position for its viewing subjects that is effectively feminine (Houston, 1984, p. 189). In part this is done through a gendered analogy in which television is domestic and subordinate (i.e. feminine) to the critically more powerful (and thus 'masculine') cinema.

My concern here is with game shows, including quizzes, which *are* gendered, but not absolutely. They may be regarded as women's programmes on the basis of their daytime screening or because they are 'trivial' (and men's programmes are regarded as 'serious'), yet many game shows are prime time, high-rating programmes with 'serious' questions. It is more accurate to consider game shows as variously gendered by both time of screening and by the type of game. The designation of weekday daytime television as women's television is more a matter of convenience than a reflection of the available audience, since undoubtedly there are more shiftworkers, retired and unemployed people, women and men, than classic full-time housewives. None the less, programmers and schedulers perceive the audience as female and address them as such.

Fashions in the popularity of particular types of game shows vary, although intellectual quizzes never seem to go completely out of favour. Apart from knowledge quizzes, which range from the intellectual (*Mastermind*) to the populist (*Sale of the Century*) (Tulloch, 1976, p. 3), there are word games (*Catchphrase*), games of physical skill (*The Generation Game*), public opinion (*Family Fortunes*), consumer knowledge (*The Price is Right*) and those, like *Blind Date* or *Love Connection*, on which I will concentrate later and which provide what John Docker has called 'space for the drama of gender' (Docker, 1988, p. 90). There are also hybrids of all these. Most of the examples in this article will be from British programmes screened during 1990 and 1991. Occasionally, I shall refer to shows from Australia or the USA.

Even ignoring for the moment the dating games, the programme types have gender implications. Gendering of the programme type may largely be a matter of the gender of the contestants, but the questions themselves may also be important. The intellectual shows tend to have a higher proportion of male contestants, but it is the similarity of the questions to those valued in traditional education (dates of battles, names of inventors) that makes them appear serious and thus more male in the eyes of schedulers, critics and reviewers. Programmes valuing consumer information, like *The Price is Right*, described by John Fiske as validating 'women's knowledge' (Fiske, 1990), feature more women and elicit greater displays of emotion. The absence of consumer game shows from British television at the time of writing, and attempts by programmes to achieve something of an internal gender balance (*Fifteen-to-One* has appealed on air for more women contestants), has reduced the evidence of this particular gendering.

'Public opinion' programmes ask contestants questions to which the 'correct' answer is the one closest to that given by the majority of a sample polled. What is being rewarded is one's knowledge of other people. This is another type of knowledge held to be more characteristic of women than men, but the design of most of the British shows of this kind (which often require male/female couples) may obscure this – except that the couple or group may need to negotiate on air to agree on their answer. Such negotiation frequently reveals the gender politics of the situation as well as the gender of the 'right' guesser.

Inasmuch as they centre around the domestic and the private, the majority of game shows are still directed more to women than to men. They usually highlight the family and emotional relationships, even when the questions deal with 'serious' matters. Contestants, women or men, appear from their private lives and only rarely, as with *Busman's Holiday*, from their public worlds.

One of the most basic dichotomies applied to game shows is that between the ordinary and the extraordinary. Except for the sub-category of the celebrity game show, contestants are 'ordinary' people. There may also be instances in which their ordinariness is offset against the extraordinariness of some other (usually professional) figure on the programme. None the less, the emphasis in all but the celebrity programmes, as well as here, is on 'ordinariness'.

Most television channels have at least one game show every day, most requiring a regular supply of 'ordinary' contestants – usually between four and eight, but up to fifteen is possible. This means that a probable minimum of a hundred and twenty different people a week are 'consumed' by game shows in the UK. (Regional variations and satellite television mean the number is almost certainly higher.) It thus seems reasonable to state that game shows provide a, possibly even the, major site for ordinary people to represent themselves on television.[1] I use the term 'represent themselves' to cover the situation that occurs when ordinary women and men are being represented neither by actors nor through documentaries or news programmes – situations in which they are framed as in some manner exceptional or exemplary. Game shows are one of the principal places on television where we can see ordinary people showing, unreflexively, what 'being a woman' or 'being a man' means. My concern here will be with aspects of this and not with the elements of competition and prize winning which may be thought to be the principal subjects of game shows.

The extraordinary people include the winner (who began as ordinary and is rarely accorded more than a moment of extraordinariness), perhaps an 'expert' and celebrities. Celebrities are people with a high recognition index. Those who appear on game shows are usually already media people, such as actors, newspaper editors or 'page three girls', even other television programme hosts. With the exception of some of those with sporting fame, they are rarely extraordinary in themselves; rather, they are extraordinary in how they are treated. They are given more time, for example. 'Celebrity' need be no more than excessive televisual presence.

The other extraordinary people associated with game shows are the hosts, who differ from celebrities only in being given even more time and, of course, on-camera control. They are nearly always male; the only female hosts I have noted are Cilla Black, Sarah Kennedy and Angela Rippon. While they do not come from the stand-up comedian circuit – the principal source for their male counterparts – all three have attained television-certified celebrity status.

Although they are becoming rarer, the main place for 'extraordinary' women is as hostesses – assistants extraordinary only in their physical appearance. They act as living set decorations, perhaps escorting contestants from place to place or manipulating props. Their function is to be displayed by the host in order to be looked at by the audience; they are objects to be consumed visually. Their absence from the most 'serious' knowledge quizzes, and from the even more 'male' sports quizzes, at first appears odd. Surely they are not provided for the female audience. Analysis, however, reveals that they accompany the older ex-comedian hosts, providing an initial trigger for their sexual repartee, before it is transferred to the contestants.

Even though solo television viewing is becoming increasingly common, watching game shows is, whenever possible, a group activity involving group mediation or negotiation of the programme.

Talking back to the television or competing in tandem with the contestants is characteristic. For both studio and home audience, participation is the norm. This acts to close the gap between viewer and contestant; they are geographically, occupationally, familially, 'just like us' and we may urge on the woman or the fellow Scot. People may choose not to watch game shows, refusing this identification, or refusing to agree with the particular definitions of what being ordinary is, especially when it seems to involve the sexist humiliation of women.

The omnivorousness of television and its requirements for more and more contestants does, however, lead to some variation from the conventional and traditional. The large number of available contestants who were unemployed was presumably an important factor in making unemployment appear 'ordinary', rather than something that could only be confessed to with a degree of shame. The most omnivorous of all game shows, *Fifteen-to-One*, with its requirement of nearly a thousand 'ordinary' people every thirteen weeks, regularly has an unemployed contestant (as well as at least one retired one) on each programme.

THE FAMILY ON THE GAME SHOW

Garry Whannel says of the public opinion shows that they 'reward normality and penalise deviance' (Whannel, 1990, p. 105). Frequently, as with *Family Fortunes* (revealingly called *Family Feud* in Australia and the USA), it is not the non-deviant individual who plays this game but the 'ordinary' family group. The shared abilities of the family to approximate (or guess at) typicality is what the show values.

Public opinion programmes of this kind are merely being a little more overt about what seems to be a dominant concern of the majority of game shows – the family. Frequently, it is a formal part of the design of the programme – either in the title, or in requirements for contestants. Contestants on all but a few shows are immediately identified by name, occupation and home town. (Visual identification adds gender and usually some idea of ethnicity and age.) On prime time programmes this is generally followed by a short chat with the host at which the most probable question to be asked is about the family. Questions are predicated on particularly strongly gender-stereotyped views of family roles, and those who admit to variations are frequently made the butt of the host's jokes. A substantial part of being ordinary involves being a member of an unremarkable family.

Individual contestants are usually asked their marital status by the host and then whether they have children (or if old enough, grandchildren). Single parents are rare and single people not usually asked further questions except along the lines of whether there is 'someone special'. Unmarried women, especially if they are attractive, may be asked why they are not married and the host may call for audience offers. This is part of the considerable encouragement to proceed along the family trajectory: childless couples will be asked about their intentions to have 'little ones', parents of married children asked if there are grandchildren on the way, and those who admit to there being someone special, whether they have yet 'named the date'. The clichés of family life are eagerly deployed. On a substantial number of programmes, a funny domestic incident is referred to – disproportionately often it is about the honeymoon, even in cases where grandchildren have been acknowledged.

This chat, and the topics on which it focuses, can be viewed as micro-confessions in which contestants reveal and place themselves. The emphasis on the honeymoon, which can seem most bizarre when it is neither recent nor related to the ostensible topic of the show, can be more readily comprehended if the programmes are seen to be part of the discourse of sexuality.

In Michel Foucault's study of the role of the confession as a highly valued technique for producing truth in western societies, he points to its pervasiveness 'in justice, medicine, education, family relationships and love relations, in the most ordinary affairs of everyday life' (Foucault, 1980, p. 59). He emphasizes how confession from the religious to the psychoanalytic, has privileged sex (ibid., p. 61). It is certainly possible to add the televisual to Foucault's list of confessional sites; only think of the endless chat shows. Seeing game shows as similar to chat shows in this way, but differing by focusing on *un*remarkable people, also helps to clarify the role of the host:

> The confession is a ritual of discourse in which the speaking subject is also the subject of the statement; it is also a ritual that unfolds within a power relationship, for one does not confess without the presence (or virtual presence) of a partner who is not simply the interlocutor but the authority who requires the confession, prescribes and appreciates it and intervenes in order to judge, punish, forgive, console and reconcile.
>
> (*Ibid., pp. 61–2*)

The host fulfils a surprisingly large number of these roles and one of the principal devices used to do this – the joke at the contestant's expense – may serve to indicate why hosts so often are stand-up comics.

Despite the pressure for family roles to conform to gender stereotypes, the scarceness of the traditional nuclear family has led, not exactly to an overt recognition of this fact, but to a recognition that (other than in gender terms) membership of a family may be quite diverse. As well as wife and husband or parent and child or (legal) multiples of either, families may now consist of cousins, aunts, in-laws and neighbours. I recall a competing 'couple' of a woman and her sister-in-law's husband. Some things remain unrepresented however – they are still too far from what can be accepted as an ordinary family. I recall no instance where ex-spouses are acknowledged as family members; and families are insistently heterosexual phenomena – even stereotypically perceived homo-sexual characteristics are permitted only of the (male) hosts.

SEX AND ROMANCE ON THE GAME SHOW

Programmes designed to display female/male compatibility were very popular on British, US and Australian television during the 1980s and are continuing to be so into the early 1990s. They are rarely simply about (hetero-)sex, since at their centre lie the dual factors of sexual attraction and cross-gender understanding. They are concerned, though certainly not overtly, with the process of *becoming* a family. There are two main ways in which the programmes are structured. The currently more popular programmes are dating games where women and men with no previous knowledge of one another choose a partner on the basis of a limited number of pieces of information. The other type usually involves (recently) established couples separately being asked questions about the other. The questions are ostensibly designed to reveal how well they know each other, but the programme's entertainment depends on misun-derstanding being revealed. The popular dating game programmes incorporate a modified element of this latter. It is this that enables Michael Pollen to say of the American versions that 'both *The New Newlywed Game* and *Love Connection* take it for granted that men and women are fundamentally incompatible' (Pollen, 1986, p. 69). To a certain extent this seems defensible, but like John Fiske's belief that dating games have the most progressive gender politics of all game shows (Fiske, 1990, p. 139), it is a very partial view of these programmes.

The miscomprehending couples programmes, like *Mr and Mrs* or, in the USA, *The New Newlywed Game*, are usually variants on the public opinion shows. One spouse is placed in an isolation booth while the other is asked questions about the isolated one's likely responses. The isolated spouse then reveals her or his actual responses, and mutual knowledge (often overtly identified as compatibility) is rewarded. The assumed pleasure of the audience, cued by the one in the studio, is, however, much more in the revelation of incompatibility and miscomprehension. There is a tension apparent between the 'ideal' of mutual understanding and the 'realistic/cynical knowledge' of persistent misunderstanding between women and men. Formally, the programme is structured by compatibility, but the anticipated pleasure in misunderstanding is, like the women's movement discourse in *Coma* (see Article 4.1), part of the contemporaneity refreshing an otherwise jaded genre.

The other type of programme is exemplified in the UK by *Blind Date*, in Australia by *Perfect Match* (now incorporating some aspects of the British programme, including its name) and in the USA by *The Dating Game* itself and *Love Connection. Perfect Match* and *Love Connection* had or have alternatives to the dater's choice – either chosen by computer or the studio audience. Both the programmes thus celebrate the concept of the ideal match while recognizing that the individual often gets it wrong. This is absent from the British *Blind Date* and from the revamped Australian one.

Fiske's description of *Perfect Match* and my observations of some episodes of the Australian *Blind Date* and of *Love Connection* reveal a world of contestants that are in most ways more homogenous than is the case for the British programme. Until the autumn 1991 series, the Australian and American programmes, which included people in their thirties and forties, were more diverse in age terms than the British, which allowed only two age groups – roughly twenty to thirty and over sixty. The British *Blind Date* is, however, less racially restrictive, and allows a wider range of definitions of what is attractive than the others, though admittedly a very high degree of 'personality' is required to compensate for much variation from the conventional. This is because the British programme has elements of the talent show as the 'datees' display their desirability. The most notable variant was called Claudia (contestants never have surnames). She was a very talented black woman, but her size – she was substantially overweight – was used as a cue for audience laughter. None the less, she was chosen as a date, and she was able to use the programme to develop her singing career. At least two end-of-season compilations have updated viewers on Claudia's progress and screened videos of her songs.

Truly central to the programme are the politics of gender and the display of the regulation of sexuality. In identifying *Perfect Match* as the game show with the most progressive sexual politics, Fiske highlighted the way in which it allows women sexual equality with men. Women may overtly choose a date, implicitly initiating sexual relations, and enjoy their sexuality without tying it to the respectability of marriage (Fiske, 1989, p. 141; 1990, p. 139).

The former is also characteristic of *Blind Date* but the latter seems less applicable. Sexuality alone is only allowed a short period of sway on *Blind Date* before being subjugated to the 'proper' familial trajectory through the introduction of romance and its purpose, marriage. (The absence of contestants in the thirty-to-sixty age range is probably because this is the age when 'ordinary' people should *already* be in families.) Much of the subjugation is achieved through the figure of Cilla Black. Whatever Cilla's talents, and as a populist presenter they are exceptional, the projection of her own sexuality deliberately is not one of them.

There is little competition between sex and romance during the programme, rather there is segregation. Whenever Cilla is prominent, sexuality is not. During the introductory chat, the closure of the choosing sequence and the reporting back, romance, individuality or non-sexual performance dominates; in those sections of the programme when the choice is being made and Cilla is absent, sexuality (rather uncomfortably) emerges. The women in particular seem ill at ease in their attempts at sexual innuendo. It is not that they seem uninterested in sex, and certainly sexual innocence is unacceptable, but they do not appear to know how to represent themselves as ordinarily sexual beings. This is not a mode of televised self-representation that it would appear 'ordinary' British women are happy with. The forced sexual repartee over, there seems general relief in returning to the Cilla-mediated world of romance. Choosers may look speculatively at lost opportunities (frequently sexually more highly charged than those selected – for the urge to choose the unthreatening seems overwhelming), but they greet the removal of any residual sexual charge avidly.

The choosing segment is followed by a reporting back from the previous week's couples. This confession of what happened on the date is complexly structured and mediated. The woman and the man are filmed separately talking about the date immediately after it has taken place. On the programme they are shown watching these comments in the studio together and with Cilla. They thus confess to each other as well as to Cilla and the studio and home audiences. There is then a joint elaboration as Cilla probes to discover what went right and wrong and how she can direct matters to the desired conclusion. There is no doubt that this conclusion is marriage. While the British *Blind Date* may emphasize this more, marriage, like the confessional report back, is a general feature of dating programmes.

The pressure on dating programmes to produce married couples is strong. The Australian sequence not only has a marriage, it has a child, but until the end of 1991, the British *Blind Date* had neither. The push to create a *Blind Date* marriage had been undisguised. The desire to be married sanctions going on blind dates; it is the end to which sexuality is represented as driving. The edition of *Blind Date* transmitted on 25 January 1991, included a report back from a couple who had been sent catwalk modelling in Paris. As the finale they had worn wedding dress. This was the focus of Cilla's interrogation. Having established that the pair, Rachel and

Chris, enjoyed themselves and that Chris 'felt good' standing as the model groom, Cilla exclaims delightedly as Rachel kisses him.

Cilla: Ooh, look at that. Well I think you make a super couple and if anything does develop, you know, let us know 'cos we'll get that wedding frock for you.

Rachel: Would you really?

Cilla: Oh yes. But you've got to marry *him*, though. Only on condition you marry him, because you do make a super, very attractive, couple. Don't they ladies and gentlemen? [audience agrees]

(*Transcription from ITV* Blind Date, *transmitted on 25 January 1991*)

The move from the (in the UK, chaperoned) date to the marriage which will license the weekly displays of sexuality is shown to be through romance. The story of the dates (usually weekends of varied activities) is at heart one that dwells on any moment of romance – a hug, a solicitous gesture and quintessentially 'the kiss'. This, as romantic gesture not sexual foreplay, is the focus of Cilla's inquisition. In the clichés that dominate game show investigations of private life, this is the moment in which the earth either did or did not move.

Sexuality is a principal focus only for those dates that fail. Perhaps it is for this reason that these are the televisually 'good' ones and the ones most enjoyed by the younger segments of the audience. The question never asked on the programme, but foremost as far as viewers are concerned (was there or was there not any sexual activity on the date?) is at least presumed answered here. Yet even the unsuccessful daters are subjected to Cilla's attempts at reconciliation as she desperately attempts to find some chink in the dislike from which she can push towards a romantic possibility.

Even within the romance-determined and marriage-bound discussions, however, there is some small basis for the application of Fiske's assertions about women's sexual equality. It is very common for men to say that they do not like making the first move, though less common for the British women away from the selection process to say that they do. Both women and men express dissatisfaction with aspects of the others' behaviour and appearance. It does not, however, seem possible for a woman to express a lack of interest in marriage. In the reporting back referred to earlier, Rachel said how she had enjoyed modelling a wedding dress, though she had never expected to wear one. Cilla instantly anchored this as diffidence ('you're putting yourself down there'), not disinclination.

I am not arguing that game shows provide some direct role models for being an ordinary person, nor for how to behave on blind dates, but rather that in providing a major site for so many non-celebrities to represent themselves, they become part of the material drawn on in the construction of our 'imagined communities' (Anderson, 1983). Even if the people on the programme may not be 'just like us', they may be just like the people we imagine to be around the corner. On game shows, these communities are more strongly identified by family than by occupation, and the regulation of sexuality can be seen as an important part of the construction of the idea of the family. *Blind Date* displays the pressures to contain sexuality in marriage as well as the commonness of the desires for sex and romance and the ordinariness of the failures of compatibility. We viewers say to the screen 'you should have known better', or 'they make a nice couple'. For the confessions are not just to Cilla Black or to another host, they are also to us. We the audience are the virtual presence Foucault referred to, we too monitor the confessions and simultaneously confess to our watching companions as we talk about what we would have done in such a situation.

Note

1 Apart from news and documentary programmes, the other sites are in difficult-to-categorize forms of light entertainment-cum-instructive programmes such as *Antiques Roadshow*, or gardening programmes, family reunion and variety magazines such as *Surprise, Surprise* and *That's Life*, and the 'real-life' comedies of humiliation.

5
PORNOGRAPHY AND REPRESENTATION

Pornography is a form of cultural representation, influenced by gender and power relations, which also represents (or takes as its subject) the relationship between gender and power. Pornography – in all its many forms – may in fact be one of the most visible forms of cultural representation which feminists can still address in terms of the slogan 'the personal is political'. That is, arguments about pornography are influenced by personal politics as well as by more broadly political concerns related to issues of censorship and legislation. Pornography is a form in which (mainly) women's bodies are represented, and about which women's (and men's) views have been presented and re-presented in a number of different ways.

The subject of pornography is impossible to approach in what might be regarded as an 'objective' academic way because it is closely linked to personal politics as they intersect with gender, race and power. The subject of pornography is therefore a 'problem' subject, related to the active subject positions of its (mostly male) makers and the passive object positions into which women (as images to be gazed at, or visually consumed) are cast. The difficulty of separating the personal from the political in the pornography debate becomes evident in most critical writing on the subject. Academic writing on pornography tends to shift into the first person, thereby implicating the author in the 'us and them' dynamic which charges the debate. Personal writing about pornography tends to include wider political references as well as personal considerations. The objective and subjective positions of the authors, or speakers, tend to blur when pornography is the subject of discussion. And discussion tends, almost always, to become debate.

Much of the debate about pornography in the feminist community has centred on two issues: the pornography/censorship debate and the distinction between pornography and erotica. Related issues are the relationship between feminism and the anti-pornography campaign, and the problems associated with mass-market production and distribution of pornographic images. One aspect of the pornography debate nearly always involves the others; yet it was necessary to attempt to narrow the scope of discussion in the selection of articles here. These articles focus on the pornography/censorship debate, though other issues are inevitably raised within them.

At the heart of the pornography debate is the question of censorship (or the imposition of limits on freedom of expression), and at the heart of the debate about censorship is the question of oppression: does pornography oppress women more or less than the imposition of limits on the freedom of the press and freedom of speech would do? This is a version of the chicken and egg dilemma: the question being whether pornography is, indeed, at the root of women's marginalized position in society, or only one manifestation of it. The relationship between pornography and violence against women has initiated considerable debate as well. Again, the key issues involved are gender and power. Race is another important factor: in much pornography (especially man-made film and video), objects of the male gaze are women of colour. Thus, racial prejudice can be seen to interact with the dynamic of gender and power which is central to the pornography problem.

In thinking about, writing for and editing this part of the book, a multiplicity of views were expressed and debated by the editorial working group in the process of negotiating a shared perspective, or set of perspectives. Several individuals held *multiple* positions, or found that a given position on the pornography problem begged questions which led towards other positions. This seems to be fairly symptomatic of the pornography problem itself: it involves engagement at both the personal and political levels, thereby allowing for conflicts of interest between personal beliefs and feelings, political perspectives, and legal or ethical principles. In choosing articles for inclusion in an academic reader of this kind, the negotiating process is further complicated by the objective (or aim) of being fairly representative of opposing views. It is impossible to include 'all' voices; yet selectivity requires choice and choice involves positioning or prioritizing of some views over others.

In one short part of this book, it is not possible to represent all sides and shades of argument in the pornography debate. Indeed, it may not be possible to do so in any amount of space. What this selection of articles offers is a range of perspectives which may be compared and contrasted, argued with and used as points of departure for fuller and more personalized debate. Five articles have been included.

The first article is by Avis Lewallen, writing on the mainstream 'pulp novel' *Lace*, with reference to Ann Barr Snitow's argument that Harlequin romance novels appeal at a certain level as 'mass market pornography' (Snitow, 1983). Lewallen's piece opens out the pornography debate by moving from discussion of man-made pornographic imagery to discussion of a novel by a woman which may also be seen to function as a kind of 'pornography'.

The second article is from Suzanne Kappeler's *The Pornography of Representation*. Kappeler argues that a limited focus on pornographic images themselves is not enough: that the process of production and distribution of those images must also be considered, since those processes are infused with gendered power struggles, and the images produced represent not only women's sexual organs but also the very real 'sale' of the woman – her body, her integrity – as a commodity in the public sphere.

The third article, from Patricia Hill Collins's 'Pornography and Black Women's Bodies', examines the links between race, power and gender in the pornography problem, and does so in academic form: through the voice of a black woman academic (Collins) who refers to another black woman creative writer and critic, Alice Walker.

The fourth article, by Gillian Rodgerson and Linda Semple, presents the views of Feminists Against Censorship. The authors argue that in choosing to censor pornography, feminists may thereby (intentionally or unintentionally) censor women's sexual experience and women's self-expression as well.

The last article provides a short overview of some of the different feminist approaches to the pornography/censorship debate. It ends with reference to Andrea Dworkin's and Catherine McKinnon's radical feminist position: one which is not discussed at length in the previous articles. This piece is intended to contextualize the other articles and to contrast key issues in the pornography debate with larger issues of cultural representation and gender as themes relevant to the book as a whole.

All the contributors to this section occupy very different spaces, or positions, on the continuum which links the various issues involved in the pornography debate. The first four articles included here were written for publication in other texts and should not be seen as 'replies' to each other. Rather, each must be evaluated on its own terms. The section as a whole is equal to no more, but no less, than the sum of its parts.

Lizbeth Goodman

Article 5.1
LACE: PORNOGRAPHY FOR WOMEN?

Avis Lewallen

Current blockbuster novels such as *Lace, A Woman of Substance, Hollywood Wives, Mistral's Daughter,* and a host of others which flood on to the market daily, it seems, comprise a genre variously described as 'shopping and fucking', or more euphemistically 'hoarding and humping'. Jane McLoughlin in a *Guardian* article describes them as '. . . second generation Mills & Boon, a kind of consumer's guide to the best beds in town' (5 June 1984). Well, they are 'second generation' romance novels in terms of moving the heroine from adolescent sexual expectation into adult sexual exploration, but they are not really a development of Mills and Boon in terms of style, structure or content. What they do have in common with the 'bodice ripper' sub-genre of romantic fiction, however, is an increase in sexual explicitness.[1]

I would like to look at the way female sexuality is being expressed in blockbusters in the context of current ideas about the representation of women. Is it possible to see within these often politically conservative, capitalist tracts, full of the ideologies of individualism, self-reliance and material wealth, a more liberated expression of female sexuality? If these texts can be classified as 'soft porn', what position is being offered to the female reader? Do they merely contribute to the further objectification of women within our misogynist society, inculcating male power, or do they offer a form of representation that facilitates the female gaze?

ROMANCE, SEX AND LIBERATION

Romance fiction has been described as a form of sexual foreplay that can function simultaneously as an expression and a containment of female desire, the fulfilment of which we imagine takes place in the nuptials promised at the close of the story. Ann Barr Snitow (1983, pp. 266–74), developing an argument put forward by Peter Parisi, contends that these romances are essentially pornographic. They return the reader to a position of 'pre-marital hopefulness', where the morality of a strictly secular world is upheld, but where sexual desire is acknowledged and articulated so that every look and touch becomes an expression of thinly disguised sexual sublimation. The heroine wants sex, but only within the marriage bed, and thus these romances illustrate women's lack of social and psychological freedom to express their sexuality. Sexuality must be anchored to an emotional attachment that will ensure, through marriage, material security. Given the double standard applied to male and female sexuality, and the material exigencies connected to the possibility of motherhood, it could be said, however, that this fiction reflects what is in fact a social reality for women as much as it promotes it.

In the early days of the Women's Liberation Movement there was the so-called 'sexual revolution', whereby women claimed the right to the same sexual freedoms as men. A number of novels in the late sixties and early seventies, such as Erica Jong's *Fear of Flying* (1974), were associated with this claim because of their explicit treatment of women's sexuality. In *The Sadeian Woman* Angela Carter claims that the essence of de Sade's philosophy, which she, with qualifications, endorses, is that women can 'fuck their way into history' (1979, p. 27). But other feminists were arguing that there were dangers for women in a 'sexual revolution' within the structure of patriarchy, which could well make them vulnerable to even greater exploitation than the old sexual double standard; that women were simply more available to be fucked by men, rather than assuming an active sexuality based on their own desires.[2]

In more recent years women writers concerned with feminist issues have tended to move away from what could loosely be described as 'social realism' (what was written in the late sixties and early seventies) to more experimental work, such as that of Kathy Acker (1984). Or they have undertaken more general analyses of sexuality and gender, particularly in the genre of science fiction, as in the work of writers like Marge Piercy (1978) or Joanna Russ (1985a). As heterosexual sex became problematic, a subject of debate, and even division, within the women's movement, so its representation in literature seemed equally problematic. Explicit representation of sex tended to be reserved for lesbian sex, which had every reason to welcome a space for public expression. The (hetero)sexual explicitness of 'bodice rippers' and blockbusters, as an effect of feminism, seems more in the nature of a hangover from the days of sexual liberation: feminist writers have become much more circumspect about the liberating possibilities of overt sexual expression in fictional form.

COMMODITY SEX

Fiction by, about and for women that shows women capable of achieving social, economic and sexual satisfaction is now extremely popular. From a feminist perspective these are contradictory texts: on the one hand, the capitalist ideology that pervades them largely ignores, on a manifest level at least, issues of class, race and gender; but on the other, they problematize and prioritize active sexuality for women in ways that might be regarded as a challenge to the exclusively male gaze of patriarchal structures.

[· · ·]

SEXBUSTERS

Lace, by Shirley Conran, is a useful example of the genre's treatment of sexuality, since a substantial part of its narrative subject matter is directly concerned with sexuality and related topics: from loss of virginity, sexual desire, sexual satisfaction and frigidity, to prostitution, rape, adultery, lesbianism and transvestism. It also deals with pornography, alcoholism, plastic surgery, childbirth, miscarriage and abortion, and makes more than passing reference to 'women's lib'. In fact, *Lace* is almost a mini-encyclopaedia of female sexuality. The novel opens with a detailed description of an abortion and closes neatly with a description of a birth. The ideological implications of this structure are readily apparent.

[· · ·]

WHATEVER TURNS US ON?

If romance fiction, through its denial of direct sexual expression, is a form of sexual sublimation, what position is offered the reader of blockbusters, where female sexuality is so prominently and explicitly placed? As Rosalind Coward (1986) argues, images are defined by their context: images of women, naked or otherwise, are not inherently pornographic, but only become so when contextualized by a 'regime of representations' – i.e. a particular set of codes with conventionally accepted meanings – defining them as such for the viewer. The way images in pornographic magazines are pinned down by captions and text presenting them explicitly for male titillation suggests that visual images alone – even of naked women in obviously provocative poses – cannot be relied upon to be unambiguous.

Whether or not *Lace* was actually written for a female readership, it has a clear appeal to women. It is women who are its central characters, while men feature mainly for their sexual (and sometimes financial) gratification. Its narrative concerns combine the professional and the personal lives of its protagonists in ways quite untypical of masculine genres of fiction, and, albeit from within a conservative discourse, challenge the conventional socio-economic position of women. And all this from a female perspective.

This is not to say that the women in the text are not objectified, but this objectification is for the female reader. It offers both glamorized images of powerful, sexy women, together with, at times, the more mundane reality assumed to lie behind the glamour. These women are not mere passive victims: even when abused and exploited, they fight back and their collective sisterhood provides them with an emotional and economic support network, which would seem to be an appropriation from feminism. The question is whether the context of this objectification alters the relationship female readers can have with it, or whether it merely colludes with conventional, sexist ways of seeing women.

It is open to question whether or not the kind of sexual scenarios to be found in *Lace* do appeal to women's masturbatory fantasies. Rosalind Coward (1986) suggests not: 'Most women still prefer the sublimated masochism of romance to explicit pornographic material and feel uneasy rather than envious about men's use of pornography.' This stems, as she sees it, from pornography's function as a sexual aid for men, which is linked to a different understanding between men and women about masturbation. She argues, rightly, that masturbation is not the problem, but that in so far as men use pornography as a kind of 'health aid', the fear is that they might view women's bodies, both in pornography and in the real world, as always 'available to meet men's sexual needs' (Coward, 1982). But while women may be uneasy about the kind of pornographic material displayed in local newsagents shops and consumed by men, they do not seem to be uneasy (if sales figures are any indication) about consuming the kind of explicit sex to be found in blockbuster novels like *Lace*, aimed presumably at women, which I would argue is quite removed from the 'masochism of romance'.

PORNOGRAPHY FOR WOMEN?

In her book, *Pornography: men possessing women*, Andrea Dworkin attempts to illustrate the direct relationship between pornography and male violence towards women. She contends that within our contemporary misogynist society men use pornography as a means to inculcate and celebrate male power. Through all pornographic forms, she argues, women are victimized by male violence, sexually objectified, humiliated and degraded.[3] The message of pornography is therefore that women exist to be used and abused, that they are contradictorily both sexually animalistic and inherently masochistic with a passive desire to be dominated. As long as pornography exists, she concludes, women cannot hope to gain sexual self-determination (Dworkin, 1981, pp. 199–202).

It is certainly true that the commercial sex industry is currently run by and for men: the women who work in it have no control over production. There is also no doubt that much of the sexually explicit material produced by it is degrading to women. But so, to differing degrees, are many other forms of representation (advertisements being the prime example) which not only exploit women as sex objects, but may more insidiously exploit them as inferior beings in all social spheres. Dworkin's pornography-equals-rape argument ignores all the other discourses through which power is mediated – of which pornography is just one, if important, constituent.

Although Dworkin argues that the original definition of 'pornography' – the depiction of whores – still underlies its now current sense of the explicit depiction of sex, she also claims that 'erotica' is merely a high-class, euphemistic way of saying the same thing. This would appear to leave us with no possibility of representing sex, or women's bodies, that is not degrading to women. On the other hand, to distinguish erotica from pornography on the grounds that 'erotic' represents sexual *love* makes the difference that between making love and fucking and returns us to the discourse of romance. Ann Barr Snitow offers an alternative definition of pornography which might point a way out of this impasse:

> Though pornography's critics are right – pornography is exploitation – it is exploitation of *everything*. Promiscuity by definition is a breakdown of barriers. Pornography is not only a reflector of social power imbalances and sexual pathologies; it is also all those imbalances run riot, run to excess, sometimes explored *ad absurdum*, exploded. Misogyny is one content of pornography; another content is the universal infant desire for complete, immediate gratification, to rule the world out of the very core of passive helplessness.

> (Snitow, 1983, p. 269; original emphases)

In other words, Snitow argues, pornography is capable of expressing sexuality beyond the typical active/passive or male subject/female object dichotomies. You can have different forms of pornography: an explicit depiction of sex that can be instructive and/or pleasurable; or one that exploits, privileging, and thereby inculcating, heterosexual power relations, whether in heterosexual or homosexual/lesbian contexts.

Snitow's argument runs into problems when we consider the ideological implications of all sexual activity: can't it ever be ideologically free? And by what criteria do we judge its ideological status? In addition, we need to ask how the context of representation affects how it is read. The same representation of lesbian sex, for example, might be acceptable to women in a lesbian context, and unacceptably pornographic in a context for male consumption.

Suzanne Kappeler suggests that we should therefore understand pornography not as a specific form of sexuality, but as a form of representation:

> The traditional debate has focused on 'porn' at the expense of 'graphy', an emphasis duly reflected in the customary

abbreviation to 'porn'. 'Porn', in this slippage, has gradually come to mean 'obscene sex' or 'violent sex' – forms of sexuality we disapprove of. We do not like them (or would not like them) in real life, therefore we do want them represented . . . Sex or sexual practices do not just exist out there, waiting to be represented; rather, there is a dialectical relationship between representational practices which construct sexuality, and actual sexual practices, each informing the other.

(Kappeler, 1986, p. 2)

I agree with Kappeler's analysis in terms of the relationship between representation and reality, but I don't think it is possible to claim that women do not get pleasure from pornographic images, 'obscene sex' or even 'violent sex' – whether or not they are represented as the object of desire, and despite the fact that this pleasure might be troubling to women.

Recent theories about the representation of women have drawn heavily on Lacan's psychoanalytic theory, which postulates that, given the phallocentricity of psychic/linguistic structures, women can only occupy the object/other position in social discourse. Therefore, it has been argued by feminists such as Laura Mulvey (1975), writing about film, that formal conventions themselves, along with the associated pleasures, must be challenged by alternative representational structures. This is because, within conventional forms, it is impossible for the female spectator not to position herself as the object, rather than the subject, of desire. In other words, it is impossible, especially with regard to sexuality, to argue for a female gaze. E. Ann Kaplan (1983) summarizes this view:

> . . . in locating herself in fantasy in the erotic, the woman places herself as either passive recipient of male desire, or, at one remove, positions herself as watching a woman who is a passive recipient of male desires and sexual actions.

In *Lace* we are presented with a number of scenarios where the female characters are 'passive recipients of male desire'. But this is not *always* the case. Just as often, the female characters *actively* desire sex, usually with men, but sometimes by themselves. They recognize their own sexuality as distinct from men's. Moreover, this occurs within a narrative in which women (almost) always occupy the dominant subject position. While the subject/object division is a pervasive component within the dualism of western thought, it is certainly not an inherent psychic structure, as Suzanne Kappeler suggests when arguing for notions of 'collectivity' and 'intersubjectivity' (1986, p. 212). While I agree with the need to challenge objectification (certainly with the need to challenge the wholesale objectification heaped on women by men), I do think that representation has to involve objectification to some extent. As Mariana

Valverde puts it: 'An eroticism that is both sexy and egalitarian is one in which both partners are simultaneously subject and object, for one another as well as for themselves' (1986, p. 46).

Part of feminism's problem in dealing with issues of pornography and erotica is that on the one hand we see ourselves bound by patriarchal discourse, and on the other we are actively desiring within them. This can be a very contradictory experience. Heterosexual feminists have been very much on the defensive in recent years, but, as Ehrenreich, Hess and Jacobs point out, not to confront the issue is tantamount to capitulation to dominant ideologies:

> Contemporary feminists who campaign against pornography do not go so far as to say that sex itself is an ordeal or insult to women, but what else can be meant by their frequent insistence that every *representation* of heterosexual sex – however 'soft-core' – is an insult to women and an assault on our rights? For if sex is the ratification of male power, then will it not always be a secret refutation of everything feminism stands for? Does feminism have any real option but to be puritanical or, what almost amounts to the same thing, utterly silent on the subject of sex?
>
> (*Ehrenreich* et al., *1987, p. 203*)

POPULAR FEMINISM?

Lace (which outrightly denounces socialist feminism at one point as a waste of time)[4] could not have been written or widely consumed as morally acceptable if the Women's Liberation Movement had not been in the vanguard of the recent challenging of traditional male views of female sexuality. The text is a testimony to the kind of contradictions involved in sexuality and representation. Through the discourse of bourgeois liberalism it offers the possibility of change for women, but only through existing structures: as a sort of mirror image of the *Cosmopolitan* type of magazine produced by characters in the novel itself. Sex is on the agenda, not only because it is an important subject, but because it sells. There is a strong didactic function that tells you how to do it, combined with passages that turn you on so that you want to do it. Sex is still firmly heterosexual (anything else is deviant) and 'real' fulfilment is still defined as penile penetration; but we do not have sublimated masochistic fantasies allied to romance and marriage. And if men and sex and love remain important to women, money – your own money – is more important. Which perhaps puts sex in its place!

Blockbuster fiction offers both the 'excitement of pre-marital romance' and the more realistic ups and downs of adult sex. I think this level of realism is one that has to be acknowledged. These novels have filled a vacuum left by feminist writers, who have moved into other genres, subjects and forms. Capitalism and its ideology have appropriated this space, articulating an active female sexuality to an individualist ethic. Some may see this as worse than a feminist hangover, but I think that feminism has managed some small, but valuable, intervention into the mass market.

Notes

1   'Bodice rippers seem to have appeared on the marketplace in the mid seventies and often portray the heroine's sexuality as "inadvertent". The bodice ripper formula transforms the hero's desire for the heroine, usually expressed through rape, into a masochistic fantasy whereby female desire is released as a product of pain and as an effect of active male desire' (Lorraine Gamman, 1987).

2   For an overall discussion of the impact of feminism on sexual ideology and the marketplace, see Ehrenreich, Hess and Jacobs (1987). Chapter 6, 'The politics of promiscuity: the rise of the sexual counter-revolution', discusses reversals in the sexual revolution, including feminist reactions to promiscuity.

3   See the opening chapter, entitled 'Power', of Dworkin (1981).

4   From Conran's *Lace* (1982, p. 495): 'Kate attended four meetings of the Women's Liberation group, but found them all disappointing. Every woman's experience was considered of utmost importance, however boring . . . The sisters never seemed to talk about practical considerations; discussion was either directed to experience-sharing or else utopian theorizing. Kate was depressed by the muddled Marxist political thinking.'

Article 5.2
OBSCENITY AND CENSORSHIP
Suzanne Kappeler

Pornography is a feminist issue. It centrally concerns women, since women are the object of pornographic representation. Feminists have produced a substantial literature on the subject.

Pornography has again become a topic of public debate: space is given over to it in the media as it is not to other feminist issues. Many men, and many experts, seem to have a special stake in this issue and contribute to the debate with an eagerness not seen when the issue is domestic work. Pornography is a topic with media appeal.

Yet as a topic of public debate, pornography does not seem to have much to do with women. Women are defined out of the question of pornography as that question is being reframed as one of obscenity and censorship or of freedom of expression. The feminist contribution to the subject is either ignored or edited out of the debate, relegated to a safeguarding footnote or a catchy title.

In the arena of debate, 'public' debate is pitted against feminist debate, without any apparent contradiction, just as we have seen 'human' rights pitted against the civil rights of women. Whilst recognizing the opposition as gender-specific – *feminist* argument, the rights of *women* – the 'public' voice and the 'human' rights lobby do not identify themselves as gendered. Instead, they hide behind ostensibly gender-neutral categories like 'human' which we are told subsume, according to the grammarians and an 1850 Act of Parliament, the gender of women (Spender, 1980, p. 150). And perhaps subsume is nearly the right word, though 'subdue' would be more explicit.

However, conjoining 'feminism' and 'pornography' enhances the media appeal of the debate. Just as of late, we are told, conjoining feminism and pornography enhances the appeal of pornography.

> The February 1980 issue of *Hustler* carried a comic strip in which astronauts subdue, through their irresistible sex-techniques, a colony of uppity space-age Amazons who worship the goddess Steinem. *Penthouse*, that same month, carried a piece called 'Stand Up and Howl' (the coverline read: 'Women's Lib: the Male Strikes Back'). Inside we find that ski instructor Clay Harris, for one, 'isn't affected by the feminist influence because he doesn't let it affect him. "I leave feminists right away," he says, "because they're a problem. I move on."'
>
> *(English, 1980, p. 22)*

Notice the two categories, 'astronauts' (gender-neutral) and 'space-age Amazons', that is to say, women astronauts. The space of the former is invaded by Amazons. Like Amazons, feminists are seen to invade the space of public debate and the turf of the experts, but the legitimate experts (no gender, nor gender interests, of course) Stand Up and Howl. Pornography, as opposed to public debate, recognizes its own gender and gender interests: the Male Strikes Back. Either subdue by dazzling and irresistible technique, of sex rather than astronautics; or don't let the feminist contribution to the debate affect you. Because it's a problem. Move on.

[· · ·]

Feminist critique is concerned with sexism, not with indecency or obscenity. The values of 'obscene' and 'indecent' change with changing mores; in particular, they are middle-class values of proven duplicity. They are part of the make-up of the society's constructed self-image. The setters of standards *to whom* indecencies and obscenities are offensive do not seem to share the values of women to whom pornography is offensive. A feminist critique of pornography is not primarily concerned with censorship – the regulation and control of 'undesired' (by whom?) representations – but with the exposition of the pervasive presence of sexism and pornographic structures throughout our culture. It is concerned with the constitution of pornography itself, rather than with how a quality, 'whatever it may be', can or cannot be circulated in the bourgeois community. And the objective is potential change based on recognition and awareness of what is wrong with pornography, rather than the touching up of the social self-image.

[· · ·]

The anxiety over a juxtaposition of art and pornography and the consequent defence of absolute boundaries between high culture and popular culture stem from an implicit recognition that the bare content of representations from either category might provide a match, just as a picture of 'fact' might be identical to a picture of 'fiction' . . . It is a tribute to the poverty of conception regarding representation with which the argument operates. The shift of focus from print to visual display, and from an élite culture to mass circulation is in fact an attempt to move out of the dead-lock conception of 'pornographic content' towards the structure of representation, through a consideration of the different media. The visual media, with their potential for display, contrast with the written medium in terms of the size of the audience. The experience of reading is, by custom, a private and individual experience (though this is a consequence of our particular cultural practice rather than of the medium's own potential): it is a communion between the white man and his guest. The visual, when displayed, is a party hosted by the white man for many white men. The concern of censorship is directed at keeping the party 'decent', and without causing offence to those not invited. Yet this shift in objective is neither systematic nor theorized, since the starting point still remains a conception of content.

Thus the concession made by the conventional conception of the problem of pornography to the fact of representation lies in a traditional notion of the private, also introduced from 'life' like the comparison of represented content with 'live' situations. It deals with the problem that what is 'done' in the scenario of a pornographic representation is published for viewing. Just as the marital bedroom is meant to be private, so the pornographic drama ought to be experienced in privacy. In the notion of a third party looking on lie both the voyeuristic titillation of the pornographic viewer and the bourgeois unease that our children might be watching too. (Hence for instance the notion of an '18' certificate (HMSO, 1979, p. 27).) The sense of the violation of privacy seems to increase with the size of the audience.

It is here that the laws on obscenity place their concern and their protection: they mean to protect the spectator, and in two different ways. The present law's most crucial operative is the 'test' of whether pornography has a 'tendency to deprave and corrupt' the spectator (ibid., p. 9). This poses the question why he is watching in the first place. The Williams Report, which recommends the abolition of this test and redefines 'harms' (ibid., p. 9),[1] makes a distinction between a voluntary and an involuntary audience, relevant in particular to the display of visual pornography in our city streets which forces itself on a large involuntary audience (ibid., p. 122ff). But as concerns the voluntary spectator, there is as much eagerness to protect his freedom of consumption as there is to protect the pornographer's freedom of expression. Just as the latter shall express himself as freely as possible, so the voluntary consumer of pornography shall consume as freely as possible (ibid., pp. 106, 116). Only, we wish to save him from corruption and depravity, that is, from getting into trouble with the law, should such a cause-and-effect relationship be established. He is protected, in other words, for his own sake, and perhaps for the sake of the moral health of the nation, rather than for the sake of any identifiable potential victims. The suggestion that those potentially so corrupted and depraved might have a tendency to assault and degrade, let alone view a particular class of potential victims, that is, real women, along the lines of pornographic representation, is disregarded by committees, experts and laymen. The concept of gender, whether with regard to consumers or with regard to victims, is absent from the expert discussion.

The concern with the involuntary audience, on the other hand, is simply that no one, in our democratic society, should be forced to consume anything unless they choose to. Hence the choice for all is kept open, inside shuttered establishments, if necessary with warning signs (ibid., p. 117), while the threat of involuntary consumption has thus been removed. The involuntary audience is not defined in terms of gender either: it consists, we are told, of 'reasonable people', and children (ibid., p. 122ff). They are, presumably, the representatives of our bourgeois community, minus their wayward sons – the voluntary consumers.

[· · ·]

In terms of the structure of representation, the distinction between one spectator or reader and a whole 'mass' audience of viewers is irrelevant. The essential positions of author and spectator – the subject positions in the representation – and the objectified 'role' of the victim, are all present, whether you gaze at a pornographic image under your pillow or in the cinema, whether you read pornographic print or peep through the slot in a peep show. The 'privacy' of the pornographic scenario is violated in each case by the presence of the spectator or reader, the alter-ego of the author of the scenario. Here, in fact, we are moving closer to the crux of the matter.

Representations are not just a matter of certain objects – books, images, films etc. The structure of representation extends to 'perceptions' and self-images, the anxious pose of the bourgeois community in front of the camera of public opinion, the self-representation through 'high culture' of a dominant social minority. Representation is thus one of the most fundamental structures of conceptualization, centred on the subject. Just as fiction is not just a matter of stories in books, but of narrative conceptualization in general, whether of factual (historical or 'true') 'contents' or of imaginary ones, perception is the representation of something to oneself, a conflation of the author and the audience in one single subject. Perception externalized inserts itself into the structure of communication between different subjects: author and audience may be separate individuals. It will therefore be expedient to look at representation in the context of communication.

The public debate about obscenity and censorship is, in fact, a little internal quibble between sections of the bourgeois community. Those in charge of censorship follow the call to keep the community's self-image clean and decent. Those who argue for the total freedom of expression on the grounds of a modern atheism in sexual mores are telling us that today all forms of sexuality and representation of sexuality are clean enough, that the standards of cleanliness have advanced. For the cultured liberal the highest source of embarrassment is the suggestion, or perception, that he might be accused of Mary Whitehouse-ism, and he shares this with the leftist. This has in a large measure prevented even those from tackling an analysis of pornography who are convinced that it is essentially a question of mass culture (bad taste, poor values) and who, true to the nineteenth-century Matthew Arnold, see themselves as the guardians of Culture against the onslaught of the 'philistinism' or the provinciality and vulgarity of 'popular culture'. This dilemma between the desire to guard Culture and regulate non-culture (popular culture) on the one hand and the fear of Mary Whitehouse-ism (the stake in 'atheism') on the other is negotiated by the liberal cultural establishment by a reinforcement and defence of the boundaries of high culture (the literary, the artistic) in preference over an outright attack on (censure of) the 'bad' culture . . .

Note

1   There is still, however, no significant shift in the conception of 'harm'. As Liz Bradbury (1985) points out, gender is rarely a factor considered in research on the effects of or responses to pornography.

Article 5.3
PORNOGRAPHY AND BLACK WOMEN'S BODIES

Patricia Hill Collins

> For centuries the black woman has served as the primary
> pornographic 'outlet' for white men in Europe and
> America. We need only think of the black women used
> as breeders, raped for the pleasure and profit of their
> owners. We need only think of the licence the 'master'
> of the slave women enjoyed. But, most telling of all, we
> need only study the old slave societies of the South to
> note the sadistic treatment – at the hands of white
> 'gentlemen' – of 'beautiful young quadroons and octo-
> roons' who became increasingly (and were deliberately
> bred to become) indistinguishable from white women,
> and were the more highly prized as slave mistresses
> because of this.
>
> (*Alice Walker, 1981a, 'Coming Apart', p. 42*)

Alice Walker's description of the rape of enslaved African women
for the 'pleasure and profit of their owners' encapsulates several
elements of contemporary pornography. First, black women were
used as sex objects for the pleasure of white men. This objectification
of African-American women parallels the portrayal of women in
pornography as sex objects whose sexuality is available for men
(McNall, 1983). Exploiting black women as breeders objectified them
as less than human because only animals can be bred against their
will. In contemporary pornography women are objectified through
being portrayed as pieces of meat, as sexual animals awaiting
conquest. Second, African-American women were raped, a form of
sexual violence. Violence is typically an implicit or explicit theme
in pornography. Moreover, the rape of black women linked
sexuality and violence, another characteristic feature of pornography
(Eisenstein, 1983). Third, rape and other forms of sexual violence
act to strip victims of their will to resist and make them passive
and submissive to the will of the rapist. Female passivity, the fact
that women have things done to them, is a theme repeated over
and over in contemporary pornography (McNall, 1983). Fourth,
the profitability of black women's sexual exploitation for white
'gentlemen' parallels pornography's financially lucrative benefits for
pornographers (Eisenstein, 1983). Finally, the actual breeding of
'quadroons and octoroons' not only reinforces the themes of black

women's passivity, objectification, and malleability to male control but reveals pornography's grounding in racism and sexism. The fates of both black and white women were intertwined in this breeding process. The ideal African-American woman as a pornographic object was indistinguishable from white women and thus approximated the images of beauty, asexuality and chastity forced on white women. But inside was a highly sexual whore, a 'slave mistress' ready to cater to her owner's pleasure.[1]

Contemporary pornography consists of a series of icons or representations that focus the viewer's attention on the relationship between the portrayed individual and the general qualities ascribed to that class of individuals. Pornographic images are iconographic in that they represent realities in a manner determined by the historical position of the observers, their relationship to their own time, and to the history of the conventions which they employ (Gilman, 1985). The treatment of black women's bodies in nineteenth-century Europe and the United States may be the foundation upon which contemporary pornography as the representation of women's objectification, domination and control is based. Icons about the sexuality of black women's bodies emerged in these contexts. Moreover, as race/gender-specific representations, these icons have implications for the treatment of both African-American and white women in contemporary pornography.

I suggest that African-American women were not included in pornography as an afterthought but instead form a key pillar on which contemporary pornography itself rests. As Alice Walker points out, 'the more ancient roots of modern pornography are to be found in the almost always pornographic treatment of black women who, from the moment they entered slavery . . . were subjected to rape as the "logical" convergence of sex and violence. Conquest, in short' (1981a, p. 42).

One key feature about the treatment of black women in the nineteenth century was how their bodies were objects of display. In the antebellum American South, white men did not have to look at pornographic pictures of women because they could become voyeurs of black women on the auction block. A chilling example of this objectification of the black female body is provided by the exhibition, in early nineteenth-century Europe, of Sarah Bartmann, the so-called Hottentot Venus. Her display formed one of the original icons for black female sexuality. An African woman, Sarah Bartmann was often exhibited at fashionable parties in Paris, generally wearing little clothing, to provide entertainment. To her audience she represented deviant sexuality. At the time European audiences thought that Africans had deviant sexual practices and searched for physiological differences, such as enlarged penises and malformed female genitalia, as indications of this deviant sexuality. Sarah Bartmann's exhibition stimulated these racist and sexist beliefs. After her death in 1815, she was dissected. Her genitalia and buttocks remain on display in Paris (Gilman, 1985).

Sander Gilman explains the impact that Sarah Bartmann's exhibition had on Victorian audiences:

> It is important to note that Sarah Bartmann was exhibited not to show her genitalia – but rather to present another anomaly which the European audience . . . found riveting. This was the steatopygia, or protruding buttocks, the other physical characteristic of the Hottentot female which captured the eye of early European travelers . . . The figure of Sarah Bartmann was reduced to her sexual parts. The audience which had paid to see her buttocks and had fantasized about the uniqueness of her genitalia when she was alive could, after her death and dissection, examine both.
>
> (Gilman, 1985, p. 213)

In this passage Gilman unwittingly describes how Bartmann was used as a pornographic object similar to how women are represented in contemporary pornography. She was reduced to her sexual parts, and these parts came to represent a dominant icon applied to black women throughout the nineteenth century. Moreover, the fact that Sarah Bartmann was both African and a woman underscores the importance of gender in maintaining notions of racial purity. In this case Bartmann symbolized blacks as a 'race'. Thus the creation of the icon applied to black women demonstrates that notions of gender, race and sexuality were linked in overarching structures of political domination and economic exploitation.

The process illustrated by the pornographic treatment of the bodies of enslaved African women and of women like Sarah Bartmann has developed into a full-scale industry encompassing all women objectified differently by racial/ethnic category. Contemporary portrayals of black women in pornography represent the continuation of the historical treatment of their actual bodies. African-American women are usually depicted in a situation of bondage and slavery, typically in a submissive posture, and often with two white men. As Bell observes, 'this setting reminds us of all the trappings of slavery: chains, whips, neck braces, wrist clasps' (1987, p. 59). White women and women of colour have different pornographic images applied to them. The image of black women in pornography is almost consistently one featuring them breaking from chains. The image of Asian women in pornography is almost consistently one of being tortured (Bell, 1987, p. 161).

The pornographic treatment of black women's bodies challenges the prevailing feminist assumption that since pornography primarily affects white women, racism has been grafted onto pornography. African-American women's experiences suggest that black women were not added into a pre-existing pornography, but rather that pornography itself must be reconceptualized as an example of the interlocking nature of race, gender and class oppression. At the heart of both racism and sexism are notions of biological determinism claiming that people of African descent and women possess immutable biological characteristics marking their inferiority to élite white men (Gould, 1981; Fausto-Sterling, 1989; Halpin, 1989). In pornography these racist and sexist beliefs are sexualized. Moreover, for African-American women pornography has not been timeless and universal but was tied to black women's experiences with the European colonization of Africa and with American slavery. Pornography emerged within a specific system of social class relationships.

This linking of views of the body, social constructions of race and gender, and conceptualizations of sexuality that inform black women's treatment as pornographic objects promises to have significant implications for how we assess contemporary pornography. Moreover, examining how pornography has been central to the race, gender and class oppression of African-American women offers new routes for understanding the dynamics of power as domination.

Investigating racial patterns in pornography offers one route for such an analysis. Black women have often claimed that images of white women's sexuality were intertwined with the controlling image of the sexually denigrated black woman: 'In the United States, the fear and fascination of female sexuality was projected onto black women; the passionless lady arose in symbiosis with the primitively sexual slave' (Hall, 1983, p. 333). Comparable linkages exist in pornography (Gardner, 1980). Alice Walker provides a fictional account of a black man's growing awareness of the different ways that African-American and white women are objectified in pornography: 'What he has refused to see – because to see it would reveal yet another area in which he is unable to protect or defend black women – is that where white women are depicted in pornography as "objects", black women are depicted as animals. Where white women are depicted as human bodies if not beings, black women are depicted as shit' (Walker, 1981a, p. 52).

[· · ·]

Developing a comprehensive analysis of the race, gender and class dynamics of pornography offers possibilities for change. Those black feminist intellectuals investigating sexual politics imply that the situation is much more complicated than that advanced by some prominent white feminists (see, for example, Dworkin, 1981) in which 'men oppress women' because they are men. Such approaches implicitly assume biologically deterministic views of sex, gender and sexuality and offer few possibilities for change. In contrast, Afrocentric feminist analyses routinely provide for human agency and its corresponding empowerment and for the responsiveness of social structures to human action. In the short story 'Coming Apart', Alice Walker describes one black man's growing realization that his enjoyment of pornography, whether of white women as 'objects' or black women as 'animals', degraded him:

> He begins to feel sick. For he realizes that he has bought some of the advertisements about women, black and white. And further, inevitably, he has bought the advertisements about himself. In pornography the black man is portrayed as being capable of fucking anything . . . even a piece of shit. He is defined solely by the size, readiness and unselectivity of his cock.
>
> (Walker, 1981a, p. 52)

Walker conceptualizes pornography as a race/gender system that entraps everyone. But by exploring an African-American man's struggle for a self-defined standpoint on pornography, Walker suggests that a changed consciousness is essential to social change. If a black man can understand how pornography affects him, then other groups enmeshed in the same system are equally capable of similar shifts in consciousness and action.

Note

1   Offering a similar argument about the relationship between race and masculinity, Paul Hoch (1979) suggests that the ideal white man is a hero who upholds honour. But inside lurks a 'black beast' of violence and sexuality, traits that the white hero deflects on to men of colour.

Article 5.4
WHO WATCHES THE WATCHWOMEN?: FEMINISTS AGAINST CENSORSHIP

Gillian Rodgerson and Linda Semple

It has been a truism for many years that anything that happens in the United States within alternative political movements surfaces in Britain about five years later. This has been proved again by the current debates surrounding the issue of pornography, erotica and other sexually explicit material.

The chronology in the USA is well known. The most significant year was 1984 when Catharine McKinnon and Andrea Dworkin co-authored an ordinance for the City of Minneapolis which allowed women to take civil action against anyone involved in the production, sale or distribution of pornography on the grounds that they had been harmed by the image of women's sexuality that it portrayed. Their definition of pornography was broad: it covered basically any depiction of women in a sexual situation. Although the 'Minneapolis Ordinance' was vetoed by the mayor, a revised version was suggested in other cities including Boston, Los Angeles and Indianapolis where it became law for a short time.

In the same year, the Feminist Anti-Censorship Task Force (FACT) was formed by feminists concerned that the anti-pornography issue was a red herring for the movement and, moreover, that the analysis was problematic since it assumed a direct relationship between pornography and violence against women which has not been proven. FACT produced an eloquent feminist argument against the ordinances which addressed the problems of sexually explicit material while arguing that censorship was not a feminist position and that supporting greater establishment power over free speech left the feminist movement hostage to fortune and open to unwanted alliances with antifeminist elements.

In 1985, after an appeal, the Indianapolis ordinance was declared unconstitutional by a circuit court judge. FACT was one of the organizers of a brief which helped this decision. Indianapolis appealed its case to the Supreme Court and Attorney-General Edwin Meese appointed a commission to 'address the serious national problem of pornography' and to find 'more effective ways in which the spread of pornography may be contained'. Despite this, in 1986, the Supreme Court declared the Indianapolis ordinance unconstitutional on the grounds that it violated the guarantee of freedom of speech contained in the First Amendment to the American Constitution, effectively closing the debate as far as legislation in the USA was concerned.

In the United Kingdom, over the same period and earlier, there had been other celebrated cases concerning censorship and obscenity law. *Gay News* was prosecuted in 1977 for blasphemous libel when it published a poem about the crucifixion; the paper and its editor were found guilty. Howard Brenton's play *The Romans in Britain* suffered a private prosecution because it contained scenes of simulated buggery. Both of these prosecutions – and most public pronouncements on the subject of pornography during the 1970s and early 1980s – were made by Mary Whitehouse and her right-wing organization, The Festival of Light (later renamed the National Viewers and Listeners Association). Both the FoL and Whitehouse were viewed as figures of fun and not as really serious threats to civil liberties or freedom of speech by the Left and feminist organizations in the UK. It was assumed that the climate of opinion would remain such that their rigid pro-family, anti-lesbian and -gay, pro-religion and anti-sexual freedom would never gain wide currency.

Midway through the first ten years of Margaret Thatcher's premiership more worrying events began to take place. Customs and Excise officers began to use their powers to seize and destroy 'offensive' material, specifically against lesbian and gay books and magazines. Lavender Menace (now West and Wilde) in Edinburgh regularly had shipments from the US destroyed and, to a lesser extent, Gay's The Word bookshop in London was targeted. Then, in the notorious 'Operation Tiger', Gay's The Word was stripped of much of its stock and its workers and directors were charged with 'conspiracy to import offensive material'. This case became one of the *causes célèbres* of general civil liberties and was a chance to highlight the different standards which pertained to sexually explicit material depicting lesbians and gays and 'straight' material. The case was taken up especially by the National Council for Civil Liberties (NCCL). It was finally dropped by the authorities two years later.

Clearly, the climate of opinion was shifting. Media hysteria was beginning to be whipped up about the issue of AIDS; gay men were being blamed for its introduction into the UK and, it has to be said, some lesbian feminists played directly into the hands of the moral right by their willingness to apportion blame to gay men's sexual practices while smugly assuming that AIDS was not a women's and definitely not a lesbian issue. At a time when parliamentarians could seriously suggest in the House of Commons that people with AIDS should be quarantined, the introduction of Clause 27 – later Section 28 – of the Local Government Act in late 1987, restricting local authorities' powers to give money to lesbian and gay groups, was no surprise.

The Thatcher Government, aided and abetted in many cases by the Opposition, seemed determined to return the country to its own version of 'The Family' and 'Victorian Values'. Concern with the sexual expression of the people was widespread and given a spurious justification with fear of AIDS which the government and its pet media blamed on promiscuity. There were calls for the electronic tagging of prostitutes, tightening of the Obscene Publications Act and greater control over broadcast media.

Meanwhile, in the subculture . . . feminists had won notable victories while the Greater London Council existed, over the licensing of violent and sexist films and against some sexist advertising on London Transport. At the opening of the London Lesbian and Gay Centre and on the Lesbian Strength and Gay Pride marches it was clear that the issue of sado-masochism within the community was still a hot potato. A short-lived group dedicated to putting the case for sexual variety and freedom – 'Sexual Fringe' – made some interventions. In the closing years of the decade the United Kingdom saw its first mail-order sex toys firm for women, 'Thrilling Bits'; the first Lesbian sex magazine *Quim* – which was banned from Sisterwrite and Gay's The Word bookshops; and the first UK collection of lesbian erotic writing, *Serious Pleasure*, published by Sheba. It was as if the stronger the repression facing activists attempting to argue the case for greater freedom in sexual choice, the more varied the manifestations of that choice were becoming.

In the late 1980s two feminist organizations were set up to combat pornography – which many women who subscribed to a radical-feminist interpretation of society considered to be one of the major causes of violence against women. Quoting the experiments by Edward Donnerstein and his colleagues (Donnerstein *et al.*, 1987) as evidence of the links between pornography and violence, and the evidence given to the Meese Commission in the USA, both the Campaign Against Pornography and Censorship and the Campaign Against Pornography launched well-publicized initiatives.

In April 1989, the NCCL voted at its annual general meeting to adopt a proposal put forward by the Campaign Against Pornography and Censorship (CAPC) to look into legal methods of fighting pornography. The CAPC justified this radical change in NCCL's position on censorship by claiming that pornography itself censors women and interferes with their civil liberties, therefore legislation to censor pornography is actually in keeping with the aims of the NCCL.

The decision by the NCCL to advocate the adoption of measures similar to the McKinnon-Dworkin bill, but tailored to British law, shocked many feminists, as did the assumption by the organization and other groups on the left that the anti-pornography position was representative of the opinion of the women's movement as a whole. On 24 May 1989 the as-yet unnamed Feminists Against

Censorship held its first meeting in London. We were among a diverse group of women united by their concern at the events of the past few weeks who met to discuss what action could be taken both to counter the influence of pro-censorship forces in the feminist movement and the larger political sphere, and to support those people who were attempting to produce alternative explicit material: that which was not sexist, racist or coercive.

By the autumn of 1989, after lively and wide-ranging discussions, the members of the group were ready to speak publicly as feminists who could not conscientiously advocate censorship of pornography. We produced a leaflet setting out our objections to the pro-censorship arguments and explaining our positions [see Figure 5.4.1]. the leaflet said:

> Women need open and safe communication about sexual matters, including the power relations of sex. We don't need new forms of guilt parading under the banner of political correctness. We need a safe, legal working environment for sex workers, not repressive laws or an atmosphere of social stigma that empowers police and punters to brutalize them. We need sexually explicit material produced by and for women, freed from the control of right-wingers and misogynists, whether they sit on the board of directors or the board of censors. We need an analysis of violence that empowers women and protects them at the same time. We need a feminism willing to tackle issues of class and race and to deal with the variety of oppressions in the world, not to reduce all oppression to pornography.

The leaflet pointed out the dangers inherent in increasing government power to ban books and magazines, noting that it is often lesbian, gay male and feminist material which first feels the bite of legislation.

When the Campaign Against Pornography and the National Union of Students launched their 'Off the Shelf' campaign, FAC attended the press conference at the London women's centre, Wesley House, to question the worth and ethics of such a campaign of 'prior censorship'.

Feminists Against Censorship has never seen the current debate as an 'Us or Them' situation. Our aim is to make certain that the pro-censorship position is not seen as the only feminist perspective on pornography. We have been very successful in that it is no longer possible for pornography to be discussed in the Press without our position being mentioned. We have been invited to speak at various colleges and universities, sometimes as part of a debate with the Campaign Against Pornography, at other times on our own.

An article in the *Guardian* on 15 February 1990, in which FAC, CAPC and CAP all stated their positions, brought more than forty positive letters and no negative ones. The requests for information and offers of help made it clear to us that we were articulating things many other women thought but had not said publicly.

The introduction of Labour MP Dawn Primarolo's Location of Pornographic Materials Bill has shown that censorship is still a popular option. FAC is lobbying MPs, encouraging them to defeat a bill which would set a dangerous precedent by removing all sexually explicit material, straight, lesbian and gay, to licensed sex shops. From there it would be a very small step to outlaw the sex shops themselves.

In its first year, Feminists Against Censorship has consisted of a small group of activists and a larger number of supporters who are kept informed of our activities and occasionally attend meetings or participate in specific projects. On 18 March, about thirty women attended a discussion day at Reeves Hotel, a women's hotel in London. There we were able to talk at greater length about some of the problems we had been presented with in public debate and to clarify our personal opinions about issues such as Racial Hatred laws, child pornography and violence. We also had the opportunity to examine some of the material that can be found on the 'top shelf' in newsagents and some more 'alternative' porn.

Strengthened by that discussion, FAC played a significant part in mobilizing opposition to censorship within the NCCL. At the 1990 annual general meeting, a strong group of speakers from FAC, the Campaign Against Censorship, the Stonewall Group and individual members was able to put a well-argued case that it is not possible to prove any causal links between pornography and sexual violence and that no state legislation in 1990s Britain would be likely to encapsulate a truly feminist definition of pornography, were such a definition possible. CAPC's motion urging NCCL to recommit itself to the search for possible legislation against pornography was defeated and NCCL policy effectively reversed and rededicated to the anti-censorship cause.

As the forces of the right continue to gather on the side of increased repression in many spheres, all feminists who are against censorship must constantly be aware of the guises this repression can assume. Simply fighting against the banning and restricting of sexually explicit images is not enough. As feminists we also have a responsibility to be critical of those images we find sexist, racist or exploitative and to counter them in the most effective way there is: if not by creating our own, then by supporting those who are creating an alternative body of sexual images for women.

The allegations made against us as a group and as individuals have been interesting. We are frequently charged with being in the pay of the pornography industry; individual members who are involved in publishing sexually explicit lesbian/feminist written and visual material have been publicly abused as 'peddlers of pornography'; there has been a worrying suggestion that opponents of our position have approached employers about our views – a tactic used against women involved in fighting against anti-pornography groups in the United States.

Such reactions serve only to prove that our tactics have been successful. It is no longer possible for anti-pornography activists to say that they, and they alone, represent the views of all women – or even, now, of all feminists. In a movement whose original tenets included belief in the right of all women to make their own sexual choices, this can only be a step in the right direction.

Figure 5.4.1
Title page of Feminists Against Censorship leaflet, summer 1989

THE PORNOGRAPHY PROBLEM
Lizbeth Goodman

Pornography can be viewed as a 'problem', or as a debate between objectivity and subjectivity, gender and power, representation and interpretation. The pornography debate is complicated and frequently discussed. It is also intricately related to many of the themes of this book, including cultural representation, gender and power.

The first four articles in this chapter argue from different points along what may be seen as a continuum of feminist thought on the pornography problem. They were not written for inclusion in this book, but, rather, were written and published in other contexts, possibly with other audiences in mind. This is ironic in that the process of choosing readings about pornography was complicated by the very same problem which is often cited as an argument against the unlimited availability of pornography in the public sphere: the danger of material intended for one audience influencing another. While there is nothing inherently dangerous in students reading about pornography, the pornography debate is difficult to discuss as an academic subject due to the conflict between personal and political perspectives which it often involves. In a parallel way, pornography itself is influenced by market values: by its intended audience(s) and the fact that modern society allows for so many different means of communication of pornographic images and representations.

This last article *has* been written for inclusion in this volume. It can therefore state its aims. The piece has three distinct functions: to provide a brief discussion of the erotica/pornography distinction, to examine some of the implications of mass communication technologies on the availability and accessibility of pornographic images, and to draw connections between the first four articles and the larger themes of the book.

EROTICA VERSUS PORNOGRAPHY

Both the terms 'erotica' and 'pornography' refer to visual or literary representations of sexual relations and imagery. The relationship between the two is difficult to define, and the attempt to distinguish between them is very contentious and often highly subjective. The term 'erotica' usually designates the mutually pleasurable, assuming an equal power base between the maker, subject and consumer of the image. Erotica further assumes the consent and equal initiative of the subject of the image, and – in cases where an erotic image involves two or more people engaged in a sexual act – there is usually an assumption of mutual desire, rather than force. In erotica, the subject of the representation is assumed to be present as an active subject: one who chose her (or possibly his) position in the representation, and who is thereby acting as a subject, rather than being designated the object of the representation. In theory, erotic imagery allows for the possibility of a politics of representation based on a 'democracy of the gaze', where the subject and the object, viewer and viewed, are 'equals'. But such a theory is not easily translated into practice in the current social order, charged as it is with unequal access to power based on differences related to gender, race and class. The term 'pornography' tends to designate an unequal power base, usually with men in positions of power over women. In pornography, an active subject (a male film-maker, photographer, writer) objectifies the body of someone else (usually a woman, or several women). The balance of power is unequal and objectification – as a form of oppression – is involved.

Feminists have taken many different approaches to the erotica/ pornography distinction. For example, Gloria Steinem defined the difference in this way: 'perhaps one could simply say that erotica is about sexuality, but pornography is about power and sex-as-weapon in the same way we have come to understand that rape is about violence, and not really about sexuality at all' (Steinem, 1985). But Joanna Russ replied: 'Maybe Gloria Steinem can tell the difference between pornography and erotica at a single glance. I can't' (Russ, 1985b).[1]

It *is* difficult to tell the difference between erotica and pornography. It can be convincingly argued that erotica is a potentially positive, liberating form of sexual expression, whereas pornography is a negative, oppressive form of patriarchal oppression. This distinction allows many feminists, as well as non-feminist women and men, to defend erotica while arguing against pornography. The tension between these viewpoints has led to much heated debate, and to the formation of several opposing 'camps' in the feminist community. If the pornography versus erotica debate may be viewed as a continuum along which feminist critics have taken many different positions, then pornographic representation may *itself* be viewed as a continuum: it is possible to think in terms of 'pornographic strategies' which are employed in advertising, news broadcasts and many other forms of cultural representation, for instance.

Not all feminists agree with the 'continuum' idea, however. Rather than viewing pornographic images as cultural manifestations of the oppression and objectification of women in symbolic terms, some feminists argue that these images reflect in 'real' terms the valuing of women in society: a valuing which cannot be disentangled from the effects of women's objectification (violence against women, limitations imposed on women's freedom of movement in society etc.).

The distinction between pornography and erotica is further problematized by these different ways of viewing and valuing the functions of cultural representations. As Sarah Franklin *et al.* have argued: 'What is at stake in the recent feminist discussions about whether it is possible to distinguish between pornography and erotica, or in disagreements about the role and relevance of censorship, are not only different understandings of pornography, but also implicit models of culture' (Franklin *et al.*, 1991, p. 182). There is not space in this short piece to discuss 'models of culture' in any satisfactory way. Instead, it is useful to discuss some of the different ways of seeing and valuing the availability of pornographic images in the public domain.

PORNOGRAPHY IN THE OPEN MARKET

Another problem in defining pornography is the contentious designating of 'objects' in the pornographic image. In many interventions in the pornography debate (feminist and non-feminist), the focus is on pornographic images of *women*. This is by far the most common form of pornography, and it is understandable that feminists (who have initiated and advanced the debate) would tend to focus on the most common form, and the form which most directly affects them (us) as women. But of course, pornographic images of women are not the only pornography. Child pornography – that is, pornographic images *of*, not *for*, children – abound. There is also an expanding market for pornography representing images of men (mostly marketed for gay men, although some is 'for' women) and there is a small but expanding market for feminist erotica (sexual/erotic images marketed for women). Some of this is lesbian erotica and some is for heterosexual women and men. Feminist erotica could include woman-made films, as well as images and fiction. It might take the form of lesbian erotica or heterosexual women's erotica.

Content and intent must be considered alongside the issue of availability, of accessibility, of pornographic images. Pornographic images are circulated today not only in photography, graphics and 'girly' magazines, but also on video and film. These media make the images more accessible in general, and immediately accessible in the case of cable porn television channels like those available in the USA. The mass-market availability of pornographic movies and videos renders pornography more visible and links it directly to the economy.

The question of accessibility is, of course, at the root of the pornography/censorship debate. The debate has surfaced in various forms in different generations, but has undergone a significant shift of focus in the past few decades. Some feminist critics – like Kate Ellis, Barbara O'Dair and Abby Talmer – have emphasized the cultural context of pornography and highlighted the problem of reception as well as that of the projection of images (Ellis *et al.*, 1990). Such arguments are significant in that they approach the pornography problem as one with shifting values which will have different implications in various contexts, cultures and generations.

Catherine King has argued – in contributing to the choice of readings for this book – that 'the acid test' of pornography is its tendency to be seen by those who may not *want* to see it, and to disturb those who are inadvertently exposed to it. Her frame of reference is that of a woman with a daughter, who finds the depiction of bound and subjugated women's bodies alienating, and who would wish not to have such images informing her view of self in the world, or that of her daughter (who might well see such images on any trip to the local newsagent). Because pornographic images have become so publicly accessible, the standard argument that 'those who don't wish to see it don't have to look at it' is no longer defensible. King argues that it should be possible to legislate against the public display of pornographic images, in the same way that British culture has legislated against 'incitement to racial hatred'.

In contributing to the negotiated perspective of the editorial group, Richard Allen suggests that there may be a paradoxical relationship between defining pornography and legislating against it. That is, the desire to see pornographic images banned requires identifying and defining the particular sets of images to be banned, thereby leaving a range of other, perhaps 'softer', pornographic images to be implicitly defined as 'acceptable' for public consumption. Yet in failing to identify specific forms of pornography to be banned, all forms of pornography may be implicitly 'approved'.

Allen's view effectively validates the view of the pornography problem as a continuum, along which different approaches to the problem of legislation emerge. Defining pornography, like defining other terms, is a process influenced by situated perspectives and power dynamics as well. Declaring a position which advocates the banning of some pornographic images, Allen argues, aligns the anti-pornography position of the individual with an 'official' or legal position. Yet the individual who wishes to see some forms of pornography banned will not necessarily wish to be aligned with the values of the 'official power structures' in other ways, since it is those very structures which encourage and contribute to the production and consumption of pornographic images in the first place. Therefore, the process of aligning an anti-pornography position with an 'authoritative' position through legislation is paradoxical and perhaps contradictory. Yet without attempting to balance these opposing dynamics, it is difficult to know where or how to begin expressing dissatisfaction with the cultural representation of pornographic imagery.

A similar argument can be taken in a different direction, by beginning on a slightly different point on the continuum. For instance, in arguing that the representation of women's bodies is symptomatic of the cultural problem of sexism, Ellen Willis contends that there is a fine line between legislating against prominent display of such images, and legislating against freedom of expression. Willis argues not only against censorship of pornography, but also against legislation which would determine which images could be displayed, and where. In Willis's words:

> There is a plausible case to be made for the idea that anti-woman images displayed so prominently that they are impossible to avoid are coercive, a form of active harassment that oversteps the bounds of free speech. But aside from the evasion involved in simply equating pornography with misogyny or sexual sadism, there are no legal or logical grounds for treating sexist material any differently from (for example) racist or anti-Semitic propaganda; an equitable law would have to prohibit any kind of public defamation. And the very thought of such sweeping law has to make anyone with imagination nervous. Could Catholics claim they were being harassed by nasty depictions of the pope? Could Russian refugees argue that the display of Communist literature was a form of psychological torture? Would pro-abortion material be taken off the shelves on the grounds that it defamed the unborn? I'd rather not find out.
>
> (Willis, 1983, p. 466)

Yet, as Catherine King argues, verbal insults are generally recognized as a form of assault or threatening behaviour; 'freedom' to assault others by means of images and words may be seen, in this view, as tantamount to a representational tyranny of sorts.

In *The Pornography of Representation*, Suzanne Kappeler also emphasizes a cultural dimension to the pornography problem. She takes a radical feminist position, summarized in the conclusion to her book:

> My argument has not been concerned with practical measures which we could take today or tomorrow in order to get rid of the problem of pornography. I have tried to show that there is no such isolated problem as 'pornography'. I have aimed, rather, to build up a critique of the underlying assumptions which make a pornographic practice of representation 'natural'. With these assumptions in place, it seems to me pointless to embark on a quick programme of reforms that would patch

up the status quo in the hope of silencing the women who are so angry. My analysis suggests that you cannot remedy the situation by appointing more women pornographers or more male victims, i.e. by achieving a more equitable quota of exploitation. Equal opportunities are out when what they are equal to is undesirable.

It is also worth saying what I am *not* implying. I am not suggesting that besides 'pornography' all other representations of women including 'art' should be censored. . . . The appeal to a cultural police force seems to me the opposite of what a feminist politics envisages.

(Kappeler, 1986, pp. 220–1)

Here, Kappeler discusses the issues at the representational level, rather than confronting questions about censorship of pornography in terms of legislation. The suggestion that some representational forms (such as 'art') should not be censored takes the discussion back to square one: the implication that there must be some way of distinguishing between pornography, erotica and 'art'. This kind of representational analysis is engaging and persuasive, but leaves some important issues unresolved.

The implication that such a distinction should somehow be made is important. But what is censorship and what is 'reasonable' elimination of damaging images from the cultural market-place? What is incitement to sexual violence and what is erotic imagery? What some call 'erotica' others call 'pornography'. What some call 'art' others call 'smut'. It is, therefore, important to recognize that it is possible to take several positions at once: to want to close the porn shop around the corner and yet to find pleasure in certain erotic novels or films; to advocate censorship at one level while reacting against it as a general rule. Taking a position on the continuum of the pornography issue is not easy, and for some, taking one position to the exclusion of all others is not possible. This sense of divided loyalties can lead to personal frustration. It can also lead to a public hesitance – even among otherwise outspoken feminists – to engage in the pornography debate.

Among those who do take positions, certain areas of overlapping concern are clearly in evidence. For instance, many feminists argue that the principle of censorship should be applied to the pornography debate, but as in the examples of *Lace* and 'mass-market romances', the issues are complex. The questions of how far censorship should be extended, what pornography will be defined *as*, who will do the defining, and how far the legislation will go, are not resolved and may not be resolvable. Rodgerson and Semple, for Feminists Against Censorship, address this question in their article, 'Who Watches the WatchWomen?', arguing against censorship.

The pornography/censorship issue is further complicated when the definition of pornography is extended to include novels and prime time television dramas as well as 'girly' magazines and videos. *Lady Chatterley's Lover* was once considered obscene, and the BBC television programme *Oranges Are Not the Only Fruit* might have fallen under this same heading, had the same definitions and restrictions applied in 1990.

The impact of mass-communication technologies has added one further obstacle to 'taking a position' in the pornography debate. As Frances Bonner has argued, video pornography has added an extra dimension to the problem by granting a new kind of power to the viewer of the video image. Bonner argues that the interaction of the viewer and the image is enhanced in video pornography, where the viewer has control of the on-off switch, the rewind and fast-forward buttons and the 'pause' or 'freeze-frame' command. Videos are usually 'consumed' privately and are not therefore amenable to public sanction. The viewer, in other words, has enhanced control over the viewing of the images. The relationship becomes a mechanized 'master–slave' dynamic which is operative in both the form of mediation of images (the video) and in the images themselves (wherein, most often, men use women's bodies physically or sexually within the frame or the image, and also in the consumption of the images themselves). This situation usurps women's subjectivity and control of self-image in two respects and is therefore, in Bonner's words: 'detrimental to feminist hopes for transforming the social order' (Bonner, 1984, pp. 38–9).

PORNOGRAPHY, OBJECTIFICATION AND RACE

Another issue of crucial importance to the pornography problem is the exploitation of racial difference. In her chapter on 'The Sexual Politics of Black Womanhood', Patricia Hill Collins argues that pornographic representations of black women's bodies are not 'an afterthought', but are, rather, a 'key pillar upon which contemporary pornography itself rests' (Collins, 1990). Several common denominators of other forms of pornography are combined in pornographic representations of black women: sexism and racism are combined and given space for expression, the power relations involved in sexual relations are exaggerated, and violence against women is not only condoned but celebrated. The objectification of black women is a double process: women are objectified as 'other than men', and black women are further objectified as 'other than white'.

One view which is not expressed in any of the previous articles is the American radical feminist perspective as articulated by Andrea Dworkin and Catharine A. McKinnon. Articulation of the pornography problem through a personal rather than an academic voice has also been under-represented in the articles. These two positions come together in Dworkin and McKinnon's *Pornography and Sexual Violence: evidence of the links*, a book which contains the first person testimonies of female survivors of pornography-related crimes, in a long transcript from the court case which resulted from Dworkin and McKinnon's proposal to the US Constitution of an amendment on the issue of pornography.[2]

One such testimony, the case of 'Ms U', supports Patricia Hill Collins's arguments about the racial element of the pornography problem. Ms U is one of a long line of witnesses who were called in turn to speak out about their experiences of sexual violence and abuse, ostensibly related to pornography. More specifically, Ms U is a native American Indian woman who describes her gang rape as evidence of a link between racial prejudice, cultural stereotype, pornographic imagery and sexual violence. This is an extract from Ms U's testimony:

> I was attacked by two white men and from the beginning they let me know they hated my people, even though it was obvious from their remarks they knew very little about us. And they let me know that the rape of a 'squaw' by white men was practically honored by white society. In fact, it has been made into a video game called *Custer's Last Stand*. And that's what they screamed in my face as they threw me to the ground. 'This is more fun than *Custer's Last Stand*.'
>
> *(Dworkin and McKinnon, 1988)*

Here, Ms U relates the comments made by her attackers about her resemblance to the cartoon caricature of an Indian 'Squaw' depicted in a popular arcade game. The game involves the (representational) violation of an Indian woman by white men. The game, as one form of pornography, is particularly disturbing because of its widespread accessibility.

Ms U's testimony, read in the context of Dworkin and McKinnon's text, suggests that Ms U was seen by her attackers (in some subliminal sense, at least) to represent the virgin country of America: a way of seeing which is encouraged and even valorized in popular 'Cowboy and Indian' movies. It also suggests that Ms U's rape was related to the familiarity of her attackers with a computerized game of sex and violence, which may have rendered them unable or unwilling to distinguish between the real person who is Ms U and the imagined Indian Squaw whom they thought 'deserved to be raped'.

The larger issue raised by Ms U's testimony is that of women's rights to live freely in both the private and public spheres without threat of physical or emotional harassment or fear of attack. One issue raised by Ms U's testimony is the interplay of mass-produced and culturally sanctioned images of violence against women. Here, Bonner's formulation of the 'master–slave' relationship between the viewer and the medium can be seen to apply to the medium of arcade games, wherein the viewer is 'master' of both the game and the image of the objectified woman projected on the screen. The viewer, who pushes the buttons, manipulates the medium and the image. When the image depicts a woman of colour, race and gender are manipulated and 'controlled' as well.

Three crucial points are raised in Ms U's story: these can be seen to inform all the other 'ways of seeing' the pornography problem discussed in this chapter. The inclusion of Ms U's testimony is used as evidence to support the claims that:

1   Pornography is linked not only to sexism, but also to racism.

2   Pornography is linked – directly or indirectly – to violence.

3   Pornography is related to freedom of movement for women in society, whether it be the freedom to go to the news-stand without seeing pornographic images, or to go out at night alone or with other women.

This last point has parallels in representations of many kinds. As Article 2.2 showed, the 'feminine' stereotype is often represented in fiction in relation to the representation of cultural ideals of female beauty and decorum. In society, freedom of movement may be related to these same personal issues. For example, the freedom to wear comfortable clothes and to sit in comfortable positions is not commonly 'granted' to women. The social convention which urges 'ladies' to sit with their knees together contrasts drastically with the position of women – legs spread apart – as commonly depicted in pornographic imagery. Pornographic images may, in this sense, be seen to depict the false dualities of 'the feminine' discussed in Chapter 2: to depict virgins and whores, and sometimes whores dressed as little girls. But these dualities are contrasted and celebrated, rather than subverted.

The points raised in the Ms U testimony are extremely contentious. There is no 'objective' way of measuring the extent to which pornography may or may not lead to violence, or contribute to sexism and racism in society. It may not be possible to determine whether pornography is the symptom or the disease: one manifestation of a cultural problem, or the problem itself. It would be possible to dismiss the three points listed above as diversionary, or to embrace them as 'truths'. Both positions, and many others in between, fall along the continuum of feminist thought on the issue of pornography.

In this article, as in the previous four, there is much to be debated, picked apart, argued with and reconsidered in the light of personal experience. Thus the question of subjectivity – one of the main themes of this book – is given new meaning in discussion of pornography. Though perspectives on pornography differ significantly from one 'school' of feminism to another, the links between pornography, representation, gender, race and power are difficult to ignore.

As Ellis, O'Dair and Talmer have observed, so it may be said of many women's positions in relation to the pornography debate: 'We are not all in agreement upon each tactic and every issue in our movement, but are committed to the belief that sexual freedom for women should not only be protected but encouraged, that free discussion of sexuality and of its representation is essential to our feminist vision' (Ellis *et al.*, 1990, p. 17). Whether that 'freedom of expression' for women should involve censorship of pornographic representations is a contentious issue. Convincing arguments for and against censorship of pornography have been put forward. It has also been argued that the issues are too complex to be summarized in a 'yes or no' answer to the censorship question, or a 'pro or con' position on the pornography problem. The debate continues.

Notes

1   For discussion of these key terms with reference to men's positions in the pornography debate, see also Heath (1987).

2   *Pornography and Sexual Violence: evidence of the links* – the complete transcript of public hearings on 'pornography as discrimination against women': Minneapolis City Council, Government Operations Committee, 12 and 13 December 1983 (Dworkin and McKinnon, 1988). See also Dworkin (1981) and Wilson (1983).

6
COMIC SUBVERSIONS

The idea of a cultural silencing of women's voices has been developed in many different ways in this book, seen in various contexts as a strategy for keeping women 'in their place'. In Chapter 1, for instance, Joan Swann discussed 'ways of speaking' which are common to women, and Dinah Birch discussed gender in relation to women's writing as another means of 'breaking the silence'. Chapters 3 and 4 offered varying perspectives on the means and modes of self-expression for women working in, and writing about, the visual arts and media. In Chapter 5, feminist critics of varying political perspectives discussed the cultural importance of speaking out against pornography, thereby opening up a debate around the subject of the representation of women's bodies. Chapter 5 also raised several complicated issues regarding the relationship between representation and self-representation, male-produced images of women's bodies versus women's representations of themselves. These same themes are also common to many other areas of women's personal and political experience, and surface in significant ways in humour and the theatre: the subjects of this last chapter in the book.

There are several interconnected ways in which a feminist perspective has been expressed through images projected of and by women in the public domain. Through cross-dressing (women dressing in men's clothes), for instance, women engage in a cultural form of representation which subverts expectation and traditional 'signs' of sexuality, status and class as measured through clothing and costuming. Cross-dressing has particular functions in the theatre, and particularly in comic theatre and lesbian performance, as one of the articles in the chapter demonstrates. Cross-dressing is a means of subverting the 'norms' of social expectations about gender.

Another method of subverting these norms is through comedy: through women 'taking the mike' and speaking out, telling jokes or arguing for different kinds of comedy altogether. Comedy can be utilized by women as a means of saying things and acting in ways which would be difficult to say or do 'straight'. One major achievement of feminism has been an effective infiltration of women into comedy, not only as spectators but also as writers, directors and performers in stand-up, cabaret, theatrical comedy and, recently, on radio and television as well. In women's stand-up comedy, the comedienne speaks directly to (and sometimes about) the audience. In the theatre, the audience–stage interaction is not so direct, but is just as important. In both cases, women 'break the silence' by speaking for themselves, and often by saying things which may be considered 'taboo' subjects in other contexts.

One factor which complicates the study of women's humour and theatre is the relationship between feminist theory and women's performance. As in other parts of this book, the practice/theory divide is important here. A good deal has been written about feminist performance theory, for instance. But not all – or even most – of this theory has been utilized by the women who make feminist theatre. Theory informs performance, and performance practice helps to shape theory. But the dynamic relationship between the two is continually shifting. Therefore, a study of gender and humour, or of comedy in feminist theatre, is both enriched and complicated by the application of feminist theory. As in everyday life, the language of theory may be seen to distance some women from others. This distancing can in itself be seen as a form of cultural silencing, and is perhaps the most serious problem facing feminist critics today.

There are only two articles in this chapter, both of which take up the ideas raised in Chapter 5, such as the recognition of gender-coded systems of oppression in society; representation of the gendered self; the inter-relationships between gender, race and power; the importance of women 'breaking the silence' and the possibility of subverting cultural norms through women's (physical, political and ideological) representation of themselves. But whereas Chapters 4 and 5 focused, for the most part, on male-produced images of women and feminist subversion and reaction to them, Chapter 6 focuses on images of women produced by women. The focus is, as in discussion of 'Pornography and Representation', partly on the representation of women's bodies, but rather than nudity and images of sexuality, this chapter examines the relationship between clothing, costume, class, comedy and power. It deals with the issue of speaking out in relation to joke telling and narrative comedy, gendered humour and comic performance.

The first article, 'Gender and Humour', compares some practical and theoretical ideas about the relationship between gender and power in comedy, and particularly in stand-up comedy. The second article, 'Comic Subversions: Comedy as Strategy in Feminist Theatre', examines the relationship between playing roles in life and on stage, with reference to the development of contemporary feminist theatre. Both articles develop a theme of satire and self-representation with reference to women's strategies for imagining and creating multiple images of self. Both articles introduce theory to practice in a way which problematizes, but also enriches, the study of comedy as a subversive strategy.

Lizbeth Goodman

Article 6.1
GENDER AND HUMOUR
Lizbeth Goodman

One day, I read a quote: 'If a woman told the truth about her life, the world would split open.' I found a stage, where I began to tell the truth about my life – because I couldn't tell the truth off the stage. And very quickly, the world began to blow apart.

(*Roseanne Barr, 1990*, My Life as a Woman, *p. 202*)[1]

POSITIONS, PERSPECTIVES, GENDER AND HUMOUR

This book has explored many different strategies for destabilizing the gendered power base of cultural representation. The idea that comedy can be a subversive strategy is not as straightforward as, for instance, the idea that visual art or fiction can be subversive forms. The complication is the 'living' quality of comedy. While visual arts and fiction require audiences of viewers and readers, the responses from those audiences do not feed back so directly to the artists and writers. Comedy, however, benefits from a live and immediate audience: an audience which shares the playing space. The exception which proves the rule is television comedy, which must often resort to the strategy of constructing a responding spectatorship in the form of simulated, or 'canned', laughter.

Comedy demands an audience: whether it is a few people listening to knock-knock jokes at a party or the paying audience in a West End theatre. Just as the knock-knock joke requires audience participation in the form of the obligatory 'who's there', stand-up comedy and comic theatre both require audience participation of some sort. Comedy has long been a woman's resource, used in prose fiction, verse, song and, more recently, in such evolving genres as feminist crime stories, science fiction, 'feminist fairy tales' and stand-up comedy. Whether it takes the form of satire, sarcasm, irony, narrative humour, or the joke, comedy underscores all these kinds of work. The question is whether some forms of comedy and humour are particular either to women or to men: that is, are gender-specific.

The relationship between gender and humour tends to be studied – if at all – in relation to one form of humour: the joke. As some of this work points out, there is a lingering general perception that women are not best suited to telling jokes, but rather to being the punchlines. This is one of the main arguments of *The Joke's on Us: women in comedy from music hall to the present*, and is the most obvious premise behind a joke such as this:

Question: How many feminists does it take to screw in a lightbulb?

Answer: That's not funny.

(*Banks and Swift, 1987*)

The idea of the joke seems simple: it is based on the assumption that 'feminists have no sense of humour', which is itself based on an assumption: that feminist politics kill the sense of humour. Yet the joke is not as straightforward as it appears to be.

This, like most jokes, is an example of an accessible and non-valorized form of social critique, which functions as a mirror of the values of the dominant culture. Many jokes belong to sets, or – in a loose application of the term – 'genres' or 'classes' of jokes: the knock-knock joke, the mother-in-law joke, the light bulb joke. Similarly, many sets of jokes take particular classes or groups of people as their 'material' or as their punchlines: Jewish people, black people, Irish people, Polish people (all classed as 'foreigners'),

lesbian and gay people, differently abled people, elderly people, and women. That women are singled out as a 'minority' group, despite the majority of women in society, is indicative of the male bias of society and its values. That women are so often the butt of jokes in western culture says a great deal about that culture. Principally, it reveals that the jokers have primarily been men, and that the listeners have been influenced by patriarchal culture to the extent that certain types of responses are 'gendered': for instance, loud laughter as opposed to quiet hand-over-the-mouth giggles.

There is, however, another way of interpreting the feminist light bulb joke. Some women, and indeed some feminists, find the joke 'funny'. It is possible to read, or hear, or even tell such a joke with a double-think mentality. This is important, for jokes are told and retold by many people who are not their 'authors' and who may have different reasons for telling them. In subverting a joke through interpretation, therefore, the hearer of the joke is as active and creative as the teller. The 'punchline' is not only aimed at women, but *is* the woman, or the feminist herself. The position of the 'teller' is harder to locate: it depends upon the interpretation of the joke.

The value of the joke is partially determined by the context of the telling and the interpretation of the hearer. The same joke may have different meanings for different tellers and different audiences. A feminist re-vision of the kind suggested by Adrienne Rich may be employed in humour as well (Rich, 1979b). This kind of re-vision or reinterpretation of the joke requires an awareness of the context of the joke's production and an ability to decontextualize the joke mentally. It can then be interpreted, not as an insult to women or feminism, but rather as a critique of the over-simplified approach to the representation of women, and particularly of feminists, which is often represented in the public sphere. In other words, the joke can be subverted: turned around on the tellers, to show them to be the dupes. In the most radical reading of the joke, it may be seen to be a product of feminist revision, rather than a reaction to it: that is, the joke may be seen to be a concise statement of feminist recognition and rejection of a generalized cultural view of feminism. In this way, feminists as the tellers and the audience can position themselves in the critical domain outside of the joke, rather than within the joke as 'the punchline'.

In re-evaluating the cultural implications of a joke like this, it is possible to decode some of the gendered implications for women and men using humour as a form of expression in the public sphere. Women have been silenced by a culture with a vested interest in not hearing women's voices: this point has been illustrated with reference to representations of women in literature and the visual arts, and in the various representations of women manufactured and proliferated by the media and popular culture. Yet comedy allows for the breaking of taboos; the saying of that which would not normally be said. In fact, much humour relies upon the breaking of taboos and the unsettling of norms of gendered response. Humour, like fiction, is an arena in which the principle of supply and demand is clearly in operation. It is possible for women to find support, and even rewards (in the form of laughter, if not money), for subverting expectation through humour: that is, so long as the subversion does not go 'too far'.

Stand-up comedy is an arena in which women have found a platform for the things they cannot say in their everyday lives, and where they can represent themselves in 'unfeminine ways' and still be accepted, perhaps even rewarded for the transgression. Yet that which women can 'get away with' in humour is allowed because it is meant to be confined to a separate sphere from the 'serious' and the 'real'. In other words, the same woman who does a hugely successful feminist routine in a comedy club or theatre will not necessarily find similar acceptance if she repeats her views at home, or at her nine-to-five job. The separation of stage and life roles has been shifted in recent years, largely through the efforts of feminist women in the wake of the modern women's movement. Humour has been a powerful tool in this cultural shift.

Women's comedy

To tell a joke is to take the subject position: to assert subjectivity. It is the subversion of traditional jokes which allows for the liberating effects of women's comedy. Whether all women's comedy is 'feminist' is as difficult to determine as whether all women's fiction is 'feminist': in both cultural forms, it depends upon who is doing the defining, and for what purposes. Broadly defined for purposes of this article, 'feminist comedy' is that comedy which purposefully subverts traditional expectations about 'what women are' or 'should be', and which also subverts the very means of expression and representation by and through which such expectations are conveyed. Some women's comedy is not feminist, and, indeed, some early women's comedy – that which emerged in the 1960s and 1970s – was what might, in retrospect, be seen as non-feminist (if not anti-feminist), in that it focused on and valorized negative images of women as objects, defined and limited by patriarchal views of women's 'proper' roles.

That women's humour which relies on satire and self-deprecation is a legacy of the cultural objectification of women. The American comedienne Phyllis Diller is known for telling audiences that when she goes to the beauty parlour, she 'always uses the emergency entrance'. Similarly, Joan Rivers is known for comments such as 'They show my picture to men on death row to keep their minds off women'. This kind of self-deprecation is now largely outdated, but can still be found in a contemporary British stand-up routine like that by The Sea Monster (Jo Brand) who begins one of her acts with a sarcastic reference to her own size and her exaggerated concern that the audience will not be able to see her behind the microphone. Brand's self-deprecation is not as extreme as those of her predecessors, but an inherited assumption of a 'norm' for women's appearance does clearly inform the act. The joke about body size relies on the audience's familiarity with 'acceptable' standards for women's appearance, as well as on Brand being willing to make fun of herself for not meeting it.

By contrast, Roseanne Barr has become known for her work in television and film comedy (she played the She-Devil in the 1990 film version of Fay Weldon's story). Barr has also used self-deprecating material in some of her work, referring to her body size and her 'failure' to live up to the superwoman image. But Barr's comedy derides the values which tell her that she ought to be thin in order to be successful. Her material tends to valorize her size and power in what can be interpreted as an embracing of her own image. Barr started as a stand-up comic doing an act about her multiple roles as housewife, mother and waitress. She created a stage persona based on the subversion of the idea that 'housewives' (a term she defines as those who have to clean up other people's messes (Barr, 1990)) are limited by their social contexts and under-valuing in society.

Barr created the persona of the 'Domestic Goddess' which, she explains, was a liberating force for her: 'I figured out that I could say everything I wanted to say by being a housewife' (ibid.). This discovery helped Barr to come to terms with her feeling of being outside the women's movement, for she had always felt that she was excluded from the movement by her class (she was a working-class woman from Iowa), by her Jewish culture, her size and her appearance. As she explained in her book: 'I threatened everyone, whether from my fat, my culture, my ideas, my marriage, or my motherhood, none of which was ever addressed by the women's movement' (ibid.).[2] Of course, feminism has advanced in recent years to embrace and discuss issues of cultural, racial and class difference. But the feeling of being excluded from feminism as well as from male culture is identifiable in the subversive and sarcastic voice of Roseanne.

The example of the Roseanne persona makes an interesting contrast to the British feminist comedy act Spare Tyre: a group which was formed in 1979 by three women with a shared concern about self-image and eating habits. The group was formed in response to Susie Orbach's publication of *Fat is a Feminist Issue* in 1978, and continues to produce popular cabaret comedy with original songs. In the groups' words: 'We always wrote songs from our own experience. All of us had been that woman sitting in her room, feeling fat, unable to do anything with her life until she'd slimmed down to the magic weight' (Spare Tyre, 1987).[3]

Spare Tyre's work encourages women to embrace their own body shapes and sizes, and to find comfort in their differences rather than trying to attain the impossible 'magic weight' or other measure of conformity to the feminine stereotype. This shift from self-deprecation to self-respect and even self-valorization has been one of the major influences of feminism on comedy. Lip Service, a comedy duo which began doing stand-up and moved into cabaret and theatrical comedy, explains the development of the self in gendered humour in this way: '. . . Coming from a feminist base gives you a confidence about yourself. That's the essential difference: you don't need to apologize for yourself . . . for the fact that you're on stage at all'.[4]

As Caroline Hirsch – founder of Caroline's Comedy Club in New York – argued in 1990: 'You really didn't see women break out in comedy until the feminist movement made it possible for women to be considered funny without degrading themselves'.[5] It was clubs like Caroline's which first encouraged women to 'take the mike'. The subsequent televising of the 'live' shows at Caroline's and other clubs helped to project women's comedy into mainstream American culture. In England, the Comedy Store and shows like *What's My Line* have had similar results. In fact, Dawn French – half of the double act French and Saunders – attributes her (their) break into comedy as a direct and fortuitous result of a certain pressure on the management of the Comedy Store to increase its 'credibility' by showcasing more women comics: a pressure put by the British women's movement in the 1970s and 1980s.[6]

Once stand-up comedy was opened up to women, radio and television comedy began to look for women performers as well, though in smaller numbers and often in shows shared with and/or written by men. The move from 'the circuit' to the mainstream is one which not all women would choose. 'Going mainstream' often means compromising on content – particularly feminist content – in order to reach larger audiences. But many comediennes are happy to make this compromise, or do not see it as a compromise at all. The development of women's humour of various kinds, as well as of the emergence of black and working-class people in what was once a white male bastion, has changed the medium of comedy itself. While women's comedy, like comedy by people of colour, was once considered definitively 'alternative', the 'alternative' has had a significant influence on the mainstream. British television comedy has featured women such as Victoria Wood, Julie Walters, Dawn French and Jennifer Saunders, Helen Lederer, Maureen

Lipman, Sandi Toksvig and Josie Lawrence. To some extent, these women no longer represent the 'alternative', but rather serve as role models for women beginning their careers in comedy.

In both the USA and the UK, the advancements of women in comedy helped to open doors for women and men of colour as well. Rhonda Hansome and Thea Vidale are two black women who have become celebrity comics in the USA; Sheila Hyde is one of Britain's few black women comics, and Donna and Kebab – who describe themselves as 'good Greek girls' – have produced live and televised comedy based on their experiences as 'representatives' of the Greek community of London. Women of colour are still relatively rare in comedy, as are working-class women, though the Chuffinelles are an important exception. The Chuffinelles are three working-class 'middle-aged' women from Sheffield who incorporate music and 'alternative themes' in their performances. Similarly, lesbian comedy acts are not yet common, though Karen Parker and Debbie Klein have made a significant impact on British audiences, as has stand-up comedienne Claire Dowie. The work of the theatrical lesbian comedy company Split Britches has had a significant impact in the USA. When humour comes from all these different positions, the possibilities for interpretation are also multiplied. The greater the differences between performers and perspectives, the greater the resulting subversion of cultural stereotypes is likely to be.

GENDER, HUMOUR AND POWER

The remainder of this article will focus on humour as a means of communication influenced by gender and power relations. Recurrent themes include the subversion of expectation through 'breaking silences and taboos' in comedy; the difference between jokes and women's forms of comedy; and the importance of role models in establishing women's comedy in mainstream culture. These points can be illustrated with reference to both feminist theory and practice.

Stand-up comedy as communication: breaking the silence

The connections between speech and silence, discourse and power, gender and humour all come together in a brief passage from Meaghan Morris's comments on 'Feminism, Reading, Postmodernism' (Morris, 1988, p. 15). Morris refers to the feminist strategy of reclaiming women from the past, and she identifies a personal and political danger in this strategy which relates to the representation of women in comedy:

> ... by resorting to the device of listing 'excluded women', women excluded for no obvious reason except that given by the discourse – their gender – I have positioned myself in a

speech-genre all too familiar in everyday life, as well as in pantomime, cartoons, and sitcoms: the woman's complaint, or *nagging*. One of the defining generic rules of 'nagging' is unsuccessful repetition of the same statements. It is unsuccessful, because it blocks change: nagging is a mode of repetition which fails to produce the desired effect of difference that might allow the complaint to end ... (A conventional comic scenario goes: she nags, he stops listening, nothing changes, she nags.) Yet there is always a change of sorts implied by repetition: in this case, her 'place' in speech becomes, if not strictly nonexistent, then insufferable – leaving frenzy or silence as the only places left to go.

(*Ibid.*)

In Morris's conception of nagging as a powerless discourse, it is easy to see its attraction for male comics as a stereotypical representation of women in jokes about nagging wives and mothers-in-law. If nagging is a powerless text, and humour is a form of communication or a speech-act involving power, then women's comedy which inverts stereotypes about nagging are subversive in the extreme.

Stand-up comedienne Helen Lederer suggests that it may be possible to subvert the power of mother-in-law jokes by reclaiming them as a useful and relevant source of material for women: she says: 'I would love to do mother-in-law jokes since I'm married and I could do some really good ones: I don't think that's a taboo area for me now'. In other words, mother-in-law jokes may have different implications when told by women about women, or by one individual about one nagging mother-in-law, rather than by men about a stereotypical and representative figure of 'the' universal mother-in-law. Part of the power of this kind of reversal of expectation comes from the very fact of the presence of the female comic on stage. In Lederer's words: 'It takes a certain audacity for a woman to go on stage and say, right, listen to me and look at me; I'm going to make you laugh'.

Lederer also refers to the power of the female voice in doing comedy. Her remarks are reminiscent of Hélène Cixous's theory that women's use of language is limited by a culture which does not encourage women to speak in public. In comedy, when women are not only speaking but also trying to gain an audible response – laughter – from an audience, the voice as the instrument for the communication of humorous ideas has an added significance. Lederer refers to the problem of her voice 'wobbling' when she is nervous; a problem she observes more generally in women's stand-up comedy as well as in public spaces such as Parliament. She compares the sound of women's voices to those of men, suggesting that women may sound less authoritative – regardless of the import of their speeches or the quality of their material – because of the volume and stability of the sound, although men may 'be talking complete rubbish but sound authoritative'. Comedy, Helen Lederer contends, is about communication, and the voice is the means of delivering the message. Therefore, she argues, part of the problem for women in comedy is learning to control their voices: to make their voices heard.

Female forms: rejecting the joke

One significant contribution of women's comedy has been a shift in the form of the medium: from jokes with punchlines to other forms like narrative comedy, theatrical comedy and cabaret. Lily Tomlin's successful one-woman show, *The Search for Signs of Intelligent Life in the Universe*, includes this example of narrative women's comedy:

At the Doctor:
You're sure Doctor? Premenstrual syndrome?
I mean, I'm getting divorced.
My mother's getting divorced.
I'm raising twin boys.

I have a lot of job pressure –
I've got to find one.
The ERA didn't pass, not long ago I lost a very dear friend,
and . . . and . . . my husband is involved . . . not just involved,
but in love, I'm afraid . . . with this woman . . .
who's quite a bit younger than I am.
And you *think* it's my *period* and *not* my life?[7]

This is narrative situational comedy. There is a punchline of sorts (the last line) but the lead-up is not contained in one feed line; rather, it is spread over a series of lines with subordinate punchlines building towards the 'climax'. The humour is diffused over the situation, rather than contained in a single phrase. This can be seen as a general characteristic of much women's comedy. Comparison of interview responses from Helen Lederer, Donna and Kebab and Lip Service all place the value of 'the joke' in the context of traditional masculine humour.

Helen Lederer on the joke:

> When a man tells a formalized joke I tend to switch off because it's quite authoritarian: you have to listen in order to get the pay off, the punchline, and then you have to laugh. It's quite strict and inflexible. It's far more interesting for me to ramble on, hopefully hitting the right targets, certainly with a throughline and certainly with an end, but not in the same formalized way. I would rather just sit and hope that it's funny.

Donna and Kebab on the joke:

> As far as jokes are concerned, there are a few in our act but . . . it's mainly observational humour. We rarely do a comedy sketch about something that we don't actually have experience of. We don't feel qualified to talk about things we haven't experienced, so when we talk it tends to be as familiar characters from within the Greek community.

Sue Ryding of Lip Service on the joke:

> The stand-up format is to do with that microphone which is a very phallic symbol, and it is to do with the fact that people expect punch lines, they expect one-liners. The main difference between women's and men's humour is that women do tend to take the essence of a situation and tell it in a more subtle way. . . . Another difference is that if you're creating characters and if you're presenting a character there is a barrier between you and the audience.

Lip Service's comments were particularly relevant to the issues of speech and silence, gender and power. In describing the audiences for their act, they explained that their earlier work (which they described as 'tub thumping feminism') was 'interesting if women came with their boyfriends or their husbands: it was as if the men had to give the women permission to laugh. You'd have women with their hands over their mouths sniggering but not feeling that they could express their laughter openly'. As in earlier discussion of visual images, it is also the case that women in comedy have 'so much they want to say'. The performance is only one side of the dynamic: the women in the audience must be free to laugh as well. Laughter is itself a form of cultural representation, or self-expression. Laughter may, for women, also be a means of subverting cultural norms by 'breaking the silence'.

Role models and representation

Helen Lederer, Lip Service and Donna and Kebab all mentioned the same few women who were influential in their acts, or who served as role models of a sort. These women include Victoria Wood, Julie Walters, Dawn French and Jennifer Saunders. But as Eve Adams of Donna and Kebab observed, the relative scarcity of women in comedy has meant that women tend to be compared to these few 'role models' in a way which seems to imply that their work is either unoriginal or largely representative: 'Men are allowed to be themselves. It's very different for women, and we're always being compared with French and Saunders because we are a double act . . . I don't look anything like Dawn French!' Adams is joking, but she is also serious: she does not 'look anything like' Dawn French. More to the point, she recognizes a tendency to see women as 'representatives' of each other in comedy as in other forms of public representation.

Adams' comments bring to mind the fact that women, like people of colour, are often seen as universally 'other'. Just as the bigoted view that 'black or Asian people all look alike' has emerged in various western cultures, so the idea that women somehow represent each other has persisted. Yet the most 'representative' of women are often the least likely to accept responsibility for representing others. For instance, Victoria Wood is often cast as the role model for young comediennes. She is assumed to be 'feminist' because the results of her act have suited the feminist cause. Yet the 'feminist' label does not necessarily reflect Wood's personal politics, as she has explained.

When asked in an interview in 1981 whether she saw herself as a feminist, Victoria Wood replied:

> I do but . . . I believe that men and women are equal, and that women had a bad time but I'm very simplistic about it. I

would never pick anything for its feminist overtones. I would only ever write about what I wanted to write about and what I knew about. Having said that I do feel very strongly that women are pressurized into feeling inadequate.[8]

The 'I do but . . .' response to the feminist label may be viewed as a 'cop out', or as an honest response to a question which is so strongly positioned that a full response is impossible to make without qualifications. Yet is is important that, regardless of her wariness about the feminist label for herself and her work, Wood is careful to point to what she sees as an undeniable link between gender, pressure, power and silencing of women's humour.

In an interview with Morwenna Banks and Amanda Swift, Wood said: 'I don't try to have an image. I just try to be myself' (in Banks and Swift, 1987, p. 87). That attempt to 'just be oneself' is complicated by the very nature of public performance. It is doubly complicated when the question of feminist representation comes into play: it is not easy for women like Victoria Wood to 'be themselves' when the image of self in performance is interpreted differently by different audiences, and when feminist politics demand a 'feminist image'. One way in which comediennes have asserted a certain kind of image is through costume. Many, like Victoria Wood, tend to wear jackets and trousers rather than skirts or dresses. The choice of costume is partially motivated by consideration of comfort, but is also intended to de-emphasize the 'feminine' image and to assert a certain power through the stronger image which masculine or gender-neutral clothing can give.

Gender and power

Power is asserted through the content of comedy material as well as through its presentation and delivery. Power is often associated with a 'male' sense of humour. When asked in an interview whether she thought her stand-up comedy was different from 'male stand-up', Claire Dowie replied: 'Well, I don't know many men who stand up and say "I'm a lesbian"' (in Banks and Swift, 1987, p. 51). Other comediennes are less forthright about the issue of the 'gendering' of their material.

One study, undertaken by critic Regenia Gagnier, suggests that the positioning of humour in gendered contexts has been a problem historically, and that it has tended to be influenced by race and class considerations as well (Gagnier, 1988). Gagnier did a large-scale 'cross-class analysis' of gender, power and humour, encompassing a wide range of sources from Victorian working women's autobiographies to contemporary feminist theory. Gagnier observed:

In none of the hundreds of working women's autobiographies I have read have I found jokes about sex or jokes at the expense of unfortunates: the sole source of humor is real or imaginary transgressions relating to social class. The form these humorous transgressions takes is not disparagement or release, nor brief laughter, but rather a process of imaginative engagement.

(Gagnier, 1988, p. 146)

With reference to contemporary manifestations of these same issues, Gagnier contends that the 'frame-breaking, democratizing, and anarchic humor' which has shown itself in women's comedy is informed – albeit indirectly – by feminist theory. She cites Hélène Cixous's 'The Laugh of the Medusa' with reference to women's breaking of silence in and through writing as an anarchic grasping of the means of communication. Gagnier's piece ends with an observation: '. . . Medusa's anarchic laughter sheds some light on why – unlike those white men secure in their absolute signification who discern in isolation the hard core of humor – the black men in the study laughed at everything and the Victorian women never laughed alone' (ibid., p. 146). Here, Gagnier pinpoints an important dynamic between race and gender, as they intersect with cultural power relations, expressed not only through the act of telling jokes but also through listening and reacting to them. Laughter is a form of expression which is dependent upon social context; only in certain contexts will certain people feel free to laugh.

The expression of laughter is important; it represents more than the value of the joke, and, in many cases, may be less informed by the joke than by the context in which it is told. Conservative analysis of humour from earlier generations made some sweeping statements about the cultural function of sexual jokes. For instance, G. Legman asserted in 1968 that:

> . . . it cannot, of course, be overlooked that the telling of sexual jokes to women by men is certainly and inevitably a preliminary sexual relation and represents a definite sexual approach, just as listening to (or telling) such jokes by women implies a readiness for or acceptance of such an approach. The telling of jokes in company also assists in this, since the permissive group often present at joke-telling sessions also allows of a much greater sexual denudation of all concerned than a woman might permit to a more or less strange man alone.

(Legman, 1968, p. 218)

The out-dated assumptions about gender and power which Legman's remarks reveal can be interpreted as 'jokes' in themselves when they are read from a contemporary perspective: cultural representation and humour have advanced considerably since Legman's study. But the same issues are at stake today. Joke telling is still a predominantly male form; joke telling is still less 'typical' for women as comediennes, and stereotypical views of women as passive and men as active makers of 'sexual advances' and jokes still inform humour to some extent, though this is changing rapidly.

As the interviews with comediennes in this piece reveal, attitudes towards the representation of women in society have affected the avenues open to women in comedy, and have also influenced the kind of material which is included in women's humour. As critic Lisa Merrill has argued: '. . . perhaps women's so-called "lack of humor" is, in fact, a refusal to comply with the *premise* of a joke' (Merrill, 1988, p. 273). Feminist writer and performer Bryony Lavery has put it another way:

> . . . if you say you are a feminist comic, you are going to have to prove you're funny. To most people there is a feeling that feminism is humourless which of course is the usual fiction, like 'women talk more than men', 'women are less funny than men', and it's all part of a huge propaganda. Humour is a weapon and if we say that women are not funny, they can't use that weapon.

(Lavery, in Banks and Swift, 1987, p. 215)

Here, Lavery identifies the premise of the light bulb joke cited earlier. As the premises accepted and encouraged by cultural representations of women change, so does the role of women in comedy, and the relationship between feminism, power, gender and humour. Humour *is* a powerful weapon, and one which feminists have not only grasped but have also learned to use in a variety of subversive ways.

Notes

1   Roseanne Barr now uses the surname Arnold.

2   See also Kathleen K. Rowe's article 'Roseanne: unruly woman as Domestic Goddess' (1990).

3   Introduction to *The Spare Tyre Song Book* (Spare Tyre, 1987). The song book and four audio-cassette recordings of Spare Tyre's songs are available from Spare Tyre, c/o Instrument House, 207 King's Cross Road, London WC1X 9DB. Spare Tyre was interviewed in 1991, in relation to a BBC/Open University radio programme on 'Women Comics'. However, since this interview took place, Spare Tyre's status has changed. Rather than performing their own shows, they now work in the community teaching others to make comic theatre.

4   The interviews with Lip Service (Maggie Fox and Sue Ryding), Helen Lederer and Donna and Kebab (Eve Adams and Martha Lewis) were conducted by Amanda Willett and Lizbeth Goodman for a BBC/Open University radio programme on 'Women Comics' in 1991 (producer: Jenny Bardwell). Quotations here are taken from the transcripts of these interviews. Lip Service was also interviewed on 28 March 1991 (research assistant: Jane Tonge).

5   'Funny Ladies' interview by Stephen Fenichell, *Philip Morris Magazine*, March–April 1990.

6   Interview with Yvonne Roberts, *The Observer*, 27 January 1991, p. 51.

7   Written by Jane Wagner; produced at the Plymouth Theatre, Broadway, New York, 1986.

8   Interview with Michael Binns, *Gambit: The International Theatre Review*, vol. 10, no. 38, 1981, p. 20.

Article 6.2
COMIC SUBVERSIONS: COMEDY AS STRATEGY IN FEMINIST THEATRE

Lizbeth Goodman

Many women are so systematically deprived of an ego that they must constantly refer to a mirror, to their physical presence, to reassure themselves that they are actually there, still in one piece. Women's lives are a series of small dramas in which they play shifting defensive roles. The necessity to do so is real, for they are under economic necessity, and often physical constraint as well, to faithfully play the parts of sister, daughter, wife, mother and lover. Many women see that these are a collection of roles, but the face behind the shifting masks is a mystery even to themselves. The only constant in their lives is misery and a never-ending unsureness of themselves. A woman must, in order to make it as a woman, reflect the desires and preconceptions of every man who has power over her. Otherwise she is out of a job, out of her parents' house, out of a marriage, with no available slot left to fill. Women have to play at being themselves – that is, their *nice* selves, the selves made to order on standard patterns. 'Just be yourself, dear,' we are told as we go off to the prom. And we wonder, 'What does that mean? What am I expected to do?'

(*Meredith Tax, 1973, 'Woman and Her Mind: The Story of Everyday Life', p. 31*)

This extract from an early radical feminist essay compares women's roles in everyday life to 'small dramas' played with inadequate financial backing and outside support. These same factors characterize the theatre. The extract also points to a striking similarity between roles played in the theatre and those which women (and men) 'play' in everyday life: roles such as mother and daughter, performer and spectator, writer and reader. Positioning is crucial. In the theatre space, only some spectators will be positioned close enough (physically and ideologically) to see beneath the costumes and makeup of the performers, and possibly to recognize self in performance. The personal–political positions of spectators and critics will always influence interpretation and reception of the play. The female majority in most theatre audiences also influences interpretation and reception by enriching the (gendered) dynamic between stage and world which is the context of any play in performance. This article argues that the gendered dynamic between the audience and the performance has particular implications for plays by and about women.

The article examines one variety of theatre: comic theatre. More specifically, it examines theatre made by women who take positions on feminism: feminist comic theatre. Not all feminist theatre conforms to the points of similarity raised in the radical feminist essay quoted above. Radical feminist theatre like that of Sarah Daniels conforms to many of these points. For instance, Daniels's play *Masterpieces* (1984) – the first major and most performed play by a woman about pornography – is an example of radical feminist theatre which deals with cultural representation in direct ways: by addressing the pornography problem as it intersects with issues of gender and power. The play continues to be a 'consciousness raiser' for its audiences, and has been received with many angry – as well as positive – reviews from theatre critics and academics.

While Daniels's plays have had significant impact on feminist audiences, they have also reached many women and men who do not tend to take a feminist perspective on social issues, much less on a night out at the theatre. But Daniels contends that labelling her work as 'feminist theatre' is problematic due to the status of the term 'feminist', rather than to the status of her work. She refers to the changing social context in which a word like 'feminism' evolves, and says: 'Feminism is now, like a panty-girdle, a very embar[r]assing word. Once seen as liberating, it is now considered to be restrictive, passé, and undesirable to wear' (Daniels, 1991, p. xii). For all that, Daniels does not deny that her work is feminist, nor that she is a feminist playwright. But she contends that these labels do not reflect the primary aims of her work, and implies that labels such as 'feminist' (and garments such as panty-girdles) have different values for different people in different contexts.

In the quotation above, as in many of her plays, Daniels makes her most powerful statement about feminist politics not through a theoretical argument or polemical diatribe, but rather through an ironic statement. The reference to the panty-girdle is an example of a playwright's use of humour as a form of communication appropriate to the theatre. Daniels's work is sometimes referred to as 'radical feminist theatre'. The label is appropriate in some respects, and not in others. But more importantly, there are many kinds of feminist theatre which cannot be conveniently categorized according to such labels as 'socialist-feminist theatre' or 'radical-feminist theatre'.

Some feminist theatre treats 'issues of comedy as issues of power', as Susan Carlson has argued in her article 'Comic Collisions: Convention, Rage and Order' (Carlson, 1987, p. 314).[1] Carlson cites

Caryl Churchill's socialist-feminist play *Cloud Nine* as an example of a piece which demonstrates the ability of comedy to disengage stereotype from traditional power structures within the text of the play. But other feminist theatre, rather than privileging personal politics and issues of cultural representation within playtexts, focuses instead on *context*. By privileging the audience's role in the performance, some feminist theatre adopts Barthes's literary critical notion of 'the death of the author' (Barthes, 1977). But this idea is complicated in feminist performance, when authors are nearly always alive and have often made their political positions public knowledge. In Jill Dolan's words:

> In theatre, much of the recent discussion over theory comes from a similar unwillingness to unsettle playwriting as one of women's primary activities. If we agree that the author is dead, how can we continue talking about women playwrights? Feminist poststructuralist theories, however, don't intend to kill off women authors a priori, but to simply enlarge the consideration of text to take into account the meanings that are constructed in peformance as well as on the page.
>
> *(Dolan, 1989, p. 64)*

There is not space here to examine all of the different kinds of feminist comic theatre. This article includes a brief introduction to feminist theatre as genre, and is followed by discussion of three feminist theatre productions: Lip Service's *Margaret III, Parts II and III*; the Dramatrix lesbian pantomime *Cinderella: The Real True Story*, and Bryony Lavery's *Her Aching Heart*. These are discussed in a context which emphasizes their qualities as comic theatre pieces with implications for their audiences, rather than as representations of particular political positions held by their writers, directors, performers, or audiences.

FEMINIST THEATRE

Feminist theatre is a genre in which women's comedy has been developed as a subversive strategy using costumes, sets and props, lighting and sound systems, experimentation with language, music and text. But what is most interesting about feminist comic theatre is context. Feminist theatre relies on a subversion of 'reality' and on the presence – imagined or real – of an audience. In defining feminist theatre, the distinction between feminist writing versus women's writing is relevant: all women's theatre is not feminist, and all feminist theatre is not necessarily 'good' theatre simply because it is feminist. Feminist theatre is defined by its politics (feminism) rather than by its form (theatre).

It is only recently that 'feminist theatre' has been recognized as a distinct form or genre. Since its emergence in the late 1960s and early 1970s, feminist theatre has changed its forms and styles considerably. The earliest 'feminist theatre' performances were the demonstrations against the Miss World and Miss America pageants held in 1970. The Women's Street Theatre Group was one of the first organized feminist theatre companies, and much of its work in the 1970s was agit prop theatre: designed to convey polemical feminist messages, or what Sue Ryding of Lip Service has called 'tub thumping feminism'. In all feminist theatre, however, feminist women have been involved in the making and interpreting of plays (whether in the 'role' of playwright, director, performer, or spectator). The image of the feminist has therefore been prioritized and because theatre is a platform for public representation, the physical appearance and costume of 'the feminist' has been publicly scrutinized.

Referring to the beauty pageant protests and first National Women's Conferences in the early 1970s, Susan Bassnett has described the development of feminist theatre in relation to the emergence of a 'feminist costume' of sorts:

> At the same time, the new feminist image began to be created. Although mocked in the press as ugly and unfeminine, a substantial number of British feminists chose to wear clothes that were practical and de-emphasized a traditional image of femininity. In Britain probably more than anywhere else, the idea of a feminist uniform became popular, and for a time in the 1970s, dungarees, laced boots and short-cropped hair were every bit as emblematic of a group identity as the old servicemen's tie and blazer. In assuming that new image, feminists were rejecting the other prevailing images of women – the Sex Object, perfumed and provocatively made up for men to ogle, and the Lady, epitomized by Margaret Thatcher in her Marks and Spencer blue suits with crimplene-bowed blouses. Women's theatre groups, like Monstrous Regiment, Beril and the Perils and the Women's Theatre Company, challenged the traditional images of women on stage, deliberately presenting images of androgyny. In addition to the campaigns for equal rights in the workplace and improved child-care conditions, British feminists emphasized the need to alter radically the image of women in society.
>
> (Bassnett, 1986, p. 156)

With the development of more subtle and refined forms of feminist theatre, there was a move away from 'tub thumping' in some quarters. But the emphasis on costume, on image, on contrasting women's social roles with theatrical roles: these aspects of early feminist theatre have remained. Contemporary feminist theatre takes many forms. It is written and produced by women of many different backgrounds and many different positions, and nearly always relies on the subversion of 'norms' or conventions which tend, as in stand-up comedy, to be male-defined.

Feminist comic theatre has particular relevance to a comparison of social and theatrical roles for women, for two reasons: it relies to a large extent on costume and cross-dressing, and it demands an enhanced audience response: not only attention and applause at the end, but laughter throughout. Feminist comic theatre is therefore more closely related, in some respects, to stand-up comedy and cabaret than it is to 'serious drama' of other kinds. In fact, many feminist theatre companies are also considered to be 'comedy acts': Spare Tyre and Lip Service are two such companies. Lip Service has developed from a stand-up act to a theatre company composed of two women: Maggie Fox and Sue Ryding.

PAYING MORE THAN LIP SERVICE TO FEMINISM IN THE THEATRE

Maggie Fox explains that she and Sue Ryding met in university, where they were both cast in rather stereotypical parts in traditional plays:

Fox: You were characterized either into being a Juliet or a character actress, which basically meant that you were fat. If you were something in between, there was nothing for you to do. We discovered in this production that we had a lot of comic talent. . . .

Ryding: Which is interesting in an Ibsen play . . .

Fox: There wasn't a lot of comic potential in Ibsen, but we found it.[2]

Their 'finding' of comedy in Ibsen was actually a finding of their dual voice and their shared dissatisfaction with the roles on offer in Ibsen and other 'canonized' drama. They formed a double act and began doing stand-up comedy. As the previous article points out, they soon found that they felt more comfortable working in comic theatre than they did doing stand-up; they preferred 'being in character' on a stage to 'being themselves' behind a microphone. Yet in writing and performing comic theatre, Fox and Ryding found that their early 'tub thumping' feminist approach to the presentation of women in theatre was limiting them to certain (positive, female) kinds of characters, while they wanted to present a range of female (and male) characters. They decided that in order to be feminist and funny but also to have a diversity of characters in their work, they would have to combine positive images of women with absurd images of women and men. It is significant that they chose Margaret Thatcher as the model for one of their most extreme characters. This is also ironic, considered in the light of Susan Bassnett's choice of Thatcher – clad in her Marks and Spencer blue suits – as the iconic antithesis of the feminist image.

Lip Service wrote *Margaret III, Parts II and III*: a play which they attribute in their programme notes – tongue in cheek – to Shakespeare (Pl. 24). The title of the play is a take-off of Shakespeare's *Henry IV: Parts I and II*, but the style is, in the words of the authors and characters, 'very modern'. The play revolves around a large open book positioned, upright, at the centre of the stage. The performers – as they very carefully and patiently explain, exaggerating their eye contact with the audience in the manner of school teachers with an unruly class – are 'on stage' when positioned in front of the book, and 'off stage' when their backs are turned, when they are out of sight behind the book, or when they are not paying attention. In this way, Lip Service mock both the style of 'the old fashioned fuddy duddy way' of delineating stage space 'frequently used by the Royal Shakespeare Company', and also the 'very modern' theatrical conventions of the post-modern theatres of newly canonized playwrights like Beckett and Pinter. The benefits of this approach, they explain, are twofold: the effect is refreshingly different, and it also 'saves a fortune on scenery'.

The central characters of the Lip Service play are the evil Queen Margaret (an obvious Thatcher parody) and her 'fool' Motley Sue. All other characters (peasants, horses, moon and star, warring tribes etc.) are played by Fox and Ryding as well. The invention of the character of Queen Margaret was a reaction to the lack of significant powerful female roles in the dramatic canon. In Maggie Fox's words: 'what we try to present is a very complex picture of women, so with *Margaret III* you've got this picture of a tyrant, and yet there is something attractive about her, because she is so extraordinary and over the top – she has the essence of Laurence Olivier about her – you can't pin her down'.

The play tells the story of the magnificent adventures of Queen Margaret: 'The tale is told how Margaret bold became fair England's Queen' by killing the eighty-nine relations standing between her and succession. The motto is encapsulated in the opening song: 'Nothing succeeds like succession'. In depicting Margaret as a power-mad murderous monarch, Lip Service illustrate some of the complicated issues surrounding female leadership. Significantly, Queen Margaret's power is 'put on' with her costume. The putting on of costumes is a central and very visible act in this play, wherein the characters demonstrate the modern theatre's preoccupation with 'demystification' by performing all costume, set and scene changes in front of the audience, as part of the play.

The first time Maggie Fox the performer becomes Margaret the mad Queen and Sue Ryding becomes Motley Sue, they pick up the sacks containing their frocks and props, and explain – with exaggerated patience – the process of their transformation to the audience:

Actor M: I'm just getting into my Margaret costume which is in here.

Actor S: I'm just getting into my Motley Sue costume which is in here. Now this is what we in modern theatre call 'demystification'. That's

Both: Demystification.

Actor S: That is we do everything in front of you –

Actor M: Everything?

Actor S: Everything.

Actor M: Everything!?

[M GOES OFF, LOOKING SHOCKED AND WORRIED.]

Actor S: So you know exactly what's going on, and you don't have any surprises.

[ACTOR M APPEARS SUDDENLY WITH A WIG ON.]

Both: Margaret III, Parts Two and Three.

[THEY GET UP AND OPEN THE BOOK TO REVEAL A LARGE CROWN.]

In this scene, which precedes the action of the play, the idea of 'demystification' is both derided and celebrated. Maggie and Sue become 'real people' distinguishable from the multiple characters they play. They are also recognizable as self-conscious wearers of 'the feminist costume' referred to by Bassnett. Thus the object of traditional acting – to 'become' or portray the character as 'believably' as possible – is subverted so that the performers themselves (Maggie and Sue) become the focus of attention. The scene serves another purpose as well: it 'demystifies' the character of Queen Margaret, who is shown early on to be uncomfortable with the idea that everything she does will be seen. Later in the play, the word 'demystification' is accompanied by clouds of very heavy mist from a smoke machine, which is carried on stage and placed in a prominent position, thereby demystifying the idea that theatrical smoke and thunder are the products of anything more 'mystical' than dry ice and amplifiers. Ironically, it is those spectators seated near the stage who are most affected by the smoke, and for whom it is consequently more difficult to see.

The play proper begins. An extract from the play shows the two performers engaged in a 'lesson' on how to decode Shakespeare's language. Because the sequence takes the form of a lesson, one character must 'play the fool' in relation to the other. Following Shakespearean tradition, it is the fool (Sue) who teaches the monarch (Margaret):

Actor M: How are you getting on with Shakespeare's language?

Actor S: Some people have a lot of trouble with Shakespeare's language.

Actor M: Because it's old fashioned.

Actor S: An example of this is 'thou'.

Both: 'Thou'.

Actor M: And what does it mean?

Actor S: You.

Actor M: (Not a sheep).

Both: You.

Actor M: You, thou.

Actor S: Thou, you.

Actor M: You, hoo.

Actor S: Another old fashioned word is 'art'.

Both: 'Art'.

Actor M: Now this does not mean a painting, or drawing.

Actor S: It means –

Actor M: Or sculpture, or music –

Actor S: It means –

Actor M: Or photography or etching –

Actor S: It means –

Actor M: Or potato printing or origami.

Actor S: It means 'are'.

Both: 'Are'.

Actor S: So if we put them both together – 'Thou art'.

Both: Thou art.

Actor M: This does not mean 'you painting'.

Actor S: It means –

Actor M: Or 'you drawing'.

Actor S: Shut up. It means 'you are'.

Both: 'You are'.

Actor S: (TO AUDIENCE) Got it?

Actor M: Yes, I think I have.

The comic lines are enhanced in performance by the absurd facial expressions and accents of both performers. The powerful position of 'the teacher role' is assigned to Motley Sue through her command of the language, while Queen Margaret shows herself to be in need of a Shakespearean vocabulary lesson. The lesson is utilized later in the play when Queen Margaret needs to decipher the 'revolutionary subtext' of a Morris-dancing sequence and to learn to 'find the point' in discussion of unemployment, and in locating battle sites on her map.

What is revealed in the last two lines of this exchange is the active role demanded of the audience in this performance. Motley Sue's last line is addressed not to Queen Margaret, but to the audience. Yet Margaret replies in the first person, on behalf of the audience (the 'royal we' condensed to an 'I') or in an obvious display of her egotistic assumption that all speech is addressed to her. But the audience is involved as well: they are asked a question ('Got it?') and are thus given a role to play within the play.

Similarly, the closing song involves the audience in the play. After Queen Margaret is slain and is allowed to die 'very dramatically' three or four times for good measure, both performers sing from the anonymous darkness of the final blackout:

Margaret star of court and battle

Daughter of St Helen's Lancs

Madder than most English cattle

For thy life we now give thanks

Dull it wasn't while you reigned

You spared no whip to make us tops

The joys of being in such pain

You feel so grateful when it stops.

This simple comic song is designed to end the play on a positive note. It involves several layers of meaning, and like the play as a whole, will appeal to different audiences in different ways. The song is, first and foremost, a rhyming verse which privileges the mundane rather than the majestic. At another level, however, the lyrics of the song are culturally specific. For instance, they refer to a town in England and to the 'mad cow disease' scare of 1990. The events of the play are also influenced by historical change in the 'real world'. Because the play was written on the eve of Thatcher's resignation and before the outbreak of the Gulf Crisis, the significance of events within the play, such as the death of Queen Margaret, has shifted since the play was first staged. Even so, the play is rendered more lasting by its comedy. The individual 'present tenses' of each audience member are invoked in the last line of the song, which functions as a statement about the power of comic theatre to raise large issues and then to allow the audience to be grateful 'when it stops'.

RECLAIMING HERSTORY IN A LESBIAN FEMINIST PANTO

The Lip Service play discussed above is unique in its depiction of a world inhabited by women, wherein women simply dress as men when the presence of 'men' on stage is required. In a different way, lesbian theatre is unique in its definition of worlds in which men do not figure, or figure only as reference points, but not often as significant characters. Lesbian comic theatre is unique in its use of cross-dressing as a form of representational liberation for women, rather than a representational mimicry of men. In this and in other ways, lesbian comic theatre provides a rich source for comparison of the playing of roles in life and in the theatre. But as Kate Davy has observed with reference to Lily Tomlin's one-woman show *The Search for Signs of Intelligent Life in the Universe*, the cultural context of lesbian performance may be its most subversive element: '. . . the fact that Tomlin and Wagner unabashedly present lesbian characters and material from a feminist perspective in a Broadway context has subversive undertones just by virtue of the way it plays, the theatre it plays in, and the spectators it plays to' (Davy, 1986, p. 46).

For these same reasons, Cheryl Moch's lesbian feminist pantomime *Cinderella: The Real True Story* is a subversive play (Pls. 21 and 22).[3] It opened off-off Broadway in 1985, and had its British premiere at London's Drill Hall in 1987. While the context of this play is not quite as 'mainstreamed' as Tomlin's one-woman Broadway performance, it is significant that Moch's *Cinderella* played to mixed audiences (women and men, lesbian, gay and heterosexual). It played as a pantomime: with all the fanfare and advertising of traditional panto adverts, but these were published primarily in 'alternative' feminist media spaces and tended to emphasize an 'alternative' scale of values. For instance, Figure 6.2.1 is the advertisement for the play which was published in *Spare Rib* in 1987, reproduced here beneath an extract from a review of the play which appeared in the same issue:

Cinderella

Does this sound familiar? Our victim/heroine Cinderella is unloved by her wicked stepmother and bullied unmercifully by her two ugly sisters (parts played traditionally by middle-aged men in drag who, to general merriment, constantly re-adjust their false breasts to show just how ridiculous the female anatomy is). Passively, she endures a life of domestic servitude, her 'feminine' saintliness wins her the ultimate reward – she is chosen by the prince as a suitable wife. . . .

As in the original pantomime, Cinderella is magically transformed and goes to the royal ball – but not in an elaborate gown. Cinderella goes in a suit, passing as a man (a dramatic reversal of the usual pantomime gender bending). To complicate matters further the prince has been replaced with a princess. The inevitable happens, the princess, to the dismay of the king, falls in love with the masculinely attired Cinderella. Courtiers visit the princess's subjects trying to find the foot to fit the leather brogue!

The second half of the evening departs from tradition. The princess and Cinderella have the challenge of making a life together despite the prejudice they initially suffer from the palace and the rest of the world.

(Kinnaird, 1987, p. 36)

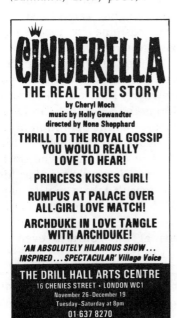

Figure 6.2.1
Advertisement for *Cinderella: The Real True Story*, published in *Spare Rib*, 1987

Cheryl Moch's version of 'Cinderella' can best be described as a lesbian feminist farce, produced by Dramatrix with a multi-racial cast, in the form of a feminist fairy tale, or revision of the traditional pantomime. The motto of the play (or the 'moral of the story') is that everyone, regardless of sexual orientation, 'deserves to have a happily ever after'. Yet the message behind the deceptively optimistic motto is quite serious. The play deals primarily with power: power as manifest in the legal status of daughters in a patriarchy, and the power of free-thinking versus the power of stereotype as embodied in cultural institutions dependent upon maintenance – or the outward signs of maintenance – of the 'norm' of heterosexuality.

Dramatrix described their motivation for performing *Cinderella* as a desire to create a form of: 'entertainment that does not rely on sexist jokes, racial stereotypes and crude innuendo for popular appeal'.[4] This version of the Cinderella story was set up in deliberate contrast to the standard endings of traditional comedies, which tend to involve dance and song in public displays of 'coming together'. In the penultimate scene of Moch's version, Cinderella and her Princess are nearly killed by a violent crowd. The happy ending is preceded by a scene of cultural violence and aggression, and is then presented as the ultimate subversion of social order: a communal 'coming out' scene. The disorder that threatened the social concord is not overcome, but overruled.

Throughout the play, the twisting of convention is taken very seriously. For instance, in scene four when the Grandmother/Clock is dressing Cinderella for the ball, she does more than uncover a man's suit beneath the tattered gown; she gives careful instructions on carrying off the wearing of the costume by practising the gendered gestures involved in cross-dressing: '. . . there's nothing to it. Just move like you're not only entitled to your own space, but like you're thinking of taking everyone else's. Walk like you're pushing, really pushing, to get somewhere. And talk the same way' (Moch, 1989a). When the Duke informs the King that Cinderella is really a woman, the King's reply reveals that his definition of cross-dressing includes only male camp: 'How can that be? . . . Maybe he's dressed as a woman today – I've heard of men who do that'. The Duke reassures the King by praising Cinderella's 'act' as highly believable with these words: '. . . It doesn't take a fool to enjoy a fine performance. Hers was splendid. I myself thought she cut a fine figure of a man'. After the Duke 'comes out', it becomes clear that the web of sexual attractions at the court is even more complicated than it at first appeared to be.

The Dramatrix production highlights the power of naming as an issue for lesbian representation. For instance, Cinderella encounters a group of birds in the nest of the Grand Inestimable Eagle. The birds are complaining about the ways in which proper bird names are made into pejoratives by humans: 'chicken livered; bird brained, hen pecked, sitting duck'. When the Eagle finally speaks, his (her) complaint is this: 'It's not just that they call us names. Our very names are made degrading'. The bird resents the use of derogatory names based on his (her) physical characteristics, just as the terms 'deaf and dumb' have been recognized as derogatory and prejudiced phrases in contemporary society. Of course, the bird's reaction to this name-calling most directly relates to use of the word 'lesbian' as an insult to Cinderella and the Princess in the penultimate scene.

The power of institutionalized heterosexuality is ingrained in the words of law, which are created and recorded by men. In this play, the traditional notion that 'the king's word is law' is called comically into question:

Princess: I want to marry her, Daddy.

King: You can't change the way things are. It's nature.

Princess: No it's not. It's law.

King: Ah, it's law then . . .

Princess: [SNUGGLING NEXT TO HIM SEDUCTIVELY] Well, you always say, 'My word is law'. Change the law Daddy. Change it for my happiness.

Just as language and power interact in this exchange, they also inform the dynamic of audience interaction inherent to the pantomime. Pantomimes tend to include audience interaction in the texts as well as in the contexts of performance. Moch's pantomime is no exception. When Cinderella enters the Gorgon's lair, she pauses in order to ask a question of the audience: 'But there's no Gorgon here, is there?' This is the next line in the script:

Audience: It's behind you!

Just as Lip Service asked their audience a question ('Got it?'), Moch asks her audience a question. But the pantomime form allows her to demand an answer as well. What the script does not say is that the question will be repeated in performance until a response is made by the audience. The performers may even refuse to carry on with the play until they receive satisfactory responses ('I can't hear you . . .'). This scene, like the entire second half of the play, is designed to engage the audience with the performers in a dynamic of recognition and identification. By including the audience in the quest, it becomes possible to include them in the happy ending as well. The chorus of the closing song is: 'lovers all deserve to have their happily ever afters'.

The cathartic effect of the play is intended and indeed clearly specified by the author. In Cheryl Moch's words: '[The play works] because of the serious purpose behind the hilarity. In this play, there's a whole lot of wish fulfilment going on' (Moch, 1989b). Moch also observed that the success of the play was closely related to the availability of an appropriate space for lesbian performance, as well as to the play's content or intent:

> The emergence, in the last ten years or so, of lesbian plays, can be traced to the emergence of lesbian, feminist and gay-controlled spaces and theatre groups as well as to the playwrights. . . . But none of what you read [in the published version of the playtext] would exist were it not for the invaluable contribution of others: performers, directors, producers, and technical crews, who, working largely as volunteers, make possible gay and lesbian theatre, giving us all the chance to gather in the dark together and watch our dreams unfold.
>
> (Ibid., p. 147)

Social and cultural contexts influence the development of texts such as Moch's *Cinderella: The Real True Story*, as well as the contexts of lesbian performance. The emergence of other varieties of feminist comic theatre was also informed by changing social contexts. Feminist theatre has been enabled by the willingness of many different people to translate 'dreams' into images in the theatre, and of audiences to engage in the interpretation and reception of different plays in a variety of imaginative ways.

BREAKING CONVENTION AND *HER ACHING HEART*

Bryony Lavery, who played one of the stepbrothers (and other characters) in the Dramatrix production of *Cinderella: The Real True Story*, is better known as a playwright than as a performer. Lavery has been involved in the development of British alternative theatre since the 1970s, and has taken part – as a performer and as a writer – in productions with many key theatre groups like Monstrous Regiment and Gay Sweatshop. In the late 1970s, for instance, she co-wrote Monstrous Regiment's cabaret *Floorshow* with Caryl Churchill and Michelene Wandor. But much of Lavery's work has taken the form of comic theatre rather than cabaret.

In 1990–91, Lavery's play *Her Aching Heart* was produced by Women's Theatre Group. The play is an example of a lesbian romantic comedy which engages with its audience (differently than the pantomime) at two levels of experience at once: that of the world of the play, and also that of the world of the play-*within*-the-play (Pl. 23).[5] This depiction of worlds within worlds is, of course, most familiar from Shakespeare's *Hamlet*. Lip Service developed a distinction between dramatic worlds in terms of 'demystification' of performers and roles, while Lavery develops it in terms of the imaginations of her characters, who transport themselves through the medium of romance into fictional and 'real' worlds.

Her Aching Heart is a subversive play: it 'demystifies' theatre traditions by pointing out that theatre history is nothing more than a composite of reviews, written mostly by men with interests and values of their own. In other words, theatre history – like all history – is biased. Lavery has drawn an analogy between theatre history and a museum run by male curators:

> At the moment the theatre seems too much like a great museum run by male curators. The glass exhibition cases are opened up and historic exhibitions taken out and shown to us all, if we can afford the entrance fee. . . . I am tired of my role as cleaner in this museum. Most of the rubbish is dropped by men.
>
> *(Lavery, 1984, p. 30)*

The serious undertones of the comic statement are supported by the available figures on women's employment and status in the British theatre (see Gardiner, 1987; Goodman, 1992a,b). But Lavery's is a unique way of seeing the problem, and one which is reflected in the characters she creates. Her work tends to offer female characters who are not politicians or superwomen, but rather shop assistants and home makers; not queens, but cleaners. This depiction does not 'degrade' women, but more in the manner of Roseanne Barr's creative persona of the 'ideal housewife as domestic goddess', it elevates the roles which women play in everyday life by representing them on stage.

Some of Lavery's earlier work contains the germs of the ideas which were developed so successfully in *Her Aching Heart*. At the core of much of that early work is the developing awareness and articulation of women's place in society: a view of the theatre which is informed by an awareness of the role playing of everyday life. Lavery recalls with amusement her debut in an experimental play (by a man) called *Furniture Revolts*, in which she was cast as the left arm of a sofa: '. . . it was a three seater . . . we were all female . . .' (Lavery, 1984, p. 25). In the early 1980s, Lavery formed her own group, without a home venue let alone furniture, and called it 'Female Trouble', followed by 'More Female Trouble'. Since then, Lavery's work has developed ideas and images of class consciousness, the sexual division of labour, sexuality and sexual orientation as weapons used in society to keep women down (or treat them as furniture). *Her Aching Heart* deals with all of these themes. It is a 'lesbian historical romance' which tells two stories at once. Modern and fictional worlds collide and combine in a play which deals with issues as varied as friendship, love, sex, desire, gender roles, the function of romance and the influence of stereotype and expectation (i.e. past precedent) on forming and informing the present.

The play is set in the present, and also in a mock Gothic past or fantasy world. Like Lip Service's *Margaret III*, there is a book at the centre of the play. Unlike *Margaret III*, however, the book does not function as 'the set', but as the central prop and metaphor. Lavery uses a particular book (a novel called *Her Aching Heart: a lesbian historical romance*). The novel is read by both modern characters (Harriet and Molly) throughout the play, and functions as the metaphorical link between them and the characters who inhabit the otherwise distinct romantic world of the book's narrative (Lady Harriet of Helstone Hall and Molly the idealized 'peasant').

Because, as in Lip Service's production, there are only two performers, each plays multiple roles. Lavery 'demystifies' the multiplicity of persona for comic effect. She contrasts the modern women with the romantic heroines they admire. For example, in an early scene when Lady Harriet goes out riding, her costume is specified in the stage directions and her words are ridiculously overblown:

Harriet: [IN RIDING HABIT]
  What a fresh, fine, sharp Cornish morning!
  I declare . . . it lifts my heart like a sparrow . . .
  tossing it in winged joy on gently-wafting currents of air!
  The trees rustle in the light wind!
  The sun streaks like a basset hound across the fields!
  The sea gallops like a thoroughbred mare pounding its shiny
  hooves upon the rocks along the shore! . . .
  (*Lavery, 1991*)

Elsewhere, the characters are always 'dressed' by Lavery in 'historical underwear' of various kinds. Lavery's stage directions do not indicate tone or mood so much as visual effect, and where they do indicate mood, they do so sarcastically, in phrases which cannot be easily translated into action. For instance, her stage directions include lines like these: 'SHE IS BROKEN-HEARTED', 'SHE MOOCHES AROUND', and: 'A WOMAN ENTERS. SHE IS DRESSED IN A SHIFT. HER HEART IS ACHING. ANGUISH CLOUDS HER SWEET EYES'. The best illustration of Lavery's comic stage directions is in the sequence wherein Molly, melodramatically straining under the weight of her love and lust, repeats Harriet's name and attempts to emphasize it differently each time (as the stage directions instruct her to do). As usual, the stage directions include an indication of her costume:

Molly: FAST AND FURIOUS
 SHE PICKS UP A BLACK GARMENT,
 WIPES HER EYES UPON IT.
 SHE PUTS IT ON . . .
 SHE PUTS ON A WHITE CLOSE FITTING HOOD.
 . . . SHE PUTS ON A CROSS.
 . . . SHE PUTS ON A WIMPLE.
 Harriet.
 WITH WARM AFFECTION. Harriet.
 WITH LUST. Harriet.
 WITH LONGING: Harriet.
 WITH HATRED. Harriet.
 WITH EMPTINESS. Harriet.
 SHE PICKS UP A BIBLE AND EXITS.

Here, as in *Margaret III*, the stage directions and 'demystification' of changes of costume are part of the performance. And as in *Cinderella: The Real True Story*, the importance of naming is also stressed. The intrusion of comedy material into the stage directions is typical of Lavery's style; the mingling of text and context is part of her subject matter, as well as her form of presentation.

Lavery, like Moch, is aware of the social context in which her lesbian feminist plays are performed. She is also aware of the power of the small circle of male critics who review British theatre. In 1988, Lavery said: 'We need to get angry again about the number of plays by women which get produced, and the constant negative criticism we get from the [male critics] of this world, who of course want to see plays about them'.[6] In other words, the project of writing and producing feminist theatre must be set in the context of contemporary society, which is 'reviewed' by critics who prefer to see images which are familiar to them, or about them (i.e. about men).

Her Aching Heart is a play about women, and about romantic fiction, and about the reality it reflects. Yet it is a play very obviously informed by an awareness of social context. It is a play about women entranced by images of women offered in popular fiction and other forms of cultural representation; about desire and lesbian love and friendship, and about subverting expectation. The closing song is celebratory, as were the closing songs of both *Margaret III* and *Cinderella: The Real True Story*. Lavery's song is a love song:

Song: I am not myself again
 ready, steady, go again
 . . . oh, oh, my aching heart again . . .
 . . . oh, oh, in love again.

THE END.

In a play which, like the other two discussed, is purposefully 'larger than life' in many respects, the words of this song are reassuringly simple.

SUBVERTING THE STORY TO REACH THE HAPPY ENDING

The three plays discussed share several common themes and devices. First, all share cross-dressing and gendered power relations as key themes. *Cinderella* is a classic story about class privilege and the influence of dress (rich clothes catch the princess or prince). In Moch's pantomime version, Cinderella does not only dress up, but also cross-dresses in order to win the *woman* of her dreams. But the princess remains a princess, needing considerable assistance in getting into her own rich clothes: the issue of class difference is glossed over rather than resolved. In Lip Service's play, two female performers play a variety of male and female parts, and Margaret is seen to be most powerful when she wears her 'Queen costume'. In *Her Aching Heart*, dressing and undressing are addressed as links between past and present, class privilege and ordinary life. The wearing of 'historical underwear' and a set of outdated and exaggerated conventions is all that separates the modern readers from their fictional heroines.

All three plays present fantastic worlds, and all three have happy endings. Even *Cinderella*, which nearly ends in a mass fight scene, closes with a traditional 'rousing chorus', though one which advocates 'untraditional' relationships. All three plays use comedy as a subversive strategy. Whether the topic is politics (as in *Margaret III*) or fairy tale (as in *Cinderella*) or romance and lesbian desire (as in *Her Aching Heart*), comedy intervenes to make the topics accessible to various audiences. All three plays are also feminist: written and performed by consciously feminist women. All three suggest that feminist comedy and role playing on stage may have significant ramifications for 'real' women and men in the audience.

The degree to which feminist theatre may cause change in society has been the subject of extended debate. Feminist theatre is one platform upon which feminist theory can be seen to meet feminist practice: where performances are directed by and from political positions, and where the role of the audience in interpreting and responding to the performance is informed by personal and political positions as well. Jill Dolan has argued that theory may act as an enabling device in relation to feminist theatre and feminist critical practice:

> Theory enables me to describe the differences within me and around me without forcing me to rank my allegiances or my oppressions. As feminist critic Gayle Austin would say, theory

enables the divided subject to fall into the cracks of difference and to theorize productively from there, knowing that truth is changeable, permeable, and finally, irrelevant.

(Dolan, 1989, p. 65)[7]

Theory may meet practice in feminist theatre. But theatre is theatre, not 'real life'. Whether the subversive strategies of comedy in theatre have any real, lasting effects on relationships in everyday life is a questionable matter. Life in the modern world requires role playing of various kinds, and as the opening extract by Meredith Tax points out, it is difficult to find a comfortable position between these multiple roles in which it is possible to 'be yourself'.

The advantage of performing in the theatre is the release from having to 'be yourself'. The advantage of watching a theatre performance is similar: it is possible to recognize self in characters on stage, but also possible to learn from and then leave the resemblance behind. This is called catharsis: the purging of emotion through identification aroused in performance, which is a universally recognized function of theatre. In feminist comic theatre, interpretation of the play will depend as much upon the positions of the audience – physical and ideological – as upon the play itself. Each spectator, or reader of the playtext, must decide where the play ends and the role playing of 'real life' begins.

Notes

1   Carlson refers to Blau's 'Comedy Since the Absurd' in *Modern Drama*, no. XXV, 1982.

2   All quotations and references are taken from an interview conducted with Lip Service in 1991, recorded and transcribed by the BBC/Open University for a radio programme on 'Women Comics' (producer: Jenny Bardwell; interviewer: Lizbeth Goodman; pre-production: Amanda Willett) and from the play script. The script of *Margaret III* is unpublished, but can be obtained from the authors, c/o Lip Service, 13 Rosford Avenue, Manchester M14 7BW.

3   *Cinderella: The Real True Story*, by Cheryl Moch. First produced at the WOW Cafe, New York; directed by Lois Weaver, 19 December 1985. First British performance at the Drill Hall, November 1987; directed by Nona Shepphard, music by Holly Gewandter, designed by Amanda Fisk. Produced by Julie Parker and Mavis Seaman for Dramatrix Productions, with Kate Corkery, Gillian Hanna, Nicola Kathrens, Bryony Lavery, Dallas Lingham, Mary McCusker, Adele Saleem and Faith Tingle. Published in *Lesbian Plays, Volume Two*, edited by Jill Davis (Moch, 1989a).

4   Programme notes from the Drill Hall production.

5   *Her Aching Heart* by Bryony Lavery, 1990. The script is published in a collection of three of Lavery's plays, entitled *Her Aching Heart, Wicked, Two Marias* (1991).

6   Interview with Lizbeth Goodman, 20 July 1988.

7   Dolan (1989, p. 65), referring to Gayle Austin, comments made on 'Elucidating Terms and Issues', panel on Women and Theatre Programme Preconference, San Diego, CA, August 1988.

CONCLUSION

IN SEARCH OF OUR MOTHERS' GARDENS

Alice Walker

> I described her own nature and temperament. Told how
> they needed a larger life for their expression . . . I pointed
> out that in lieu of proper channels, her emotions had
> over-flowed into paths that dissipated them. I talked,
> beautifully I thought, about an art that would be born,
> an art that would open the way for women the likes of
> her. I asked her to hope, and build up an inner life
> against the coming of that day . . . I sang, with a strange
> quiver in my voice, a promise song.
>
> (*Jean Toomer*, 1975, 'Avey')

The poet speaking to a prostitute who falls asleep while he's talking –

When the poet Jean Toomer walked through the South in the early
twenties, he discovered a curious thing: black women whose
spirituality was so intense, so deep, so *unconscious*, that they were
themselves unaware of the richness they held. They stumbled
blindly through their lives: creatures so abused and mutilated in
body, so dimmed and confused by pain, that they considered
themselves unworthy even of hope. In the selfless abstractions their
bodies became to the men who used them, they became more than
'sexual objects', more even than mere women: they became 'Saints'.
Instead of being perceived as whole persons, their bodies became
shrines: what was thought to be their minds became temples
suitable for worship. These crazy Saints stared out at the world,
wildly, like lunatics – or quietly, like suicides; and the 'God' that
was in their gaze was as mute as a great stone.

Who were these Saints? These crazy, loony, pitiful women?

Some of them, without a doubt, were our mothers and
grandmothers.

In the still heat of the post-Reconstruction South, this is how
they seemed to Jean Toomer: exquisite butterflies trapped in an evil

honey, toiling away their lives in an era, a century, that did not acknowledge them, except as 'the *mule* of the world'. They dreamed dreams that no one knew – not even themselves, in any coherent fashion – and saw visions no one could understand. They wandered or sat about the countryside crooning lullabies to ghosts, and drawing the mother of Christ in charcoal on courthouse walls.

They forced their minds to desert their bodies and their striving spirits sought to rise, like frail whirlwinds from the hard red clay. And when those frail whirlwinds fell, in scattered particles, upon the ground, no one mourned. Instead, men lit candles to celebrate the emptiness that remained, as people do who enter a beautiful but vacant space to resurrect a God.

Our mothers and grandmothers, some of them: moving to music not yet written. And they waited.

They waited for a day when the unknown thing that was in them would be made known; but guessed, somehow in their darkness, that on the day of their revelation they would be long dead. Therefore to Toomer they walked, and even ran, in slow motion. For they were going nowhere immediate, and the future was not yet within their grasp. And men took our mothers and grandmothers, 'but got no pleasure from it'. So complex was their passion and their calm.

To Toomer, they lay vacant and fallow as autumn fields, with harvest time never in sight: and he saw them enter loveless marriages, without joy; and become prostitutes, without resistance; and become mothers of children, without fulfilment.

For these grandmothers and mothers of ours were not Saints, but Artists; driven to a numb and bleeding madness by the springs of creativity in them for which there was no release. They were Creators, who lived lives of spiritual waste, because they were so rich in spirituality – which is the basis of Art – that the strain of enduring their unused and unwanted talent drove them insane. Throwing away this spirituality was their pathetic attempt to lighten the soul to a weight their work-worn, sexually abused bodies could bear.

What did it mean for a black woman to be an artist in our grandmothers' time? In our great-grandmothers' day? It is a question with an answer cruel enough to stop the blood.

Did you have a genius of a great-great-grandmother who died under some ignorant and depraved white overseer's lash? Or was she required to bake biscuits for a lazy backwater tramp, when she cried out in her soul to paint watercolours of sunsets, or the rain falling on the green and peaceful pasturelands? Or was her body broken and forced to bear children (who were more often than not sold away from her) – eight, ten, fifteen, twenty children – when her one joy was the thought of modelling heroic figures of rebellion, in stone or clay?

How was the creativity of the black woman kept alive, year after year and century after century, when for most of the years black people have been in America, it was a punishable crime for a black person to read or write? And the freedom to paint, to sculpt, to expand the mind with action did not exist. Consider, if you can bear to imagine it, what might have been the result if singing, too, had been forbidden by law. Listen to the voices of Bessie Smith, Billie Holiday, Nina Simone, Roberta Flack and Aretha Franklin, among others, and imagine those voices muzzled for life. Then you may begin to comprehend the lives of our 'crazy', 'Sainted' mothers and grandmothers. The agony of the lives of women who might have been Poets, Novelists, Essayists and Short-Story Writers (over a period of centuries), who died with their real gifts stifled within them.

And, if this were the end of the story, we would have cause to cry out in my paraphrase of Okot p'Bitek's great poem:

O, my clanswoman

Let us all cry together!

Come,

Let us mourn the death of our mother,

The death of a Queen

The ash that was produced

By a great fire!

O, this homestead is utterly dead

Close the gates

With *lacari* thorns,

For our mother

The creator of the Stool is lost!

And all the young women

Have perished in the wilderness!

But this is not the end of the story, for all the young women — our mothers and grandmothers, *ourselves* – have not perished in the wilderness. And if we ask ourselves why, and search for and find the answer, we will know beyond all efforts to erase it from our minds, just exactly who, and of what, we black American women are.

One example, perhaps the most pathetic, most misunderstood one, can provide a backdrop for our mother's work: Phillis Wheatley, a slave in the 1700s.

Virginia Woolf, in her book *A Room of One's Own*, wrote that in order for a woman to write fiction she must have two things, certainly: a room of her own (with key and lock) and enough money to support herself.

What then are we to make of Phillis Wheatley, a slave, who owned not even herself? This sickly, frail black girl who required a servant of her own at times – her health was so precarious – and who, had she been white, would have been easily considered the intellectual superior of all the women and most of the men in the society of her day.

Virginia Woolf wrote further, speaking of course not of our Phillis, that 'any woman born with a great gift in the sixteenth century [insert 'eighteenth century', insert 'black woman', insert 'born or made a slave'] would certainly have gone crazed, shot herself, or ended her days in some lonely cottage outside the village, half witch, half wizard [insert 'Saint'], feared and mocked at. For it needs little skill and psychology to be sure that a highly gifted girl who had tried to use her gift for poetry would have been so thwarted and hindered by contrary instincts [add 'chains, guns, the lash, the ownership of one's body by someone else, submission to an alien religion'], that she must have lost her health and sanity to a certainty.'

The key words, as they relate to Phillis, are 'contrary instincts'. For when we read the poetry of Phillis Wheatley – as when we read the novels of Nella Larsen or the oddly false-sounding autobiography of that freest of all black women writers, Zora Hurston – evidence of 'contrary instincts' is everywhere. Her loyalties were completely divided, as was, without question, her mind.

But how could this be otherwise? Captured at seven, a slave of wealthy, doting whites who instilled in her the 'savagery' of the Africa they 'rescued' her from . . . one wonders if she was even able to remember her homeland as she had known it, or as it really was.

Yet, because she did try to use her gift for poetry in a world that made her a slave, she was 'so thwarted and hindered by . . . contrary instincts, that she . . . lost her health . . .' In the last years of her brief life, burdened not only with the need to express her gift but also with a penniless, friendless 'freedom' and several small children for whom she was forced to do strenuous work to feed, she lost her health, certainly. Suffering from malnutrition and neglect and who knows what mental agonies, Phillis Wheatley died.

So torn by 'contrary instincts' was black, kidnapped, enslaved Phillis that her description of 'the Goddess' – as she poetically called the Liberty she did not have – is ironically, cruelly humorous. And, in fact, has held Phillis up to ridicule for more than a century. It is usually read prior to hanging Phillis's memory as that of a fool. She wrote:

The Goddess comes, she moves divinely fair,

Olive and laurel binds her *golden* hair.

Wherever shines this native of the skies,

Unnumber'd charms and recent graces rise. [My italics]

It is obvious that Phillis, the slave, combed the 'Goddess's' hair every morning; prior, perhaps, to bringing in the milk, or fixing her mistress's lunch. She took her imagery from the one thing she saw elevated above all others.

With the benefit of hindsight we ask, 'How could she?'

But at last, Phillis, we understand. No more snickering when your stiff, struggling, ambivalent lines are forced on us. We know now that you were not an idiot or a traitor; only a sickly little black girl, snatched from your home and country and made a slave; a woman who still struggled to sing the song that was your gift, although in a land of barbarians who praised you for your bewildered tongue. It is not so much what you sang, as that you kept alive, in so many of our ancestors, *the notion of song.*

Black women are called, in the folklore that so aptly identifies one's status in society, 'the *mule* of the world', because we have been handed the burdens that everyone else – *everyone* else – refused to carry. We have also been called 'Matriarchs', 'Superwomen', and 'Mean and Evil Bitches'. Not to mention 'Castraters' and 'Sapphire's Mama'. When we have pleaded for understanding, our character has been distorted; when we have asked for simple caring, we have been handed empty inspirational appellations, then stuck in the farthest corner. When we have asked for love, we have been given children. In short, even our plainer gifts, our labours of fidelity and love, have been knocked down our throats. To be an artist and a black woman, even today, lowers our status in many respects, rather than raises it: and yet, artists we will be.

Therefore we must fearlessly pull out of ourselves and look at and identify with our lives the living creativity some of our great-grandmothers were not allowed to know. I stress *some* of them because it is well known that the majority of our great-grandmothers knew, even without 'knowing' it, the reality of their spirituality, even if they didn't recognize it beyond what happened in the singing at church – and they never had any intention of giving it up.

How they did it – those millions of black women who were not Phillis Wheatley, or Lucy Terry or Frances Harper or Zora Hurston or Nella Larsen or Bessie Smith; or Elizabeth Catlett, or Katherine Dunham, either – brings me to the title of this essay, 'In Search of

Our Mothers' Gardens', which is a personal account that is yet shared, in its theme and its meaning, by all of us. I found, while thinking about the far-reaching world of the creative black woman, that often the truest answer to a question that really matters can be found very close.

In the late 1920s my mother ran away from home to marry my father. Marriage, if not running away, was expected of seventeen-year-old girls. By the time she was twenty, she had two children and was pregnant with a third. Five children later, I was born. And this is how I came to know my mother: she seemed a large, soft, loving-eyed woman who was rarely impatient in our home. Her quick, violent temper was on view only a few times a year, when she battled with the white landlord who had the misfortune to suggest to her that her children did not need to go to school.

She made all the clothes we wore, even my brother's overalls. She made all the towels and sheets we used. She spent the summers canning vegetables and fruits. She spent the winter evenings making quilts enough to cover all our beds.

During the 'working' day, she laboured beside – not behind – my father in the fields. Her day began before sun-up, and did not end until late at night. There was never a moment for her to sit down, undisturbed, to unravel her own private thoughts; never a time free from interruption – by work or the noisy inquiries of her many children. And yet, it is to my mother – and all our mothers who were not famous – that I went in search of the secret of what has fed that muzzled and often mutilated, but vibrant, creative spirit that the black woman has inherited, and that pops out in wild and unlikely places to this day.

But when, you will ask, did my overworked mother have time to know or care about feeding the creative spirit?

The answer is so simple that many of us have spent years discovering it. We have constantly looked high, when we should have looked high – and low.

For example: in the Smithsonian Institution in Washington, DC, there hangs a quilt unlike any other in the world. In fanciful, inspired, and yet simple and identifiable figures, it portrays the story of the Crucifixion. It is considered rare, beyond price. Though it follows no known pattern of quilt-making, and though it is made of bits and pieces of worthless rags, it is obviously the work of a person of powerful imagination and deep spiritual feeling. Below this quilt I saw a note that says it was made by 'an anonymous Black woman in Alabama, a hundred years ago'.

If we could locate this 'anonymous' black woman from Alabama, she would turn out to be one of our grandmothers – an artist who left her mark in the only materials she could afford, and in the only medium her position in society allowed her to use.

As Virginia Woolf wrote further, in *A Room of One's Own*:

> Yet genius of a sort must have existed among women as it must have existed among the working class. [Change this to 'slaves' and 'the wives and daughters of sharecroppers.'] Now and again an Emily Brontë or a Robert Burns [change this to 'a Zora Hurston or a Richard Wright'] blazes out and proves its presence. But certainly it never got itself on to paper. When, however, one reads of a witch being ducked, of a woman possessed by devils [or 'Sainthood'], of a wise woman selling herbs [our root workers], or even a very remarkable man who had a mother, then I think we are on the track of a lost novelist, a suppressed poet, of some mute and inglorious Jane Austen ... Indeed, I would venture to guess that Anon, who wrote so many poems without signing them, was often a woman ...

And so our mothers and grandmothers have, more often than not anonymously, handed on the creative spark, the seed of the flower they themselves never hoped to see: or like a sealed letter they could not plainly read.

And so it is, certainly, with my own mother. Unlike 'Ma' Rainey's songs, which retained their creator's name even while blasting forth from Bessie Smith's mouth, no song or poem will bear my mother's name. Yet so many of the stories that I write, that we all write, are my mother's stories. Only recently did I fully realize this: that through years of listening to my mother's stories of her life, I have absorbed not only the stories themselves, but something of the manner in which she spoke, something of the urgency that involves the knowledge that her stories – like her life – must be recorded. It is probably for this reason that so much of what I have written is about characters whose counterparts in real life are so much older than I am.

But the telling of these stories, which came from my mother's lips as naturally as breathing, was not the only way my mother showed herself as an artist. For stories, too, were subject to being distracted, to dying without conclusion. Dinners must be started, and cotton must be gathered before the big rains. The artist that was and is my mother showed itself to me only after many years. This is what I finally noticed:

Like Mem, a character in *The Third Life of Grange Copeland*, my mother adorned with flowers whatever shabby house we were forced to live in. And not just your typical straggly country stand of zinnias, either. She planted ambitious gardens – and still does – with over fifty different varieties of plants that bloom profusely from early March until late November. Before she left home for the fields, she watered her flowers, chopped up the grass, and laid out new beds. When she returned from the fields she might divide clumps of bulbs, dig a cold pit, uproot and replant roses, or prune branches from her taller bushes or trees – until night came and it was too dark to see.

Whatever she planted grew as if by magic, and her fame as a grower of flowers spread over three counties. Because of her creativity with her flowers, even my memories of poverty are seen through a screen of blooms – sunflowers, petunias, roses, dahlias, forsythia, spirea, delphiniums, verbena ... and on and on.

And I remember people coming to my mother's yard to be given cuttings from her flowers; I hear again the praise showered on her because whatever rocky soil she landed on, she turned into a garden. A garden so brilliant with colours, so original in its design, so magnificent with life and creativity, that to this day people drive by our house in Georgia – perfect strangers and imperfect strangers – and ask to stand or walk among my mother's art.

I notice that it is only when my mother is working in her flowers that she is radiant, almost to the point of being invisible – except as Creator: hand and eye. She is involved in work her soul must have. Ordering the universe in the image of her personal conception of Beauty.

Her face, as she prepares the Art that is her gift, is a legacy of respect she leaves to me, for all that illuminates and cherishes life. She has handed down respect for the possibilities – and the will to grasp them.

For her, so hindered and intruded upon in so many ways, being an artist has still been a daily part of her life. This ability to hold on, even in very simple ways, is work black women have done for a very long time.

This poem is not enough, but it is something, for the woman who literally covered the holes in our walls with sunflowers:

> They were women then
> My mama's generation
> Husky of voice — Stout of
> Step
> With fists as well as
> Hands
> How they battered down
> Doors
> And ironed
> Starched white
> Shirts

How they led
Armies
Headragged Generals
Across mined
Fields
Booby-trapped
Kitchens
To discover books
Desks
A place for us
How they knew what we
Must know
Without knowing a page
Of it
Themselves.

Guided by my heritage of a love of beauty and a respect for strength – in search of my mother's garden, I found my own.

And perhaps in Africa over two hundred years ago, there was just such a mother; perhaps she painted vivid and daring decorations in oranges and yellows and greens on the walls of her hut; perhaps she sang – in a voice like Roberta Flack's – *sweetly* over the compounds of her village; perhaps she wove the most stunning mats or told the most ingenious stories of all the village storytellers. Perhaps she was herself a poet – though only her daughter's name is signed to the poems that we know.

Perhaps Phillis Wheatley's mother was also an artist.

Perhaps in more than Phillis Wheatley's biological life is her mother's signature made clear.

REFERENCES

ACKER, K. (1984) *Blood and Guts in High School Plus Two*, London, Picador.

ADAMS, M.J. (n.d.) 'The Harriet Powers pictorial quilts', *Black Art*, vol. 3, no. 4, pp. 12–28.

ALEXANDER, K. (1987) Review of *She's Gotta Have It*, *Spare Rib*, no. 176.

ALLEN, P.G. (1990) *Spider Woman's Granddaughters: traditional tales and contemporary writing by Native American women*, London, The Women's Press.

ALVARADO, M., GUTCH, R. and WOLLEN, T. (1987) *Learning the Media*, London, Macmillan Education.

ANDERSON, B. (1983) *Imagined Communities*, London, Verso.

ANG, I. (1985) *Watching Dallas*, London, Methuen.

ANGENOT, M. (1979) 'The absent paradigm: an introduction to the semiotics of science fiction', *Science Fiction Studies*, vol. 6, no. 1, pp. 9–19.

ANSCOMBE, I. (1984) *A Woman's Touch: women in design from 1860 to the present day*, London, Virago.

ATTFIELD, J. (1989) 'Inside pram town: a case study of Harlow house interiors, 1951–61', in Attfield, J. and Kirkham, P. (eds) *A View from the Interior: feminism, women and design*, London, The Women's Press, pp. 215–38.

ATTILLE, M. and BLACKWOOD, M. (1986) 'Black women and representation', in Brunsdon, C. (ed.) *Films for Women*, London, British Film Institute.

BAILEY, C. (1990) 'Black Country working women', *Oral History* (The Crafts), no. 18, pp. 75–8.

BANK, M. (1979) *Anonymous was a Woman*, New York, St Martin's Press.

BANKS, M. and SWIFT, A. (1987) *The Joke's On Us: women in comedy from the music hall to the present*, London, Pandora Press.

BANKS, O. (1981) *Faces of Feminism: a study of feminism as a social movement*, New York, St Martin's Press.

BARON, S. (1987) 'Kiss me in black and white', *City Limits*, no. 282 (26 February–5 March).

BARR, R. (1990) *My Life as a Woman*, London, Fontana.

BARRETT, M. (1980) *Women's Oppression Today: problems in Marxist feminist analysis*, London, Verso.

BARTHES, R. (1977) *Image-Music-Text*, essays selected and translated by Stephen Heath, New York, Noonday Press.

BARTHES, R. (1986) 'The death of the author', Howard, R. (tr.), in Barthes, R. *The Rustle of Language*, Oxford, Blackwell.

BASSNETT, S. (1986) *Feminist Experiences: the women's movement in four cultures*, London, Allen and Unwin.

BAUMANN, M. (1979). 'Two features of "women's speech"?', in Dubois, B.L. and Crouch, I. (eds) *The Sociology of the Languages of American Women*, papers in Southwest English IV, San Antonio, Trinity University.

BAXANDALL, M. (1972) *Painting and Experience in Fifteenth-Century Italy*, London, Oxford University Press.

BECKETT, J. and CHERRY, D. (1989) Review of *The Spectacle of Women: imagery of the Suffrage campaign 1907–14*, 1987, by Lisa Tickner, in *Art History*, vol. 12, no. 1, p. 125.

BEER, G. (1979) 'Beyond determinism: George Eliot and Virginia Woolf', in Jacobus, M. (ed.) *Women Writing and Writing about Women*, London, Croom Helm.

BELL, L. (ed.) (1987) *Good Girls/Bad Girls: feminists and sex trade workers face to face*, Toronto, Seal Press.

BENJAMIN, J. (1983) 'Master and slave: the fantasy of erotic domination', in Snitow, A., Stansell, C. and Thompson, S. (eds) *Powers of Desire: the politics of sexuality*, New York, Monthly Review Press, The New Feminist Library.

BENNETT, S. and GIBBS, J. (1980) 'Racism and classism in the lesbian community', in Bennett, S. and Gibbs, J. (eds) *Top Ranking*, Brooklyn, NY, February 3rd Press.

BENSTOCK, S. (ed.) (1988) *The Private Self: theory and practice of women's autobiographical writing*, London, Routledge.

BERGER, J. (1972) *Ways of Seeing*, London, BBC Books.

BETTERTON, R. (1987a) 'Pornography: the politics of representation', in Betterton, R. (ed.) *Looking On: images of femininity in the visual arts and media*, London, Pandora Press, pp. 143–50.

BETTERTON, R. (ed.) (1987b) *Looking On: images of femininity in the visual arts and media*, London, Pandora Press.

BLOOM, H. (1975) *The Map of Misreading*, Oxford and New York, Oxford University Press.

BONNER, F. (1984) 'Women and the new media', in the Third Women and Labour Publications Collective (eds) *All Her Labours: embroidering the framework*, Sydney, Hale and Iremonger.

BORNSTEIN, D. (1978) 'As meek as a maid: a historical perspective on language for women in courtesy books from the Middle Ages to *Seventeen Magazine*', in Butturff, D. and Epstein, E.L. (eds) *Women's Language and Style*, Akron, OH, Department of English, University of Akron.

BOWMAN, R. and ADRIAN, D. (eds) (1990) *Sylvia Sleigh*, Milwaukee, WI, Milwaukee Art Museum.

BRADBURY, L. (1985) 'Pornography the theory, rape the practice?', unpublished BA dissertation, Cambridge College of Art and Technology.

BRADFORD, S. (1974) *Harriet Tubman: Moses of her people*, Secaucus, NJ, Citadel.

BROOKS, F. (1990) 'On the work of Claudette Johnson', in Sulter, M. (ed.) *Passion: discourses of blackwomen's creativity*, Hebdon Bridge, Urban Fox Press.

BROOKS, P. (1976) *The Melodramatic Imagination: Balzac, Henry James, melodrama and the mode of excess*, New Haven, CT, Yale University Press.

BRUNSDON, C. (1981) 'Crossroads − notes on soap opera', *Screen*, vol. 22, no. 4.

BUCKLEY, C. (1986) 'Designed by women' (review of Anscombe, I. *A Woman's Touch: women in design from 1860 to the present day)*, *Art History*, vol. 9, no. 3, pp. 400–3.

BURKE, C. (1980) 'Rethinking the maternal', in Eisenstein, H. and Jardine, A. (eds) *The Future of Difference*, Boston, MA, G.K. Hall, pp. 107–13.

BURNISTON, S., MORT, F. and WEEDON, C. (1978) 'Psychoanalysis and the cultural acquisition of sexuality and subjectivity', in Women's Studies Group, Centre for Contemporary Studies, University of Birmingham (ed.) *Women Take Issue*, London, Hutchinson.

BURROWS, I. (1989) Members' Focus, *Women's Art*, no. 30, p. 31.

CAMERON, D. (1985) *Feminism and Linguistic Theory*, Basingstoke, Macmillan.

CAMERON, D. (1991) 'Survival guide: language and gender', *Women's Art*, no. 39, p. 11.

CAMERON, D., MCALINDEN, F. and O'LEARY, K. (1988) 'Lakoff in context: the social and linguistic functions of tag questions', in Coates, J. and Cameron, D. (eds) *Women in Their Speech Communities*, London, Longman.

CARLSON, S. (1987) 'Comic collisions: convention, rage and order', *New Theatre Quarterly*, vol. III, no. 12.

CARNEGIE, D. (1957) *How to Help Your Husband Get Ahead*, New York, Pyramid Books.

CARTER, A. (1979) *The Sadeian Woman: an exercise in cultural history*, London, Virago.

CARTER, A. (1982) 'The sweet smell of romance', in *Nothing Sacred: selected writings*, London, Virago.

CARTER, A. (ed.) (1986) *Wayward Girls and Wicked Women: an anthology of stories*, London, Virago.

CARTER, A. (ed.) (1990) *The Virago Book of Fairy Tales*, London, Virago.

CHADWICK, W. (1990) *Women, Art and Society*, London, Thames and Hudson.

CHERRY, D. (ed.) (1987) *Painting Women: Victorian women artists*, exhibition catalogue.

CHODOROW, N. (1978) *The Reproduction of Mothering: psychoanalysis and the sociology of gender*, Berkeley, CA, University of California Press.

CHRISTIAN, B. (1985) 'Alice Walker: the black artist as wayward', in Evans, M. (ed.) *Black Women Writers*, London, Pluto Press.

CIXOUS, H. (1980) 'The laugh of the Medusa', Cohen, K. and Cohen, P. (trs), in Marks, E. and de Courtivron, I. (eds) *New French Feminisms*, Amherst, MA, University of Massachusetts Press.

CIXOUS, H. (1981a) 'The laugh of the Medusa', Cohen, K. and Cohen, P. (trs), in Marks, E. and de Courtivron, I. (eds) *New French Feminisms*, Brighton, Harvester, pp. 245–64. (First published in *Signs*, summer 1976.)

CIXOUS, H. (1981b) 'Sorties', Liddle, A. (tr.), in Marks, E. and de Courtivron, I. (eds) *New French Feminisms*, Brighton, Harvester, pp. 90–8. (First published in *La Jeune Née*, 1975.)

CLARK, K. (1980) *Feminine Beauty*, London, Weidenfeld and Nicolson.

CLIFF, M. (ed.) (1978) *The Winner Names the Age*, New York, W.W. Norton.

COATES, J. (1986) *Women, Men and Language*, London, Longman.

COATES, J. (1988) 'Gossip revisited: language in all-female groups', in Coates, J. and Cameron, D. (eds) *Women in Their Speech Communities*, London, Longman.

COLLINS, P.H. (1990) *Black Feminist Thought*, Boston, MA, Unwin Hyman.

COLLIS, R. (1988) 'Pleasure is a risky business', *Spare Rib*, no. 191, pp. 10–14.

CONRAN, S. (1982) *Lace*, New York, Simon and Schuster. (Harmondsworth, Penguin Books; 1983.)

COOTE, A. and CAMPBELL, B. (1982) *Sweet Freedom: struggle for women's liberation*, London, Pan Books.

COWARD, R. (1980) 'Underneath we are all angry': open letter to Advertising Standards Authority on brassiere ad. 'Underneath they're all lovable', in *Time Out*, no. 567, pp. 6–7. (Reproduced in Parker, R. and Pollock, G., 1987, *Framing Feminism: art and the women's movement 1970–85*, London, Pandora Press.)

COWARD, R. (1982) 'Sexual violence and sexuality', *Feminist Review*, no. 11.

COWARD, R. (1986) 'Porn: what's in it for women?', *New Statesman*, 13 June.

CROWLEY, H. and HIMMELWEIT, S. (1992) *Knowing Women: feminism and knowledge*, Cambridge, Polity Press.

D'ACCI, J. (1987) 'The case of *Cagney and Lacey*', in Baehr, H. and Dyer, G. (eds) *Boxed In: women and television*, London, Pandora Press.

DANIELS, S. (1991) Introduction to *Plays: One*, London, Methuen.

DAVEY, D. (1980) *A Sense of Adventure*, SE1 People's History Project.

DAVIS, A. (1971) 'The black woman's role in the community of slaves', *Black Scholar*.

DAVY, K. (1986) 'Constructing the spectator: reception, context and address in lesbian performance', *Performing Arts Journal*, vol. 10, no. 2.

DE BEAUVOIR, S. (1974) *The Second Sex*, Harmondsworth, Penguin Books. (First published in 1949.)

DELANY, S.R. (1976) *Triton*, New York, Bantam Books.

DE LAURETIS, T. (1984) *Alice Doesn't: feminism, semiotics, cinema*, Bloomington, IN, Indiana University Press.

DE LAURETIS, T. (1989) 'The essence of the triangle or, taking the risk of essentialism seriously: feminist theory in Italy, the US and Britain', *Differences*, vol. 1, no. 2, pp. 3–37.

DOCKER, J. (1988) 'In defence of popular TV: carnivalesque v. left pessimism', *Continuum*, vol. 1, no. 2, pp. 83–99.

DOLAN, J. (1988) *The Feminist Spectator As Critic*, Ann Arbor, MI, University of Michigan Press.

DOLAN, J. (1989) 'Materialist feminism, postmodernism, poststructuralism . . . and theory', *TDR: The Drama Review*, T123.

DONNERSTEIN, E., LINZ, D. and PENROD, S. (1987) *The Question of Pornography: the research findings and policy implications*, London, Collier-Macmillan.

DOUGLAS, A. (1990) Review of *Gracie Fields' Live Art Communities*, Rochdale Art Gallery, in *Women's Art*, no. 37, pp. 6–7.

DUBOIS, B.L. and CROUCH, I. (1975) 'The question of tag questions in women's speech: they don't really use more of them, do they?', *Language in Society*, no. 4, pp. 289–94.

DWORKIN, A. (1981) *Pornography: men possessing women*, London, The Women's Press; New York, Perigee.

DWORKIN, A. and MCKINNON, C. (1988) *Pornography and Sexual Violence: evidence of the links*, London, Everywoman Publications.

DYER, D. (1980) *Stars*, London, British Film Institute.

DYER, R. (ed.) (1981) *Coronation Street*, London, British Film Institute.

ECKENSTEIN, L. (1896) *Women Under Monasticism*, Cambridge.

EHRENREICH, B., HESS, E. and JACOBS, G. (1987) *Re-making Love: the feminization of sex*, London, Fontana.

EISENSTEIN, H. (1983) *Contemporary Feminist Thought*, Boston, MA, G.K. Hall.

ELLET, E. (1859) *Women Artists of All Ages and All Countries*, New York.

ELLIS, K., O'DAIR, B. and TALMER, A. (1990) 'Feminism and pornography', *Feminist Review*, no. 36.

ELSAESSER, T. (1972) 'Tales of sound and fury: observations on the family melodrama', *Monogram*, no. 4. (Reprinted in Gledhill, C., ed., 1987, *Home is Where the Heart Is*, London, British Film Institute.)

ELWES, C. (1985) 'Floating femininity: a look at performance art by women', in Kent, S. and Morreau, J. (eds) *Women's Images of Men*, London, Pandora Press.

ENGLISH, D. (1980) 'The politics of porn: can feminists walk the line?', *Mother Jones*, April.

EVANS, M. (ed.) (1985) *Black Women Writers*, London, Pluto Press.

FAIRBAIRNS, Z., MAITLAND, S., MINER, V., ROBERTS, M. and WANDOR, M. (1978) *Tales I Tell My Mother: a collection of feminist short stories*, London, Journeyman.

FAUSTO-STERLING, A. (1989) 'Life in the XY corral', *Women's Studies International Forum*, vol. 12, no. 3, pp. 319–91.

FISHMAN, P.M. (1983) 'Interaction: the work women do', in Thorne, B., Kramarae, C. and Henley, N. (eds) *Language, Gender and Society*, Rowley, MA, Newbury House.

FISKE, J. (1989) *Reading the Popular*, Boston, MA, Unwin Hyman.

FISKE, J. (1990) 'Women and quiz shows: consumerism, patriarchy and resisting pleasures', in Brown, M.E. (ed.) *Television and Women's Culture*, London, Sage.

FORTNUM, R. and HOUGHTON, G. (1989) 'Women and contemporary painting: representing non-representation', *Women's Art*, no. 28, p. 4.

FOUCAULT, M. (1980) *The History of Sexuality Volume 1: an introduction*, New York, Vintage Books.

FOUCAULT, M. (1988) *Politics, Philosophy, Culture: interviews and other writings 1977–1984*, Kritzman, L.D. (ed.), Sheridan, A. *et al.* (tr.), London, Routledge.

FOX, B. (1990) 'Selling the mechanized household: 70 years of ads in *Ladies Home Journal*', *Gender and Society*, vol. 4, no. 1, pp. 25–40.

FRANKLIN, S., LURY, C. and STACEY, J. (1991) 'Feminism and cultural studies', *Media, Culture and Society*, vol. 13, p. 182.

FRASER, J. and BOFFIN, T. (1991) *Stolen Glances: lesbians take photographs*, London, Pandora Press.

FRIEDAN, B. (1963) *The Feminine Mystique*, New York, W.W. Norton. (Harmondsworth, Pelican; 1982.)

FUSS, D. (1989) *Essentially Speaking*, New York and London, Routledge.

GAGNIER, R. (1988) 'Between women: a cross-class analysis of status and anarchic humor', in Barreca, R. (ed.) *Last Laughs: perspectives on women and comedy*, New York, Gordon and Breach.

GAMMAN, L. (1987) 'Dirty looks in the bodice ripper', unpublished paper presented at Middlesex Conference Centre, 5 September.

GAMMAN, L. and MARSHMENT, M. (eds) (1988) *The Female Gaze*, London, The Women's Press.

GARDINER, C. (1987) *What Share of the Cake? The employment of women in the British theatre*, The Women's Playhouse Trust.

GARDNER, C. (n.d.) 'Street on the dole', *City Limits*, quoted in *Inside Television: soap comes clean*, the programme for the Institute of Contemporary Arts Television Season, 29 September 1982.

GARDNER, T.A. (1980) 'Racism and pornography in the women's movement', in Lederer, L. (ed.) *Take Back the Night: women on pornography*, New York, William Morrow, pp. 105–14.

GERAGHTY, C. (1981) 'The continuous serial – a definition', in Dyer, R. (ed.) *Coronation Street*, London, British Film Institute.

GILBERT, S. and GUBAR, S. (1979) *The Madwoman in the Attic: a study of women and the literary imagination in the nineteenth century*, New Haven, CT, Yale University Press.

GILBERT, S. and GUBAR, S. (1986) Preface to 'Shakespeare's sisters: feminist essays on women poets', in Eagleton, M. (ed.) *Feminist Literary Theory: a reader*, Oxford and New York, Basil Blackwell. (First published as Gilbert, S. and Gubar, S., eds, 1979, *Shakespeare's Sisters: feminist essays on women poets*, Bloomington, IN, Indiana University Press.)

GILBERT, S. and GUBAR, S. (1988) *No Man's Land: the place of the woman writer in the twentieth century, I*, New Haven, CT and London, Yale University Press.

GILMAN, S.L. (1985) *Black Bodies, White Bodies: toward an iconography of female*, New York, Perigee.

GLEDHILL, C. (1984) 'Recent developments in feminist film criticism', in Doane, M.A., Mellencamp, P. and Williams, L. (eds) *Re-Vision: essays in feminist film criticism*, Frederick, MD, University Publications of America, in association with the American Film Institute.

GLEDHILL, C. (1987) 'The melodramatic field', in Gledhill, C. (ed.) *Home is Where the Heart Is*, London, British Film Institute.

GOMBRICH, E.H. (1960) *Art and Illusion: a study in the psychology of pictorial representation*, London, Phaidon.

GOODMAN, L. (1992a) *British Feminist Theatre: survey and analysis*, Manchester, University, The Feminist Praxis Journal Monograph Series. Double issue no. 37/40.

GOODMAN, L. (1992b) 'Feminist theatre: a survey and a prospect', *New Theatre Quarterly*, vol. VIII, no. 32.

GOODWIN, M.H. (1980) 'Directive–response speech sequences in girls' and boys' task activities', in McConnell-Ginet, S., Borker, R. and Furman, N. (eds) *Women and Language in Literature and Society*, New York, Praeger.

GOSSETT, T.F. (1965) *Race: the history of an idea in America*, New York, Schocken Books.

GOULD, S.J. (1981) *The Mismeasure of man*, New York, W.W. Norton.

GOUMA-PETERSON, T. and MATHEWS, P. (1987) 'The feminist critique of art history', *The Art Bulletin*, LXIX, pp. 326–57.

GRADDOL, D. and SWANN, J. (1989) *Gender Voices*, Oxford, Basil Blackwell.

GRAMSCI, A. (1971) *Selections from the Prison Notebooks*, Hoare, Q. and Nowell-Smith, G. (eds and trs), London, Lawrence and Wishart.

HACKETT, N. (1985) *XIX Century British Working Class Autobiographies: an annotated bibliography*, New York, AMS.

HALL, J.D. (1983) 'The mind that burns in each body: women, rape and racial violence', in Snitow, A., Stansell, C. and Thompson, S. (eds) *Powers of Desire: the politics of sexuality*, New York, Monthly Review Press, The New Feminist Library, pp. 329–49.

HALL, S. (1980) 'Encoding/decoding', in Hall, S. *et al.* (eds) *Culture, Media, Language*, London, Hutchinson.

HALPERN, D. (1986) *Sex Differences in Cognitive Abilities*, Hillsdale, NJ, Lawrence Erlbaum Associates.

HALPIN, Z.T. (1989) 'Scientific objectivity and the concept of "the other"', *Women's International Studies Forum*, vol. 12, no. 3, pp. 285–94.

HANAFORD, P.A. (n.d.) *Daughters of America*, Augusta, ME, True.

HARAWAY, D. (1988) 'Situated knowledges: the science question in feminism and the privilege of partial perspective', *Feminist Studies*, vol. 14, no. 3, pp. 575–99.

HASKELL, M. (1975) *From Reverence to Rape: the treatment of women in the movies*, London, New English Library. (Harmondsworth, Penguin Books; 1979.)

HAYTHORNE, E. (1990) *On Earth To Make the Numbers Up*, Castleford, Yorkshire Art Circus.

HEATH, S. (1974) 'Lessons from Brecht', *Screen*, vol. 15, no. 2.

HEATH, S. (1987) 'Male feminism', in Jardine, A. and Smith, P. (eds) *Men in Feminism*, New York and London, Methuen. (Reprinted in Eagleton, M., ed., 1991, *Feminist Literary Theory*, Longman.)

HEDGES, E. and WENDT, I. (eds) (1980) *In Her Own Image: women working in the arts*, New York, The Feminist Press.

HEILBRUN, C. (1989) *Writing a Woman's Life*, London, The Women's Press.

HEILBRUN, C.J. (1991) 'Margaret Mead and the question of woman's biography', in *Hamlet's Mother and Other Women*, London, The Women's Press.

HERRERA, H. (1989) *Frida: biography of Frida Kahlo*, London, Bloomsbury Publications.

HERRNSTEIN-SMITH, B. (1983) 'The contingency of value', *Critical Inquiry*, no. 10, pp. 1–35.

HIMID, L. (1989) in Araeen, R. *The Other Story: Afro-Asian artists in post-war Britain*, London, Hayward Exhibition Catalogue, pp. 78–81, 122–4, 145.

HINZ, R. (ed.) (1981) *Käthe Kollwitz: graphics, posters, drawings*, Writers and Readers Publishing Co-operative.

HMSO (1979) *Report of the Committee on Obscenity and Film Censorship*, London, HMSO.

HOCH, P. (1979) *White Hero, Black Beast: racism, sexism and the mask of masculinity*, London, Pluto Press.

HOLMES, J. (1986) 'Functions of *you know* in women's and men's speech', *Language in Society*, no. 15, pp. 1–22.

HORDYK, A. (1986) 'Assertion and confidence training with girls', in ILEA, *Secondary Issues*, London, Inner London Education Authority.

HOSSAIN, R.S. (1988) *Sultana's Dream and Selections from The Secluded Ones*, Jahan, R. (ed. and tr.) (with an Afterword by H. Papanek), New York, The Feminist Press at The City University of New York.

HOUSTON, B. (1984) 'Viewing television: the metapsychology of endless consumption', *Quarterly Review of Film Studies*, vol. 9, no. 3, pp. 183–95.

HULL, G.T., SCOTT, P. BELL and SMITH, B. (eds) (1981) *All the Women are White, All the Blacks are Men, But Some of Us are Brave*, New York, The Feminist Press.

HUNT, M. (1990) 'The de-eroticization of women's liberation: social policy movements and the revolutionary feminism of Sheila Jeffreys', *Feminist Review*, no. 34, pp. 23–46.

JACKSON, G. (1971) *Soledad Brother: the prison letters of George Jackson*, Harmondsworth, Penguin Books.

JACOBUS, M. (1979) 'The difference of view', in Jacobus, M. (ed.) *Women Writing and Writing about Women*, London, Croom Helm.

JACOBUS, M. (1982) 'Is there a woman in this text?', *New Literary History*, no. 14, pp. 117–41.

JELINEK, E. (1986) *The Tradition of Women's Autobiography: from antiquity to the present*, Boston, MA, Twayne Publishers.

JOHNSTON, C. (1973) 'Notes on women's cinema', *SEFT*. (Reprinted by *Screen*, 1991.)

JOLLEY, E. (1986) 'The last crop', in Carter, A. (ed.) *Wayward Girls and Wicked Women: an anthology of stories*, London, Virago.

JONES, D. (1980) 'Gossip: notes on women's oral culture', in Kramarae, C. (ed.) *The Voices and Words of Women and Men*, Oxford, Pergamon.

JOUVE, N.W. (1991) *White Woman Speaks with Forked Tongue: criticism as autobiography*, London, Routledge.

JOWITT, J. (1844) *Memoirs of Jane Jowitt, the Poor Poetess, Aged 74 Years, Written by Herself*, Sheffield, J. Pearce.

KALCIK, S. (1975) '". . . like Ann's gynecologist or the time I was almost raped": personal narratives in women's rap groups', *Journal of American Folklore*, no. 88, pp. 3–11.

KAPLAN, A. (1983) *Women and Film: both sides of the camera*, New York, Methuen.

KAPLAN, C. (1986) *Sea Changes: essays on culture and feminism*, London, Verso.

KAPLAN, E.A. (1983) 'Is the gaze male?', in Snitow, A., Stansell, C. and Thompson, S. (eds) *Powers of Desire: the politics of sexuality*, New York, Monthly Review Press.

KAPPELER, S. (1986) *The Pornography of Representation*, Cambridge, Polity Press.

KEARNS, M. (1976) *Käthe Kollwitz: woman and artist*, New York, The Feminist Press.

KENT, S. and MORREAU, J. (eds) (1985) *Women's Images of Men*, London, Pandora Press.

KINNAIRD, L. (1987) Review of 'Cinderella the Real True Story', *Spare Rib*, no. 185.

KIRKUP, G. and KELLER, L.S. (1992) *Inventing Women: science, technology and gender*, Cambridge, Polity Press.

KOEDT, A., LEVINE, E. and RAPONE, A. (eds) (1973) *Radical Feminism*, New York, Quadrangle Books.

KRAMARAE, C. and TREICHLER, P.A. (1985) *A Feminist Dictionary*, London, Pandora Press.

KUHN, A. (1982) *Women's Pictures: feminism and cinema*, London, Routledge and Kegan Paul.

KUHN, A. (1984) 'Women's genres: melodrama, soap opera and theory', *Screen*, vol. 25, no. 1. (Reprinted in Gledhill, C., ed., 1987, *Home is Where the Heart Is*, London, British Film Institute.)

KUZWAYO, E. (1990) *Sit Down and Listen: stories from South Africa*, London, The Women's Press.

LAKOFF, R. (1975) *Language and Woman's Place*, New York, Harper and Row.

LANDRY, D. (1990) *The Muses of Resistance: labouring class women's poetry in Britain, 1739–1796*, Cambridge, Cambridge University Press.

LAPLACE, M. (1987) 'Producing and consuming the woman's film: discursive struggle in *Now, Voyager*', in Gledhill, C. (ed.) *Home is Where the Heart Is*, London, British Film Institute.

LAURET, M. (1989) 'Seizing time and making new: feminist criticism, politics, and contemporary feminist fiction', *Feminist Review*, no. 31, pp. 94–106.

LAVERY, B. (1984) 'But will men like it? Or living as a feminist writer without committing murder', in Todd, S. (ed.) *Women and Theatre: calling the shots*, London, Faber and Faber.

LAVERY, B. (1991) 'Her aching heart', in *Her Aching Heart, Wicked, Two Marias*, London, Methuen.

LEE, S. (1986) *Film Comment*, October, Film Society of Lincoln.

LEE, S. (1987) *Ebony*, BBC1 transcript, ref. 1/NBM JH 646T.

LEFANU, S. (1988) *In the Chinks of the World Machine: feminism and science fiction*, London, The Women's Press.

LEGMAN, G. (1968) *No Laughing Matter: an analysis of sexual humor*, vol. 1, Bloomington, IN, Indiana University Press.

LEITH, D. (1983) *A Social History of English*, London, Routledge and Kegan Paul.

LEJEUNE, P. (1980) *Je Est Un Autre: l'autobiographie de la literature aux medias*, Paris, Le Seuil.

LEJEUNE, P. (1986) *Le Moi Autobiographique*, Paris, Le Seuil.

LEVITAS, R. (1990) *The Concept of Utopia*, New York and London, Philip Allan.

LIDOFF, J. (1982) 'Fluid boundaries: the origins of distinctive women's voice in literature', work in progress, University of Texas at Austin.

LIGHT, A. (1986) '"Returning to Manderley" – romance fiction, female sexuality and class', in Eagleton, M. (ed.) *Feminist Literary Theory: a reader*, Oxford and New York, Basil Blackwell, pp. 140–5. (First published in *Feminist Review*, no. 16, 1984.)

LINKER, K. (1990) *Love for Sale: the words and pictures of Barbara Kruger*, New York, Abrams.

LIPKING, L. (1983) 'Aristotle's sister: a poetics of abandonment', *Critical Inquiry*, no. 10.

LIPPARD, L. (1976) *From the Center: feminist essays on women's art*, New York, Dutton.

LOVELL, T. (1980) *Pictures of Reality: aesthetics, politics and pleasure*, London, British Film Institute.

LOVELL, T. (1981) 'Ideology and *Coronation Street*', in Dyer, R. *et al.*, *Coronation Street*, London, British Film Institute Television Monograph 13.

LOVELL, T. (1983) *Pictures of Reality: aesthetics, politics and pleasure*, London, British Film Institute.

LURIE, A. (1983) *The Language of Clothes*, Feltham, Hamlyn.

MACCABE, C. (1974) 'The politics of separation', *Screen*, vol. 15, no. 2.

MAINARDI, P. (1973) 'Quilts: the great American art', *The Feminist Art Journal*, no. 2. (Reprinted in Broude, N. and Garrard, M.D., eds, 1982, *Feminism and Art History: questioning the litany*, New York, Harper Collins, pp. 331–46.)

MARTIN, P. (1990) *Chaucer's Women*, London, Macmillan.

MATRIX (1984) *Making Space – women and the manmade environment*, London, Pluto Press.

MCNALL, S.G. (1983) 'Pornography: the structure of domination and the mode of reproduction', in McNall, S. (ed.) *Current Perspectives in Social Theory, Vol. 4*, Greenwich, CT, JAI Press, pp. 181–203.

MCQUISTON, L. (1988) *Women in Design*, London, Trefoil Books.

MCVANE, H. (1980) Introduction, *Women Writers of the Short Story: a collection of critical essays*, Englewood Cliffs, NJ, Prentice Hall.

MERRILL, L. (1988) 'Feminist humor: rebellious and self-affirming', in Barreca, R. (ed.) *Last Laughs: perspectives on women and comedy*, New York, Gordon and Breach.

METZ, C. (1975) 'The imaginary signifier', *Screen*, vol. 16, no. 2.

MILLER, C. and SWIFT, K. (eds) (1981) *The Handbook of Non-Sexist Writing*, London, The Women's Press.

MINOGUE, S. (1990) Introduction, *Problems for Feminist Criticism*, London, Routledge.

MITCHELL, H. (1968) *The Hard Way Up: the autobiography of Hannah Mitchell, Suffragette and Rebel*, London, Faber and Faber.

MITCHELL, H. (1984) *The Hard Way Up: the autobiography of Hannah Mitchell, Suffragette and Rebel*, London, Virago.

MOCH, C. (1989a) 'Cinderella the Real True Story', in Davis, J. (ed.) *Lesbian Plays, Volume Two*, London, Methuen.

MOCH, C. (1989b) published Afterword in Davis, J. (ed.) *Lesbian Plays, Volume Two*, London, Methuen.

MODLESKI, T. (1982a) *Loving with a Vengeance: mass produced fantasies for women*, New York, Methuen. (Hamden, CT, The Shoe String Press, 1982; London, Methuen, 1984.)

MODLESKI, T. (1982b) 'Never to be thirty-six years old: *Rebecca* as female Oedipal drama', *Wide Angle*, vol. 5, no. 1.

MODLESKI, T. (1987) 'Time and desire in the woman's film', in Gledhill, C. (ed.) *Home is Where the Heart Is*, London, British Film Institute.

MOERS, E. (1976) *Literary Women* (New York, Oxford University Press, 1985).

MORLEY, D. (1980) *The Nationwide Audience*, London, British Film Institute Television Monograph 11.

MORLEY, D. (1986) *Family Television: cultural power and domestic leisure*, London, Comedia.

MORRIS, M. (1988) 'Feminism, reading, postmodernism', in *The Pirate's Fiancée*, London, Verso.

MORRISON, T. (1975) *Sula*, New York, Bantam.

MORRISON, T. (1989) 'Unspeakable things unspoken: the Afro-American presence in American literature', *Michigan Quarterly Review*, vol. 38, no. 1.

MOYLAN, T. (1986) *Demand the Impossible: science fiction and the utopian imagination*, London, Methuen.

MULVEY, L. (1975) 'Visual pleasure and narrative cinema', *Screen*, vol. 16, no. 3.

MULVEY, L. (1981) 'Afterthoughts on "Visual pleasure and narrative cinema" inspired by Duel in the Sun', *Framework* (15/17).

NOCHLIN, L. (1971) 'Why are there no great women artists?', in Gornick, V. and Moran, B. (eds) *Women in Sexist Society*, New York, pp. 481–510.

NOCHLIN, L. (1989) *Women, Art and Power and Other Essays*, London, Thames and Hudson.

O'BARR, W.M. and ATKINS, B.K. (1980) '"Women's language" or "powerless language"?', in McConnell-Ginet, S., Borker, R. and Furman, N. (eds) *Women and Language in Literature and Society*, New York, Praeger.

O'NEALE, S. (1985) 'Reconstruction of the composite self: new images of black women in Maya Angelou's continuing autobiography', in Evans, M. (ed.) *Black Women Writers*, London, Pluto Press.

OOSTHUIZEN, A. (ed.) (1986) *Stepping Out: short stories on friendship between women*, London, Pandora Press.

ORBACH, S. (1978) *Fat is a Feminist Issue*, London, Arrow Books.

OSTRIKER, A. (1986) *The Mother/Child Papers*, Boston, MA, Beacon Press.

PAINTER, N.I. (1990) 'Sojourner Truth in life and memory: writing the biography of an American "Exotic"', *Gender and History*, vol. 2, no. 1, pp. 3–16.

PALLISTER, D. (1991) 'Under pressure', *The Guardian*, 27 March.

PALMER, P. (1989) *Contemporary Women's Fiction: narrative practice and feminist theory*, Hemel Hempstead, Harvester Wheatsheaf.

PARKER, R. (1984) *The Subversive Stitch: embroidery and the making of the feminine*, London, The Women's Press.

PARKER, R. and POLLOCK, G. (1981) *Old Mistresses: women, art and ideology*, London, Routledge.

PARKER, R. and POLLOCK, G. (eds) (1987) *Framing Feminism: art and the women's movement 1970–1985*, London, Pandora Press.

PATERSON, R. and STEWART, J. (1981) 'Street life', in Dyer, R. (ed.) *Coronation Street*, London, British Film Institute.

PETERSEN, K. and WILSON, J.J. (1976) *Women Artists: recognition and reappraisal from the early Middle Ages to the twentieth century*, New York, New York University Press.

PIERCY, M. (1979) *Woman on the Edge of Time*, London, The Women's Press.

POLLEN, M. (1986) 'What's love got to do with it', *Channels of Communication*, vol. 5, no. 6, pp. 68–9.

POLLOCK, G. (1988) *Vision and Difference: femininity, feminism and the histories of art*, London, Routledge.

PREISLER, B. (1986) *Linguistic Sex Roles in Conversation: social variation in the expression of tentativeness in English*, Berlin, Mouton de Gruyter.

RADWAY, J. (1987) *Reading the Romance: women, patriarchy and popular literature*, London, Verso.

RICH, A. (1963) *Snapshots of a Daughter-in-Law* (London, W.W. Norton, 1980).

RICH, A. (1977) *Of Woman Born: motherhood as experience and institution*, London, Virago.

RICH, A. (1979a) *On Lies, Secrets and Silence*, New York, W.W. Norton.

RICH, A. (1979b) 'When we dead awaken: writing as re-vision', in *On Lies, Secrets and Silence*, New York, W.W. Norton.

RICHARDSON, J. (1972) *Manet*, London, Phaidon.

ROBINSON, H. (ed.) (1987) *Visibly Female: feminism and art today*, London, Camden Press.

ROSZINSKA, R. and WIGHTMAN, C. (1990) *Black Country Working Women*, Wolverhampton Art Gallery, Exhibition Catalogue.

ROWE, K.K. (1990) 'Roseanne: unruly woman as Domestic Goddess', *Screen*, no. 4, pp. 408–19.

RUSS, J. (1985a) *The Female Man*, London, The Women's Press.

RUSS, J. (1985b) 'Being against pornography', in Kramarae, C. and Treichler, P.A. (eds) *A Feminist Dictionary*, London, Pandora Press.

RUSSELL, E. (1991) 'The loss of the feminine principle in Charlotte Haldane's *Man's World* and Katherine Burdekin's *Swastika Night*', in Armitt, L. (ed.) *Where No Man Has Gone Before: women and science fiction*, London, Routledge.

SAAR, B. (n.d.) 'Interview with Houston Conwill', *Black Art*, vol. 3, no. 1, p. 9.

SAXTON, J. (1991) 'Goodbye to all that . . . ', in Armitt, L. (ed.) *Where No Man Has Gone Before: women and science fiction*, London, Routledge.

SCHREINER, O. (pseudonym Ralph Iron) (1883) *The Story of an African Farm* (a novel in two volumes), vol. II, London, Chapman and Hall.

SCHULTZ, M. (1975) 'The semantic derogation of women', in Thorne, B. and Henley, N. (eds) *Language and Sex: difference and dominance*, Rowley, MA, Newbury House.

SEXTON, A. (1960) *To Bedlam and Part Way Back*, New York, Houghton Mifflin.

SEXTON, A. (1962) *All My Pretty Ones* (New York, Houghton Mifflin, 1973).

SHAHAR, S. (1983) *The Fourth Estate: a history of women in the Middle Ages*, London, Cambridge University Press.

SHOWALTER, E. (1977) *A Literature of Their Own: British women novelists from Brontë to Lessing*, Princeton, NJ, Princeton University Press.

SHOWALTER, E. (ed.) (1985) *The New Feminist Criticism: essays on women, literature and theory*, New York, Pantheon.

SMITH, L. (1949) *Killers of the Dream*, New York, W.W. Norton.

SMITH, L. (1978a) 'The mob and the ghost', in Cliff, M. (ed.) *The Winner Names the Age*, New York, W.W. Norton.

SMITH, L. (1978b) 'Words that chain us and words that set us free', in Cliff, M. (ed.) *The Winner Names the Age*, New York, W.W. Norton.

SMITH-ROSENBERG, C. (1975) 'The female world of love and ritual: relations between women in nineteenth-century America', *Signs*, no. 1, pp. 1–29.

SNITOW, A. (1983) 'Mass market romance: pornography for women is different', in Snitow, A., Stansell, C. and Thompson, S. (eds) *Powers of Desire: the politics of sexuality*, New York, Monthly Review Press, The New Feminist Library, pp. 266–74.

SNITOW, A., STANSELL, C. and THOMPSON, S. (eds) (1983) *Powers of Desire: the politics of sexuality*, New York, Monthly Review Press, The New Feminist Library.

SOBCHACK, V. (1987) *Screening Space* (second enlarged edn), New York, Ungar.

SPACKS, P.M. (1976) *The Female Imagination*, New York, Avon.

SPARE TYRE (1987) *The Spare Tyre Song Book*, London, Virago.

SPENCE, J. and HOLLAND, P. (eds) (1991) *Family Snaps*, London, Virago.

SPENDER, D. (1980) *Man Made Language*, London, Routledge and Kegan Paul.

STANLEY, J.P. and WOLFE, S.J. (ROBBINS) (1978) 'Toward a feminist aesthetic', *Chrysalis*, no. 6, pp. 57–71.

STEINEM, G. (1985) 'Erotica and pornography: a clear and present difference', in Kramarae, C. and Treichler, P.A. (eds) *A Feminist Dictionary*, London, Pandora Press.

STETSON, E. (1981) 'Studying slavery', in Hull, G.T., Scott, P. Bell and Smith, B. (eds) *All the Women are White, All the Blacks are Men, But Some of Us are Brave*, New York, The Feminist Press.

STEVEN, P. (ed.) (1985) *Jump Cut: Hollywood, politics and counter-cinema*, New York, Praeger.

STUBBS, P. (1979) *Women and Fiction: feminism and the novel 1880–1920*, London, Methuen.

SULTER, M. (1990/91) 'Reviewing lesbian erotica', *Spare Rib*, no. 219, pp. 42–4.

SUVIN, D. (1979) *Metamorphoses of Science Fiction*, New Haven, CT and London, Yale University Press.

SUVIN, D. (1988) *Positions and Presuppositions in Science Fiction*, London, Macmillan.

TAX, M. (1973) 'Woman and her mind: the story of everday life', in Koedt, A., Levine, E. and Rapone, A. (eds) *Radical Feminism*, New York, Quadrangle Books.

THORNE, B., KRAMARAE, C. and HENLEY, N. (1983) *Language, Gender and Society*, Rowley, MA, Newbury House.

TOOMER, J. (1975) *Cane*, New York, Liveright.

TUFTS, E. (1974) *Our Hidden Heritage*, New York, Paddington.

TULLOCH, J. (1976) 'Gradgrind's heirs – the quiz and the presentation of knowledge by British television', *Screen Education*, no. 19, pp. 3–12.

VALVERDE, M. (1986) *Sex, Power and Pleasure*, Toronto, Women's Press of Canada.

WALKER, A. (1977) 'In search of our mothers' gardens', in Ruddick, S. and Daniels, P. (eds) *Working It Out*, New York, Pantheon.

WALKER, A. (1981a) 'Coming apart', in *You Can't Keep a Good Woman Down*, New York, Harcourt Brace Jovanovich, pp. 41–53.

WALKER, A. (1981b) 'One child of one's own', in Hull, G.T., Scott, P. Bell and Smith, B. (eds) *All the Women are White, All the Blacks are Men, But Some of Us are Brave*, New York, The Feminist Press.

WALLACE, M. (1979) *Black Macho and the Myth of the Superwoman*, London, John Calder.

WALTERS, M. (1979) *The Nude Male: a new perspective*, Harmondsworth, Penguin Books.

WARNER, M. (1987) *Monuments and Maidens: the allegory of the female form*, London, Picador.

WARNOD, J. (1981) *Suzanne Valadon*, Bonfini Press.

WELDON, F. (1984) *The Life and Loves of a She-Devil*, London, Coronet Books.

WEST, C. and ZIMMERMAN, D. (1977) 'Women's place in everyday talk: reflections on parent–child interaction', *Social Problems*, no. 24, pp. 521–9.

WEST, C. and ZIMMERMAN, D. (1983) 'Small insults: a study of interruptions in cross-sex conversations', in Thorne, B., Kramarae, C. and Henley, N. (eds) *Language, Gender and Society*, Rowley, MA, Newbury House.

WHANNEL, G. (1990) 'Winner takes all: competition', in Goodwin, A. and Whannel, G. (eds) *Understanding Television*, London and New York, Routledge.

WHITE, F. (1938) *A Fire in the Kitchen: the autobiography of a cook*, London, J.M. Dent.

WHITE, J. (1986) 'The writing on the wall: beginning or end of a girl's career?', *Women's Studies International Forum*, vol. 9, no. 5, pp. 561–74.

WILLIAMS, L. (1987) '"Something else besides a mother": *Stella Dallas* and the maternal melodrama', in Gledhill, C. (ed.) *Home is Where the Heart Is*, London, British Film Institute.

WILLIAMS, R. (1977) *Marxism and Literature*, Oxford, Oxford University Press.

WILLIAMSON, J. (1986) 'The problems of being popular', *New Socialist*, September.

WILLIS, E. (1983) 'Feminism, moralism and pornography', in Snitow, A., Stansell, C. and Thompson, S. (eds) *Powers of Desire: the politics of sexuality*, New York, Monthly Review Press, The New Feminist Library.

WILSON, E. (1983) *What Is To Be Done About Violence Against Women?*, Harmondsworth, Penguin Books.

WOLFF, J. (1990) *Feminine Sentences: essays on women and culture*, Cambridge, Polity Press.

WOOLF, V. (1978) *A Room of One's Own*, London, Hogarth Press. (First published in 1928.)

SOURCE LIST OF ARTICLES

Article 1.1   Making things mean: cultural representation in objects
Catherine King
Commissioned article.

Article 1.2   Analysing representations   Richard Allen
Commissioned article.

Article 1.3   Gender and genre   Dinah Birch
Commissioned article.

Article 1.4   Ways of speaking   Joan Swann
Commissioned article.

Article 2.1   The feminist critical revolution   Elaine Showalter
from Showalter, E. (ed.) (1985) *The New Feminist Criticism: essays on women, literature and theory*, New York, Pantheon.

Article 2.2   Supply and demand: women's short stories
Lizbeth Goodman
Commissioned article.

Article 2.3   Towards a better way of being: feminist science fiction
Frances Bonner
Commissioned article.

Article 2.4   A wild surmise: motherhood and poetry
Alicia Ostriker
from Ostriker, A. (1983) *Writing Like a Woman*, Ann Arbor, MI, University of Michigan Press.

Article 2.5   'Moment of faith': worksheets   Carol Rumens
from Sellers, S. (ed.) (1989) *Delighting the Heart: a notebook by women writers*, London, The Women's Press.

Article 2.6   Criticism as autobiography   Nicole Ward Jouve
from Jouve, N.W. (1991) *White Woman Speaks with Forked Tongue: criticism as autobiography*, London, Routledge.

Article 2.7   Our life: working-class women's autobiography in Britain   Wendy Webster
Commissioned article.

Article 3.1   The politics of representation: a democracy of the gaze   Catherine King
Commissioned article.

Article 3.2   Object into subject: some thoughts on the work of black women artists   Michelle Cliff
from Robinson, H. (ed.) (1987) *Visibly Female*, London, Camden Press. (Also published in *Heresies*, 1984, vol. 4, no. 3, issue 15).

Article 3.3   Beyond the mirror: women's self portraits
Felicity Edholm
Commissioned article.

Article 3.4   Feminist arts   Catherine King
Commissioned article.

Article 4.1   Pleasurable negotiations   Christine Gledhill
from Pribram, E.D. (ed.) (1988) *Female Spectators: looking at film and television*, London, Verso.

Article 4.2   *She's Gotta Have It*: the representation of black female sexuality on film   Felly Nkweto Simmonds
from *Feminist Review* (1988), no. 29, Spring.

Article 4.3   A woman's space: women and soap opera
Christine Geraghty
from Ch. 3 of Geraghty, C. (1991) *Women and Soap Opera: a study of prime time soaps*, Cambridge, Polity Press.

Article 4.4   Confession time: women and game shows
Frances Bonner
Commissioned article.

Article 5.1   *Lace*: pornography for women?   Avis Lewallen
from Gamman, L. and Marshment, M. (eds) (1988) *The Female Gaze: women as viewers of popular culture*, London, The Women's Press.

Article 5.2   Obscenity and censorship   Suzanne Kappeler
from Kappeler, S. (1986) *The Pornography of Representation*, Cambridge, Polity Press.

Article 5.3   Pornography and black women's bodies
Patricia Hill Collins
from Collins, P.H. (1990) *Black Feminist Thought: knowledge, consciousness and the politics of empowerment*, Boston, Unwin Hyman.

Article 5.4   Who watches the watchwomen?: feminists against censorship   Gillian Rodgerson and Linda Semple
from *Feminist Review* (1990), no. 36, Autumn.

Article 5.5   The pornography problem   Lizbeth Goodman
Commissioned article.

Article 6.1   Gender and humour   Lizbeth Goodman
Commissioned article.

Article 6.2   Comic subversions: comedy as strategy in feminist theatre   Lizbeth Goodman
Commissioned article.

Conclusion   In search of our mothers' gardens   Alice Walker
from Walker, A. (1985) *In Search of Our Mothers' Gardens*, London, The Women's Press.

ACKNOWLEDGEMENTS

Grateful acknowledgement is made to the following sources for permission to reproduce material in this book:

Text

Chapter 2: Article 2.1: Showalter, E. (1985) *The New Feminist Criticism*, Virago Press. And: from *The New Feminist Criticism* by Elaine Showalter. Copyright © 1985 by Elaine Showalter. Reprinted by permission of Pantheon Books, a division of Random House, Inc.; *Article 2.4:* Ostriker, A. (1983) *Writing Like a Woman*, University of Michigan Press; *Article 2.5:* Rumens, C. (1989) '"A moment of faith": worksheets', in Sellars, S. (ed.) *Delighting the Heart: a notebook by women writers*, The Women's Press Ltd, © 1989 by Carol Rumens; *Article 2.6:* Ward Jouve, N. (1991) *White Woman Speaks With Forked Tongue*, Routledge.

Chapter 3: Article 3.2: Cliff, M. (1984) 'Object into subject: some thoughts on the work of black women artists', *Heresies*, 1984, vol. 4, no. 3, issue 15 (abridged version).

Chapter 4: Article 4.1: Gledhill, C. (1988) 'Pleasurable negotiations', in Pribram, E.D. (ed.) *Female Spectators*, Verso; *Article 4.2:* Simmonds, F.N. (1988) 'She's gotta have it', *Feminist Review*, no. 29, Spring 1988, © Felly Nkweto Simmonds, Senior Lecturer in Sociology, Newcastle Polytechnic; *Article 4.3:* Geraghty, C. (1991) *Women and Soap Opera*, Basil Blackwell Ltd. This is an edited extract of the original.

Chapter 5: Article 5.1: Lewallen, A. (1988) '*Lace*: pornography for women?', in Marshment and Gamman (eds) *The Female Gaze*, The Women's Press Ltd; *Article 5.2:* Kappeler, S. (1986) *The Pornography of Representation*, Polity Press; *Article 5.3:* from *Black Feminist Thought* by Patricia Hill Collins, reprinted by permission of the publisher Routledge, Chapman and Hall; *Article 5.4:* Rodgerson, G. and Semple, L. 'Who watches the watchwomen?: Feminists against censorship', *Feminist Review*, no. 36, Autumn 1990.

Conclusion: Walker, A. (1984) *In Search of Our Mothers' Gardens*, The Women's Press Ltd.

Extracts from *Margaret III* in Lizbeth Goodman's Article 6.2 reproduced by permission of Lip Service, 13 Rosford Avenue, Manchester M14 7BW.

Illustrations

p. 6: Bülbül ' My name was Helen …' , cartoon from *Dissecting Doctor Medi-corpse*, 1974, by permission of the artist; *p. 9:* 'Stone Age Man … did they have women in those days?'. Reproduced from Casey Miller and Kate Swift (1977) *Words and Women*, London, Victor Gollancz Ltd, by permission of the publishers; *p. 135, Figure 3.1.1:* Barbara Kruger 'I can't look at you and breathe at the same time' tee shirt, photograph by Enrique Cubillo, 1987. Private collection. Reproduced in *Love for Sale*, 1990, New York, Abrams; *p. 171, Figure 3.3.1:* woodcut of Suzanne Valadon, poster for benefit of L'Aide Amicale des Artistes, 1927 (self portrait). Musée National d'Art Moderne, Centre Georges Pompidou, Paris; *p. 172, Figure 3.3.2:* Suzanne Valadon, preliminary drawing for poster for benefit of L'Aide Amicale des Artistes, 1927 (self portrait). Musée National d' Art Moderne, Centre Georges Pompidou, Paris; *p. 188:* GUERRILLA GIRLS, 'The advantages of being a woman artist …'. Reproduced by permission of Guerrilla Girls/Leeds Postcards; *p. 273, Figure 5.4.1:* Feminists Against Censorship, title page of leaflet 'Ask yourself … do you really want more censorship?', Summer 1989. Reproduced by permission of

Feminists Against Censorship, 38 Mount Pleasant, London WC1X 0BP; *p. 287:* Nicole Hollander Sylvia, 'Gender based differences in humor', © Nicole Hollander. Reprinted by permission of the artist; *p. 293:* Nicole Hollander Sylvia, 'Preliminary steps toward a national humor survey', © Nicole Hollander. Reprinted by permission of the artist; *p. 299:* Nicole Hollander Sylvia, 'Results of a national humor survey conducted at 2:00 A.M. ...', © Nicole Hollander. Reprinted by permission of the artist; *p. 311, Figure 6.2.1: Cinderella: The Real True Story,* Drill Hall Arts Centre, London, production poster 1987.

Colour Plate Section

Colour Plate 1: Maud Sulter, Alice Walker as *Thalia, One of The Muses,* from Zabat series 1989. Reproduced by courtesy of the artist; *Colour Plate 2:* Alexis Hunter, *Struggle Between Ambition and Desire,* 1983, oil on canvas, 171 x 190 cm. Collection of the artist; *Colour Plate 3:* Christine Merton, *Tree Tomb,* 1988, wood and earth, 305 cm. high. Private collection. Photograph by courtesy of the Women Artists Slide Library; *Colour Plate 4:* Harriet Powers, *The First Bible Quilt, c.* 1886, pieced cotton with cotton and metallic thread. National Museum of American History, Smithsonian Institution, Washington, DC; *Colour Plate 5:* Harriet Powers, *Pictorial Quilt,* 1895–1898, 175 x 267 cm., pieced and appliquéd cotton and printed cotton embroidered with plain and metallic yarns. Bequest of Maxim Karolik, courtesy, Museum of Fine Arts, Boston; *Colour Plate 6:* Betye Saar, *The Liberation of Aunt Jemima,* 1972, mixed media, 30 cm. high. University Art Museum/Pacific Film Archive, University of California at Berkeley. Purchased with funds from the National Endowment for the Arts; *Colour Plate 7:* Frida Kahlo, self portrait with thorn necklace and humming bird, 1940, oil on canvas, 63.5 x 49.5 cm. Harry Ransom Humanities Research Center, University of Texas at Austin. Reproduction authorized by Instituto Nacional de Bellas Artes y Literatura; *Colour Plate 8:* Frida Kahlo, *My Nurse and I* (Mi nana y yo), 1937, oil on sheet metal, 30 x 37 cm. Collection of Fundacion Dolores Olmedo. Photograph: Archivio CENIDIAP-INBA. Reproduction authorized by Instituto Nacional de Bellas Artes y Literatura; *Colour Plate 9:* Frida Kahlo, *Roots,* 1943, oil on sheet metal, 30.5 x 49.9 cm. Collection of Fundacion Dolores Olmedo. Photograph: Archivio CENIDIAP-INBA. Reproduction authorized by Instituto Nacional de Bellas Artes y Literatura; *Colour Plate 10:* Suzanne Valadon, self portrait with the necklace in maturity, 1931, oil on canvas. Private collection. Photograph by courtesy of Gilbert Petrides; *Colour Plate 11:* Detail from *Women's Rights Quilt, c.* 1850, cotton, 177 x 176 cm. From *Heart and Hands: the influence of women and quilts on American society* by Pat Ferrero, Elaine Hedges and Julie Silber. Quilt from the collection of Dr and Mrs John Livingston and Mrs Elizabeth Livingston Jaeger; *Colour Plate 12:* Florence Claxton, *Women's Work: A Medley,* 1861, oil on panel, 51 x 61 cm. Private collection. Photograph: A.C. Cooper; *Colour Plate 13:* Janie Terreno, Suffragette Handkerchief, worked in Holloway, showing Mrs Pankhurst and Christabel, 1912, silk, 51 x 45.5 cm. Museum of London; *Colour Plate 14:* Sally Ranson (1870–1956) of New Seaham, border patterned cotton quilt, *c.* 1890. The North of England Open Air Museum, Beamish; *Colour Plate 15:* Sylvia Sleigh, *Turkish Bath,* portraying the art critics Paul Rosano, Laurence Alloway, Scott Burton, John Perrault and Carter Ratcliff, 1973, oil on canvas, 193 x 259 cm. Reproduced by courtesy of the artist; *Colour Plate 16:* Monica Sjoo, *God Giving Birth,* 1969, oil on hardboard, 183 x 122 cm. Collection of the artist. Photograph by courtesy of Women Artists Slide Library; *Colour Plate 17:* Lesley Sanderson, *Time for Change,* 1989, oil on canvas, 240 x 350 cm. Reproduced by courtesy of the artist. Photograph: David Amy; *Colour Plate 18:* Sonia Boyce,

Talking Presence, 1988, mixed media on photographic paper, 165 × 120 cm. Reproduced by courtesy of the artist; *Colour Plate 19:* Lyn Malcolm, *Why Have We So Few Great Women Artists?*, mixed media installation, 1982, life-size. Courtesy of the artist. Photograph by Paul Guest; *Colour Plate 20:* Lubaina Himid, *We Will Be*, 1983, hardboard cutout, larger than life-size. Installation photograph by courtesy of the artist.

Black and White Plate Section

Plate 1: Barbara Kruger, *(Untitled) We Won't Play Nature to Your Culture*, black and white photograph, 1983, 186 × 124.46 cm. Ydessa Hendeles Art Foundation; *Plate 2: The Quakers Meeting*, engraved by Egbert van Heemskirk and Marcel Lauron, after a painting by Heemskirk [late seventeenth century], satirical engraving contemptuous of women preaching. Reproduced by permission of the Library Committee of the Religious Society of Friends; *Plate 3:* Janine Wiedel, *The Chainmaker*, Cradley Heath, Birmingham, photograph, 1977. Reproduced by permission of Janine Wiedel; *Plate 4:* Harriet Powers, portrait photograph, *c.* 1890. Courtesy, Museum of Fine Arts, Boston; *Plate 5:* Edmonia Lewis, portrait photograph, *c.* 1875. Boston Atheneum, AA/5.4/Lewis e(no1)(no2); *Plate 6:* Edmonia Lewis, *Forever Free*, 1867, marble, 105 cm. high. The Howard University Gallery of Art, Washington, DC. Photograph: Jarvis Grant; *Plate 7:* Edmonia Lewis, *Hagar*, 1875, marble, 133.6 × 38.8 × 43.4 cm. National Museum of American Art, Smithsonian Institution, Washington, DC. Gift of Delta Sigma Theta Sorority, Inc.; *Plate 8:* Elizabeth Catlett, *Homage to My Young Black Sisters*, 1969, cedar wood, 180 cm. high. Collection of the artist; *Plate 9:* Judy Chicago, *Sojourner Truth*, ceramic plate from *The Dinner Party*. Copyright Judy Chicago, 1979; *Plate 10:* Elizabeth Catlett, *Harriet Tubman*, 1975, linocut, 28 × 23 cm. Museum of African American Art, Los Angeles; *Plate 11:* Käthe Kollwitz, self portrait, 1889, aged 22, pen, sepia, pencil, 22 cm. signed with maiden name Schmidt. Kupferstich-kabinett, Staatliche Kunstsammlungen, Dresden; *Plate 12:* Käthe Kollwitz, self portrait, 1910, aged 43, etching, 15.4 × 13.7 cm. National Gallery of Art, Washington, DC, Rosenwald Collection; *Plate 13:* Käthe Kollwitz, self portrait, 1934, aged 67, lithograph, 20.8 × 18.7 cm. National Gallery of Art, Washington, DC, Rosenwald Collection; *Plate 14:* Suzanne Valadon, self portrait, 1883, aged 18, pastel. Musée National d'Art Moderne, Centre Georges Pompidou, Paris; *Plate 15:* Suzanne Valadon, *Family Portraits* (Portraits de famille), 1912, oil on canvas. Private collection. Photograph by courtesy of Musée National d'Art Moderne, Centre Georges Pompidou, Paris; *Plate 16:* Barbara Leigh-Smith, *Ye Newe Generation*, 1855, pen and ink. Reproduced by permission of the Mistress and Fellows of Girton College, Cambridge; *Plate 17:* Sojourner Truth seated with knitting, photograph, 1864. Sophia Smith Collection, Smith College, Massachusetts; *Plate 18:* Sheila Levrant de Bretteville, *Pink Poster*, created in response to a request from AIGA and put up in Los Angeles, 1974. Reproduced by courtesy of the artist; *Plate 19:* Geneviève Bujold as Dr Susan Wheeler in *Coma*, 1977, directed by Michael Crichton. Photograph: John Kobal Collection; *Plate 20:* Tracy Camilla Johns as Nola Darling, Redmond Hicks as Jamie Overstreet, in *She's Gotta Have It*, 1985, directed by Spike Lee. Photograph: John Kobal Collection; *Plate 21:* Lizzie Minim as Cinderella, Bridget Long as Princess '… Stay close to me, darling, stay very close …', Act II, Scene 26 of *Cinderella: The Real True Story* by Cheryl Moch. Hull University production by Jools Gilson, 1991. Photograph: John Spencer, Hull University; *Plate 22:* Detail from *Cinderella: The Real True Story* by Cheryl Moch. Dramatrix production, 1987, Drill Hall, London; *Plate 23:* Detail from *Her Aching Heart*. By courtesy of Sheila Burnett; *Plate 24:* Detail from *Margaret III*. Lip Service production.

INDEX

*(Note: Page numbers in **bold** indicate articles by these authors)*

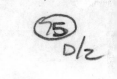